THE

AUTOBIOGRAPHY OF A SEAMAN.

VOL. II.

THOMAS, TENTH EARL OF DUNDONALD, G.C.B.

Admiral of the Red, Rear Admiral of the Fleet &c.

THE

AUTOBIOGRAPHY OF A SEAMAN.

BY

THOMAS, TENTH EARL OF DUNDONALD, G.C.B.

ADMIRAL OF THE RED; REAR-ADMIRAL OF THE FLEET,
ETC. ETC.

VOLUME THE SECOND.

CONSTABLE · LONDON

This edition published in Great Britain 1996
by Constable and Company Ltd
3 The Lanchesters, 162 Fulham Palace Road
London W6 9ER
Originally published in London in 1860
by Richard Bentley
Printed in Great Britain by
St Edmundsbury Press Ltd
Bury St Edmunds, Suffolk

A CIP catalogue record for this book
is available from the British Library

CONTENTS

OF

THE SECOND VOLUME.

CHAP. XXVI.

A NAVAL STUDY—*continued*.

CHAP. XXVII.

CONDUCT OF THE COURT-MARTIAL.

CHAP. XXVIII.

THE VOTE OF THANKS.

CHAP. XXIX.

REFUSAL OF MY PLANS FOR ATTACKING THE FRENCH FLEET IN THE SCHELDT.

CHAP. XXX.

MY PLANS FOR ATTACKING THE FRENCH COAST REFUSED, AND MYSELF
SUPERSEDED.

CHAP. XXXI.

VISIT TO THE ADMIRALTY COURT AT MALTA.

CHAP. XXXII.

NAVAL LEGISLATION HALF A CENTURY AGO.

CHAP. XXXIII.

OPENING OF PARLIAMENT, 1812.

CHAP. XXXIV.

MY SECRET PLANS.

AUTOBIOGRAPHY OF A SEAMAN.

CHAPTER XXIV.

A NAVAL STUDY FOR ALL TIME.

CHARTS, ETC., SUPPLIED BY THE PRESENT GOVERNMENT.—REFUSED BY A
FORMER GOVERNMENT. — ALTERATION MADE IN THE CHARTS. — MR.
STOKES'S AFFIDAVITS.—LETTER TO SIR JOHN BARROW. — SINGULAR
ADMIRALTY MINUTE.—SECOND LETTER TO SIR JOHN BARROW.—THE
CHARTS AGAIN REFUSED. — MY DEPARTURE FOR CHILI. —RENEWED
APPLICATION TO THE ADMIRALTY.—KINDNESS OF THE DUKE OF SOMER-
SET.—DIFFERENCE OF OPINION AT THE ADMIRALTY.

IT will be asked, "How is it that the matters recorded
in the present volume are, after the lapse of fifty years,
for the first time made public?"

The reply is, that it was not till after the publication
of the preceding volume that I have been enabled to
place the subject in a comprehensible point of view *,
and that only through the high sense of justice manifested by the late and present First Lords of the

* This concession will, in the future narrative, render necessary a
slight recapitulation of some matters contained in the previous
volume, but not to any appreciable extent.

Admiralty, in furnishing me with charts and logs, access to which was prohibited by former Boards of Admiralty. On several previous occasions the attempt has been made, but from the obstinate refusal of their predecessors to afford me access to documents by which alone truth could be elicited, it has not hitherto been in my power to arrive at any more satisfactory result than that of placing my own personal and unsupported statements in opposition to the sentence of a court-martial.

The necessary materials being now conceded, in such a way as to enable me to prepare them for publication in detail, it is, therefore, for the first time in my power to vindicate myself. A brief recapitulation of former refusals, as well as of the manner in which I became possessed of such documentary testimony as will henceforth exhibit facts in a comprehensive point of view, is desirable, as placing beyond dispute matters which would otherwise be incredible.

My declaration previous to the court-martial—that it was in my capacity as a member of the House of Commons alone that I intended to oppose a vote of thanks to Lord Gambier, on the ground that no service had been rendered worthy of so high an honour—will be fresh in the remembrance of the reader*; and also that when, at the risk of intrenchment on the privilege of Parliament, the Board of Admiralty called upon me officially to accuse his lordship, I referred them to the logs of the fleet for such

* See my conversation with Lord Mulgrave, vol. i. pp. 345, 346.

information relative to the attack in Aix Roads as they might require * ;—it nevertheless became evident that I was regarded as his lordship's prosecutor! though, *throughout the trial, excluded from seeing the charts before the Court, hearing the evidence, cross-examining the witnesses, or even listening to the defence!* †

On the acquittal of Lord Gambier, the ministry did not submit the vote of thanks to Parliament till six months afterwards, viz. in the session of the following year, 1810. To myself, however, the consequences were -— as Lord Mulgrave had predicted — immediate ; bringing me forthwith under the full weight of ministerial displeasure. The Board of Admiralty prohibited me from joining the *Impérieuse* in the Scheldt.

The effect of this prohibition in a manner so marked as to be unmistakeable as to its cause, produced on my mind a natural anxiety to lay before the public the reasons for a proceeding so unusual, and, as a first step, I requested of the Board permission to inspect the charts upon which— *in opposition to the evidence of officers present at the attack* — the decision of the court-martial had been made to rest. The request was evaded, both then and afterwards, even though persisted in up to the year 1818, when it was officially *denied* that the original of the most material chart was in the possession of the Admiralty. Even inspection of *a copy admitted to be in their possession* was refused.

An assertion of this nature might be dangerous were not ample proof at hand.

---

* See my letter to the Secretary of the Admiralty, vol. i. p. 408.

† See Minutes of Court-martial, p. 228.

It having come to my knowledge, from certain affi-davits filed in the Court of Admiralty by Mr. Stokes, the master of Lord Gambier's flagship, on whose chart the acquittal of Lord Gambier had been based — that, *after the lapse of eight years from the court-martial!* material alterations had been made *by permission of the Board itself, and under the direction of one of its officers* —I naturally became suspicious that the charts might otherwise have been tampered with ; the more so, as neither at the court-martial, nor at any period sub-sequent to it, had I ever been allowed to obtain even a sight of the charts in question.

The very circumstances were suspicious. On the application for head-money to the Court of Admiralty in 1817, the Court had refused to receive Mr. Stokes's chart, on account of its palpable incorrectness. On this, Mr. Stokes applied to the Admiralty for permission *to alter his chart!* The permission was granted, and in this altered state it was received by the Court of Admiralty, which, on Mr. Stokes's authority, decreed that the head-money should be given *to the whole fleet,* contrary to the Act of Parliament, *instead of the ships which alone had taken part in the destruction of the enemy's vessels.*

Fearful that material erasures or additions had been made, I once more applied to the Board for permission to *inspect* the alterations. The request was again refused, though my opponents had been permitted to make what alterations and erasures they pleased.

The following are extracts from the above-mentioned affidavits of Mr. Stokes :—

Extract from the affidavit, sworn before the High Court of Admiralty on the 13th of November, 1817, of Thomas Stokes, master of the *Caledonia*, as to the truth of the MSS. chart, upon which the acquittal of Lord Gambier was based; *before* the Court of Admiralty rejected his chart, and *before* the alterations were made.

"And this deponent maketh oath that the annexed paper writing marked with the letter A, being a chart of Aix Roads, *is a true copy* * *made by this deponent* of an original French chart found on board the French frigate *L'Armide* in September, 1806, which *original chart is now in the Hydrographic Office in the Admiralty*, and by comparing the same with the original chart he is enabled to depose, and *does depose that the said chart is correct and true,* and that the soundings therein stated accurately describe the soundings at low water, to the best of his judgment and belief."

Extract from a second affidavit, sworn by Mr. Stokes, before the High Court of Admiralty, on the 17th of April, 1818, *after* the Court had refused to admit his chart from its incorrectness; and *after* the alterations had been made !

"Appeared personally, Thomas Stokes, master in the Royal Navy, and made oath that the original MSS. chart found on board the French frigate *L'Armide*, and marked A, annexed to his affidavit of the 13th of November, 1817, were delivered at the Hydrographic Office at the Admiralty, and this deponent for *greater convenience of reference !* *inserted a scale of a nautic mile ! !* the original manuscript chart having only a scale of French toises; that in inserting a scale of a nautic mile, this deponent *had allowed a thousand French toises to a nautic mile,* and that Mr. Walker, the Assistant-Hydrographer, accordingly made the erasures which now appear on the face of the chart !" &c.

In these affidavits Mr. Stokes first distinctly swore

---

* The original was neither produced at the court-martial nor before the Court of Admiralty. A far greater and more deliberate error will appear in a future chapter.

that his chart, copied from a French MSS. was *correct*; 2ndly—when detected by the Court of Admiralty—that it was *incorrect*; 3rdly—that the original was *deposited in the Hydrographic Office at the Admiralty.*

My application to Sir John Barrow, then Hydrographer to the Admiralty, was as follows :—

" May 4th, 1818.

" Sir,—As it appears by the affidavit of which I enclose a copy that two charts of Aix Roads, the one stated to be a copy of the other, were deposited in the Hydrographic Office, and that the one *purporting to be the copy* has been delivered up for the purpose of being exhibited as evidence on the part of my opponents in a cause now pending in the High Court of Admiralty, and as it further appears that *an alteration* in the last-mentioned chart was made by Mr. Stokes, and a further alteration by Mr. Walker, Assistant-Hydrographer, I have to request that the Right Honourable the Lords Commissioners will be pleased to permit me to see the other or original chart of Mr. Stokes still remaining at the Hydrographic Office, in order that I may be enabled to judge for myself of the nature and effect of the alterations now acknowledged to have been made on the charts. The reasonableness of this request will, I presume, be manifest to their Lordships, and the more especially, seeing that my opponents *are not only allowed similar access, but have been permitted to withdraw one of the said charts for the purpose of exhibiting it in evidence,* notwithstanding that a variation from the original has been avowedly made therein.

I have, &c.,

" Cochrane.

" Sir John Barrow, Hydrographer, &c."

To this request Sir John Barrow, on the 6th of May, returned the following refusal :—

" As Mr. Stokes's charts have been restored to him, and *a copy* made for the use of the office, I am directed to acquaint your Lordship that my Lords cannot comply with your request in respect *to the original chart,* and as to *the copy* of the chart made in this office and now remaining here, their Lordships *do not feel themselves at liberty to communicate it.*

"I have the honour, &c.

"JOHN BARROW."

This refusal was accompanied by the following copy of a minute from the Admiralty: in which it was pretended that Stokes had only *lent* the original chart to the Hydrographer's office, *to be copied for the use of the Hydrographic Department* — though it had been made use of to acquit an admiral, to the rejection of the charts of the fleet, as will presently be seen.

"Mr. Stokes *lent* the original chart to the Hydrographer's office, to be copied for the *use of that department.*

"Mr. Stokes then went abroad.

"On his return he applied for his chart, which being *mislaid* they gave him the *copy.*

"Stokes, finding the alteration objected to in a court of law, applied about a month since for his own chart, the *original* of which was *restored to him,* copy being made."— 23, 141, 147.

To this singular communication and minute I returned the subjoined reply:—

"13, Henrietta Street, Covent Garden.
18th May, 1818.

"SIR,—Your letter of the 6th of May was delivered to me as I was going out of town, consequently I had no opportunity of referring to documents which I have since consulted, in order to refute the statements which the Lords of the Admiralty appear to have received.

"You inform me, by command of their Lordships, that ' it appears by a report from the Hydrographer that Mr. Stokes had become possessed of the original chart which he *lent* to the Hydrographer's office for the use of that department.' This appears to imply that Mr. Stokes became possessed of the original chart at the time of the attack in the *Charente* under Lord Gambier, whereas Mr. Stokes made oath that it was taken from the *Armide* in 1806, two years and a half previous to the attack in question. As it does not appear from the Minutes of the court-martial on Lord Gambier that the original chart was then produced, and as it is not now forthcoming in the cause now pending in the Court of Admiralty, I am compelled to disbelieve its existence, or at least to believe that it underwent material alterations after it came into Mr. Stokes's possession. The original ought to have been exhibited with the copy at the trial of Lord Gambier, and both either were or ought to have been filed in the office of the Admiralty with the Minutes of the proceedings; but whether *either* are so filed their Lordships *have not permitted me to ascertain.*

" If the original were filed, it could not afterwards have been ' *lent* by Mr Stokes to the Hydrographer's office to be copied for the use of that department.' Even had the copy only been filed — sworn as it was by Mr. Stokes ' *to be correct!* ' there could have been no necessity — if Mr. Stokes was deemed worthy of belief—for the Hydrographer to *borrow the original. Eight years* having elapsed since the court-martial on Lord Gambier, you inform me that ' Mr. Stokes on his return from abroad applied for his chart accordingly, which chart happening to be mislaid, he was furnished *with the copy* in question,' viz. that ' made for the use of the Hydrographer's department.' It is important to observe that *this is completely at variance with the affidavit* of Mr. Stokes, who swears that ' *he himself made the copy*,' and that ' *both the copy and the original were delivered at the Hydrographic Office!* ' It cannot fail to be observed, that to ' deliver ' a chart at the Hydrographic Office, and to ' *lend* a chart to be copied for the use of that department ' — the language of the letter before me — are different expressions, conveying widely different meanings.

"It is also material to observe that it is strange alterations *at all* should have been made on a chart represented to be a *copy* of an *original,* and exhibited as evidence in a court of law. That such original *is not forthcoming* is a very material and a very *suspicious circumstance.* If it be true, or if there really be any other chart than that which is described as a copy and *admitted* to be altered, I may fairly infer that such altered copy differs so materially and so fradulently from the original, or that the original — so called — is itself so palpable a fabrication, or has so obviously been altered, that Mr. Stokes and his employers *do not dare to exhibit it in a court of law;* and have withdrawn it from the Hydrographer's office for the purpose of suppressing so convincing a proof of the fraud practised on Lord Gambier's trial.

"Exclusive of the glaring contradiction between the statements of Mr. Stokes on the court-martial, and that which you have been commanded to make to me, when it is considered that Mr. Stokes is detected in *having altered* a document which he exhibits in a court of law as a correct copy of an original, and that he is no sooner detected than he endeavours to defend the alteration by declaring that it proceeded from the Hydrographer's office, where the *original was deposited;* and that upon such defence leading to an application for leave to inspect the *original,* answer is made that such original *had merely been borrowed of Mr. Stokes,* and had been returned to him *at his own request,* and that request, too, made in consequence of the alteration in the alleged copy *having been detected* — it is impossible not to infer a juggle between Mr. Stokes, the Hydrographic Office, and others whom I shall not here undertake to name, for the purpose of defeating the ends of justice.

"COCHRANE.

"Sir John Barrow, Hydrographer, &c."

Receiving no reply to this letter, I subsequently addressed the following to the Secretary of the Admiralty.

" 9, Bryanstone Street, Portman Square,
2nd July, 1818.

" SIR,—I feel it proper to inclose to you, as Secretary of the Admiralty, a copy of an affidavit, accompanied by a general outline of the chart of Basque Roads, the originals of which are filed in the High Court of Admiralty, by which their Lordships will clearly perceive that five more ships of the line *might* and *ought* to have been taken or destroyed, had the enemy been attacked between daybreak and noon on the 12th of April.   And I have to request, Sir, that you will have the goodness to lay these documents before their Lordships (as well as the inclosed printed case which they have already partly seen in manuscript), with my respectful and earnest desire that their Lordships may be pleased to cause the facts therein set forth to be verified by comparing them with the original documents, logs, charts, and records in their Lordships' possession.   I am the more solicitous that the present Lords Commissioners of the Admiralty should adopt this mode of proceeding, as it will enable them decisively to judge on a subject of great national importance, and also to ascertain (what a portion of the public know) that it is not by false evidence from amongst the lower class of society alone that my character has been assailed, in order not only to perpetuate the concealment of neglect of duty, but to prevent an exposure of the perjury, forgery, and fraud by which that charge was endeavoured to be refuted.

" I beg, Sir, that you will assure their Lordships on my part, that as a deep sense of public duty alone induced me formerly to express a hope that the thanks of Parliament might not be pressed for the conduct of the affair in Basque Roads, so, in addition to that feeling, which made me disregard every private interest, I have formed a fixed determination never, whilst I exist, to rest satisfied until I expose the baseness and wickedness of the attempts made to destroy my character, which I value more than my life.

" As the affidavits of Captains Robert Kerr and Robert Hockings (which, as well as my own, are filed in the High Court of Admiralty) may immediately be made the subject of indictment in a court of law, and as the proceedings in the Admiralty Court have been put off under the pretence of obtaining further evidence in support of the mis-statements of these officers and the claim of Lord Gambier, I have respectfully to request that when the Lords Commissioners of the Admiralty shall have instituted an inquiry into the logs, charts, and documents, and ascertained the conduct of the before-named officers, they will be pleased to cause public justice to be done in a matter involving the character of the naval service so deeply.

" If, Sir, through their Lordships' means, a fair investigation shall take place, it will be far more gratifying than any other course of proceeding.

" I have the honour to be, &c. &c.,

" COCHRANE.

" Jno. Wilson Croker, Esq., Secretary, &c., Admiralty."

After the above correspondence I gave up, as hope-less, all further attempts to obtain even so much as a sight of the charts without which any public expla-nation on my part would have been unintelligible.

In the year 1819 — when nearly ruined by law expenses, fines, and deprivation of pay — in despair moreover, of surmounting the unmerited obloquy which had befallen me in England — I accepted from the Chilian government an invitation to aid in its war of independence ; and removed with Lady Cochrane and our family to South America, in the vain hope of find-ing, amongst strangers, that sympathy which, though interested, might, in some measure compensate for the persecutions of our native land.*   I will not attempt

---

* The malice of offended faction pursued me even to this remote part of the globe, in the shape of a " Foreign Enlistment Act " (59th George III. cap. 69). This Act was introduced by the At-

to describe the agonised feelings of this even temporary exile under such circumstances from my
country, in whose annals it had been my ambition to
secure an honourable position.   No language of mine
could convey the mental sufferings consequent on finding
aspirations — founded on exertions which ought to
have justified all my hopes — frustrated by the enmity
of an illiberal political faction, which regarded services
to the nation as nothing when opposed to the interests
of party.

On my return to England, from causes which will
appear in the sequel, the subject of the charts was not
again officially renewed.

Latterly, however, considering that at my advanced
age there was a probability of quitting the world with
the stigma attached to my memory of having been
the indirect cause of bringing my commander-in-chief
to a court-martial — though in reality the charges were
made by the Admiralty — I determined to make one
more effort to obtain those documents which alone
could justify the course I had deemed it my duty to
pursue.   In the hope that the more enlightened policy
of modern times might concede the boon, which a
former period of political corruption had denied, I
applied to Sir John Pakington, late First Lord of the
Admiralty, for permission to inspect such documents
relative to the affair of Aix Roads as the Board might
possess.

torney-General, Sir Samuel Shepherd, for the express purpose of
preventing any one from assisting the South American States then
at war with Spain; the Act being thus especially levelled at me,
though injuriously driven from the service of my own country.

Permission was kindly and promptly granted by Sir John Pakington ; but Lord Derby's ministry going out of office before the boon could be rendered available, it became necessary to renew the application to the successor of the Right Honourable Baronet, viz. his Grace the Duke of Somerset, who as promptly complied with the request. The reader may judge of my surprise on discovering, in its proper place, bound up amongst the Naval Records, in the usual official manner, the *very chart the possession of which had been denied by a former Board of Admiralty !*

The Duke of Somerset, moreover, with a consideration for which I feel truly grateful, ordered that whatever copies of charts I might require, should be supplied by the Hydrographic Office; so that by the kindness of Captain Washington, the eminent hydrographer to the Board, tracings of the suppressed charts have been made, and are now appended to this volume. His grace further ordered that the logs of Lord Gambier's fleet should be submitted to the inspection of Mr. Earp, with permission to make extracts ; an order fully carried out by the courtesy of Mr. Lascelles, of the Record Office, to the extent of the logs in his possession.

It is, therefore, only after the lapse of fifty-one years and in my own eighty-fifth year,—a postponement too late for my peace, but not for my justification,—that I am, from official documents, and proofs deduced from official documents which were from the first and still are in the possession of the Government, enabled to remove the stigma before alluded to, and to lay before the public such an explanation of the fabricated chart, together with an Admiralty copy of the chart itself, as from that evidence shall place the whole matter beyond the possibility of dispute.   It will in the present day be difficult to credit the existence of such practices and evil influences of party spirit in past times as could permit an Administration, even for the purpose of pre- serving the *prestige* of a Government to claim as a glorious victory ! a neglect of duty which, to use the mildest terms, was both a naval and a national dis- honour.

The point which more immediately concerns myself is, however, this :—that the verdict founded on this fabri- cated chart, together with the subsequent official enmity directed against me in consequence of my determina- tion to oppose the vote of thanks to Lord Gambier, was persevered in year after year, till it reached its climax in the consequences of that subsequent trial which was made the pretext for driving me from the navy, in defiance of remonstrance at the Board of Admiralty itself.   I have not long been aware of the latter fact. Admiral Collier has recently informed me that Sir W. J. Hope, then one of the Naval Lords of the Ad- miralty, told him that considering the sentence passed against me cruel and vindictive, he refused to sign his name to the decision of the Board by which my name was struck off the Navy List.

CHAP. XXV.

A NAVAL STUDY—*continued.*

THE charts to which the reader's attention is invited
are those alluded to in the last chapter, as having,
after the lapse of fifty-one years, been traced for me
by Captain Washington, by the order of his Grace
the Duke of Somerset. The subject being no longer
of personal but of historical interest, there can be no
impropriety in laying before the naval service, for its
judgment, materials so considerately supplied by the
present First Lord of the Admiralty.

CHART A

is a correct tracing of Aix Roads from the *Neptune
François,* a set of charts issued by the French Hydro-
graphical Department — bound in a volume, and supplied for the use of the French navy previous to

1809 *; copies from the same source being at that period supplied under the auspices of the Board of Admiralty for the use of British ships on the French coasts — these, in fact, forming the only guides available at that period.

Chart A shows a clear entrance of two miles, without shoal or hindrance of any kind, between Ile d'Aix and the Boyart Sand ; the soundings close to the latter marking thirty-five feet at low water, with from thirty to forty feet in mid-channel. The chart shows, moreover, a channel leading to a spacious anchorage between the Boyart and Palles Sands, marking clear soundings at low water of from twenty to thirty feet close to either sand, with thirty feet in mid-channel. In this anchorage line-of-battle-ships could not only have *floated*, without danger of grounding, but could have effectively operated against the enemy's fleet, even in its entire state before the attack, wholly out of range of the batteries on Ile d'Aix, as will hereafter be corroborated by the logs and evidence of experienced officers present in the attack, and therefore practically acquainted with the soundings. To a naval eye, it will be apparent that, by gaining this anchorage, it would not at any time have been difficult for the British force to have interposed the enemy's fleet between itself and the fortifications on Ile d'Aix in such a way as completely to neutralise the fire of the latter.

Further inspection of the chart will indicate an inner

* Sets of these charts, bound as described, were found on board the grounded ships captured in the afternoon of the 12th of April, and were therefore available for the purposes of the court-martial, had it been deemed expedient to consult them.

anchorage, called *Le Grand Trousse*, to which any British vessel disabled by the enemy's ships—two only of which, out of thirteen, remained afloat,—might have retired with safety to an anchorage capable of holding a fleet—the soundings in *Le Grand Trousse* marking from thirty to forty feet at low water. Between these anchorages it will be seen on the chart that there is no shoal, nor any other danger whatever.*

The rise of tide marked on the chart was from ten to twelve feet†, consequently amply sufficient *on a rising tide* for the two-deckers and frigates to have been sent to the attack of the enemy's ships aground on the Palles Shoal, as testified by the evidence of Captains Malcolm and Broughton.‡ The flood-tide making about 7·0 A.M. gave assurance of abundant depth of water by 11·0 A.M., which is the time marked in the commander-in-chief's log § as that of *bringing the British ships to an anchor!* in place of forwarding them to the attack of ships on shore!

This chart was tendered by me to the Court, in explanation of my evidence. It was, however, rejected,

* This anchorage was plainly marked on the French charts supplied to the British ships, as deposed to by the officers present in the action. (See the evidence of Captain Broughton, *Minutes*, p. 222, and that of Captain Newcomb, p. 198). The correctness of the chart furnished by me being thus clearly established in evidence.

† In reality, from eighteen to twenty feet, at spring tides, as appeared from the testimony of various officers, Admiral Stopford amongst others. Even Mr. Stokes marked on his chart a rise of twenty-one feet, so that there was abundance of water for the operation of ships of the largest class. The defence of the Commander-in-chief was, that there was not sufficient water at half-flood to float the ships!

‡ See pp. 58 and 63.

§ Erroneously, according to the logs of the other ships.

because I could not *produce the French hydrographer to prove its correctness!* though copies of a similar chart, as has been said, were furnished to British ships for their guidance! Being thus repudiated, my chart was flung contemptuously under the table, and neither this nor any other *official* chart was afterwards allowed to corroborate the facts subsequently testified by the various officers present in the action, they being imperatively ordered to base their observations on the chart of Mr. Stokes alluded to in the last chapter, as having been — eight years after the court-martial — pronounced by the Court of Admiralty so incorrect as to require material alteration before it could be put in evidence in a court of law! To this point we shall presently come.

A singular circumstance connected with the rejected chart should rather have *secured its reception,* viz. that it was taken by my own hands out of the *Ville de Varsovie* French line-of-battle ship shortly before she was set fire to, and therefore its authenticity, as having been officially supplied by the French government for the use of that ship, was beyond doubt or question. I also produced two similar charts, on which were marked the places of the enemy's ships aground at daylight on the 12th of April, as observed from the *Impérieuse,* the only vessel then in proximity. The positions of the grounded vessels are marked on Chart B.

The manner of the rejection by the Court — at the suggestion of the Judge-Advocate — of the chart tendered by me, is worthy of note.

PRESIDENT.—" I think your lordship said just now, that you

thought there was water enough for ships of any draught of water ? "

LORD COCHRANE. — " Yes."

PRESIDENT. — " Have you *an authenticated chart,* or any evidence that can be produced to show that there is *actually* such a depth of water ? "

LORD COCHRANE *(putting in the charts)*. — " It was *actually* from the soundings we had going in, provided the tide does not fall more than twelve feet, which I am not aware of. I studied the chart of Basque Roads for some days before. The rise of the tide, as I understand from that, is from ten to twelve feet. It is so mentioned in the French chart. I have no other means of judging." *

Judge-Advocate. — " THIS CHART IS NOT EVIDENCE BEFORE THE COURT, BECAUSE HIS LORDSHIP CANNOT PROVE ITS CORRECTNESS ! ! "

PRESIDENT. — *No ! It is nothing more than to show upon what grounds his lordship forms his opinion on the rise and fall of the tide ! ! "* †

---

* This was fully corroborated by Captain Malcolm, when, having said that "there were *no obstacles* to prevent the frigates and some ships of the line from going into Aix Roads, he was asked by the President, " if he made known to the Commander-in-chief that by keeping close to the Boyart Shoal the ships *might have gone in ?* "

The reply was in every way remarkable.

CAPTAIN MALCOLM. — " I do not know that I mentioned this to the Commander-in-chief. THE CHARTS SHOWED IT."—*Minutes*, p. 214. A complete corroboration of the correctness of my charts tendered to but rejected by the Court; though as these had been supplied under the sanction of the Admiralty, it was out of the question to reject them as the basis of evidence, inasmuch as there could be none other of a reliable nature.

† The following extract from my evidence, and the singular remark from Admiral Young, are extracted from the minutes of the court-martial.

" The Commander-in-chief had the same charts as I was in possession of, and from these I formed my conclusion with respect to the anchorage. In reconnoitring the enemy's fleet, *so near as*

It was not put in for any purpose of the kind — for I had expressly said that I had no opinion as to the rise and fall of the tide, except as marked on the French official charts. The object of my putting in those charts was to *show the truth of the whole matter before the Court.* The president, however, flung the chart under the table with as much eagerness as the Judge-Advocate had evinced when objecting to its reception in evidence.*

The object of the chart was in fact to prove, as indeed *was subsequently proved* by the testimony of eminent officers, and *would* have been proved even by the ships' logs had they been consulted, that there was plenty of channel room to keep clear of the batteries on Ile d'Aix, together with abundant depth of water † ; and that the commander-in-chief, in ordering all the ships to *come to an anchor,* in place of sending a portion ‡ of the British

to induce him to open a fire from almost his whole line, I reported to the Commander-in-chief the ruinous state of Ile d'Aix, *the inner fortifications being completely blown up and destroyed.* There were only 13 guns mounted."

ADMIRAL YOUNG.—" Will you consider, my Lord Cochrane, before you go on, HOW FAR THIS IS RELEVANT " ! ! ! — *Minutes,* p. 58.

My assertion of the fact that the Commander-in-chief's charts were identical with my own, as having come from the Admiralty, was considered *irrelevant,* because, had they been put in, or mine not rejected, there could have been no doubt of the result of the court-martial.

* It is a singular circumstance that notwithstanding the chart was flung under the table and rejected by the Court, I found it *bound up amongst the Admiralty records !*

† The ships which were sent in though too late were untouched by shot or shell. For the depth of water they found on going in, see page 71.

‡ My signals were, " *half the fleet* can destroy the enemy." Then, " the *frigates alone* can destroy the enemy." Yet in his defence

ships to the attack of the enemy's vessels aground
on the north-west part of the Palles Shoal, on the
morning of the 12th of April, had displayed a "*mollesse*"
— as it was happily termed by Admiral Gravière —
unbecoming the Commander-in-chief of a British force,
superior in numbers, and having nothing to fear from
about a dozen guns on the fortifications of Aix ; which,
had the ships been sent in along the edge of the
Boyart, could have inflicted no material damage, either
by shot or shell.*

These were precisely the points which the ministry
did not want proved, and which — as will presently be
seen—the Court was no less anxious to avoid proving.
Had the French chart been received in evidence, as
it ought to have been — I do not say mine, but
those on board the flagship itself, or indeed *any copy*
supplied by the Admiralty to the fleet—a vote of thanks
to Lord Gambier would have been *impossible*, and with
the impossibility would have vanished the Government *prestige* of a great victory gained by their commander-in-chief, under their auspices.†

The French official chart being thus adroitly got rid
of by the Judge-Advocate, the other charts tendered
by me to mark the positions of the enemy's ships

Lord Gambier assumed that I had signalled for the fleet at a time
when, as he alleged, it could not have floated for want of water ?

* See Captain Malcolm's evidence, page 58.   Also Captain Godfrey's, of the *Etna*, who "*thinks* some of the enemy's shot went
over them " (*Minutes*, p. 173), but admits that not a mast, yard,
or even a rope-yarn was touched.

† "I was furnished by Lord Cochrane with a French chart, *and
considered it a good one.*"—*Evidence of Captain Newcomb*, p. 199.

"I had for several years been in the possession of official French
charts, which, in my previous cruises, had not been found defective,

aground shared the like fate, though not open to the same objection.   The exactness of the positions was moreover confirmed by the evidence of Mr. Stokes, the master of the *Caledonia*, Lord Gambier's flagship; though his chart, substituted for those in use amongst the British ships, was in direct contradiction to his oral evidence.

The positions, of the ships aground as marked on my charts, were as follows.

The *Ocean*, three-decker, bearing the flag of Admiral Allemand, and forming a group with three other line-of-battle ships close to her, lay aground on the north-west edge of the Palles Shoal, nearest the deep water, where even a gun-boat, had it been sent whilst they lay on their bilge, could have so perforated their bottoms, that they could not have floated with the rising tide.   All were immoveably aground, and were therefore incapable of opposition to an attacking force*; whilst each of the

and from those charts I had at all times drawn my conclusions with respect to the depth of water, or other circumstances which related to the navigation on the enemy's coast."

PRESIDENT.—" The coast of the enemy, I suppose you mean ? "

LORD COCHRANE.—" I refer to the French coast."

ADMIRAL YOUNG.—" When did you discover that there was this anchorage in deep water ? "

LORD COCHRANE.—" I have said that in going in I found the soundings correct, and that, in fact, I had such confidence in the chart, that I had said to Admiral Keates, when we were off there, and to Admiral Thornborough, that there *could be no difficulty in going in there and destroying the enemy's fleet.*   I took the chart on board Admiral Thornborough's ship."—See my Letter to Admiral Thornborough, vol. i. p. 195.—*Lord Cochrane's Evidence*, p. 57.

* " Till *about noon*, the Ocean, three-decker, was *heeling considerably, and appeared to me to be heaving her guns overboard.*"— *Captain Malcolm (Minutes*, p. 209).   She escaped about two o'clock P.M., just before I advanced in the *Impérieuse*, lest all should escape.

group of three lay so much inclined towards each other as to present the appearance of having their yards locked together.* They had, in fact, drifted with the same current, into the same spot, and being nearly of the same draught of water, had grounded close to each other. The one separate was a vessel of less draught than these, and had gone a little further on the shoal.

The correctness of these positions, as marked on my chart, was completely confirmed by Mr. Stokes, master of the flag-ship, in his oral evidence as subjoined.

QUESTION. — " State the situation of the enemy's fleet on the morning of the 12th of April."

MR. STOKES. — " At daylight I observed *the whole of the enemy's ships, except two of the line, on shore.* Four of them *lay in group,* or lay together on the western part of the Palles Shoal. The three-decker (*L'Océan,* flagship) was *on the north-west edge* of the Palles Shoal, with her broadside flanking the passage ; *the north-west point nearest the deep water."* * — (*Minutes,* page 147.)

This was the truth as to the positions of the grounded ships which escaped ; these being referred to in Mr. Stokes's evidence precisely as marked on my rejected chart. That is, his evidence showed, in corroboration of my chart, the *utter helplessness of an enemy which a British admiral refrained from attacking, though aground !*

* "I *think* their yards were not locked."—*Evidence of Mr. Fairfax, Minutes,* p. 144. It was, however, *so nearly,* that Mr. Fairfax, a witness carefully in Lord Gambier's interest, could only *think* about it. He reluctantly admitted that all lay "*within a ship's length of each other,*" and ships lying aground on their bilge inclined towards each other at an angle of thirty degrees are—if not locked together—completely incapable of resistance.

The French charts produced by me being thus rejected, those in the possession of the Commander-in-chief not produced, and those connected with the fleet not being called for, the court decided to rely upon two charts professedly constructed for the occasion by the master of the *Caledonia*, Mr. Stokes, and the master of the fleet, Mr. Fairfax, *neither of whom was present in the attack.**

*   *   *   *   *

CHART C

was tendered to the Court by Mr. Stokes, the master of Lord Gambier's flag-ship *Caledonia*.

This chart professed to show, and was sworn to by Mr. Stokes as showing, the positions of the enemy's ships aground *on the morning of the* 12*th of April,* before the *Ocean* three-decker, together with a group of three outermost ships near her, had been permitted by the delay of the Commander-in-chief to warp off and escape. Instead, however, of placing these on his chart as they lay helplessly aground " nearest the deep water " as *he had sworn in his evidence,* they were placed in

---

* It is a remarkable fact that many of the witnesses chiefly relied on by the Commander-in-chief, in confirmation of his having done his duty, *had not been in Aix Roads at all,* and could therefore have no knowledge of anything, except their remaining inactive with the fleet whilst the enemy's ships were warping off. Mr. Stokes was of this number; yet all were questioned on points known only to officers intimately acquainted with Aix Roads, and present at the action. But for the court to adopt *exclusively,* as will presently be seen, a chart constructed by a man who admitted that an important portion had been laid down *from hearsay,* was monstrous; the more so, as the official charts, would have shown the truth.

on the other side of the sand, in the positions occupied *after their escape !* and *to this Mr. Stokes swore as their* position *when first driven ashore!* The *Ocean* three-decker, and group in particular, which, according to Mr. Stokes's oral evidence, must, as already stated, have been an easy prey to a gunboat had such been sent on the first quarter instead of the last quarter flood, was thus placed on his chart where no vessel could have approached them ! *

This falsehood on Mr. Stokes's chart, in opposition to his oral evidence just given, as well as to the evidence of other officers, formed one of the principal grounds of Lord Gambier's acquittal ; and it was for this end that the official French charts presented by me for the information of the court were rejected by the judge-advocate.

On the presentation of Mr. Stokes's chart to the court, the subjoined colloquy took place as to the methods adopted in its construction.

MR. BICKNELL. — " Produce a chart or drawing of the anchorage at Isle d'Aix, with the relative positions of the

---

* Mr. Stokes, moreover swore, in his evidence, that the *Ocean* three-decker lay *on the north-west edge of the Palles Shoal*, and that the group lay on the *western* part of the same shoal, though the latter observation was incorrect, as the group lay around the *Ocean*, which formed a part of it. On his chart these vessels are placed to the SOUTH-EAST of the shoal, and *the remainder* nearly DUE EAST ! ! That is, in place of being " *nearest the deep water,*" where they were easily attackable, they were placed on the chart " *farthest from the deep water,*" where they were not attackable. He swore too that they lay with their broadsides "*flanking the passage* " to Aix Roads. On his chart, not one of them "flanks the passage," but all are made *to flank the opposite direction ;* so that they could not have fired on any British ship which might have been sent in.

British and French fleets, and other particulars, on and previous to the 12th of April last."

The Witness produced it.

MR. BICKNELL. — " Did you prepare this drawing, and from what documents, authorities, and observations; and are the several matters delineated therein accurately delineated, to the best of your knowledge and belief?"

MR. STOKES. — " I prepared that *drawing* (Chart C), partly from the knowledge I gained in sounding to the southward of the Palles Shoal, and the anchorage of the Isle of Aix.* *The outlines of the chart are taken from the Neptune François,* and the position of the enemy's fleet from Mr. Edward Fairfax, and from the French captain of the *Ville de Varsovie,* and the British fleet from my own observation." The distance between the sands was copied from a French MS. which will be produced, and that *I take it* is correct.

MR. BICKNELL.—" Are the matters and things therein accurately described?"

MR. STOKES. — " They are."

PRESIDENT (*inspecting Mr. Stokes's chart*). — " There was a large chart you lent me?"

---

* In his subsequent evidence Mr. Stokes admitted that he had *never sounded there at all* previous to the action !

QUESTION.—" Had you any knowledge of that anchorage previous to the 12th of April?"

MR. STOKES.—" NONE WHATEVER ! " — *Minutes,* p. 148.

He swears that everything on his chart is *accurately described* — then, that " the distance between the sands," which was one of the most important points of the court-martial, *was copied from a French MS. !* the name of whose author he does not think proper to communicate, nor does the court ask him ! nor was any MSS. produced in Court. Yet, as master of the Admiral's flagship, Mr. Stokes must have navigated her by the French charts supplied by the Admiralty, though these when tendered by me to the Court had been rejected. The fleet could, in fact, have had no other for its guidance, as no British survey of Aix Roads was in existence. Such charts were surely a better guide in any case than an anonymous MSS.

MR. STOKES. — "That is the chart I allude to.   This chart I produce as containing the *various positions*."

JUDGE-ADVOCATE (*to the President*). — " THIS CHART IS PRODUCED TO SAVE A GREAT DEAL OF TROUBLE ! ! " (*Minutes*, pp. 23, 24.)

No doubt — the trouble of confirming the Commander-in-chief's neglect of duty in not following up a manifest advantage, as would have been shown had the court allowed the *Neptune François itself* to have been put, in evidence; for it would have shown a clear passage of *two miles* wide, extending beyond reach of shot, instead of the *one mile* passage in Mr. Stokes's "*accurate outlines*" of the French chart, and no shoal where he had marked only twelve feet of water ! *   That the president should have allowed this to pass, after having himself detected the imposition practised on the court, is a point upon which I will not comment.

Mr. Stokes further admitted his chart to be valueless, as regarded the position of the enemy's fleet ashore, for he said that position was taken "*from Mr. Edward Fairfax and the captain of the Ville de Varsovie*, and the British fleet *from " his own observations*." That is, he confessed to know nothing but from hearsay as to the position of *the enemy's fleet*, the important object before the court; but only of the position *of the British fleet*, lying at anchor nine miles from the enemy's fleet ashore, a matter with which the court had nothing to do ; he being all the time on board the flagship, at that distance.   Yet the court insisted on this chart being *ex-*

---

* Compare charts A and C.

clusively referred to throughout the court-martial! * It is strange that such a chart should have been used at all, when the charts of the fleet were available, but more strange that, when the court saw the two miles passage in the French chart was reduced to little more than *one mile* in Mr. Stokes's chart, he was not even asked the reason why he had not conformed to the scale of the French chart, *to the correctness of the outlines of which he had sworn!*

But the most glaring contradiction of Mr. Stokes's chart is this : he swore to his chart as truly depicting the positions of the *Ocean* and other grounded ships, as they lay *on the morning of the* 12*th of April, which was the point before the Court;* but being further questioned, reluctantly admitted that he had marked the *Ocean*

---

* The President thus dictated to Captain Beresford :—" Captain Beresford *must* say whether the ships are marked on *that* chart (Mr. Stokes's) as they appeared to him." Captain Beresford took no notice of the order.

Captain Bligh was less independent when asked to vouch for the accuracy of Mr. Stokes's chart. He " *thinks* the enemy's ships, on the morning of the 12th, were as there represented, though Mr. Stokes, in contradiction to his own chart, had sworn *that they were not so marked, but only those that were destroyed!* "

When asked if the ships aground could have annoyed the British ships had they been sent in ? Captain Bligh replied, " I *think* they were capable of annoying the British ships." — *Minutes*, p. 154. He, however, immediately afterwards stated that the ships "were not within reach of the guns of the British squadron."

Captain Kerr " *thinks* the situation of the enemy's fleet on the morning of the 12th was marked on Mr. Stokes's chart *as nearly as it can be*. There were seven sail-of-the-line ashore, and two afloat." — *Minutes*, p. 166. What had the numbers ashore or afloat to do with their exact position ? A palpable evasion of the question was permitted by the court.

as she lay on the 13*th of April,* viz. *on the following day when an attack was made on her by the bomb vessel!* though he had just sworn to the positions of the ships on the chart as being those *on the morning of the* 12*th,* immediately after having run ashore to escape destruction.

The fact was, as will be seen on inspection of the chart, that *not one* of the ships under the cognizance of the court is marked on Stokes's chart as they lay on the morning of the 12th, which position, and not that on the 13th, was the subject of inquiry. Though as already said this misrepresentation was detected by the President, the court nevertheless persisted in the exclusive use of Mr. Stokes's chart throughout the trial, in accordance with the suggestion of the Judge-Advocate, that it was produced to " *save a great deal of trouble.*"

The President thus commented on the manifest contradiction.

PRESIDENT.—"I observe in the chart I had from you the situation of the *Ocean* particularly is *not marked on the* 12*th. She is marked on the* 13*th as advanced up the Charente!* "

MR. STOKES.—" The *only ships* marked on the chart *on the* 12*th* are *those that were destroyed.* The reason I marked her on the 13th is, that a particular attack was made on her by the bombs. *I observed her from the mizentop of the Caledonia* *, and I *also had an observation from an officer,* so that I have no doubt her position is put down within a cable's length." (Minutes p. 147.)

There is something in this evidence almost too re-

---

* Nine miles off. This answer shows most forcibly the nature of the data on which Mr. Stokes's chart was constructed.

pugnant for observation. Mr. Stokes first swore that his chart accurately described the positions of the enemy's ships ashore on the *morning of the* 12*th*. He then admitted that the most material ship of the enemy's fleet was marked as she lay *on the* 13*th ! !* On this misstatement being detected by the president, he then swore that the only ships marked on the 12th were *those which were destroyed*, viz. *on the evening and night of the* 12*th !*—a matter foreign to the subject of inquiry ; which was *how the ships lay on the morning of the* 12*th, and whether Lord Gambier was to blame for refraining from attacking them at that particular time ?* So that the positions of the enemy's ships aground on the morning of the 12th, according to Mr. Stokes's own admission, *were not marked on his chart at all!* though he had sworn to this very chart *as giving those positions accurately to the best of his knowledge and belief;* and with the full knowledge that their position on the *morning* of the 12th, when they were helplessly aground, was the point before the court, — not their position *in the evening,* and on the following day after their escape to a spot where the British ships could not have pursued them.

The fact is, Mr. Stokes swore to their positions *after their being warped off in consequence of the British fleet being prematurely brought to an anchor*— as being their positions *previous to their escape!* which was the matter of inquiry before the court, viz. as to whether the Commander-in-chief had not committed a neglect of duty in permitting them to escape *by the rising tide,* when and before when the British force *could have operated with every advantage in its favour.*

The court had nothing whatever to inquire about with regard to the ships which were *destroyed*, respecting which there could be no question ; the subject of inquiry being whether the escape of the *other* ships run ashore from terror of the explosion vessels on the night of the 11th, and *still ashore* on the morning of the 12th, ought to have been prevented.

Not so much as one of the ships marked on Mr. Stokes's chart formed part of the " group" to which he had sworn, in his oral evidence, as lying on the " western and northernmost edge of the Palles Shoal, *nearest the deep water*, all of which escaped towards the Charente, where he truly enough placed the *Ocean* three-decker, but as she lay on the 13th instead of the 12th, he having sworn to the truth of his chart as showing her position on the morning of the 12th ! It was a desperate venture, and can only be accounted for by the supposition that, in reality, Mr. Stokes had never seen the chart to which he was swearing. It was no wonder, as proved in the first chapter, that Mr. Stokes applied to the Admiralty for permission to *alter his chart* before producing it in a court of law, where it must have fallen under my inspection !

I will indeed so far exonerate Mr. Stokes from a portion of blame, by declaring my belief that he never had looked at the chart to which he had sworn. There is little question in my mind but that this chart had been fabricated under the auspices of Mr. Lavie, Lord Gambier's solicitor, the only hope of success consisting in affirming a false position for the grounded ships ; the chart being then given to Stokes for paternity. Had it been otherwise, Stokes could not possibly have

sworn to a chart in diametrical opposition to his oral
evidence, which truly stated that on the morning of
the 12th, the *Ocean* and group lay on "*the north-west
edge of the Palles shoal, nearest the deep water*," where
they were easily attackable.   On his chart they were
placed on the *opposite side of the shoal!* where no ship
could have got near them.

Lord Gambier no doubt saw the mistake committed
by the evidence of his Master, and adroitly relieved
him from the dilemma, by putting a question of a
totally different nature.   With this course the court
complacently complied, notwithstanding that the president had detected a discrepancy so glaring.

Another material point on Mr. Stokes's chart was his
marking *a shoal* between the Boyart and the Palles
Sands, where Capt. Broughton and others present in the
action, who *actually sounded there*, testify in corroboration of the French chart to there being *no shoal whatever*.* Yet Mr. Stokes marks only from twelve to
sixteen feet, in the deepest part.   That this statement
was a misrepresentation on the part of Mr. Stokes, is
proved by Lord Gambier himself, who, in his defence,
says that "Mr. Stokes found on this bar or bank from
fourteen to nineteen feet (*Minutes*, p. 134). When closely
questioned on the point, Mr. Stokes deposed to these
soundings as "*having been reported to him to have been
found*"! (*Minutes*, p. 150.) The *Neptune François*
gives from twenty to thirty feet at low water, which
was no doubt correct.

But even had there been only nineteen feet of water
Mr. Stokes again forgot his chart when he gave *oral*

* See p. 68.

evidence that " the rise of tide in Aix Roads is *twenty-one* feet, which is more than we ever found in Basque Roads " (*Minutes*, p. 150). I had put the rise of tide at *twelve feet* only, so that by the oral evidence of Mr. Stokes there was abundance of water for the British force to have operated with full effect.

A still further falsification of the chart was, that it reduced the channel by which the British fleet must have passed to the attack to little more than *a mile* in width, in defiance of the fact that on all the official French charts the minimum distance between the Boyart Sand and the fortifications on Ile d'Aix was nearly *two miles*, and that Admiral Stopford, the second admiral in command, confirmed the correctness of the French charts so far as to admit a width of *a mile and a half*. The object of Mr. Stokes's statement was to prove the danger to which, in a channel *only a mile wide*, the British ships would have been exposed from the batteries on Ile d'Aix had they been sent to the attack. To this end was the chart no doubt produced, and as narrowing the channel to a mile only — to meet the occasion — gave a colour to this view, his chart was accepted by the court, whilst the French charts which *marked two miles*, were rejected.

A yet more flagrant contradiction is — that within pistol shot of the *western* and *north-western* edge of the Palles Shoal, where Mr. Stokes first truly swore " the *Ocean* three-decker and a group of four lay *aground* on the morning of the 12th," he has placed *the attacking British ships*, where their logs show that they never touched the ground, notwithstanding that they took up their positions on a *falling tide.* If they could float in safety much more could other ships have done so at 11 a.m. on *a rising tide?* How such a manifest discrepancy could have passed without comment from any member of the court-martial, is a point which is not in my power to explain.

Such are some of the leading features of this famous chart, upon which the acquittal of Lord Gambier was made to rest, though the chart was admittedly constructed—not from personal observation, otherwise than from the mizentop of the *Caledonia,* nine miles off—but from unofficial sources—from an anonymous manuscript, and *even from hearsay !*

Yet Lord Gambier did not scruple to introduce this chart for the guidance of the court, in the following terms :

" I have to call the attention of the Court to the plan drawn by Lord Cochrane of the position of the enemy's ships as they *lay aground on the morning of the* 12*th of April,* and to that position marked upon the chart verified by Mr. Stokes; the former laid down from uncertain data, the latter *from angles measured and other observations made on the spot* *; the difference between the two is too apparent to escape the notice of the Court, and the respective merits of these charts will not, I think, admit of a comparison." (*Minutes,* p. 133.)

This statement was made by Lord Gambier in face of the admission previously made by Mr. Stokes, that his observations were taken from the mizentop of the *Caledonia,* three leagues off — that he had never

---

* See note, p. 26.

sounded in Aix Roads — that the soundings were only reported to him, the name of the reporter being omitted — and that he had only marked upon his chart, " *the ships that were destroyed*" on the evening and during the night of the 12th, the destruction, in fact, not being complete till the morning of the 13th.

This contradiction is so important to a right comprehension of what follows, that I will, at the risk of prolixity, bring into one focus Mr. Stokes's admissions as to his *data* for the construction of his chart.

"I prepared that drawing partly from the knowledge I gained *in sounding* to the southward of the Palles Shoal. The outlines of the chart are taken from the *Neptune Français* (narrowed from two miles to one!). The positions of the enemy's fleet are from Mr. Fairfax and the captain of the *Ville de Varsovie.* For the distance between the sands I must refer the court to a chart *which I copied from a French manuscript!*" (*Minutes*, pp. 23, 24.)

For this confused jumble from unauthoritative sources, the French charts were rejected as not being trustworthy, and Lord Gambier did not hesitate to endorse Mr. Stokes's fabrication as being "from angles measured and other observations taken on the spot;" whilst by this act he decried the use of the French charts by which his own fleet had been guided!

Comment, whether on Lord Gambier's statement or on Mr. Stokes's involuntary contradiction thereof in his oral evidence, is superfluous. If such were wanted, it must be sought for in the fact already adduced in the first chapter, viz. that, in 1817 and 1818, Mr. Stokes, when conscious that his fabrication must become public, and that it might fall into my hands, thought it prudent to make affidavit before the Court of Admiralty that this chart, produced at the court-martial nine years before, *was incorrect*, and *therefore required alteration! !* for which purpose the Admiralty gave him back his chart, though this, as already observed, remains to this day bound up amongst the Admiralty records. The affidavits of Mr. Stokes will be in the remembrance of the reader.

In a national point of view, Mr. Stokes's chart has another and even more important feature. A comparison between the French chart and that produced by Mr. Stokes will show that the latter narrowed the entrance to Aix Roads — which on the French charts is two miles wide — to one mile, and that it filled a space with shoals where scarcely a shoal existed. Of the imaginativeness of Mr. Stokes in this respect, the French Government appears to have taken a very justifiable naval advantage, calculated to deter any British admiral in future from undertaking in Aix Roads offensive operations of any kind.

A chart of the Aix Roads based on a modern French chart has recently been shown me, as on the point of being issued by the Board of Admiralty, on which chart the main channel between Ile d'Aix and the Boyart sand is laid down according to charts copied from fabricated charts produced on Lord Gambier's court-martial, and not according to the hydrographic charts of the *Neptune François*. The comparatively clear anchorage shown in the new chart is also filled with Mr. Stokes's imaginary shoals! the result being that no British admiral, if guided by the new chart,

would trust his ships in Aix Roads *at all*, though both
under Admiral Knowles and at the attack in 1809
British ships found no difficulty whatever from want
of water, or other causes, when once ordered in.

The solution of the matter is not difficult.   For
the purpose of deterring a future British fleet from
entering Aix Roads, the modern French Government
appears to have followed the chart of Mr. Stokes in
place of their former official chart; and the British
Admiralty, having no opportunity of surveying the
anchorage in question, has copied this modern French
chart; so that in future the fabrications of Mr. Stokes
or rather I should say, the ingenuity of Lord Gambier's
solicitor, or whoever may have palmed the chart on
Mr. Stokes, will form the best possible security to one
of the most exposed anchorages on the Atlantic coast
of France.   Assuredly no British Admiral, with the
new chart in his hands,—should such be issued—would
for a moment think of operating in such an anchorage
as is there laid down, notwithstanding that former
British fleets have operated in perfect safety so far as
soundings were concerned.

CHART D

was constructed by Mr. Fairfax, the Master of the
Fleet, and was used by the Court as confirmatory
of Mr. Stokes's chart, agreeing with it, in fact, on
nearly every point; a circumstance not at all extraordinary, as in his examination Mr. Stokes first
says that "his *marks* arose from the knowledge he
gained in sounding in the anchorage of Aix" (*Minutes*,

p. 23), whilst Mr. Fairfax swore that he " GAVE MR. STOKES THE MARKS."!!* A fact subsequently proved by Mr. Stokes, who admitted that he had " *never sounded there at all* " The credibility of either witness may be left to the reader's judgment.

In one respect, the chart of Mr. Fairfax might have been considered by those interested to be an improvement on that of Mr. Stokes. The latter gentleman had narrowed the *two mile* channel of the French charts to a *little more than a mile*, but the chart of Mr. Fairfax reduces it to *a mile* only!

Mr. Fairfax's chart was introduced to the Court with the same flourish as had been that of Mr. Stokes.

MR. FAIRFAX.—" This chart shows the state of the enemy's ships at daylight on the 12th of April. *This chart is correct*, except that the head of the *Calcutta* is placed by the engraver *too far to the southward*. It should have been about N.W. by compass, and the head of the three decker *Ocean* is to the eastward, but *not sufficiently far to the northward by compass*."

Not much correctness here, but abundance of misrepresentation. Mr. Fairfax is very particular about the positions of the *heads* of the grounded ships, but, like Mr. Stokes, not at all particular to a league or two as to where they lay aground. For instance, he is very sensitive about the position of the *Ocean's* head, yet the *Ocean* herself is *not to be found on his chart!!*

* I GAVE MR. STOKES THE MARKS!!! and I have all the different angles *in my pocket*, with the different soundings! (*Mr. Fairfax's Evidence, Minutes*, p. 140.) This evidence is truly wonderful. Yet the Court made no comment! and I was excluded from listening to the evidence!

though the names of other enemy's ships aground, not far from where she had lain before her escape, are given, to mark the care with which the chart had been constructed!

I will not in this place make any further observations upon Mr. Fairfax's chart, this being identical with that of Mr. Stokes. The exposure of the one in the next chapter will serve for the confutation of the other. The reader will, from what has been stated, be able to form a pretty correct idea as to why — in, and subsequently to 1809 — inspection of these charts was refused to me. At that period it was in vain that I published explanations, which, without access to the charts, were incomprehensible to the public; my unsupported declarations, as has been said, falling to the ground unheeded, even if they were not the cause of attributing to me malicious motives towards the commander-in-chief, after his acquittal by sentence of a court-martial. But for the consideration of his Grace the Duke of Somerset a stigma must have followed me to the grave. It is now otherwise, and I am content to leave the matter to the judgment of posterity. I must, however, remark, that neither the charts of Mr. Stokes or Mr. Fairfax were shown to me on the court-martial, though shown to nearly every other witness, one — Capt. Beresford — being told that he " *must* " base his observations on those charts. Had they been shown to me, I should in an instant have detected their fallacy.

CHAP. XXVI.

A NAVAL STUDY—*(continued)*.

THE matters related in the preceding chapter will
appear yet more extraordinary when contrasted with,
and confirmed by, the evidence of eminent officers
present in the action of Aix Roads; that is, of such
officers commanding ships as were permitted to give
their testimony, for those who were suspected of
not approving the Commander-in-chief's conduct, *were
not summoned to give evidence before the court-martial!*
In one instance— that of Captain Maitland, of the
Bellerophon, whose opinions on the subject had been
freely expressed — this gallant officer was ordered to

join the squadron in Ireland, so as to render his testimony unavailable.

To a gallant officer still living, Admiral Sir Francis William Austen, K.C.B., who was present in Basque Roads, but, like other eminent officers, *not examined on the court-martial*, I am indebted for a recently-expressed opinion as to the causes why the majority of the enemy's ships were suffered to escape beyond reach of attack, as well as of the persecution which I afterwards underwent, in consequence of my conscientious opposition to a vote of thanks to the Commander--in-chief.

The following is an extract from the gallant Admiral's letter : --

"I have lately been reading your book, the 'Autobiography of a Seaman,' and cannot resist the desire I feel of stating how much pleasure I derived from its perusal, especially of that part which has reference to the movements of the fleet in the Mediterranean from 1798 to 1800. Having been serving for the greater part of those years on that station, your narrative excited in my mind a vivid recollection of former times -- as it were living that part of my life over again.

"With reference to the latter part of the volume which details the proceedings in the attack on the enemy's squadron in the Charente, I wish to say as little as possible which may inculpate the conduct of the Commander-in-chief, to whom, as you probably know, I owe a debt of gratitude for his kindness to me.

"But at the same time I cannot but admit that he appears to me to have acted injudiciously. It would have been far better had he moved the squadron to a position just out of reach of the batteries on Isle d'Aix, when he would have been able to see the position of the enemy's ships, and thus have decided for himself whether they could have been attacked without needless risk, and not have been compelled to form his determination entirely on the report of others.*

"Had he done so, it seems probable that he would have seen things in a different point of view, and decided to send in a force sufficient to have captured or destroyed the whole.

" I must, in conscience, declare that I do not think you were properly supported, and that had you been so the result would have been very different. *Much of what occurred I attribute to Lord Gambier's being influenced by persons about him who would have been ready to sacrifice the honour of their country to the gratification of personal dislike to yourself, and the annoyance they felt at a junior officer being employed in the service.*†

"I will only add that I consider your services in the *Speedy, Pallas,* and *Impérieuse* will entitle you to the warmest thanks of your country, as well as to the highest honours which have been awarded for similar services.   Instead of whĭch, you have in numerous instances been persecuted in the most cruel and unrelenting manner.

" I desire to subscribe myself, with much respect and esteem,

" My dear Lord Dundonald,

" Yours very faithfully,

" FRANCIS W. AUSTEN.

" Admiral the Earl of Dundonald."

If anything could alleviate the remembrance of the bitter persecutions originating with this one-sided court-martial, it is an unsolicited expression of opinion like that of the gallant Admiral Austen, whose name, for evident reasons, was *not* included in the list of those summoned to give testimony on that remarkable occa-

* Who were more interested in the failure of the action than its success, from the fact shown in the first volume of the ill-feeling manifested towards me in consequence of my being a junior officer temporarily appointed, though against my own will, and after all others had declined the enterprise.

† Though I had suggested the plan, after all other suggestions had failed to satisfy the Board of Admiralty.

sion. That other gallant officers still living entertain
similar sentiments, I make no doubt, for the simple
reasons that, as honourable men, it is impossible for
them to entertain other opinions. What would have
been the result of the court-martial had such testimony
as that of Admiral Austen been permitted, may safely
be left to public decision.

The gallant Admiral and the naval public at large
will perhaps be surprised to learn that my persecutions
have not ceased at this day. Despite my restoration to
rank and honours, my banner has never been restored
to its place in Henry the Seventh's Chapel, the unjust
fine inflicted on me in 1814 has never been remitted,
nor other rights withheld during my forced expulsion
from the Navy conceded ; the excuse being want of
precedent, though with that of the gallant Sir Robert
Wilson fresh in the archives of the nation.*

A few words may here be devoted to a point intimately connected with this subject. In several reviews
on the first volume of this work, the public has been
told of the handsome rewards which have been bestowed
for my services. The reader will perhaps be scarcely
prepared to learn, in answer to such statements, that
with the exception of the ordinary good service pension
granted for general service in 1844, thirty-five years
after the action in Aix Roads, I never in my life received
a recompense from my country in any shape, the Order of
the Bath alone excepted. For my services in the *Pallas*,

---

* This fact, together with the particulars of Sir Robert Wilson's
restoration, was obligingly communicated to me by that distinguished
patriot Joseph Hume, together with a letter expressive of his surprise that my restoration had not been rendered complete. This
letter and the enclosures will be given in another place.

that of destroying three heavily-armed French corvettes at the embouchure of the Garonne, and cutting out the *Tapageuse*—all performed in one day—not a shilling was awarded to myself, officers, and crew, though in the late war with Russia I have been told that the destruction of a Russian gunboat was scrupulously paid for. For my services on the coast of Catalonia in the *Impérieuse*, to which Lord Collingwood testified that, single-handed, I had stopped the advance of a French army, not a farthing was conceded, whilst the thanks of Lord Collingwood were the only expressions of the kind ever awarded for what English historians have eulogised even more highly than did his Lordship.

For the partial destruction of the enemy's fleet in Aix Roads not a farthing was given to myself, officers, or crew ; but nine years afterwards, when told that I might take my share of head-money with the rest of the fleet, I replied by refusing both the offer and the money, on the ground that the ships only which took part in the action had a right to it.

The reader will pardon this brief digression, which has arisen from Admiral Austen's allusions to the persecutions unworthily inflicted on me, and I have chosen the opportunity to set the public right on a subject which has been much misapprehended, to the detriment of myself and family. Neither directly nor indirectly have my services throughout my whole career ever cost the country a *penny* beyond the ordinary pay and the ordinary good service pension to which my rank entitled me ; nor did any of my family ever receive a place under government, other than that to which they have risen in the ordinary course of naval promotion.* After this positive assurance on my part, I feel confident that the portion of the press which has expressed an opinion that " I had been amply rewarded for my services," will do me the justice to acknowledge an unintentional error.

Since the receipt of Admiral Austen's letter, I have been favoured with another, from Capt. Hutchinson, who,

---

* My third son is a post-captain, and my youngest a commander in the navy, both having won their rank by services in action. With regard to my eldest son, Lord Cochrane, the public shall judge of the favour shown to him on my account. He was originally placed in the navy, in which he served four years, but was driven from the service by the animosity excited by the imputations against his father. After this he entered the army, in which he served eighteen years. He was engaged throughout the Canadian rebellion, and subsequently for eight consecutive years in the pestilential climate of China during the war. He there served under Lord Clyde, acted as aide-de-camp to Major-General D'Aguilar, and subsequently as Quartermaster-General. His health having at length broken down under the arduous nature of his duties—he having been, as I have reason to believe, the only officer who remained for so long a period on a station proverbially unhealthy—he was ordered home on sick leave, and had to undergo the unusual mortification of being periodically, and that too at short intervals, ordered to appear before the Medical Board in London. This was actual persecution, nor did it cease till Major-General D'Aguilar himself went to the Horse Guards and remonstrated against such conduct being pursued towards an officer whom he had sent home as being worn out by eight consecutive years' hard duty. On my son's asking for an unattached majority *by purchase*, he was told that his length of service, from 1833 to 1851, was insufficient, notwithstanding that he gave the precedent of earlier promotion in the case of an officer who had married the daughter of the Master-General of the Ordnance, and who got his majority in eleven years. Finding no prospect of promotion, my son sold out, quitting the army as a captain, as the state of his health did not warrant him in returning to his regiment. I adduce this as a specimen of the kind of reward bestowed on me or my family.

at the time of the action in Aix Roads, was a lieutenant in the *Valiant*, one of the two line-of-battle ships reluc-tantly sent to the assistance of the *Impérieuse*, when engaged single-handed with three of the enemy's ships. Captain Hutchinson was, therefore, in action throughout the whole affair, but, like Admirals Austen and Mait-land, *was not summoned to give evidence on the court-martial.*

Capt. Hutchinson's letter, whether in point of fact or ability, deserves to be put on record as a proof that when naval officers have the opportunity of speaking their minds on any subject connected with their noble profession, there are few amongst them who will let self-interest outweigh the honour of the service. So complete is the information voluntarily given by Capt. Hutchinson, with whom I have not the pleasure of being even personally acquainted, that it might have saved me much of the lengthened critical explanation into which my sense of duty to the naval service, as well as to my own reputation, has compelled me to enter. As a further corroboration of my own proofs, written before the reception of Capt. Hutchinson's letter, I can only tell that gallant officer how highly I ap-preciate it, and shall be surprised if the rest of my brother officers do not form the same judgment.

Cumberland House, Chilham, Canterbury,
June 8th, 1860.

"MY LORD,

"I have read, with very great interest, the first volume of your Autobiography, and if the second is not yet pub-lished, it is possible that what I have to communicate may be

of some service in any further notice you may give of the
attack upon the French fleet in Aix Roads. I would not
otherwise have taken the liberty of writing merely to express
the interest taken in your Memoirs, since I can only entertain
that in common with every naval officer who has any true
love for his profession, and of esteem for those who have so
eminently adorned it by their gallantry and skill.

"I was fifth or junior lieutenant of the *Valiant*, on the
mortifying occasion above mentioned, and can bear testimony
to the indignation which pervaded the whole fleet in wit-
nessing the total want of enterprise, and even common sense
of duty, which then permitted so many of the enemy's ships
to escape, when they were entirely at our mercy.

"I have, however, to mention some circumstances which
may throw light upon the mystified despatch of Lord Gambier, which certainly surprised all those who were present.
In the first place, Lord Gambier can have given no *positive*
orders to Capt. Bligh of the *Valiant* to *attack* the French
ships which were aground at the time indicated in the despatch, for after we had anchored off the Boyart Shoal, Capt.
Bligh, seeing you go in with the *Impérieuse unsupported*
(after waiting some time, expecting to be *ordered* by the
Commander-in-chief to assist you) went in his gig on board
the *Caledonia* to *volunteer his services.* Lord Gambier
expressed himself greatly obliged, but said some other ship
must accompany, upon which Capt. Bligh selected the *Re-*
venge, from regard for Capt. Kerr, who had been acting for
him in the *Valiant* some time before, when he had occasion
to go on leave of absence for private affairs.

"We accordingly ran in, as your Lordship has detailed, and
I have nothing to remark as to what followed but one circumstance, of which your Lordship does not appear to have been
aware. No doubt you would have observed that on the
evening of the 12th the crews of the *Ocean* and two other
enemy's line-of-battle ships near her, were evidently *flying*
from them in a panic, numerous boats from the shore as-
sisting in conveying them from the ships.

" This was so apparent that our Captain, Bligh, went in his gig, with two other Captains, as soon as it was dark, to reconnoitre these ships, with a view to take possession of them with boats, if they were deserted.

" These Captains returned, however, reporting that they had found them surrounded by boats, &c., and that, consequently, they could not be attacked. In the morning, however, no boats were near them, nor were any persons seen stirring on board them; and it was not till about ten o'clock, I think, that the crews, *finding that we had not taken possession, took courage, ventured to return on board their ships, and immediately began to warp them out of our reach.*

" Captain Bligh was a man of the firmest nerve I ever knew, and therefore I can only suppose that the boats he saw were still engaged carrying the crews on shore, though I believe it was at least ten o'clock at night when he went to reconnoitre, and I know we were greatly puzzled at the time to account for the presence of these boats. As a proof that these ships *were* totally deserted that night, I need only refer your Lordship to the account of Admiral Gravière, quoted by you, where he says, ' *The panic was so great, that ships which had not even been attacked were abandoned by their crews.*'

" But, my Lord, we heard soon after this disgraceful affair, by means of some French vessel which had been boarded or taken, that such was the case. I do not now perfectly recollect *how* this information reached us, but we had no doubt of the fact at the time, it being only in accordance with our own observations and conjectures. I exceedingly regret that I did not make note of this at the time, but the belief in the fact of the crews having deserted those three ships was so general and undoubted, that it never occurred to me that it might be questioned.

" The report went further, and added one singular circumstance — that there was *one* man who *did* remain when all the remainder of the crews had quitted. This was a quarter-master on board the *Ocean*, who, indignant at the cowardly desertion of the ships, *hid himself*, when the crews were ordered to quit, and this was the salvation of that three-decker and the two other ships, in a very extraordinary way. A little midshipman belonging to one of our smaller vessels (I believe a brig) had been sent in a jolly-boat that night with a message to another ship, and having delivered it, instead of returning immediately to his own vessel, he proposed to his men to go and look at the French ships from which the crews had been seen to fly.   His men of course were willing, and they approached cautiously *very near* to the three-decker (the night was very dark) before they could observe any stir on board or around her.   They were then suddenly hailed by the quarter-master before mentioned with a loud "Qui vive!" Of course the poor little midshipman took it for granted that the ship was occupied by more than that one man, and he hastily retreated, glad to escape capture himself; but had he known the truth, *that little midshipman, with his jolly-boat and four men, might have taken possession of a three-decker and two seventy-fours!*

"This seems more like a story of romance than an actual occurrence, and I greatly regret that I did not then make note of every name and circumstance, which at this distance of time I cannot call to mind, but I have never entertained any doubts as to the facts here detailed, and I have always mentioned them in speaking of that most unsatisfactory affair of Basque Roads.   Admiral Gravière's account is a positive confirmation of what we observed and fully believed as to the abandonment of the ships, and I only wonder that he should not have mentioned the noble conduct of the quarter-master.

"Admiral Gravière, however, would probably not have heard of the approach of the boat, and the quarter-master himself would not perhaps have reflected upon the possible danger the ships were in from the approach of only *one little boat;* yet if he had not been there to hail that boat, it is more than probable that the little midshipman would have continued cautiously to approach, till he discovered that the ships were entirely deserted, and he would either have ventured to take possession himself, or would certainly have returned to report the circumstance, and a proper force would have been despatched to take advantage of the abandonment, if it had been found to be as he reported.

" It was the supposed abandonment of the ships, indeed, which induced him to approach them at all, and it was this also which induced Capt. Bligh to reconnoitre. These, my Lord, are the only circumstances I had to communicate, and no doubt they will be in some degree interesting, though not wholly satisfactory, from my inability to establish the perfect correctness and truth of them. I *have* not, and never *had,* any doubt myself, though I am by no means inclined to believe cock-and-bull stories. Of one thing I am very certain, that there was a universal conviction, that, but for the ingenious ruse adopted by your lordship of *running in singly with the Impérieuse, and then making a signal of distress,* or *rather of want of assistance, nothing whatever would have been effected against the French fleet.*

"I remain, my Lord,
"Your very obedient servant,
"CHAS. HUTCHINSON, Capt. R.N.
" The Right Honble. the Earl of Dundonald."

To return to the testimony of eminent officers at the court-martial, by which evidence Admiral Austen and Captain Hutchinson will be pleased to find their disinterested opinions corroborated.

The first evidence adduced shall be that of another distinguished officer, also still living, viz. Admiral Sir George Francis Seymour, K. C. B., G. C. H., who commanded the *Pallas* frigate at the action in Aix Roads, and remained by me when the line-of-battle ships left the roads on the morning of the 13th of April.*

* See vol. i. p. 392.

An attempt was made to stop the evidence of Captain Seymour nearly at its commencement, by Lord Gambier remarking that he had "*no further questions to propose to Captain Seymour;*" who however promptly asked whether he was not "bound by his oath to relate *every circumstance* within his knowledge, respecting the proceedings of the fleet." (*Minutes*, p. 190.)

To this pertinent query the President replied; "If the questions that *are asked you* should not seem to embrace all the circumstances *to which it refers*, you are still bound to relate them." (*Minutes*, p. 190.)

CAPT. SEYMOUR.—"From what period am I to give my answer?"

PRESIDENT.—"From the time of your being *sent in to attack the enemy*, and your having remained there."

CAPT. SEYMOUR.—"*Without going back to the* 11*th?*"

PRESIDENT.—"No! *I take it from your going in on the* 12*th*." (*Minutes*, p. 193.)

The President thus authoritatively stopped Captain Seymour from saying a single word relative to the neglect of the Commander-in-chief in not having sent ships to the attack before the *Ocean* and group floated away, as the *Pallas* and the other vessels were withheld until *the afternoon of the* 12*th*. This, however, did not prevent Captain Seymour from taking the course which he had evidently proposed to himself.

CAPT. SEYMOUR.—"I think the ships *might* have floated in sooner; that they might have come in on the last half of the flood-tide."*

* Which rose as high as the last quarter of the ebb tide, when two line-of-battle ships were sent in and remained without grounding.

PRESIDENT.—" How much sooner would that have been than the time they actually did go in ? "

CAPT. SEYMOUR.—"At eleven o'clock."

PRESIDENT.—" What time did the line-of-battle ships go in ? "

CAPT. SEYMOUR.—" Within a short time after two o'clock." (*Minutes*, p. 193.)

These three hours made all the difference in the result of the action, and were in fact the point of inquiry before the court. At eleven o'clock the whole fleet came to an anchor in Little Basque Roads, instead of detaching a force to attack the enemy, as Captain Seymour testifies they *might* have done. The French ships were at that time helplessly aground. Seeing the British fleet come to an anchor, the enemy took heart, and strained every nerve to warp off, in which, being unmolested, they succeeded — by throwing their guns and stores overboard — and soon after *one o'clock* had *effected their escape.*

At *two o'clock*—seeing me go in with the *Impérieuse*, in order to prevent the other ships from escaping also, and rightly appreciating the risk I was running single-handed, the Commander-in-chief then, but not till then, reluctantly sent in two line-of-battle ships and some frigates, and this only after repeated signals — the final one necessarily being *in want of assistance.* So that *no attack* was made on the enemy's ships till *after* the escape of the *Ocean*, and all those nearest the deep water, though these were most easily attackable ; nor would any attack have been made *at all*, but for my last signal. Had Admiral Seymour been permitted to speak to this point, his evidence would have been most conclusive, as the President must have seen when he ordered the witness to speak only as to what occurred *after* he was sent in; that is, after the French ships had escaped, which was the subject of inquiry, about which Admiral Seymour was thus ordered to say nothing!

This forms, in fact, the history of the whole affair; three French ships only being attacked in the afternoon, after all the outermost had been quietly permitted to heave off and escape during the morning, and with a rising tide in favour of the British force. Captain Seymour's highly honourable pertinacity in giving the above important opinion as to what was clearly the duty of the Commander-in-chief at *eleven o'clock*, after he had been cautioned by the President not to speak of anything which occurred previous to *two o'clock*, when the *Pallas* was sent in, will be regarded — as it deserves to be regarded — in the light of truth and honour holding itself superior to power. For the sake of the service no less than for that of Admiral Seymour, I am proud to record this instance in which self-interest weighed nothing in comparison with the interest of the country, and the service which Captain Seymour evidently considered to be at stake.

This reply of Captain Seymour took the Court by surprise, as opening the very point sought to be avoided. This led to the subjoined angry remonstrance from Admiral Young.

ADMIRAL YOUNG.—"The general question is not meant to subject the general conduct of the Commander-in-chief to the opinions of all the officers serving under his command.

If you think the two ships (*Revenge* and *Valiant*) not going in so early as you think they might have floated to be an instance of neglect, it is your duty to state it, that we may *inquire into it*, and hear *any other evidence* upon it."

The tendency and peculiarity of this remark to Captain Seymour, is worthy of note. It more than insinuates that he was incapable of forming a correct judgment, and plainly tells him that his evidence will go for nothing, but " *to hear any other evidence* " upon it. A perusal of the minutes of the court-martial will show the meaning of this expression, viz. that when any officer in command spoke his mind on the subject, the next witness was a master or other inferior officer *to contradict his evidence*. For this purpose masters and others were recalled over and over again — which is one of the most curious features of the court-martial.

Captain Seymour had said nothing about the *two ships*, but that *the ships* — meaning the British line-of-battle ships — might have gone in to the attack *at eleven o'clock*, and thus replied to the insinuation.

CAPT. SEYMOUR.—" I have already stated that I cannot say it was misconduct. I STATE THE FACT AND LEAVE THE COURT TO JUDGE."

ADMIRAL YOUNG.—" You state an opinion that *the fleet* would have floated in at eleven o'clock."

CAPT. SEYMOUR.—" Yes, THAT THERE WAS WATER ENOUGH."

ADMIRAL YOUNG. — " Is that all you mean to say, that there would have been water enough for them to have floated in ? "

CAPT. SEYMOUR.—" Yes. That is all I *have* said."

ADMIRAL YOUNG.—" When you say that the ships of the

line would have floated in at eleven o'clock, do you mean to speak to the depth of water alone?"

CAPT. SEYMOUR.—"I confine myself to the *meaning of the words*, that there WOULD HAVE BEEN WATER ENOUGH FOR THE LINE-OF-BATTLE SHIPS TO HAVE FLOATED IN. That is what I mean to say. With regard to the opposition they would have met with, THE COURT HAVE AS MUCH BEFORE THEM AS I HAVE."* (*Minutes,* p. 195.)

That is, in Captain Seymour's opinion, the fleet ought to have proceeded to the attack at eleven o'clock instead of then coming to an anchor, and by that act, giving the enemy's ships aground ample time to warp off and escape, which they would not otherwise have attempted ; a point on which all French writers agree.

Attention must here be drawn to Admiral Young's constantly repeated expression "*floated in.*" The expression appears to have been used, not more to prevent Captain Seymour from using any other, than to convey the idea that there was no room in the Channel for operations, but that the ships, if sent to the attack, must have *floated* or *drifted* in, exposed to the fire of the enemy, had Lord Gambier directed them so to do !

At the conclusion of Captain Seymour's evidence, so

---

* Two ships of the enemy's line afloat, viz. the *Foudroyant* and *Cassard !!* "These," said Lord Gambier in his defence, "*must have entirely crippled every one of our ships in their approach through so narrow a channel.* Besides which, *some of the grounded ships were upright !!* and could have brought their guns to bear on the entrance." (Lord Gambier's Defence, *Minutes,* p. 125.) Two enemy's ships, both of which made sail for the Charente the moment the escaped ships had got off, "*must have entirely crippled*" a powerful British squadron !!!

clear and so conclusive, the Commander-in-chief had the bad taste to remark that he "*did not consider it of the least consequence!*" (*Minutes,* p. 196.) An opinion in which posterity will assuredly not coincide.

I must here repeat that I was not permitted to be present in the court during the examination of the witnesses, *or to know who had been summoned to appear*, the evidence of Captain Seymour, and that of several other eminent officers, would not have been taken at all, had I not contrived to ascertain the names of those summoned. Finding that most of these had either not been present in the action, or were known to be in the interest of the Commander-in-chief, I went on the half deck of the *Gladiator*, and wrote a note to the Court, pointing out the unfairness of such proceeding, and naming other officers who ought to be examined. They were *then* summoned, and their evidence will be conclusive to the reader, as it ought to have been to the Court, and would have been so had not the Court itself been picked by the Government, *i.e.* principally composed of officers who had been ordered to hoist their flags to qualify them for sitting on the court-martial, which, being ended, they were ordered again to strike their flags!

As a contrast to the evidence of Captain Seymour, I will turn to that of three officers who were *not present in the action*, and in fact, do not appear to have been in Aix Roads at all, either before or after it; though without a minute knowledge of those Roads they could not be competent to give even a general opinion on the subject. Without reason assigned —

as indeed it was not in their power to assign any —
each thus delivered his testimony.

QUESTION (*put to each in succession*).—"Was everything
in your judgment done that could be done, to effect the de-
struction of the enemy's ships?"
CAPT. BURLTON.—"I *think* there was."
CAPT. BALL.—"I *think* there was everything done."
CAPT. NEWMAN.—"Perfectly so."
QUESTION. — "From the time the Commander-in-chief
arrived in Basque Roads to the time of your quitting it, can
you state any instance of neglect, misconduct, or inattention
on his part to the public service?"
CAPT. BURLTON.—"I know of none."
CAPT. BALL.—"No; I cannot."
CAPT. NEWMAN.—"None."

Widely different was the testimony of Captain Malcolm of the *Donegal*—the late Admiral Sir Pulteney
Malcolm—whose love of truth, like that of Captain
Seymour, was not to be fettered by negatives in reply
to leading questions. Captain Malcolm thus spoke of
the only two enemy's ships afloat, *Foudroyant* and
Cassard, which two ships Lord Gambier in his defence
said "*must have entirely crippled*" the whole British
force, had it attempted to pass the channel leading
to Aix Roads.

"When those ships quitted their stations there was then
no obstacle to prevent the small ships from going in; by
which I mean the *frigates*, or even SEVENTY-FOURS. The
fire from Isle d'Aix they nearly *avoid* by keeping near the
Boyart." (Capt. Malcolm's evidence, *Minutes*, pp. 208,
209.)

Lord Gambier had stated in his defence that he refrained from sending in the ships on account of the danger from the fire of the fortifications. Mr. Stokes supported this view by swearing that the ships would have been "within point-blank range of shot." The assertion of Captain Malcolm that they would be nearly out of reach of shot, which was true, was *malapropos*, though not to be shaken by the testimony of an inferior officer. It was therefore dangerous to recal Mr. Stokes in opposition to so high an authority as Captain Malcolm; Captain Kerr was consequently recalled whilst Captain Malcolm *was under examination!* to say that his ship was *once* hit from the batteries. After which extraordinary interruption Captain Malcolm was suffered to proceed with his testimony.

PRESIDENT.—" Was the enemy's three-decker in a situation on the morning of the 12th to have done any mischief to ships that had been sent in?"

CAPT. MALCOLM.—" Till about noon she was heeling considerably, *and appeared to me to be throwing her guns overboard.* When she righted, she could have annoyed ships coming in."

QUESTION.—"At what time did the three-decker remove from the situation where you saw her on shore *heeling?*"

CAPT. MALCOLM.—"About two o'clock. I took no note of the time."

QUESTION.—" Would you have sent ships in before the two ships were removed and the three decker got off?"

CAPT. MALCOLM.—" Had it appeared to me that there was no other chance of destroying those ships *but by such an attack,* I certainly think it *ought to have been made.* It was understood that they must all again ground in the mouth of the Charente where it was the *received opinion* they could be attacked by bombs, gun-vessels, and fire-ships again, *without risk.*"

QUESTION.—" Upon the whole, are you of opinion that, of all the French ships which got ashore on the night of the 11th of April, any more could have been destroyed than were destroyed had the British ships been earlier sent in on the 12th of April to attack them ? "

CAPT. MALCOLM.—" Had they been attacked by the British ships, in my opinion *they could not have been warped off from the shore, as it was necessary to lay out anchors to heave them off*. Those that were not aground had always the option of running further up the Charente. It should be understood that it must have been at the risk of our fleet, as I have already mentioned. (*Minutes*, pp. 209 to 211).

Of course, every naval combat must be at the risk of fleets ; such risk, in my judgment, forming the chief object in building fleets for the purpose of encountering it. But the risk to a whole squadron from two ships afloat, and a three-decker ashore, " *heeling over, and throwing her guns overboard*," is what no brave seaman would ever take into consideration. The chief risk, as has been alleged by Lord Gambier, was from the fire of the batteries on Ile d'Aix, which he had shortly before pronounced " *no obstacle*." What this was, may be judged from the fact that Captain Seymour, in the *Pallas*, Captain Woolfe, in the *Aigle*, and myself in the *Impérieuse*, lay for two days in this formidable position without loss of any kind.

The reply to the next question put to Captain Malcolm ought to have been conclusive with the Court.

QUESTION.—" *Would you, had you commanded the British fleet, have sent in ships to attack the enemy's ships on shore?* "

CAPT. MALCOLM.—" The moment that the two ships quitted

their defensive position the risk was then small of sending ships, and, OF COURSE, I WOULD HAVE SENT THEM IN INSTANTLY." (*Minutes*, p. 212.)

This was spoken like a seaman.   No greater contrast can be set in juxtaposition with such evidence than that of the chartmaker Stokes, the master of Lord Gambier's flagship, who, though of no higher rank than that of a warrant officer, was gravely consulted as to what, in his opinion, was the Commander-in-chief's duty!!

The subjoined evidence of Mr. Stokes is very curious, not only from its effrontery in contradiction of superior officers, but in its own flat and unblushing contradiction to itself.   The portion of Mr. Stokes's evidence placed in a double column is truly wonderful; but it is more wonderful that any tribunal should have so far forgot itself as to act upon it.

"The ships would have been at half range of shell and point-blank shot." (*Minutes*, p. 148.)

"They would have remained under the fire of the enemy's batteries till the tide floated them to the southward of the Palles Shoal; but this retreat, in my opinion, they would not have been able to have gained." (P. 148.)

"If we had made the attack on the morning of the 12th, we should have sacrificed our own ships without making any impression on the enemy, or destroying *any* of their ships." (P. 148.)

"The enemy's ships were *fast on the ground* with their sterns to the westward; and they *could not bring their guns to bear on the ships*	"The three decker lay with her *broadside flanking the passage*. They all three could have fired with *complete effect on any ships that*

that attacked them. Had the *might approach ! ! !* " (P.
French ships *grounded with* 149.)
their broadsides flanking the
passage, they could not have "Had four sail of the line
been attacked with the least run into Aix Roads when
prospect of success." (P. Lord Cochrane made the
151.) signal, the whole fire of Isle
d'Aix, as well as the fire of
"I told Sir H. Neale that the *Foudroyant, Cassard,* and
perhaps we might destroy *Ocean, three-decker,* would
some of their ships, but that *have been directed on them!!*"
we should sacrifice our own."* (P. 152.)
(P. 151.)

The only comment here necessary is, that nothing in
the evidence volunteered by Titus Oates in former years
displayed greater effrontery. The evidence of the other
chartmaker Fairfax is almost as astounding.

QUESTION.—" Would ships of the line sent in have been
within range of shells and shot from the enemy's batteries?"
MR. FAIRFAX. — " From every chart I have seen they
certainly would."
QUESTION.—" Could any of the enemy's ships before they
run up the Charente have *annoyed and raked* (*!!*) any of the
king's ships that might have been sent to attack them?"
MR. FAIRFAX.—" *They certainly lay in a favourable place*
for it." † (*Minutes,* p. 144.)

* This was said with the full knowledge that when " our own "
were reluctantly sent in, *no damage was sustained.* To use Lord
Gambier's own words in making his defence, " *Not one, even of the*
smallest of our vessels employed, has been disabled from proceeding
on any service that might have become necessary." (*Minutes,*
p. 138.)—A circumstance not at all expected by the country when
the destruction of the enemy's fleet was required.
† This reply is very characteristic. He knew, as Stokes swore,
that the " *enemy's ships were aground with their sterns to the*
westward," and that not only could they not return a fire, but that

QUESTION.—" Had even two or three ships of the line been sent in to attack those two ships, were *any of the enemy's ships aground* (!) in a position to annoy our ships, either in the anchorage or in their approach to it ? "

MR. FAIRFAX. — " *Some of them certainly were.*"   (P. 145.)

QUESTION.—" If a part of the fleet had gone into Aix Roads when the *Impérieuse* made the first signal, must it have remained within three quarters of a mile of the batteries till the ebb made ? "

MR. FAIRFAX.—" *They might have shifted with the flood!* " (P. 146.)

The ingenuity of Mr. Fairfax in avoiding straightforward answers to embarrassing questions is remarkable. He was one of Lord Gambier's tract distributors spoken of in the first volume, but though he had no objection to construct an imaginary chart to serve his chief, his conscience would not permit him to swear to its contents. Nevertheless such evasion ought not to have been tolerated by any tribunal. Yet on the charts and evidence of Stokes and this man was the result of the court-martial made to rest, in opposition to the testimony of officers of standing and character.

The opinion of another eminent officer, Captain Broughton of the *Illustrious*, will be even more to the purpose.

PRESIDENT.—" From the first attack on the ships of the

a broadside from a British ship must have gone clean through them from stern to bow ; but, unlike Stokes, he would not swear that ships in such a position could have " *annoyed and raked the king's ships.*" The enemy's ships were merely " *in a favourable place for it ! !* " And so they were, had they been *afloat* instead of helplessly *ashore*, heeling over at an angle of thirty degrees.

enemy on the evening of the 11th of April to the time of
your leaving Basque Roads, according to your judgment, was
everything done that could be done to effect the destruction
of the enemy's ships?"

CAPT. BROUGHTON.—"I think it would have been more
advantageous *if the line-of-battle ships, frigates, and small
vessels had gone in at half flood,* which I take to be at
about *eleven o'clock* A.M. *or twelve.*"*

"The French admiral and two more got off and made
sail towards the river, very soon after the two that were
afloat."

QUESTION.—"By the French admiral you mean the *Ocean?*"

CAPT. BROUGHTON.—"Yes."

QUESTION.—"As the two ships that remained at anchor did
not change their position till about noon, and the *Ocean* continued in her position till about the same time, if the British
fleet had been ordered in at eleven o'clock, which you thought
would have been the proper time —— "

CAPT. BROUGHTON.—"I would rather say between eleven
and twelve, which, in my judgment, was more advantageous."

QUESTION.—"Would not the ships sent in have been exposed to the fire of the *two ships* that remained at anchor,
the French Admiral's ship, and the batteries of Isle d'Aix, at
the same time?"

CAPT. BROUGHTON.—"Certainly; but I conceive they were
partly *panic struck,* and on the appearance of a force coming
in might have been induced to cut their cables, and try to
make their escape up the river." (*Minutes,* pp. 219—221.)

There was not much to be feared from a "*panic-
struck*" enemy, with only two ships afloat out of
thirteen, eleven being on shore.   Yet those who peruse

---

* Precisely the time at which Lord Gambier ordered the fleet to
come to an anchor, after it had been got under weigh with every
indication of proceeding to an attack.

the minutes of the court-martial will marvel to find these two ships set up as bugbears to a British fleet.

I will next adduce Captain Broughton's testimony as to the trifling opposition to be anticipated from the batteries on Isle d'Aix, which three weeks previous to the action had been pronounced " *no obstacle* " by the Commander-in-chief, in his letter to the Admiralty*, but were now considered formidable enough to pre-vent a British fleet from passing within two miles of them !

It may here be remarked that Captain Broughton was well acquainted with these batteries, from having previously been here under Admiral Keats, as they were familiar to me from having been employed on the same spot under Admiral Thornborough, and having, in fact, engaged the *Minerve* frigate under their fire†, which I held so cheap as not to consider them or their ineffectual fire worthy attention. As Admiral Austen well remarks—all Lord Gambier knew respecting them was from the reports of others, who had not even ventured closely to reconnoitre the bat-teries. The report of Captain Broughton, who had reconnoitred them, was not acted upon.

PRESIDENT.—" In your services in Basque Roads had you any opportunity of making observations upon the state of the enemy's fortifications on Isle d'Aix ? "

CAPT. BROUGHTON.—" Yes, I had."

PRESIDENT.—" Narrate those observations."

CAPT. BROUGHTON.—" I was on board the *Amelia* when she was ordered to dislodge the enemy from the Boyart

---

* See vol. i. p. 342.   † See vol. i. p. 191.

Shoal, and, being *nearly within gunshot**, I observed the fortifications. They appeared to me in a very different state to what I observed them when serving two or three years before under Sir Richard Keats. I thought they were repairing the works from the quantity of *rubbish that was thrown up;* and I counted on a semicircular battery which commanded the roadstead where the enemy lay between *fourteen and twenty guns,* I am not positive as to the exact number. There was a small battery lower down, nearer the sea. I do not know the exact number of guns; there might be *six* or *nine,* I suppose. What I had before taken to be a blockhouse above the semicircular battery seemed to have *no guns whatever;* it appeared to be a barrack for containing the guard. I thought from this observation that the fortifications of the island, at least in that part, were *not so strong as we supposed,* and I reported my opinion to that effect to Lord Gambier."

PRESIDENT.—"Are those the only guns you observed on Isle d'Aix that could bear upon the anchorage?"

CAPT. BROUGHTON.—"They were all that I observed; there might be more."

QUESTION.—"Did it appear to you that the enemy was constructing new works in front of the old ones, and nearer to the sea?"

CAPT. BROUGHTON.—"I think the *rubbish* was the remains of the old works that *had been taken down.*

PRESIDENT.—"Would your Lordship wish to ask any questions on the subject?"

LORD GAMBIER.—"I would wish Capt. Broughton to point out on the chart the situation of the *Amelia* when he was on board her and made those observations?"

CAPT. BROUGHTON.—"The south point of Isle d'Aix was

---

* Mr. Stokes said the ships going in must have been "*at half range of shell and point blank shot!*" (*Minutes,* p. 148.) Mr. Stokes's observation was taken "from the mizentop of the *Caledonia;*" that of Captain Broughton from actual exposure to the fire of the batteries.

just shut in with Fouras Castle, and I think the bearing was nearly S.E. and by E. when it was open.   When it was touching the point we were JUST OUT OF GUNSHOT FROM BOTH SIDES. THEY FIRED AT US FROM BOTH SIDES, BUT THE SHOT DID NOT REACH US."   (*Minutes*, pp. 218, 219.)

This was decisive, and in his defence, the Commander-in-chief thus attempted to evade the facts which had been officially reported to him by Captain Broughton.   To contradict them was impossible.

" With respect to the force of the Aix batteries, I apprehend what appeared to Lord Cochrane and to the master of his ship as ruins of the fort were, in fact, materials for *improving or increasing the work!*   Indeed, can it be natural to *suppose* that the enemy, who are so active in forming batteries wherever they can be useful, and whose engineers are considered to be equal to any, would, of all moments, choose that for dismantling or blowing up works when they expected those works would be most required; for it is very certain the enemy was as fully apprised of *our intentions of attacking their fleet as myself ! ! !* *   And it will perhaps be considered less likely that the enemy should *weaken their defences* on Isle d'Aix, *raised evidently for the protection of their fleet,* when at the same time they were endeavouring to form others on the Boyart Shoal as a protection for it." (*Minutes*, p. 135.)

* Lord Gambier had just before written to the Admiralty that an attempt with fireships would be " *hazardous if not desperate.*"   He had no intention of attacking otherwise.   And after the enemy's ships had been driven ashore by the explosion vessels, Captain Broughton testifies to Lord Gambier's expressions that he did not intend to make any attack, as the object of their destruction seemed to be already accomplished.   That is, neither before nor after the action did he intend to make any attack with the fleet, nor would he have done so unless a partial attack had been forced on him by my signal on the *afternoon* of the 12th of April.

There was no " *supposition* " in the matter, nor any necessity for hypothesis, in face of the fact that the fortifications were for the most part *débris*, or as Captain Broughton termed them, a mass of " *rubbish.*"   No one said that they had been " *blown up*," or that the enemy were *weakening their defences!* The fact is, that only a month before the action Lord Gambier had himself set the matter at rest, by writing to the Admiralty as follows :—" The advanced work between the Isles of Aix and Oleron, I *find* was injured in its foundation, and is in no state of progress, *it is therefore no obstacle to our bombarding the enemy's fleet**," yet it was now an " obstacle " to even attempt attacking ships on shore ; and Lord Gambier condescended to resort to the just quoted assertions, in contradiction to his own letter to the Admiralty.

On the utter worthlessness of the batteries, as calculated to impede the operations of a British fleet, there was abundant evidence before the Court, as will be seen on an examination of the minutes of the court-martial, such testimony confirming the correctness of Lord Gambier's letter to the Admiralty on the 11th of March, and completely disproving his Lordship's contradictory assumptions in his extraordinary defence read to the Court.

Captain Broughton was next examined with reference to the imaginary shoal, which forms so conspicuous an object on Mr. Stokes's chart (C).

" If the ships had been damaged in masts and rigging,

---

* See vol. i. page 342.

considering the direction and strength of the wind at that time, was there any place those ships could have retired to?"

CAPT. BROUGHTON. — "I think as the wind was north-westerly and northerly, they might have found safe anchorage and protection in what is called in the French chart I had on board " *Le Grand Trousse*" (see Chart A), *where there is thirty or forty feet of water* OUT OF RANGE OF SHOT OR SHELLS IN ANY DIRECTION."

QUESTION. — "How many ships would you have thought it necessary to send into Aix Roads to attack the enemy?"

CAPT. BROUGHTON. — "I should think *five or six ships* of the least draught of water."

"I conjecture that the *discomfited* French squadron *would have made very little resistance.*"

"From the situation in which the enemy were, *not having recovered from the fright of the night before, I think our loss would have been very little,* as few of the French ships were in a situation to FIGHT THEIR GUNS !!"

QUESTION. — "Do you know that from the anchorage in Aix Roads to the anchorage you have just now described, that *there is* A BAR GOES ACROSS?"

CAPT. BROUGHTON.—"No! I do not know anything of it; I *sounded* from the wreck of the *Varsovie* to that anchorage, and FOUND NO SHOAL THERE !!"

PRESIDENT. — "*That is not the place!* It *is* marked in *some* of the charts that between the Boyart and the tail of the Pallas there *is* a bar!"

CAPT. BROUGHTON. — "*I sounded as I came in from the fleet* BUT DID NOT FIND ANY BAR." (*Minutes,* pp. 221—233.)

The extraordinary conduct of the President in saying " *That is not the place,*" and then that " in *some* of the charts there *is* a bar," in the place which was "*not* the place," needs no comment. The evidence of Captain Broughton, who *had* sounded there, should have been fatal to the chart of Mr. Stokes, who *had not* by his own admission taken soundings. The fact was, that this bar, made for the occasion, formed one of the main points in the Commander-in-chief's defence, and Mr. Stokes's chart was retained in spite of the testimony of those who, from having sounded, could alone know anything of the matter.

But Mr. Stokes shall first *prove* and then disprove his imaginary *bar or shoal.*

Notwithstanding that Mr. Stokes admitted that his knowledge of the supposed shoal between the Palles and the Boyart was only founded on an anonymous French MS., he subsequently forgot the admission, and swore to his own *personal knowledge of the minutest particulars* connected with the imaginary shoal!!

LORD GAMBIER. — " Is there not a bank between the Boyart and the Palles Shoal ? "

MR. STOKES. — " Yes."

" What water is there generally upon that bank at low water ? "

MR. STOKES. — " From *twelve to sixteen feet in the deepest part,* but that part is *very narrow.*"

" If there are only *sixteen feet,* line-of-battle ships could not pass over it at all times ? "

MR. STOKES. — *No*, not until nearly two-thirds flood.* You must reckon on going over that part at *twelve feet.*"

" To get to the anchorage, it *is* necessary to pass over the bank just mentioned ? "

MR. STOKES. — " IT IS."

ADMIRAL YOUNG. — " Is there a channel of sixteen feet all across ? "

MR. STOKES. — " *There is a channel of sixteen feet all*

---

* It is marked on Mr. Stokes's chart that the rise of tide is *twenty-one feet.*

across, but that is *narrow.* There are about the middle of it patches of twelve feet."

PRESIDENT. — " *There is* no going into the channel of sixteen feet without, in *some instances,* passing over that of twelve feet ? "

MR. STOKES. — " You *may* go over the channel of sixteen feet, but *it is so narrow* that I should calculate going over that part which is *only twelve feet.*"

PRESIDENT. — " It is *so intricate,* you *must* count on passing over some part with only *twelve feet?* "

MR. STOKES. — " I should calculate on going over part of the twelve feet, because *it is so narrow,* it is *difficult to hit* the passage of *sixteen feet.*" *

This is pretty minute for a man who was not present in the action, who confessed that he was "ignorant of the distance between the sands," and had, in fact, "never sounded there at all," that his survey had been made from the mizentop of the *Caledonia,* nine miles off, and that he had his information from Mr. Fairfax and an "anonymous French MS.," which was not even produced in Court, nor demanded by the Court, so that it is not known to this day who was the author of that MS., or, indeed, whether it ever existed ; a matter which, from its non-production, I do not hesitate to doubt.

The President was, however, bent on confirming Mr. Stokes's shoal, but the result was most unfortunate. In order further to substantiate the alleged fact, Captain Woolfe of the *Aigle,* which vessel was present during the action, thus replied to an interrogation on the point.

---

* Yet Captain Broughton had " hit " it, and that without finding any shoal at all !

"I think *four or five sail of the line* might have lain clear of the enemy's batteries. I lay there with the *Pallas* and *fifteen or sixteen brigs, gun-brigs, cutters, and schooners!*" (*Minutes*, p. 86.)

PRESIDENT.—"*Would the casting your eye upon this chart* (Stokes's) *give you a clearer comprehension!!!*"

CAPT. WOOLFE. — "No! I have it all in my mind. *I received orders to assist Mr. Stokes on a survey.*

PRESIDENT. — "What was the report of the depth of water at any particular time of tide in the situation *I have pointed out between the Palles and the Boyart, if you can recollect it?*"

CAPT. WOOLFE. — "Mr. Stokes said HE HAD FOUND DEEPER WATER AND A LITTLE MORE ROOM FARTHER TO THE SOUTHWARD."

Is it not wonderful that in face of such facts, the Court should have acted on Mr. Stokes's chart or his evidence? Where Mr. Stokes had found "*deeper water*" he had marked on his chart a shoal, on which no admiral in his senses would have trusted a frigate, though the *Revenge* and *Valiant* line-of-battle ships, with five or six frigates had found plenty of water, and, whilst destroying two enemy's ships, remained there through a whole tide without grounding! The following are extracts from the logs of the ships present.

"3·0 P.M. Shortened sail and anchored *in 7 fathoms*, near the outer ship of the enemy, *Valiant* in company." (*Log of the Pallas.*)

"3·30. Came to with the best bower *in 6 fathoms*." (*Log of Valiant.*)

"4·0. Anchored *in 5½ fathoms*." (*Log of Unicorn.*)

"3·30. Anchored *in 7 fathoms*." (*Log of Indefatigable.*)

"2·30. Anchored *in 6 fathoms*." (*Log of L'Aigle.*)

The subjoined evidence of Mr. Spurling, the master

of the *Impérieuse*, will render further allusion to the subject unnecessary.

" Where we anchored, which was *out of the reach of shot and shell*, we lay *in five and a half fathoms at low water.* Three or four cables' length *nearer* to the Pallas Shoal than we lay, was a good berth for three or four sail of the line to anchor in five and a half or six fathoms *dead low water.* The marks for such anchorage I took myself." " I know this from my own observation. It was marked on the French chart, but I did not choose to trust it, but wished to prove it. The lead was kept going the whole of the time on both sides."

PRESIDENT. — " What water did you find in working out between the tail of the Pallas Shoal and the shoal towards the Boyart, when working to and fro ?"

" *From six and a half to seven fathoms.*"

" Did you make any observation before you began to engage ?"

" Yes. On the morning of the 12th I was desired by Lord Cochrane to lay a buoy on the Boyart Shoal, which I did in *six and a half fathoms water*, a sufficient distance to allow *any ship* to tack round that buoy."

The reader must not imagine that I am too minutely descending into particulars. I am writing history — naval history — in which Lord Gambier is nothing — myself less, except as unavoidably connected with the proceedings of the court-martial. I have no wish to speak of Lord Gambier where it can be avoided. The subject is, however, one in which the nation is collectively interested, and the national, no less than naval character, involved. Now that the justice of the Duke of Somerset has given me the means of incontrovertible explanation, I am personally gratified in availing myself of it; but I repeat that my object is now, as it ever was, national; and having at length those means, it is my duty, no less than my pleasure, to use them as a warning to future generations of the noble service to which I have the honour to belong.

I must reluctantly turn for a moment to the evidence founded on Mr. Fairfax's chart (D). First premising, that when Mr. Fairfax was asked to "state the situation of the enemy's ships at noon," he replied, that "at *eleven o'clock* he went down below, and did not come up again till near two." (*Minutes*, p. 143). That is, during the whole of the three hours' delay, and the consequent escape of the grounded ships, which constituted the question before the Court, Mr. Fairfax had been, by his own voluntary admission, in his berth, recovering himself from the fatigues of the previous night.

During these three hours, as has been said, the *Océan*, three-decker, and the three other line-of-battle ships had *quietly hove off*, and were running into the Charente. This was proved by the concurrent testimony of *all* the witnesses, and their escape formed the neglect, if any, of the Commander-in-chief. Yet Mr. Fairfax unblushingly testified that his chart showed their position on the morning of the 12th, and that when at two o'clock he returned from his *three hours' nap*, the enemy's ships were " NEARLY IN THE SAME POSITION as when he went below at *eleven o'clock!* " All the other witnesses, without exception, stating the fact that they had warped off and escaped beyond reach ! Yet the Court made no comment on Mr. Fairfax's evidence.

When pressed to describe their position more minutely, Mr. Fairfax, with real or assumed indignation,
replied, " *I have described them in the chart produced
by me.*" The Court complacently declined further question, and Mr. Fairfax thus escaped the struggle between
his chart and the truth, which had so much embarrassed Stokes, who had not the sagacity to perceive
that his silence would have been more acceptable than
his volubility.

Mr. Fairfax's minute description of the " nearly same
position " of the ships which had *escaped while he was
below !* is yet more extraordinary.

" Were any of the enemy's ships aground lying so close
together as to have the yards of two of them locked
together ? "

MR. FAIRFAX. — " By perspective those near the *Tonnerre*
seemed to be *very close.* If you draw a line they appear in
one."

PRESIDENT. — " The question is, whether these two ships
were lying so close together that their masts and yards might
be locked in, or whether they were distinct ? "

MR. FAIRFAX. — " They were *distinct at night !*"

" Were you in any situation which enabled you to determine that they were *not* near each other ? "

MR. FAIRFAX. — " No; it was prior (*i. e.* before daylight)
that I distinguished them separate."

" Can you determine *how far* they were asunder ? "

MR. FAIRFAX. — " I should think a ship's length from each
other, *those three.*"

Yet even the reluctant vision of Mr. Stokes, at a
distance of nine miles, could perceive *at daylight* four
of the enemy's vessels lying helplessly " in a group."
Mr. Fairfax — from whom a straightforward answer

could not be got — said, when pressed, that amidst *pitch* darkness, and by "*perspective*," he could plainly distinguish them as distinct from each other ; and was thus, with difficulty, made to tell almost the truth as to how they lay when driven ashore on the preceding night. He could see in the darkness that their yards were not locked together, but they were only " a ship's length from each other " — a distinction almost without a difference.

The whole affair was made to turn on the evidence of these two masters, Stokes and Fairfax, who unhesitatingly contradicted in that evidence the testimony of the most experienced officers present in the action, though the latter, had it not been for my pertinacity, as before described, *would not have been allowed to give evidence before the Court.* It has been shown that the charts of Messrs. Stokes and Fairfax were used to the exclusion of the actual charts of the enemy's coast supplied under sanction of the Admiralty itself, because there were none more reliable in existence.

It would be easy to extract from the evidence of Fairfax much more to the same effect ; but the subject is nauseating, and the naval reader may, if he choose, search the *Minutes* of the court-martial for himself. The young officer could scarcely occupy himself more profitably, if he wish to become acquainted with the practice of the service fifty years ago.

A short extract from Mr. Fairfax's evidence relative to the explosion vessel and the *Mediator* is necessary, as Lord Gambier avowed in his defence that the " explosion vessels *failed in their object;* " and to corroborate this, Mr. Fairfax falsely placed on his chart the spot where the explosion took place, in a false position, in order to confirm to the *eye* of the Court the asseverations of the Commander-in-chief in his defence. Like Mr. Stokes, Mr. Fairfax swore the *truth* in his evidence in contradiction to his chart.

The assertion of the Commander-in-chief in his defence, with regard to the explosion vessels, is as follows :—

" The explosion vessels, conducted by Lord Cochrane, *failed in their object,* as will be seen with reference to the *small chart* which I now deliver into Court. (Mr. Fairfax's chart D.) This points out where two of them blew up. The situation in which, and the time when, those vessels blew up, *proved prejudicial to the enterprise in several respects.* . . . In fact, had not Captain Wooldridge and some of the other officers, wholly disregarding the explosion, taken their fireships in *a proper direction* for the enemy, it is more than probable that *none of them would have produced any effect on the enemy's fleet.*" (Lord Gambier's Defence, *Minutes,* p. 124.)

Lord Gambier uttered this with the full knowledge that NOT A SINGLE FIRESHIP DID TAKE EFFECT ON THE ENEMY'S FLEET, a fact which his lordship openly states in another part of his defence ; so prematurely were the fireships kindled, and so badly were they directed. That Captain Wooldridge took his fireship in " a proper direction," is wholly disproved by the very man upon whose chart his lordship relies; viz. Fairfax, who states in his evidence that *after* the explosion had taken place he " *hailed the Mediator* to ALTER HER COURSE, OR SHE WOULD MISS THE FRENCH FLEET ! !

I am sorry to bring such evidence as the subjoined

to confute the unfounded assertions of a British admiral, but justice to myself leaves me no alternative.

QUESTION. — " Do you recollect when and where the explosion vessel blew up on the night of the 11th of April ? "

MR. FAIRFAX. — " She was about *two cables' length from the Lyra.* The *Lyra* is marked in the chart produced by me, as well as the explosion vessel. *When she blew up the fire vessels all seemed to steer for that point.* I hailed four of them and the *Mediator,* and *desired the Mediator to steer south-east, or else she would miss the French fleet."*

Here Mr. Fairfax proved ; 1st, that the explosion-vessel took effect before a single fireship was kindled. 2ndly, that the *Mediator* was steering in a *wrong direction,* not a *"proper direction,"* as alleged by Lord Gambier. 3rdly, and that therefore the boom was destroyed before the *Mediator* could have got near it. The *Mediator's* log is, however, luckily amongst the Admiralty records, and is carried up to the time the ship was set on fire, viz. 9·30 P. M., but not a word is said of breaking any boom, or even coming in contact with one, though had she done so the shock must have shook her from stem to stern. The subjoined are the *Mediator's* last log entries previous to her being set on fire.

" 8·30 P.M. Cut the cable and made sail for the French squadron.

" 9·30. *Set the ship on fire."*

The preceding extract from Mr. Fairfax is taken from the " *revised* " minutes. He says : "*When the explosion vessel blew up all the fire-vessels seemed to steer from that point.* What he really said was, " *I was below at the time of the first explosion !* " which I supposed was some shells bursting in the top, but I got on deck time enough to see her blow up!" This was expunged, and the above version substituted. The fact was, as every seaman will comprehend in a moment, that there was not a grain of powder, or a single shell, anywhere but in *a mass in the hold*, and this, as a matter of course, exploded *in an instant!* I do not say that Mr. Fairfax can be accused of this perversion of his evidence, as it was evidently the work of the person who *revised* the minutes for publication by a Portsmouth bookseller.

The *Mediator's* log was taken out of her previously to her being set on fire, and is subsequently continued up to midnight, two hours and a half afterwards, but still not a word is mentioned of coming in contact with a boom. This should be conclusive on the subject, and it is not my fault that a fact beyond dispute, must necessarily disprove the asseverations of the Commander-in-chief in his defence before the court-martial. These, however, are both facts. Let the reader make the most of them.

Yet in his letter to the Admiralty of April 14th, Lord Gambier stated that " the weight of the *Mediator* broke the boom," in that letter also ignoring the effect of the explosion vessels altogether. His Lordship says, in his defence, that they were *signals for the fireships!!* The subjoined are his Lordship's words :—" Their explosion was to point out *the proper time for the officers commanding the fireships to set fire to their respective vessels*, and to intimidate and prevent the enemy from towing off the fireships."* Three explosion vessels

* *Minutes*, p. 123.

fitted at an enormous cost for ammunition, &c., to do that which a signal rocket could have done as well!! If the explosion vessels did not strike terror into the enemy assuredly nothing did, for at page 125 of his defence he admits that " *not one of the enemy's ships was actually destroyed by means of fireships.*"

This perseverance on the part of the Commander-in-chief in persisting that the explosion vessels " failed in their object," though according to his own admission that the fireships failed also, was attempted to be corroborated by the evidence of Mr. Fairfax, but in a different way, viz. by swearing that she blew up at too great a distance from the enemy to produce any effect at all!

PRESIDENT. — " To the best of your judgment, what was the distance of the explosion vessel from the enemy when she blew up ? "

MR. FAIRFAX. — "About a mile."

ADMIRAL YOUNG. - - " What sort of a night was it ? "

MR. FAIRFAX. — " Very dirty, and blowing strong. The *Lyra* was pitching bows under."

" Was the night light or dark ? "

MR. FAIRFAX. — " *Very dark at intervals.*"

" How then did you, in a *very dark night,* ascertain that the explosion vessel blew up *within a mile* of the enemy?"

MR. FAIRFAX. — " By her computed distance from us in the *Lyra,* judging the distance she was from the enemy." (*Minutes,* p. 177.)

At first sight, these questions on the part of the Court seem impartial, but their object was to make Mr. Fairfax say that she might have been *more* than a mile from the enemy, as appears from the subsequent evidence. Mr. Fairfax would not say this. He, however, placed her on his chart on this " *very dark* " *night near the Boyart shoal*, and not *close to the Ile of Aix and the boom*, where Captain Proteau, who was lying under the lee of the boom, says she blew up.

Unfortunately for the veracity of Mr. Fairfax on this point, he had previous to the trial unwittingly written a letter to the editor of the *Naval Chronicle*, evidently not for publication, but in explanation of a chart. The editor of the *Naval Chronicle*, however, published the explanatory remarks, which are in complete contradiction to Mr. Fairfax's evidence on the court-martial —in fact, this portion of the letter tells the truth in the following language :—

" I have it from good authority that the fuses on board one of the explosion vessels only burned six minutes and a half, instead of twenty.* Had they burned twelve minutes longer *nothing could have been better placed!* I saw the French ships with lights up *immediately after the explosion, before any of the fireships got near!!* — EDWARD FAIRFAX." (*Naval Chronicle for* 1809, vol. xxii. p. 49.)

With this glaring contradiction between his evidence and his previous *honest* assertion to the editor of the *Naval Chronicle*, I take my leave of Mr. Fairfax and the subject, being quite content to rest my character on the contradictory evidence of those suborned to serve the cause of an administration in want of the prestige of a victory, at the expense of truth and even common sense, had such been relied on in the investigation.

---

* This is incorrect. They were calculated to burn twelve minutes, and exploded in about half that time.

I will conclude with the remark, that had I been permitted access to the charts *before the lapse of fifty-one years* from the date of the action — or could I after the court-martial have prevailed on Parliament to investigate the matter, by demanding the production of the minutes of the court-martial before voting thanks to the Commander-in-chief, the Administration of that corrupt day would never have dared to treat me as an officer maligning my Commander-in-chief unjustly, nor to have followed up their malignity to its final consummation of driving me from the British Navy, on the imputation of an offence of which I had not the smallest cognisance, as will by and by appear as plainly, and I trust as satisfactorily, as do these extraordinary revelations concerning a court-martial which will stand a beacon and a warning to the naval service as long as that service may exist. God grant that the records of that noble service to the latest day of its existence may never again be sullied in like manner!

CHAP. XXVII.

CONDUCT OF THE COURT-MARTIAL.

LORD GAMBIER'S DEFENCE. — SECOND DESPATCH IGNORING THE FIRST.
—ATTEMPT OF THE COURT TO STOP MY EVIDENCE. — EVIDENCE RE-
CEIVED BECAUSE OPPOSED TO MINE.—I AM NOT PERMITTED TO HEAR
THE DEFENCE. — THE LOGS TAMPERED WITH. — LORD GAMBIER'S
DEFENCE AIMED AT ME UNDER AN ERRONEOUS IMPUTATION. — MY
LETTER TO THE COURT CONFUTING THAT IMPUTATION. — ADMIRALTY
ACCUSATION AGAINST LORD GAMBIER ON MY REFUSAL TO ACCUSE HIS
LORDSHIP.—HIS INSINUATIONS AGAINST ME UNCALLED FOR.—ASSUMES
THAT I AM STILL UNDER HIS COMMAND.—ENEMY ESCAPED FROM HIS
OWN NEGLECT. — THE SHOALS PUT IN THE CHART TO EXCUSE THIS.
— ATTEMPT TO IMPUTE BLAME TO ME AND CAPTAIN SEYMOUR. —
THE TRUTH PROVED BY CAPTAIN BROUGHTON THAT LORD GAMBIER
HAD NO INTENTION OF ATTACKING. — LORD HOWE'S ATTACK ON THE
AIX FORTS. — CLARENDON'S DESCRIPTION OF BLAKE.

THE most damnatory point connected with the court-
martial is — that on finding me inflexible with regard
to the vote of thanks to Lord Gambier, the Board of
Admiralty ordered his lordship, AFTER HIS RETURN TO
ENGLAND, to *write a second despatch containing fresh
details of the action!* thus superseding the first despatch
written by himself as Commander-in-chief at the time
of the action!!

With this extraordinary demand Lord Gambier appears to have gladly complied on the 10th of May, 1809 ;
so that there are two despatches (Appendix A, *written
on the spot*, and B, *written in England*), the first highly
praising me for what I neither did nor intended to
do—the second IGNORING MY SERVICES ALTOGETHER!!

In fact, only mentioning me by name, as *lying* " *about three miles from the enemy.*" One step more in the second despatch, viz. that I was not in Aix Roads at all! would only have been in keeping with the assertion just quoted. Were not these contradictory documents now adduced, the denial of such an act by suppressing all mention of it in the despatches would be incredible. Nevertheless, I fearlessly assert, that to my personal conduct of the explosion vessel was solely attributable the panic produced in the enemy's fleet, and that such conduct was one of the most desperate acts on record There, however, they are—printed in the Appendix at the end of this volume. The naval reader may regret their reproduction, as I do, for the sake of the service, but he can no more ignore them than I can pass them over.

There is nothing like this in the records of the British or any other naval service, and the reasons for a precedent so unusual must themselves have been extraordinary. It is clear to me, that from the order of the Board of Admiralty to the Commander-in-chief to make a second report of the action in Aix Roads the court-martial took its cue. This may be a harsh conclusion, and perhaps would be so were it not corroborated by circumstances, not the least significant of which was, that the Commander-in-chief's official report had been long before *published in the Gazette!* No naval reason to invalidate this official report was alleged, or could have existed.

During my examination before the Court I alluded to the fact of having " reported to the Commander-in-chief the ruinous state of the Ile of Aix, it having the *inner fortifications completely blown up and destroyed.* This I not only ascertained from the deck of the *Impérieuse* with perfect precision as to the side towards us, but also as to the opposite side, from personal observations made from the main-topgallant mast-head. There were thirteen guns mounted." (*Minutes*, p. 58.)

This evidence, if admitted, and its truth was fully proved by the testimony of other officers, completely confirmed Lord Gambier's previous statement to the Admiralty, that " *the fortifications were no obstacle.*" But now it was expedient that these fortifications should constitute the bugbear which, as was asserted, would have destroyed any British ships sent in to attack the enemy's ships aground! and that the issue of the court-martial mainly rested on establishing the formidable character of the fortifications, a second despatch was called for. When, in my evidence, I was explaining to the Court the little danger to be apprehended from these fortifications—one of the principal points before the Court, Admiral Young stopped me with the query, "Will you consider, my Lord Cochrane, before you go on, HOW FAR THIS IS RELEVANT?"

On my insisting upon further explanation the Judge-Advocate attempted to stop me, by demanding—" CAN THIS RELATE TO THE QUESTION ASKED?" The President— seeing that I would not be stopped—remarked—" *Lord Cochrane states this as his reason for not taking a particular line of conduct.*" I stated it for no purpose of the kind, but to show that opposition from such fortifications was hardly worth taking into consideration, and thus continued:—

" I have felt that if I had answered ' *Yes* ' or ' *No* ' to all
the questions which had been put to me, I ought to be hung,
and that if a court-martial were held upon me and only the
answers ' *Yes* ' or ' *No* ' appeared to those questions, I *should*
be hung for them."

JUDGE-ADVOCATE. — " *I believe nobody has desired your
Lordship to answer merely ' Yes ' or ' No ! ' * "

A still more striking instance of the animus of the
Court was the following attempted stoppage of Captain
Beresford's evidence.

CAPT. BERESFORD. — " The only thing I know with respect
to the *Calcutta* being fired, was by a conversation between
Lord Cochrane and myself in the presence of Captain Bligh,
Captain Maitland, and others."

PRESIDENT. — " *Is this strictly evidence, Mr. Judge-
Advocate ?* "

JUDGE-ADVOCATE. — " *Yes ! I should think it is;* BE-
CAUSE I CONCEIVE IT IS TO AFFECT THE EVIDENCE OF LORD
COCHRANE ! ! !" (*Minutes*, p. 163.)

At the present day such proceedings in any tribunal
would be thought impossible. There, however, they are
on record — showing that the openly-avowed object of
the court-martial was the suppression and invalidation
of my evidence by any means that could be brought to
bear, rather than an inquiry into the conduct of the
Commander-in-chief on the merits of the case.

One point more must be noticed, relative to the
manner in which the Court was conducted. Having
reason to believe, as has been shown, that the inquiry
was being directed against myself, I was naturally
anxious to be present at the reading of the Commander-
in-chief's defence, in order to judge how far I might
thereby stand affected. With this view I presented

myself at the Court on the fifth day of the inquiry, when it was known that the defence would be made.

To my surprise the Court saw fit to refuse the privilege.

PRESIDENT. — " All the witnesses must withdraw."

LORD COCHRANE. — " With all due respect to the Court, in some former courts-martial the witnesses have been permitted to hear the defence."

PRESIDENT. — " *I never heard such a thing in my life*. The Court have ruled the point."

LORD COCHRANE. — " The case of Admiral Harvey is a case in point."

PRESIDENT. — " Lord Cochrane, the Court have determined the contrary."

" (*Lord Cochrane withdrew*".)   (*Minutes*, p. 105.)

One of my reasons for wishing to be present was to ascertain what use would be made of the logs of the small vessels present in the action; it being quite clear from circumstances which had come to my knowledge that some of these had been tampered with.   As such an assertion may readily be doubted, it must be confirmed.

When Mr. Earp inspected the logs at the Record Office, several, for the date of the action, were found missing from the log books.   One—the log of a line of battle ship — *had been torn out and was put back loose !* This, however, is after-knowledge, I will rather rest the matter on circumstances at the time.

When the master of the *Beagle* was under examination, the subjoined conversation took place :—

PRESIDENT (*to the Master*). — " Were these things written (in the log) day by day as they occurred ? "

MASTER. — " Yes ; everything was written every day at twelve o'clock."

" Then what is called the log of the 6th of April *was* written on the 6th of April ? "

MASTER. — " Yes."

" And what is inserted here as of the 7th, *was* written on the 7th in this book ? "

MASTER. — " Yes."

" Is this the identical book into which it was copied from the board ? "

MASTER. — " Yes."

" And there never was any other log-book kept ? "

MASTER. — " No."

" Who kept this ? "

MASTER. — " I kept it myself."

PRESIDENT. — " It is written so fair and so neat that *it bears every mark of being a fair copy !* "

JUDGE-ADVOCATE. — " *I tell the gentleman I am sure no imputation rests upon him !* "

PRESIDENT. — " No ; *not the least !* "* (*Minutes,* pp. 30, 31.)

It was nevertheless a fact that it *had* been tampered with, as was unwittingly elicited by Mr. Bicknell from the same witness.

QUESTION. — " You say, on your oath, that you believe everything in this log to be correct."

MASTER. — " Yes."

QUESTION. — " How does it happen that the signals of the *Impérieuse* are inserted in the margin of the log amongst the columns, and *not in the body of the log ?* "

---

* Inspection of more than one of the logs can leave no doubt, from the neatness of the handwriting, that those relating to the date of the action had been recopied, and could not have been written from day to day ; which from the difference in the pen and other little circumstances must have shown itself as in other logs. In one instance portions of the signal book have been transcribed into the ship's log. G. B. EARP.

MASTER. — "I wrote that *at the same time the log was written!*"

"Why did you not put it in the body of the log in the narrative?"

MASTER. — "*I made a mistake!* in copying it from the log-board!" (*Minutes*, pp. 29, 30.)

It will thus be seen that my most material testimony was attempted to be stopped by the Court as "irrelevant;"—that the Judge-Advocate gave as a reason for receiving testimony *really irrelevant*, that it *ought* to be received because "*it would affect the evidence of Lord Cochrane;*"—that garbled logs were resorted to —that the whole proceedings were directed against me, and carefully in favour of Lord Gambier, by leading questions which abound in almost every page, that I was not allowed to be present whilst the witnesses were under examination, so that I had no opportunity of cross-examining them in my own vindication—a right granted to every man by the constitution of his country; and that I was *refused admission* to the Court during the delivery of Lord Gambier's defence, *by the Judge-Advocate himself!* a most unusual course, that defence being full of the most injurious insinuations against my honour, though these were not borne out by evidence. In short, I was refused admission to the Court, though I quoted a precedent *not two months old*, in support of my right to be present — a right the more important to me if only from the fact of Lord Gambier having written a second despatch relative to the action in Aix Roads, in which despatch my services were altogether omitted, notwithstanding his lordship's praises of my conduct

in his first despatch written on the spot, where everything had transpired under his own observation.

I must now briefly advert to his lordship's defence,
but only so far as personally concerns myself.

Lord Gambier stated at the outset of his defence,
that he had been compelled to demand a court-martial
in consequence of " the insinuations thrown out against
him by Lord Cochrane, which not only compromised
his own honour, but that of brave officers and men
serving under his command." (*Minutes*, p. 105.)

I never threw out against his lordship a single insinuation, nor does one exist, either on the records
of the Court or elsewhere. I merely told Lord
Mulgrave, as narrated in the first volume, that I did
not consider Lord Gambier's services worthy of a vote
of thanks from Parliament, and that on this ground,
as bound by public duty to my constituents, I should
resist it. As will presently be seen, this was also the
opinion of many eminent men in Parliament, and on
the same ground too — that of public duty. If I committed any offence in this, it was that of refusing to
have my name coupled with that of Lord Gambier in
the vote of thanks, and resisting an offer of an independent squadron and a regiment*, not to persist in my
determination of opposing it.

That my objection to the vote of thanks to Lord
Gambier included any of the officers serving under
him was a gratuitous assumption to secure sympathy
for himself. As I have shown, the opinions of those
officers present in the action, whose opinions were to

* See vol. i. p. 404.

be relied on, were *anything but in Lord Gambier's
favour.* Not a single word did I utter against any
officer; though, on the ninth and last day of the court-
martial, it was with the greatest difficulty, and *after a
positive refusal,* that I succeeded in getting a denial of
Lord Gambier's unfounded assertion attached to the
Minutes. It will be better to give the whole transaction.

The Right Honourable Lord Cochrane called in.

PRESIDENT.—" Lord Cochrane, I have received the note
which you addressed to me, and have taken the sense of the
Court upon it. The decision of the Court is, that as the
matter to which your lordship refers *does not at all bear
upon the trial of Lord Gambier they cannot enter into
it.*"

LORD COCHRANE.—" I would request, sir, that that letter
may appear as an official letter to you, and that it may be
entered upon the Minutes."

PRESIDENT.—" The Court will take that into their consideration."

The Court was cleared.

The Court was re-opened at one o'clock.

PRESIDENT.—" Lord Cochrane, the Court have taken into
their consideration the note you addressed to them, and have
agreed that it shall be attached to the Minutes."

The letter was read, and is as follows : —

" August 4, 1809.

" SIR,— Having learnt from my brother officers that a
report has gone abroad that I censured, in general terms, the
conduct of the officers employed in the Road of Aix, on the
12th of April, I wish to have an opportunity to declare the
truth on oath; considering reports of that nature highly
injurious to the service of our country. I am also desirous
to lay before the Court the orders given to the fireships for

their guidance, as these will tend to elucidate and clear some
of those who consider that blame has been imputed to them.

"I have the honour to be, sir,

"Your most obedient humble servant,

"COCHRANE.

"Admiral Sir Roger Curtis, President."

Let the reader mark that expression of the president, "*it does not at all bear upon the trial of Lord
Gambier!*" Though the very first sentence of Lord
Gambier's defence was an accusation of myself upon
an assumption for which there was no foundation
whatever. Nothing but fear of a parliamentary debate
caused that letter to be attached to the Minutes.

So clumsily was this accusation made against me,
that Lord Gambier, despite the unwarrantable assumption just quoted, subsequently admitted my objection to the vote of thanks to have *been solely aimed
at himself*, and not, as he had just said, at the officers
and men of the fleet. Here are his lordship's words :—

" Lord Cochrane *warned* the noble lord at the head of the
Admiralty that if this measure (the vote of thanks) were
attempted he should, if standing alone, oppose it ; thus,
without specifically objecting to thanks being given for the
service performed, directing his hostility *personally at me.*'
(*Minutes*, p. 107.)

That is—I should not have objected to a vote of
thanks to the officers and men of the fleet, but only to
himself *personally*. Yet in the same breath he accused
me of traducing the officers and men of the fleet ;
with the intention, no doubt, of sheltering himself
under the pretence of my having traduced them also.
Could anything be more puerile ? I gave no other

"*warning*" to Lord Mulgrave than that which Lord Gambier correctly stated, and that I certainly did give, but without a word which could give rise to the slightest imputation on the officers and men of the fleet.

The fact is, that I never accused Lord Gambier at all, *not even to Lord Mulgrave*, to whom I only expressed an intention of opposing a parliamentary vote of thanks. It was the Board of Admiralty who accused him. Here are their accusations in full:—

"*By the Commissioners for executing the office of Lord High Admiral of the United Kingdom of Great Britain and Ireland, &c.*

"Whereas Admiral the Right Hon. Lord Gambier bas, by his letter to our Secretary, of the 30th of May, 1809, requested that his conduct, as Commander-in-chief of the Channel Fleet employed in Basque Roads, between the 17th day of March and the 29th day of April, 1809, may be inquired into by a court-martial:

"And whereas, by the log-books and minutes of signals of the *Caledonia, Impérieuse,* and other ships employed on that service, *it appears to us* that the said Admiral Lord Gambier, on the 12th day of the said month of April, the enemy's ships being then on shore, and the signal having been made that they could be destroyed, did, for a considerable time, neglect or delay taking effectual measures for destroying them: We, therefore, in compliance with his lordship's request, and *in consequence of what appears in the said log-books and minutes of signals,* think fit that a court-martial shall be assembled for the purpose of examining into his lordship's conduct, and trying him for the same: We send you herewith his lordship's said letter, and also his letter of the 10th of the said month therein referred to, together with an attested copy of a letter of our Secretary, dated the 29th of last month, and addressed to Lord Cochrane, and his lordship's reply thereto, with the log-books and minutes of signals above-mentioned: and we do hereby require and direct you to assemble a court-martial on Monday the 19th day of this month (if the witnesses shall be then ready, and if not then ready, as soon after as they shall be so) to try the said Admiral the Right Hon. Lord Gambier, for his conduct in the instance hereinbefore mentioned; and also to inquire into his whole conduct as Commander-in-chief of the Channel Fleet employed in Basque Roads, between the 17th day of March and the 29th day of April, 1809, and to try him for the same accordingly.—Given under our hands the 5th day of June, 1809.

(Signed)   " MULGRAVE.

" R. BICKERTON.

" WM. DOMETT.

" R. MOORSOM.

" To Sir Roger Curtis, Bart., Admiral
   of the White, and Commander-in-
   chief of his Majesty's ships and
   vessels at Spithead and in Portsmouth Harbour.

" By Command of their Lordships,

" W. W. POLE."

There is nothing here from which it can be inferred that—to use Lord Gambier's own words in his defence —I had driven him " to defend himself against the *loose and indirect accusations* of an officer so much his inferior in rank." I had made no accusation whatever against him, having merely and only declared that the service rendered was not worth the thanks of Parliament; the frequency of such thanks for trifling service being at that period so notorious as to become subject for sarcasm, as will appear in the next chapter. Had Lord Gambier construed my parliamentary opposition rightly, he might have thanked me for saving him from himself, and would have done so, had not his peculiar failing, vanity, demanded an ovation for services which under evil advice he had prevented from being fully consummated. So far from accusing Lord Gambier, *I was ordered by the Admiralty to do so*, and refused, to my own detriment*; telling the Board *to go to the logs of the fleet, and frame their own accusations, if they had any.* Yet, even this consideration did not prevent Lord Gambier from giving utterance to the following bombast ;—

" Whether Lord Cochrane supposed that he might with impunity endeavour to lower me in the opinion of my country and of my sovereign, signal marks of whose favour had at that instant been exclusively conferred upon himself,— whether his Lordship thought to *raise his own reputation at the expense of mine,*— and whether he expected that his *threat* would intimidate me to silence, I know not." (*Minutes,* p. 108.)

How could I " raise my own reputation " at the expense of Lord Gambier, who had, in his first despatch, said that my conduct in the action of Aix Roads " could not be exceeded by any feat of valour hitherto achieved by the British navy ;" though in his second despatch, substituted for the first after his return to England, and that too by order of the Board of Admiralty, he only remembered that I " lay with my ship about three miles from the enemy ! " His lordship was not once within gunshot of the enemy, whilst my frigate was throughout engaged, and for some time single-handed, against two line-of-battle ships, and a fifty gun ship, the *Calcutta,* which I captured.

* See vol. i. p. 407.

So far from "raising my reputation at the expense of Lord Gambier's," I voluntarily stated on the court-martial, that "the feelings of Lord Gambier for the honour and interest of his country were as strong as my own." (*Minutes*, p. 40.) For which mark of good nature, his lordship said in his defence, that even "in the present proceedings, Lord Cochrane stands in a situation only as an officer *under my command!*" (*Minutes*, p. 107) the meaning of which evidently was that I ought not to say anything but by order. The expression could not have had any other meaning.

I will not enter further into Lord Gambier's unfounded recriminations upon myself, further than to remark, that even had they any foundation, in no way did they bear upon the subject of the trial, much less were they in any way connected with his defence to the inquiry as to *why it was, that with a favourable wind, a rising tide, and plenty of water, he had refrained from attacking eleven ships helplessly ashore, allowing all but three to escape? This was the inquiry before the court, which, departing from the subject of inquiry, connived at its being substituted for recriminations on me for accusing Lord Gambier — though I had never done so.*

Upon the real point Lord Gambier in his defence wisely abstained from trusting himself, except in such terms as the following. "*If* he had sent in any ships, and they should have been necessitated to remain a whole tide in the Roads of Aix ; *if* they had been crippled in going in ; *if* the wind, which was favourable for carrying them in, should not have shifted so as to bring

them out again ; and that even, *if* the wind were fair
and they should lose their foremasts, the crews would
not have been able to get the ships before the wind."
To this, I will add that "*if,*" instead of conjuring up
these absurd dangers to be apprehended from an enemy
of whom Lord Gambier had said to Captain Broughton,
that they were "*already destroyed,*" his Lordship had
sent in ships to finish the work, the court-martial
would never have been heard of, and he would have
enjoyed a legitimate triumph. I was not his enemy.
Those who persuaded him not to second my efforts
were so unquestionably.

Quitting these "*ifs,*" and calculations of possible risk
and conjectural disasters, one or two points professionally connected with the defence remained to be noticed.

Lord Gambier knew, that during the ebb and rising
tide, the enemy's ships ashore were preparing to warp
off with the flood, and he also knew that the only two
enemy's ships at anchor, the *Foudroyant* and *Cassard*,
which at the court-martial were converted into bugbears to the whole British fleet, would be prepared in
case of the attack which they naturally expected, to
cut or slip, and so run for the mouth of the Charente
as they did, the moment the ships aground had warped
off and escaped.

When the British fleet weighed from Basque Roads,
the enemy was, as Captain Broughton testified "*panic
struck.*" When, in place of proceeding straight on to
the attack, the British ships *came to an anchor* in Little
Basque Roads, the enemy, as their own writers declare,
considered "*la mollesse de Lord Gambier*" an un-

expected stroke of good luck, and set energetically to work to warp off their ships from the bank on which they were stranded.   As Captain Broughton rightly says, had the frigates and smaller vessels been *then* sent in, and a demonstration only made of others ready to follow, the destruction of the whole must have been complete.   This is neither a matter of naval tactics nor science, but a commonplace consequence. It was this which caused Captain Malcolm to say, " Had it appeared to me that there was no other chance of destroying them, but by such an attack, *I certainly think it ought to have been made.*" (*Minutes*, p. 211.)   And again, " Had they been attacked by the British ships, they could not, in my opinion, *have been warped off from the shore*, as to do so, it was necessary to lay out anchors to heave them off."   (*Ibid.*)   There are no " *ifs* " or contingent disasters in Captain Malcolm's opinion, which, as Captain Hutchinson pertinently remarks, was that of every officer in the fleet.

But even after the enemy's ships had escaped, and the two at anchor, the *Foudroyant* and *Cassard had* run for the Charente, the Commander-in-chief allowed an hour and a half to escape before a single ship was sent into the inner roads, nor would any have been sent at all had not I taken the *Impérieuse* in alone, and then hoisted the signal " in want of assistance." Had not this been done, not a single ship of the enemy's fleet would have been destroyed, unless from the impossibility of getting her again afloat, and I am not aware that any such instance occurred.

To excuse this neglect, the hypothesis of banks and

shoals, in the charts of Messrs. Stokes and Fairfax was resorted to, for they neither existed in the French charts, nor in reality. Coupled with this was the alleged danger of point blank shot from the dilapidated batteries!

" Scarcely," says Lord Gambier, "had the *Cæsar* reached Aix Roads, before she grounded, and lay *in a perilous situation exposed to the point blank shot of the batteries.*" (*Minutes*, p. 128.) Unfortunately for this hypothesis, a careful search in the *Cæsar's* log shows that *she was never once touched by shot or shell !!* and that in place of grounding in Aix Roads, she grounded on the Boyart Sand—on her way to Aix Roads—and that she lay there beyond the reach of shot ; thus proving what other officers testified, viz. that there was plenty of room in the channel to avoid shot. The *Cæsar* only went a few feet too far, and came off next morning without damage of any kind.

A still less worthy part of the defence was, in laying the fault on myself and Captain, now Admiral Seymour, of the *Pallas* that nothing more was done. " Lord Cochrane," says the Commander-in-chief, " *remained* in the Road of Aix, during the 13th and 14th, accompanied by the *Pallas*, sloops and gun-brigs, but nothing was attempted by those two frigates." (*Minutes*, p. 129.) The fact was, that in the fight with the line-of-battle ships destroyed on the evening of the 12th, before any assistance came, the *Impérieuse* was severely damaged, so much so, as to occupy the whole of the 13th in repairs. This was why Admiral Seymour so gallantly stood by us, and the 14th was occupied in vain attempts even then to get a force sent in. Had

Admiral Seymour run the *Pallas* alone amongst the line-of-battle ships which remained, at the mouth of the Charente, he would not have earned the high reputation he now enjoys. But when Lord Gambier threw out this questionable insinuation, he forgot to mention that Admiral Stopford lay at a short distance with two line-of-battle ships and half a dozen frigates, besides having our two frigates and all the smaller vessels under his command. Had Admiral Stopford been asked why, with such a force under his orders, he remained inactive, the reply would have not been to the Commander-in-chief's credit. Admiral Stopford would not have been a spectator only, could he have helped himself.

I now quit this miserable subject for ever. The real fact is, that from over-persuasion of those who were jealous of a junior officer originating and being appointed to carry out plans deemed impossible by others, Lord Gambier declined to second my efforts, as Admiral Austen has plainly said in his letter previously quoted, the fact being as completely confirmed by Captain Hutchinson. This decision of his lordship was no doubt arrived at, when a council of officers were summoned on board the flag-ship, on the morning of the 12th, at which time the enemy's fleet was lying helplessly ashore.

That, after such council, his Lordship never intended to make *any attack at all* on the French ships, is proved *beyond question*, by the subjoined testimony of Captain Broughton.

"A ship or two might have been placed, in my opinion

against the batteries on the southern part of Ile d'Aix, so as to take off their fire AND SILENCE THEM. I mentioned to Sir H. Neale, when the signal was made for all captains in the morning, that I thought *they were attackable* — speaking of the confused state in which the French ships appeared to be at the time."

" *I heard my Lord Gambier the same morning say* (at this council) it *had been his intention to have gone against the batteries I now speak of, but as the enemy were on shore he did not think it necessary to run any unnecessary risk of the fleet when the object of their destruction seemed to be already obtained.*" (*Minutes*, pp. 221, 222.)

That is, he admits my exertions to have destroyed the French fleet, (which was not destroyed — all except three ships having escaped) and plainly tells Captain Broughton that *he will do nothing more !* This should for ever decide the point.

If, however, proof be still wanted of the utter worthlessness of any opposition in the power of the enemy to offer, whether by fortifications or ships, it is to be found in the following statement at the close of Lord Gambier's defence :—

" I conclude by observing that the service actually performed has been of great importance, as well in its immediate effects as in its ultimate consequences; for the Brest fleet is so reduced as to be no longer effective. It was upon this fleet the enemy relied for the succour and protection of their West India colonies, and *the destruction of their ships was effected in their own harbour, in sight of thousands of the French. I congratulate myself and my country that this important service has been effected, under Providence, with the loss only of ten men killed, thirty-five wounded, and one missing.* NOT EVEN ONE OF THE SMALLEST OF OUR VESSELS EMPLOYED HAS BEEN DISABLED FROM PROCEEDING ON ANY SERVICE THAT MIGHT HAVE BECOME NECESSARY." (*Minutes*, p. 138.)

By this voluntary admission of Lord Gambier I am willing to be judged — feeling certain that posterity will be as fully convinced of the inability of the enemy to inflict material damage on our ships, as was Lord Gambier himself, according to his own testimony, as quoted in the above passage. As Lord Gambier truly says, no damage worth mentioning *was* done to any of our ships, to which I shall add, that at no period after the enemy's ships were driven ashore were they in a condition to inflict damage. This his lordship not only admits, but *proves*, in the concluding paragraph of his defence, and yet the whole point of the trial is made to rest on the surmise that had Lord Gambier done *anything* against the enemy's ships aground, *the destruction of the British force must have been the consequence.* That is, *by doing nothing the enemy's ships were destroyed; though by doing anything our own would have been in danger ! ! !*

The subjoined chart B will show, at a glance, the whole affair.

A. *Ocean* three-decker and group on the north-west edge of the Palles Shoal. These were permitted to escape.

B. *Calcutta*, captured by the *Impérieuse* and set on fire.

C. *Ville de Varsovie*, hauled down her colours to the assisting ships. Afterwards burned.

D. *Tonnerre*, ditto, ditto.

The last three were destroyed *on the falling tide*, but no others! These being the only enemy's ships which, after the escape of the other four, remained assailable.

E. The position taken up by the *Impérieuse*, she being at the time of the arrival of the assisting force engaged with the *Calcutta*, and with the other two ships.

F. Position of the British ships sent in after the *Ocean* and group had warped off, viz. within pistol shot of the sand on which the escaped ships lay till 1 p.m. aground.

The best comment, perhaps, on the whole affair of
Aix Roads is what had previously been effected with a
less force than that under Lord Gambier, and when
the fortifications were perfect. The subjoined historical
facts should for ever put an end to all controversy on
the subject, and at the same time to the untenable
defence set up at this memorable court-martial.

"A well-planned and vigorous attack on the coast of
France being in 1757 much desired, with a view to give a
decisive blow to the marine of that kingdom (*the very purpose for which Lord Gambier was sent, and which Lord
Mulgrave especially impressed on me*), a fleet was ordered to
be got in readiness, under the command of Sir E. Hawke,
Rear-Admiral Knowles being appointed second in command.
On the 20th of September the fleet made the Island of Oleron,
and Sir E. Hawke ordered the Vice-Admiral to proceed to
Basque Road, to stand in *as near* to Ile d'Aix as the pilot
would carry him, with such ships of his division as he thought
necessary, and *to batter the fort, until the garrison should
either abandon it or surrender.*"

"On the 22nd of September the fleet entered the bay
called the Road of Basque, between the islands of Rhé and
Oleron. *About eight the next morning* Admiral Knowles
in the *Neptune*, with the *Magnanime, Barfleur, America,
Alcide, Burford,* and *Royal William, made sail towards
Aix.* Captain Howe (*afterwards Earl Howe*) in the *Magnanime* led the van. At *half-past twelve* the fort upon the
island began to fire, but he continued to advance without
exchanging a single shot, continually urging his pilot to lay
his ship as close to the fort as possible. *He dropped his
anchor under the very walls.* It was, however, near an hour
before the fort struck its colours." (*Biographical Memoir
of Earl Howe in the Naval Chronicle,* vol. i. 1799 ; see also
Campbell's Lives of the Admirals.)

This was the very fort, only now *in ruins,* — or to

use Lord Gambier's words, " *no obstacle, from the dila-pidated condition of the fortifications* " — that his lord-ship adduced as a reason for not endangering the British fleet by exposing the ships to its fire. Admiral Harvey had perhaps Lord Howe's exploit in his mind's eye when he told Lord Gambier to his face that " had Nelson been there, he would not have waited for fire-ships, but would have dashed at once at the enemy ; " an assertion of which there can be no doubt, though poor Harvey was dismissed the service for this and similar opinions.

Another extract, from Lord Clarendon's remarks on Admiral Blake, shall close the subject.

" He despised those rules which had been long in practice, to *keep his ship and men out of danger, which had been held in former times a point of great ability and circum-spection; as if the principal art requisite in the captain of a ship had been to be sure to come home safe again !* He was the first man who brought ships to contemn *castles on shore,* which had been thought ever very formidable, and were discovered by him to *make a noise only, and to fright those who could be rarely hurt by them.*" (CLARENDON'S *History of the Rebellion.*)

CHAP. XXVIII.

THE VOTE OF THANKS.

FROM this time forward I never trod the deck of a
British ship of war at sea, as her commander, till
thirty-nine years afterwards I was appointed by her
present most gracious Majesty to command the West
India squadron ; the greater portion of the interval
being marked by persecution of which the court-martial
on Lord Gambier was only the starting-point.

The commencement of the parliamentary session in
1810, was remarkable for its votes of thanks, and the
refusal of all information which might justify them.
This led Lord Milton to declare in the House of Commons, that " votes of thanks, from their frequency, had
lost their value, and ceased to be an honour. They
had got so much into the habit of voting thanks that
it was almost an insult not to vote them." (Feb. 1st.)

On the 25th of January 1810, Lord Grenville ad-

verted in the House of Lords to notice of motion for
a vote of thanks to Lord Gambier, for *his* services in
destroying the enemy's ships in Basque Roads; and
observed that as the last intimation on the journals
respecting Lord Gambier was his arrest, it would be
necessary that the *minutes* of the court-martial should
be laid before the House, in order to enable it to judge
of the necessity for a vote of thanks.   To this Lord
Mulgrave strongly objected, on the ground that it
" would appear as if it was wished to retry the case."
Laying the sentence of acquittal only before the House,
said his lordship, would be " sufficient to render their
proceedings regular, and would answer all the purposes
of the noble lord."   With this the House was obliged
to be content, though how that sentence had been
obtained the reader is now made aware.

On the 29th of January, in pursuance of notice previously given, I made a motion for the production of
the *minutes of the court-martial* in the House of Commons; as being, from the extraordinary discrepancy
between the nature of the evidence and the sentence,
absolutely necessary, in order to enable members fairly
and impartially to decide whether the thanks in contemplation of ministers *were due* to Lord Gambier for
the part he took in what had been by them denominated a victory in Basque Roads.*

In support of this production of the minutes, I
adverted to a previously expressed opinion of the

* The action took place in Aix Roads.   The only victory gained
by Lord Gambier in Basque Roads was that of bringing his ships
to anchor there whilst the enemy's ships were quietly heaving off
from the banks on which they had been driven, nine miles distant
from the fleet.

Chancellor of the Exchequer (Mr. Perceval), that Lord Gambier had been honourably acquitted, but that an officer's having done no wrong *did not entitle him to the thanks of the House;* which, if bestowed on trifling, or, indeed, on any but brilliant achievements, would dwindle into contempt, even with those on whom they should be conferred. Votes of thanks were already lightly esteemed in the Navy, and I pledged myself — if the House would insist on the production of the minutes — to prove that " Lord Gambier's defence was contradicted by itself — by his lordship's official letters — and by his own witnesses ; many of whom, as to essential facts, were at variance with themselves and with each other." Lastly, I undertook to prove to the House, that the chart of the 12th of April was " in a most material point false — and in every respect a fabrication."

I will not inflict on the reader a recapitulation of the long discussion which followed, but the opinions of some whose names are to this day held in respect are too much to the point to be passed over. The opinion expressed by Mr. Tierney is so remarkable that I shall give it entire as reported.

" The question was not as to the noble lord's (Gambier) innocence, but as to his claim to a most distinguishing reward. The honours of the House were high things, dear and valuable ; but dear only because they implied merit, valuable only because that merit must be rare. Honours too frequently bestowed lost their value, and became signs of nothing but the weakness which lavished them, or the worthlessness on which they were to be thrown away.

" He would vote for the minutes, but in his vote he begged to be understood as merely calling for matter to enable him to shape his opinion. He could mean no slight to Lord Gambier. He respected his lordship's character. He had some opportunities of hearing him spoken of, and it was always in a high strain of praise and estimation. But he had never understood that Lord Gambier took *any share* of the merit of the achievement to himself. *He had not approached the French fleet nearer than seven miles.* Ministers had praised Lord Gambier for discretion ; *he hoped they had not intended this* as an instance in the enumeration of its proofs.

"It became the House to be cautious of being prodigal of honours entrusted to their distribution. Lord Cochrane ought to be heard; his judgment and character, his signal gallantry and signal honours* deserved the serious attention of the House. Even his feelings, led as they were, perhaps, astray by an excess of strength and sensibility, deserved all the attention which could be paid to them."

The opinions of Mr. Whitbread are no less remarkable. Sir C. Hamilton had said that the reason why no more ships were destroyed was solely attributable *to me!* and that he would engage to prove it to the House.† Mr. Wynne also declared, on behalf of the Ministry, that the evidence was *all on Lord Gambier's side!* and opposed to it only my solitary evidence. This called up Mr. Whitbread, whose remarks are reported as follows :—

"The noble lord (Cochrane) had done wrong in returning any answer to the application of the Admiralty.‡ He ought to have told them, as a member of the House of Commons, he had no answer whatever to make ; and if they thought the logs *inconclusive* why did they not manfully come down and try the question in that House ?

* The red ribbon.
† He however omitted so to do.
‡ Demanding the reasons for my opposition to the vote of thanks. See vol. i. p. 404.

" The hon. gentleman (Mr. Wynne) talked of the injustice of trying an officer in that House! Must not the merits of every officer be inquired into when it is proposed to confer on him a vote of thanks? Was he not *then* on his trial? Was not that a species of trial to which any officer must necessarily be exposed before he could receive the high honour of the thanks of Parliament? After a court-martial, by which Lord Gambier had been acquitted, did it follow, as a matter of necessity that they must grant him the thanks of that House? He presumed this by no means followed.

" What then was the situation to which the House was reduced? The noble lord (Cochrane) had committed himself more than he had ever heard man do in that House to prove his statements respecting the conduct of Lord Gambier. And now a member (Sir C. Hamilton) came forward and said that the duty intrusted to Lord Cochrane had not been properly executed, and that if it had been he might have done far more injury to the enemy's ships. The hon. baronet (Hamilton) said that at the time Lord Cochrane was in command, and made signals to the vessels employed under him, ' *some of them obeyed and others disobeyed* the instructions they received, and that those who disobeyed were ultimately successful, whilst those who obeyed at the moment failed.' The worthy baronet also added that ' those who *disobeyed* the signals were promoted, whilst those who *obeyed* were not.' What would become of the subordination of our Navy if our officers were to be informed, in any one instance, that those who obeyed the instructions of their superior officer were to be *passed by*, while those who disobeyed his signals *might expect to be promoted!* *

" From the disagreeable situation in which the House was placed on both sides, he thought they must unavoidably have the *Minutes*."

* This admission by a ministerial partisan was true. It was chiefly owing to this that the fireships, to use Lord Gambier's words, "failed to take effect on the enemy's ships;" viz. by kindling them where they drifted on the shoals or went wide of the enemy's fleet.

Various other opinions were expressed. Mr. Wilberforce thought acquiescence in my motion for the production of the minutes " most important, as throwing a *stigma on all the members of the court-martial;* " which was true enough, one of my objects being to show that the influence of a corrupt government had been used to vitiate a tribunal upon which the very safety of the Navy depended. How far I should have succeeded in this may be left to the reader's judgment.*

Mr. Ponsonby would not agree to the motion because its adoption would be a violation of the fundamental principles of jurisprudence. Sir Francis Burdett said, that " Lord Gambier's plan seemed to be a desire *to preserve his fleet* — my plan, to destroy the enemy's fleet. He had never heard that the articles of war held out an instruction to preserve the fleet. What if Nelson, at the Nile or Trafalgar, had acted on this principle? He had never heard that Lord Gambier, in the affair of Basque Roads, pretended to have done any hard, or even important service. His only merit seemed to consist in what he omitted to do."

Having thus been put on my defence by direct accusation on the part of a Ministerial supporter that I had not done my duty, I implored the House to give me an opportunity, not only of defending myself, but of laying bare matters of more importance to the country than either my judgment or character. I again pledged myself to prove all I had asserted, and to stake everything

* See Lord Grey's expressions, *infra.*

that was valuable to man on the issue, at the same time telling the House that, if the minutes were granted, I would expose such matters as might make the country tremble for its safety — and entreating it well to consider that there was another tribunal to which it was answerable, that of posterity, which would try all our actions and judge impartially.

Neither argument nor a sense of justice availed, and the word "*sentence*" was substituted for "*minutes*," in an amendment carried by a large majority of the faction, in that day dependent on and wielded by Ministers — of whose general conduct Lord Grey, in the opening debate of the session, thus thought it necessary to express himself: — "He was glad to find from the humble and chastened tone of Ministers that they *appeared to feel some remorse for the numerous miseries which, by their imbecility and misconduct they had inflicted on their country. Had it been otherwise, he should have supposed the Almighty vengeance was hanging over this nation, and that therefore the hearts of its rulers had been hardened in proportion as their understandings were darkened.*" This merited censure from one of the great lights of that day and of all time, passed unheeded in the conduct of the session, which outdid its predecessors in acts of subserviency to the faction in power by whose supremacy it was felt that the rotten-borough interest could alone maintain itself against the national execration which was now beginning to make itself heard.

At the conclusion of the preliminary debate, the Chancellor of the Exchequer rose to move a vote of thanks to Lord Gambier for *his eminent services in destroying the French fleet* in the Basque Roads! My name, as having effected anything, was *purposely and very ingeniously left out!* but warm thanks were accorded to those who directed the fireships,—not against the enemy, but against the banks of the Boyart and Palles shoals!

The passage in the vote of thanks is curious : "for their gallant and highly meritorious conduct on this glorious occasion, *particularly marked by the brilliant and unexampled success of the difficult and perilous mode of attack by fireships, conducted under the immediate direction of Captain Lord Cochrane!*" Yet Lord Gambier stated in his defence, "The success of the first part of the enterprise arose from the terror excited by the *appearance* of the fireships! *as they failed in the principal effect they were intended to produce.*" (*Minutes*, p. 131.) If the House had been in the possession of the minutes of the court-martial, would they have voted thanks to officers of whom the Commander-in-chief says that they "*failed in their object*"? Not a word of thanks to me for having conducted it, but to the Commander-in-chief, then twelve miles off, his only merit consisting in coming three miles nearer, anchoring out of gunshot—and to men whom a ministerial supporter had praised by saying they had been promoted for "*disobeying my signals!*" And this though the First Lord of the Admiralty had offered me his own regiment—a squadron of frigates, with *carte blanche* to do what I pleased with them—and a vote of thanks, conjointly with Lord Gambier, if I would not offer any opposition!

The value of such a vote under such circumstances had been rightly estimated, even by those who acquiesced in it. The value of the service rendered was paltry, in comparison with what it ought to have been ; and the vote, either to myself or my superiors, would have been worthy of it. I had from the first refused to have my name coupled with such pretence, as a fraud on national honours.

Yet, leaving me altogether out of the vote of thanks, so long as thanks were voted, and giving them to the Commander-in-chief and the officers under " my immediate direction," was a specimen of party spite so transparent that it could deceive nobody. The Chancellor of the Exchequer, either ashamed of his subject, or forgetting the purpose in hand, most unaccountably gave me in his harangue *the credit of the whole affair!* He could only have done this from two motives. Either he was too much a gentleman to permit his personal honour to be trampled under foot by his colleagues, or he could not have read the vote of thanks till he came to it at the conclusion of his speech. There is, however, a third hypothesis. The subjoined eulogy might have been pronounced to blind the House.

" The attack having thus recommenced on the night of the 13th successively* was followed up on the next day by the noble lord (Cochrane) † with peculiar gallantry. The

---

* There was no attack at all on the night of the 13th, for all the ships taken were destroyed on the afternoon and night of the 12th.

† No such thing. I followed up nothing on the 14th, except trying to evade Lord Gambier's signals of recall. A pretty clear proof that the Chancellor had never even read the despatches, and less the minutes of the court-martial !

consequence was that no less than three sail of the line and a fifty-gun ship were completely destroyed. The House would not, therefore, he trusted, be disposed to refuse its thanks *for eminent services when performed under such great peril and risk*, whilst the enemy were possessed of the protection of their own batteries*, and other advantages which they could bring into play for the security of their own vessels. *It was an enterprise of great and peculiar hazard and difficulty.* The result had been highly injurious to the enemy, and had the effect of not only disabling but of removing the enemy's whole squadron from the possibility of being for a considerable time available for the purposes of the naval campaign. *Was not this an object of great magnitude?*"

From this speech it is clear that the Chancellor of the Exchequer considered that the whole success was attributable to my exertions, and it is no less apparent that he contemplated my being included in the vote of thanks.

Then why leave me out of the vote of thanks, and give thanks to those who had nothing to do with this "*work of great magnitude?*"

Lord Mulgrave made no such blunder in the House of Lords, nor even mentioned my name *except in terms of reprobation* — possibly because I refused his lordship's temptation of a squadron and a regiment to hold my peace! Yet it may be that the Chancellor of the Exchequer made no mistake. His eulogy might have been merely intended to appeal to the popular ear, whilst contemptuously excluding me

---

* About which I did not trouble myself, and by which the *Impérieuse* was not once hit.

from the vote. Be this as it may, the trick succeeded, and my voice was drowned amidst the clamour of faction, as were the voices of those who supported me in the House.

Still I was not disposed to allow the vote to pass without further protest. I again warned the House that " even their verdict was not conclusive upon character, but that there was another tribunal to which even that House was amenable, and that the public would one day exercise a judgment, even though the House might shrink from a just decision. I inquired what portion of Lord Gambier's exploit merited thanks, or what had been the nature of his exploit? He lay at a distance — never brought his fleet to the place of action, or even within danger, and yet for such supineness he was to receive the highest honours of his country! The ground taken by ministers was frivolous — that where the subordinates admittedly deserved the praise, the superiors must receive it. The public *would one day read the minutes, though the House would not. The public would judge from the facts, though the House would not. The public would not submit to have its eyes bound because the House chose to keep theirs shut.* Let a single reason be adduced for this vote of thanks, and I was ready to vote for it — but the *reasons* which had been obtruded on the House were unworthy the name of *arguments*."

Sir John Orde, of all the supporters of the ministry, gave the only honest reason for his vote in favour of Lord Gambier, though probably his argument might

not pass current at the present day. It was this :— " As
thanks to his Lordship have been proposed, I shall
vote for them, because I entertained this opinion of
Lord Gambier's conduct before the prorogation of
Parliament, *and their Lordships of the Admiralty appeared to do the same ! !*" Poor Sir John ! He must
have had better reasons for his arguments than arguments for his reasons.

A few more reasonable opinions than that of worthy
Sir John shall be transcribed *verbatim,* and first those
of Sir Francis Burdett :—

" Sir Francis Burdett wished to know whether the service
of Lord Gambier was worth the thanks of Parliament, even
admitting it to have all the value attributed to it by anything
but the unblushing and profuse spirit of ministerial favour-
itism.* He would not ask whether, on the other hand, there
was not the full and decided testimony of a man competent
to give his judgment, and of whose admirable valour and
good fortune the House and the nation had but one opinion ?
He felt that in making these observations he might be tread-
ing on perilous ground. He was probably bringing on himself some charitable retorts, particularly those of a gentleman
whose charity was of a very peculiar nature. But he was
careless about such remarks ; for though he deprecated that
person's charity, he would not shun but would rather court
his hostility.†

" Had there been anything said to make out a reason of
the vote demanded ? Where was the evidence of the Com-

* Lord Gambier had recently been a colleague of the Lords of
the Admiralty.

† Mr. Croker, who did not, however, respond to the challenge of
my excellent colleague. Had he done so, the House would, no
doubt, have been highly amused at the result. But Mr. Croker
was " wise in his day and generation."

mander-in-chief's *intrepidity or skill?   Of that boldness
which bursts its way through all obstacles?   Of that genius
before which obstacles vanish?*   In place of this, the House
was insulted with a dry catalogue of negatives, and an account
as to how the noble Admiral inspected the action *at a distance
of seven miles.** The question had been treated lightly;
but levity was unbecoming the grave matter for their
deliberation."

Mr. Windham said :—

"The thanks of that House did not deserve to be lavished
on any man, unless his services were of that rank which forced
itself into universal report and universal admiration.   It was
not to be evolved in some obscure process of official che-
mistry, not to be drawn out under bundles of obscure records,
not to be elicited by any keen, cunning, recondite, subtilising
process† beyond the practice or perception of the general
mass of mankind.   To be praised, it must be known; to
become matter of thanks, it must be matter of public fact.

In voting thanks it was time to pause.   These old rewards
had become worthless.   It had been said that nothing was
left but the peerage, and even of that high honour ministers
had been most lavish.   This was the natural process when
there was no distinct scale of merit and reward.   It was high
time to stop.   They had in their hands the great provision
for national virtue.   They had the honours of the country
intrusted to them, and it became them as legislators not to
suffer its streams to be idly diverted, nor to be prodigally
and profusely poured forth to slake the thirst of undeserving
ambition, still panting, still insatiable."

Argument and fact were alike unavailing, and Sir
John Orde's extraordinary reasons and opinions prevailed.   To 161 of the Admiralty opinion, only 39

---

* Nine.   † Alluding to the court-martial.

could be found alive to a true sense of legislative dignity or functions.

A few remarks on what passed in the House of Lords, where similar thanks were voted, are necessary.

Lord Mulgrave said that it was with great surprise that he first heard that a noble lord serving under the noble Admiral, and a member of another House, had intimated his intention to oppose the vote of the House of Commons, on the ground that his commander had not done his duty to *the utmost*. Lord Mulgrave, of course, alluded to my conversation with him nine months before, though I never said anything of the kind to his Lordship. What I said was, " that the Commander-in-chief had not done anything deserving the thanks of Parliament." Had the *minutes* been allowed to be produced in either House, this would have been proved beyond question, in spite of the *sentence of acquittal*, which was alone laid on the table.

Lord Mulgrave was no less unjust in attempting to convince the peers that I had done nothing but carry out *Lord Gambier's plan of fireships;* referring them to Lord Gambier's letter of March 19th, 1809, in which, instead of recommending an attack by fire-ships, Lord Gambier had denounced such an attempt as " *hazardous, if not desperate*," * as would have appeared had the minutes of the court-martial been laid before them.

Mine, as explained in the first volume, was not an attack by fireships alone, for such an attack could only have ended in the boarding of the fireships by the

* See Lord Gambier's letter, Vol. I. p. 342.

enemy's row-boats, and the murdering of the crews. It was an attack by means of explosion-vessels, which should impress the enemy with the idea that every fire-ship was similarly charged, so as to have the effect of deterring them from boarding, and thus, the fireships, had they been properly directed, must have done their work in spite of the enemy's row-boats.

Yet Lord Mulgrave followed Lord Gambier in this " *suppressio veri.*" On the very day Lord Gambier had *not* recommended the use of fireships—though Lord Mulgrave's speech would lead the House, in the absence of the minutes of the court-martial, to infer that he *had* recommended their use—the Commander-in-chief had stated that an attack with fireships would be " *hazardous, if not desperate.*" A curious way, truly, of recommending the use of fireships; though, had he recommended them, they would have been of no use without the explosion-vessels, the terror created by which formed the very essence of my plan, and was the sole cause even of the trifling success gained. Again, said Lord Mulgrave :—

"Lord Cochrane arrived at Plymouth. He had on a former occasion been employed in blockading Rochefort, and was acquainted with the coasts. He was, therefore, consulted, and *spoke with greater confidence of the success of the attempt than those who wrote from that quarter.* It was not, however, merely the zeal and *desire of execution* he showed, but also the talent he displayed in meeting the objections *started by naval men,* which induced the Admiralty to employ his Lordship."

This representation was thoroughly incorrect. So far from there being any " desire of execution " on my part, I tried every means in my power to avoid being intrusted with the execution of my own — not Lord Gambier's,— plans as Lord Mulgrave insinuated. He, however, unconsciously admitted that other naval men " started " such objections, that they could not be got to undertake an attack with fireships, and therefore the duty was *thrust* on me, with the addition of the explosion-vessels I had suggested, thus convincing the Admiralty Board that an attack, on my plan, was both easy of execution and certain in its result. Lord Mulgrave's expression of "those who wrote from that quarter," viz. Lord Gambier, showed that the Commander-in-chief had *no confidence* in fireships. Neither had I, unless accompanied by my plan of explosion-vessels.

Still persisting that this was an attack by fireships merely, Lord Mulgrave told the House that it was nothing new, which was the case, if the explosion-vessels were left out, but that—

"In the course of the last century there were two services performed by fireships; the first in 1702 at Vigo, and the second off Minorca in 1792. But *what was the present service?* Recollect, a fleet protected by *shoals and currents,* in sight of their own coast, and in presence of their countrymen. *Nothing in the annals of our Navy was more brilliant!*"

Who, then, performed that "*brilliant*" service, than which nothing could be more satisfactory? Lord Mulgrave told the House that Lord Gambier did, *whilst lying with his fleet nine miles off,* and reluctantly sending two line-of-battle ships and some frigates to my "assistance," when almost too late to rescue me from the dilemma into which, in sheer despair of anything being done, I had voluntarily rushed, with the determination that if my frigate was sacrificed, while he was calmly looking on, he should take the consequences, and what they would have been I need not say. It was this act of mine, and this only, which caused the paltry service to be effected of destroying two line-of-battle ships and a store ship, instead of the whole enemy's fleet!

Lord Mulgrave's statements were severely rebuked by Lord Holland :—

"Lord Holland represented in strong terms the light in which ministers placed themselves before Parliament and the country by coming forward, so hastily in the first instance to procure thanks, and then suddenly sending Lord Gambier to a court-martial *with the thanks on their lips.* He thought that in a case of parliamentary thanks the case should be *clear and strong* to receive such a reward. What said Lord Cochrane in his reply to the Admiralty?* ' *Look at and sift the log-books!* and not ask me for accusations.' He (Lord Holland) condemned the precipitancy of ministers, who by their measures had endeavoured to *stultify the House as they had already stultified their own administration.*

"After sending Lord Gambier through the ordeal of a court-martial, Lord Mulgrave now came down, pronounced his praises, and called upon the House to vote him their thanks! It was not in this manner that the French government conducted itself towards their admirals and generals. They instituted a very severe inquiry as to this affair at Basque Roads, and many of their commanders were most severely punished.† They did not give thanks to General

* See Vol. I. p. 408.

† For having, as Buonaparte afterwards said (see Vol. I. p. 421), suffered themselves to be terrified by the explosion-vessels, so as to

Monnet for his defence of Flushing, but, on the contrary, censured his conduct most severely. *

"If the barren thanks of both Houses of Parliament were *often to be voted in this way, they would soon cease to be of any value.* The noble Lord (Mulgrave) had said a great deal about the battle of Talavera, and the resistance made to the vote of thanks in that instance. Now it did not appear to him (Lord Holland) that the battle of Talavera could have anything to do with the action of Basque Roads or with the conduct of Lord Gambier. But if resistance to the vote of thanks to Lord Wellington were adduced as a proof of party motives, it might well be considered a proof of party spirit on the other side to bring forward motions of thanks for services of such a description as were those of Lord Gambier."

The remarks of other noble lords were more to the purpose :—

"Earl Grosvenor did not think the services of Lord Gambier of such a nature as to require the particular thanks of the House. He thought such should only be given on very signal and important victories. Nobody could doubt they were due to Lord Howe for his victory on the 1st of June, to Lord Duncan for his victory at Camperdown; to Lord St. Vincent for his glorious achievements near the cape which gave him his title, or to the immortal Nelson for the splendid exploits with which he had adorned our naval his-

take every fireship for one, and then to run their ships ashore in order to avoid the impending danger ; this result forming the very essence of my plan. Poor Captain Lafon of the *Calcutta* was shot, *not for surrendering to Lord Gambier's fleet*, but to the *Impérieuse* frigate under my command, she being a vessel of inferior force to the *Calcutta*.

* Though he had thwarted, but not so effectively as he might have done, the powerful armament mentioned at the commencement of the next chapter.

tory. These were things which spoke for themselves, and
nobody could doubt the propriety of voting thanks, as it
were, by acclamation. He thought, however, *the services of
Lord Gambier were of a very inferior description, and
called for no such reward.*"

"Earl Darnley had no objection to the vote of thanks,
but at the same time he thought the present vote one of the
efforts now too often resorted to *to throw a false lustre on
the Government.* To compare the services rendered by Lord
Gambier at Basque Roads with the battles of the Nile or
Trafalgar would be the height of presumption!"

Lord Darnley was right; the vote itself, no less
than the assumption of victory, where, through the pusil-
lanimity of the Commander-in-chief, none had been
achieved, had no other object than to " throw a false
lustre upon a Government" powerful in rotten-borough
influence, but justly mistrusted by all besides, whether
in Parliament or out of it. Because I acted practically
and conscientiously on these sentiments, I have been
marked through life an object of party malevolence.

However dexterous might be the ministerial leger-
demain which could convert into victory the admitted
intention of the Commander-in-chief *not to fight**, Lord
Melville alone exposed the real secret of the matter :—

"Lord Melville conceived the Admiralty to have acted
extremely wrong in giving to Lord Cochrane a command so
contrary to the usual rules of the service, and which must
have been so galling and disgusting to the feelings of other
officers in Lord Gambier's fleet. He respected as much as
any man could the zeal, intrepidity, and enterprise of Lord
Cochrane, but it was wrong to presume that these qualities

* See Captain Broughton's Evidence, p. 95.

were wanting in officers of that fleet of superior standing to his Lordship. Such a selection naturally put Lord Cochrane upon attempting enterprises whereby great glory might be obtained."

Here lies the gist of the whole matter. Had I devised the plan of attack, and had the Board of Admiralty acceded to my earnest wish, and left it to my seniors to execute, or had I persisted in my determination to refuse a command which the Admiralty literally forced upon me, all would have been well. Even had Lord Mulgrave fulfilled his promise of satisfying the *amour-propre* of the fleet—which he neither did nor intended to do—all might have been well. As it was, I was exposed to the full amount of hostility which formed my reason for declining the command in the first instance.

It was felt — as Admiral Austen plainly says — by the officers of the fleet in Basque Roads, that a decisive victory would elevate me in national estimation over my seniors, as it unquestionably would have done. Lord Gambier was an easy man, and the " shoal and current " bugbear was successfully used to bring the fleet to an anchor in place of going on to the attack, he knowing no better, and having taken no trouble to ascertain the fact ; in short, confining himself to mere blockade. This was the fault of the Commander-in-chief, but it did not justify him in bringing forward charts made up for the purpose of proving imaginary dangers from ruined fortifications and shoals where none existed. * Nor did it justify the evidence of influenced

* See Captain Broughton's evidence, p. 64.

witnesses to *prove* danger — in defiance of his Lordship's own admission that *no ship suffered injury !* *
It did not justify his Lordship in assuming many
things in his defence, which were not in evidence
at all, and many more things that were totally at
variance with the evidence contained in the minutes.
To have declined pushing an advantage to victory, in
deference to the jealousy of senior officers, was one
thing ; to trump up a story of *an old storeship breaking
up a boom of more than a mile in lineal extent, and
moored with a hundred anchors, was another.*

It will now be seen why the Government of that day
refused the production of "*minutes* of the court-martial,
almost every page of which would have rendered the defence of the Commander-in-chief — or rather that of his
solicitor, Mr. Lavie, for I will do Lord Gambier the
justice of believing that he did not write the defence
read to the Court by the Judge-Advocate — untenable
for a moment. That the Ministry of that corrupt day
should have resorted to such a subterfuge can, however,
scarcely add to the contempt with which history already
regards them.

I told the House of Commons that "*posterity would
judge their acts.*" Here, then, is matter for that judgment. That it was not made public at the time arose
from two causes. First, that in those days the bulk of
the press was influenced by the Ministry ; and a jackal
howl, from one end of the kingdom to the other, would
have been—and was, the reward of my pains. Secondly,
that until his Grace the Duke of Somerset gave me, a

* See Lord Gambier's defence, p. 100.

few months since, the chart and other official materials requisite to lay the matter before posterity, it was not in my power to do so ; except, as on my previous attempts at justification, by assertions, which would have had no more effect on the public mind than now would those of the factions which persecuted me. As I belonged to no party in the House, I found no friends but the few who, like myself, stood alone in their independence of party. Those were themselves disorganised, and deceived by the well-timed eulogy of the Chancellor of the Exchequer, into the belief that the vote of thanks included me also. The numbers of the independent party were, however, as nothing compared to the organised masses in power, or eager to place themselves in power. The debate was felt to have most seriously damaged the party to whom I was politically opposed, and that party ever afterwards made me a mark for their revenge. In this brief sentence may my whole subsequent history be comprised.

CHAP. XXIX.

REFUSAL OF MY PLANS FOR ATTACKING THE FRENCH FLEET IN THE SCHELDT.

REFUSED PERMISSION TO REJOIN MY FRIGATE. — I AM REGARDED AS A MARKED MAN. — NO SECRET MADE OF THIS. — ADDITIONAL CAUSE OF OFFENCE TO THE MINISTRY. — THE PART TAKEN BY ME ON THE RE-FORM QUESTION, THOUGH MODERATE, RESENTED.—MOTION FOR PAPERS ON ADMIRALTY COURT ABUSES.—EFFECT OF THE SYSTEM.—MODES OF EVADING IT. — ROBBERIES BY PRIZE AGENTS. — CORROBORATED BY GEORGE ROSE. — ABOMINABLE SYSTEM OF PROMOTION. — SIR FRANCIS BURDETT COMMITTED TO THE TOWER. — PETITIONS FOR HIS LIBER-ATION INTRUSTED TO ME. — NAVAL ABUSES. — PITTANCES DOLED OUT TO WOUNDED OFFICERS. — SINECURES COST MORE THAN ALL THE DOCKYARDS.—MY GRANDMOTHER'S PENSION.—MR. WELLESLEY POLE'S EXPLANATION.—OVERTURE TO QUIT MY PARTY.—DEPLORABLE WASTE OF PUBLIC MONEY. — BAD SQUIBS. — COMPARISON WITH THE PRESENT DAY.—EXTRACT FROM "TIMES" NEWSPAPER.

JUST at the period of the court-martial on Lord Gam-bier, great national expectations were excited by the combined military and naval expedition to Walcheren, under the Earl of Chatham and Sir Richard Strachan. The object of this armament, the most formidable England had ever sent forth, was the capture or de-struction of the French fleet in the Scheldt, and of the arsenals and dockyards of Flushing, Terneuse, and Antwerp, at the latter of which ports Buonaparte was carrying on naval works with great vigour.

The force employed for this purpose comprised

40,000 troops, 35 sail-of-the-line, 2 fifty gun-ships, 3 forty-four gun-ships, 18 frigates, and nearly 200 smaller vessels, besides dockyard craft; the first portion of the expedition quitting the Downs on the 28th of July, 1809, and anchoring the same evening near the coast of Walcheren.

To the reader acquainted with the views expressed in the first volume of this work, it will not be surprising that I viewed the departure of this force with regret ; as had one half of the troops been placed, as suggested in my letter to Lord Mulgrave, on the islands of the French coast, and had half the frigates alone been employed, as had been the *Impérieuse* and other vessels in the Mediterranean, not a man could have been detached from Western France to the Spanish peninsula, from which the remaining portion of the British army might have driven the French troops already there.

Full of these views, and knowing that short work might be made of the Walcheren expedition, so as to liberate both the naval and military force for service elsewhere, I laid before the Admiralty a plan for destroying the French fleet and the Flemish dock-yards, somewhat analogous to that which would have proved completely effectual in Basque Roads, had it been followed up by the Commander-in-chief. My new plan had, moreover, received an important addition from the experience there gained, and was now as formidable against fortifications as against fleets.

The first measure of indignation against me for my late services to my country was the summary rejection of my plan, and not only this, but a refusal by Admiralty letter, given elsewhere, to proceed to the Scheldt to join my frigate, which had been sent there under the temporary command of the Hon. Captain Duncan, a most excellent and gallant officer.

Of the disastrous failure of the Walcheren expedition —the destruction of a large portion of the army by disease—and the retreat of the remainder, I shall not speak ; these matters being already well known to the student of English history. I will, however, assert — and the assertion will be borne out by the plan of attack submitted by me to the Admiralty — that had my recommendation been adopted, even though not carried out under my own supervision, nothing could have saved the French fleet in the Scheldt from a similar fate to that which had befallen their armament in Aix Roads. Even—as with the disaster in Aix Roads fresh in remembrance, is probable — had the French fleet in the Scheldt taken refuge above Antwerp, it could only have placed itself in a *cul-de-sac ;* whilst there was ample military and naval force to operate against the dockyards and fortifications during the period that my appliances for the destruction of the enemy's fleet were in progress ; for I in no way wished to interfere with the operations of the general or admiral commanding, but rather to conduct my own operations independently of extraordinary aid from either.

The cost of this plan to the nation would have been ten rotten old hulks, some fifty thousand barrels of powder, and a proportionate quantity of shells. The cost of the expedition, which failed—in addition to the

thousands of lives sacrificed—was millions; and the
millions which followed by the prolongation of the
war, by the refusal of the Admiralty to put in operation any naval expedition calculated to effect a beneficial object — who shall count? So much for war
when conducted by cabinets! But I was now a
marked man, and the Government evidently considered
it preferable that the largest force which England had
ever despatched from her shores should incur the chance
of failure in its object, than that the simple and easily
applied plans of a junior post-captain should again jeo-
pardise the reputation of his Commander-in-chief.

It was very curious that whilst this animosity was
being directed against me in my professional capacity,
I had shortly before received from His Majesty George
the Third the highest decoration of the order of the
Bath for my professional services !

So little secret did the Government make of their
determination not to employ me again, that the public
press regarded this determination as a settled matter.
It was nothing that I had been instrumental in destroying the fleet so much dreaded by our West India merchants and the nation generally, or that I had offered
to serve the French fleet in the Scheldt in the same
way. I was now an obnoxious man, and the national
expenditure of millions for defeat, was by the ministry
of that day deemed preferable to cheap victory if
achieved by a junior officer, to whom the Chancellor
of the Exchequer — whilst denying him thanks for the
service — had attributed the destruction of a fleet
quite as formidable as the one in the Scheldt.

It may be scarcely credible to the present age that the Government should have openly announced such a determination. On the principle adopted throughout this work, of adducing nothing without proof, it will be necessary to place the preceding facts beyond dispute. From one of the most talented periodicals of the time I extract the following passage : " The worst injury which the radical reformers have done the country, has been *by depriving it of Lord Cochrane's services, and withdrawing him from that career* which he had so gloriously begun."* The pretence was, that I had *withdrawn myself!* at the time I was entreating the Admiralty to permit me to return to my frigate! This matter will shortly be made very clear.

One grave cause of offence to the Ministry, in addition to my determination to oppose the vote of thanks to Lord Gambier, had been the part I took at the famous meeting held at the Crown and Anchor in the Strand. For a junior naval officer in that day to associate with such persons as Sir Francis Burdett and Major Cartwright was bad enough, but that he should *act* with them was a thing unheard of in the naval service.

At this meeting many irritating things were said, though not by me. The late trial of the Duke of York was freely handled, and Colonel Wardle, the principal promoter of it, held up to public admiration. The " borough-mongering faction," as it was forcibly termed by Sir Francis Burdett, was painted as involving the country in perpetual misfortune, and consigning to

* Ed. An. Reg. vol. iv. p. 107.

hopeless imprisonment all who ventured to expose their practices ; whilst, it was said, even His Majesty could not carry on his fair share of government, being compelled to choose his ministers from a faction which not only oppressed the people, but controlled the King himself.

The resolutions moved by good old Major Cartwright at this celebrated meeting were at that time regarded as treason, though at the present day sound doctrine, viz. that " so long as the people were not fairly represented corruption must increase—our debts and taxes accumulate—our resources be dissipated—the native energy of the people be depressed, and the country be deprived of its best defences. The remedy was only to be found in the principles handed down to us by the wisdom and virtue of our forefathers, in a full and fair representation of the people in Parliament."

This was perfectly true, and singularly enough, after the lapse of fifty-one years, the very same question forms the principal feature of the present session of Parliament, the debates on the subject in our day differing very little from their predecessors of half a century ago, if we may credit the following picture from a *Times* leader of April 23rd last. " Call Reform what you will, it is almost anything you please, except legislation. *The belligerent parties will fight and cheat one another, and both together will cheat the people !*"

If after a battle of fifty years the people have not achieved the victory which early Reformers began, I have some right to call on the public to estimate the amount of obloquy which befell myself for my volun-

tary enrolment amongst the combatants on their side ;
and in the belief that the public of the present day
will do my memory that justice which through life has
been denied me, I shall not shrink from laying these
matters before them.   If such a picture of our present
legislators be truly drawn, what must have been that
of the faction against which I had to contend?

The speech made by me at the Crown and Anchor
was very moderate, and indeed was spoken of by the
ministerial organs as expressing less of the spirit of
faction than any which had been delivered on that day.
The worst part of it, so far as I can recollect, was that
generally recorded, that " I hoped the time would come
when ministers would not be employed all day in
thinking what they were to cavil about all night, and
all night in useless debate — whereby the real business
of the country was neglected ; so much so indeed, that
when the newspapers had reached me abroad, I felt
ashamed at the manner in which the government of
my country was conducted."

I had even gone further in moderation, though the
Ministry did not know it, viz. by observing to Sir
Francis Burdett that I thought he was going *too far*.
His reply was characteristic.   " My dear Lord Coch-
rane you don't know ministers.   If you wish to get
anything from them, you must go for a great deal more
than you want.   Even then you will get little enough."
" Oh !" replied I, " if those are your tactics, go on,
I'll follow."

The real grievance was, however, my support of the
motions in Parliament which arose from the meetings

at the Crown and Anchor. Mr. Madocks distinctly charged the Ministry with trafficking in seats, offering to prove to the House that Lord Castlereagh had, through the agency of the Honourable Mr. Wellesley, been instrumental in purchasing for Mr. Quintin Dick the borough of Cashel; and that when in the matter of the Duke of York Mr. Dick had determined to vote according to his conscience, Lord Castlereagh intimated to that gentleman the necessity of voting with the Government, or resigning his seat, which was accordingly done. The Ministry declined to accept the challenge.*

The subsequent motion of Mr. Curwen went further. But I must not forget that I am writing my autobiography, and not political history; I never made pretensions to parliamentary eloquence, and shall not inflict on the reader my humble efforts, excepting only those connected with the naval service.

On the 19th of February I moved for certain papers relative to the conduct of the Admiralty Court, and as my speech on that occasion was sufficiently compre-

---

* The defence to these charges consisted of what was termed eloquence, but which was nothing but empty declamation, without the slightest attempt at argument. The subjoined effort of Mr. Canning on this very occasion is a specimen : —

" Good God ! was this the time to suppose that the character of the House of Commons was lost, and that the most hazardous experiments should be made to restore it ! It was the character and influence of that House which achieved all our blessings ! and distinguished the character and condition of this country from that of any other country in the world ! Was the source from which such blessings flowed to be stigmatised as a sink of corruption ? "

Even at the present day this is amusing.

hensive, I will adduce it with some slight explanations
indicative of the practices which at that time were in
full operation :—

"If these papers are granted it will be in my power to
expose a system of abuses in the Admiralty Court unparalleled in this country, even exceeding those prevalent in
Spain under the infamous administration of Godoy.

"The whole navy of England was, by the existing system,
compelled to employ one individual to carry on its business
before the Admiralty Court; a person perhaps in whose
competence or honesty they might have no confidence. But
admitting his ability and integrity to be unquestionable, still
the thing was preposterous. Would any man like to employ
an attorney who at the same time did business for the other
side? Was such a regulation consistent with equity or
common sense?

"Even the personal liberty of naval officers was answerable
for some seizures, the produce of which notwithstanding went
to the Crown, and the most abominable compromises sometimes took place. Whether the profits of these compromises
found their way into the pockets of any particular individual
I was not absolutely sure, but had evidence to presume that
this was the fact. What indeed could be the design of confining the captors to one proctor, except that secrecy as to
these questionable transactions may be preserved."

One case was my own. In the first volume of this
work is narrated the capture of the *King George* privateer, or pirate, for which seizure by any vessel of war
a reward of 500*l.* had been issued. The *King George* in
part actually belonged to parties connected with the
Maltese Admiralty Court. As her condemnation was
unavoidable, she was condemned as a *droit* to the
Crown; and costs to the extent of 600*l.* were decreed
against myself, officers, and crew, for having taken

her! A subject which will hereafter have to be further alluded to.

The effect of this system was to indispose officers to look after prizes, and thus many an enemy's vessel was suffered to escape. One of my reasons for harassing the French on the coasts of Languedoc and Catalonia was, that it appeared more advantageous to effect something of service to the country, than to take prizes for no better end than to enrich the officers of the Maltese Admiralty Court, and at the same time to be ourselves condemned in costs for our trouble.

Some curious stories might be told of the effect of the system. It was my own practice, when any money was captured in a prize, to divide it into two portions, first, the Admiral's share, and next our own. We then buried the money in a sand-bank, in order that it might not be in our possession; and, as opportunity occurred, it was afterwards taken up, the Admiral's share being transmitted to him, our share was then distributed at the capstan, in the usual proportions. As I never made any secret of my own transactions, the Maltese officials regarded me with perfect hatred; they, no doubt, honestly believing that by appropriating our own captures to our own use, we were cheating them out of what they had more right to than ourselves! By their practices they appeared to entertain one idea only, viz. that officers were appointed to ships of war for the sole purpose of enriching them!

In a case narrated in the first volume, where I had, in Caldagues Bay, taken thirteen vessels laden with corn for the French army in Barcelona, after having

sunk two small ships of war protecting them —we sold
the corn vessels and their cargo to the Spaniards for a
trifle, dividing the dollars amongst us, after sending
Lord Collingwood his share. We afterwards took the
vessels of war after raising them to Gibraltar, where I
purchased one as a yacht. Had I sent those corn
vessels to Malta, and had them condemned there—
in place of obtaining anything for the capture, a
heavy bill of costs for the condemnation of such small
vessels would have greatly exceeded the sum realised
by their sale.

To return to my address to the House :—

"The Navy was paralysed by this corrupt system. The
most insignificant vessels were condemned at an expense
equal to that of the largest, so that the condemnation of a
fishing lugger might be swelled up to the expense of condemning an Indiaman, the labour of capture ending in
nothing but putting money into the proctor's pocket. As an
instance within my own knowledge, Moses Griffin, a Jew
agent at one of the outports, received two thirds out of the
produce of a vessel, the remaining third being the whole
share distributed for admiral, captain, inferior officers, petty
officers, seamen, and marines. What was the effect of such
a system but to paralyse the Navy? It prevented exertion
on the part of the officers. Could it possibly be necessary to
have 120 ships of the line in commission to blockade twenty-
three ships of the enemy, if proper exertions were made. To
insure alacrity in harassing the shipping and commerce of
the enemy, the abuses of the Admiralty must be stopped,
and nothing else would be effectual."

A more startling practice was the following :—

"The commerce of the enemy was carried on to an immense extent by a system of licenses, which permitted the

enemy to trade where they pleased. These licenses, issued by us, *formed an article of common sale* in Hamburgh and other places, and by means of such licenses the enemy's ships were seen coasting along by hundreds in perfect security, even filling the river Thames, contrary to the Navigation Act! We were thus raising up sailors for Buonaparte, *to whose commerce and navy our ministers were the best friends.*"

My representations were met by Sir William Scott, the Judge of the Admiralty Court, with the inquiry as to "how that Court could possibly be answerable for the accounts of the agents on which I had founded my invectives? Lord Cochrane was a prompt accuser, but an unfortunate one, and he pledged his credit these accusations would prove as unfortunate as any that had preceded them."

Unluckily for Sir William Scott's allusion to my " unfortunate habit of making unfounded accusations," Mr. Rose, the treasurer of the Navy, got up and officially confirmed my statements, by admitting the abuses complained of!

"This evil," said Mr. Rose, " had been so strongly represented to him, that soon after he had become treasurer to the Navy he had bestowed many days and nights in its investigation. The result was, that *he had before him no less than 153 cases, nine out of which were now before the judge of the Admiralty Court* (Sir W. Scott himself!) *in consequence of the enormous charges which their accounts contained.* In one case the charges of an agent at Portsmouth, who had 62,000*l.* to distribute, *amounted to* 9462*l., of which* 1200*l. was stated to be for postage!* "

Mr. Rose recommended me to alter my motion, and to move for papers relative to a particular ship. I took this advice and moved for documents relating to two vessels, which was carried. Sir William Scott, however, never forgave me.

On the 9th of March, when these papers were laid before the House, I moved for others in order to elucidate them. This gave rise to another debate, in which some curious facts were brought to light by Colonel Wardle:—

"In the Navy Pay Office it was usual to promote junior clerks over the heads of men who were many years their seniors in the service. One junior clerk, eleven years in the office, was promoted to a place of 300*l.* a year, over the heads of senior clerks from twenty-seven to thirty years in the service. In another case a gentleman was obliged to retire against his will on 170*l.* per annum, and a *boy of fourteen* was appointed to his situation *with a raised salary,* and over the heads of many senior clerks. The Secretary of the Sick and Hurt Office was pensioned off at his full salary of 500*l.,* and an assistant appointed in his stead *with a salary of* 1000*l. ! !* "

On the 12th of March, my respected colleague, Sir Francis Burdett, than whom a purer patriot never breathed, moved that Mr. Gale Jones should be discharged from Newgate, to which prison he had been committed by order of the House, for placarding a handbill, the contents of which were construed into a violation of the privileges of the House. Sir Francis—conceiving that the people had privileges as well as those claiming to be their representatives, or rather that the popular voice constituted the power of their representatives—demanded the release of Mr. Jones, on the ground that the House possessed no privilege to commit a man for asserting his right to discuss its measures, and that neither legally nor constitutionally could such privilege exist.

The debate which ensued, not coming within the scope of this work, may be omitted. Suffice it to say that Sir Francis published in *Cobbett's Weekly Register* a revised account of his speech, in which he declared that the House of Commons sought to set aside Magna Charta and the laws of England by an order founded on their own irresponsible power.

Accompanying this revised speech was a letter addressed by Sir Francis to his constituents of Westminster; and these coupled together the House chose to construe into a breach of their privileges also. The result, as every one knows, was a motion for the committal of Sir Francis Burdett to the Tower.

My worthy colleague, however, refused to surrender. As there was no knowing to what lengths the despotism of the House might extend, a rumour of breaking into the honourable Baronet's house being prevalent, a number of his friends, myself amongst them, assembled at his residence in Piccadilly to see fair play; but one morning, during our absence, an officer, armed with the Speaker's warrant, forcibly entered, and Sir Francis was carried off to the place of his imprisonment.

It is quite unnecessary to detail these circumstances, as they are well known to every reader of English history. On the day after my excellent colleague's capture the electors of Westminster held a meeting in

Palace Yard, and adopted a petition which fell to my lot to present to the House.

The petition went even farther than had Sir Francis, by denouncing the House as "prosecutor and juror, judge and executioner," and denying its right to exercise these combined offices. It taunted the House with evading the offer of a member to prove at the bar that two of the ministers had been distinctly charged with the sale of a seat on their benches, and that such practices were "as notorious as the sun at noonday." They therefore prayed not only for the release of their member, but for a reform of the House itself, "as the only means of preserving the country from despotism."

To have committed the whole of the electors of Westminster for adopting such a petition would have been inconvenient. To have committed me for presenting it would have been scarcely less dangerous, as depriving Westminster of both its representatives. The predominant feeling in the House appeared to be that of astonishment that a naval officer should dare to meddle with such matters. One member opposed its reception at all, another begged me to withdraw it, which I refused to do ; and, therefore, the House adopted the only possible alternative of "ordering it to lie on the table." The feeling towards myself may be conceived.

A similar petition from the freeholders of Middlesex was presented by Mr. Byng, and denounced by Mr. Perceval as a "deliberate and unparalleled insult to the House ; " the petition denying the right of the

House to imprison Sir Francis, and accusing Mr. Perceval and Lord Castlereagh by name as openly trafficking in seats; the petitioners further declaring that the presence of Sir Francis Burdett in the House was necessary to " enforce his plan of reform." Angry debate followed, but neither Sir Francis nor Mr. Jones were released till the following month of June.

On the 11th of May Mr. Croker proposed a vote for the ordinances of the Navy, when I embraced the opportunity of making what was at the time termed " one of the most remarkable speeches ever delivered in that House." The speech indeed was remarkable — not for its eloquence, for it had none, but for some very awkward statistics which *my enforced leisure* had enabled me to collect and arrange. And let me here remark, that when my parliamentary speeches are adduced, the object is to give a faithful picture of the condition as well of the House as of the Navy at that period, not as specimens of an eloquence to which I had no pretension. My parliamentary efforts, such as they are, are on record, and the reproduction of a portion may save both myself and the reader the trouble of further dilating thereon.

One besetting sin of the Administration was the bestowal of pensions, which was carried on to a wonderful extent. Wives, daughters, distant relatives, &c., of all sorts of people who had votes or influence claimed a pension as a matter of right. Another besetting sin of the Government was doling out pittances scarcely sufficient for the support of life to those who had fought and bled for their country.

Bearing this in mind, the reader will readily comprehend the following "remarkable" address — as it has been termed by historical writers—to the House of Commons:—

"An admiral, worn out in the service, is superannuated at 410*l.* a year, a captain at 210*l.*, a *clerk of the ticket office retires on* 700*l. a year!* The widow of Admiral Sir Andrew Mitchell has *one third* of the allowance given to the widow of a Commissioner of the Navy!

"I will give the House another instance. Four daughters of the gallant Captain Courtenay have 12*l.* 10*s.* each, the daughter of Admiral Sir Andrew Mitchell has 25*l.*, two daughters of Admiral Epworth have 25*l.* each, the daughter of Admiral Keppel 24*l.*, the daughter of Captain Mann, who was killed in action, 25*l.*, four children of Admiral Moriarty 25*l.* each. That is — thirteen daughters of admirals and captains, several of whose fathers fell in the service of their country, receive from the gratitude of the nation a sum *less than Dame Mary Saxton, the widow of a commissioner.*

"The pension list is not formed on any comparative rank or merit, length of service, or other rational principle, but appears to me to be dependent on parliamentary influence alone. Lieutenant Ellison, who lost his arm, is allowed 91*l.* 5*s.*, Captain Johnstone, who lost his arm, has only 45*l.* 12*s.* 6*d.*, Lieutenant Arden, who lost his arm, has 91*l.* 5*s.*, Lieutenant Campbell, who lost his leg, 40*l.*, and poor Lieutenant Chambers, who lost both his legs, has only 80*l.*, *whilst Sir A. S. Hamond retires on* 1500*l. per annum.* The brave Sir Samuel Hood, who lost his arm, has only 500*l.*, *whilst the late Secretary of the Admiralty retires, in full health, on a pension of* 1500*l. per annum!*

"To speak less in detail, 32 flag officers, 22 captains, 50 lieutenants, 180 masters, 36 surgeons, 23 pursers, 91 boatswains, 97 gunners, 202 carpenters, and 41 cooks, in all 774 persons, cost the country 4028*l. less than the nett-proceeds of* *the sinecures of Lords Arden* (20,358*l.*), *Camden* (20,536*l.*), *and Buckingham* (20,693*l.*).

"All the superannuated admirals, captains, and lieutenants put together, have but 1012*l.* more than Earl Camden's sinecure alone! All that is paid to the wounded officers of the whole British navy, and to the wives and children of those dead or killed in action, do not amount by 214*l.* to as much as Lord Arden's sinecure alone, viz. 20,358*l.* What is paid to the mutilated officers themselves is *but half as much!*

"Is this justice? Is this the treatment which the officers of the Navy deserve at the hands of those who call themselves His Majesty's Government? Does the country know of this injustice? Will this too be defended? If I express myself with warmth I trust in the indulgence of the House. I cannot suppress my feelings. Should 31 commissioners, commissioners' wives, and clerks have 3899*l.* more amongst them *than all the wounded officers of the Navy of England?*

"I find upon examination that the Wellesleys receive from the public 34,729*l., a sum equal to* 426 *pairs of lieutenants' legs, calculated at the rate of allowance of Lieutenant Chambers's legs. Calculating for the pension of Captain Johnstone's arm, viz.* 45*l., Lord Arden's sinecure is equal to the value of* 1022 *captains' arms! The Marquis of Buckingham's sinecure alone will maintain the whole ordinary establishment of the victualling department at Chatham, Dover, Gibraltar, Sheerness, Downs, Heligoland, Cork, Malta, Mediterranean, Cape of Good Hope, Rio de Janeiro, and leave* 5460*l. in the Treasury. Two of these comfortable sinecures would victual the officers and men serving in all the ships in ordinary in Great Britain, viz.* 117 *sail of the line,* 105 *frigates,* 27 *sloops, and* 50 *hulks. Three of them would maintain the dockyard establishments at Portsmouth and Plymouth.* The addition of a few more would amount to as much as the whole ordinary establishments of the royal dockyards at Chatham, Woolwich, Deptford, and Sheerness; whilst the sinecures and offices executed wholly by deputy

would more than maintain the ordinary establishment of all
the royal dockyards in the kingdom !

"Even Mr. Ponsonby, who lately made so pathetic an
appeal to the good sense of the people of England against
those whom he was pleased to term demagogues, actually
receives, for having been *thirteen months in office*, a sum
equal to nine admirals *who have spent their lives in the
service of their country;* three times as much as all the
pensions given to all the daughters and children of all the
admirals, captains, lieutenants, and other officers who have
died in indigent circumstances, or who have been killed in
the service! "

This portion of the speech, true in every figure, was
not incorrectly termed "remarkable;" and it made an
enemy of every sinecurist named, as I had afterwards
but too good reason to know. Nevertheless, the Administration had made a mistake. I was not permitted
to be employed *afloat*, and was determined to effect all
the good I could for the naval service by advocating
its interests *ashore.*

But the worst was yet to come. My very excellent
grandmother, of whom I have spoken in the first
volume of this work in terms feebly expressive of her
worth, had a pension of 100*l.* for the services of her
gallant husband, Captain Gilchrist; and *though she had
been dead eight years*, some patriotic individual had
been *drawing her pension, as though she were still
living !* Given, a hundred dead widows, with a pension
of 100*l.* each, and some one was at the national expense the richer by 10,000*l.* per annum!

On this point, I thus proceeded, no doubt to the
intense disgust of the party enjoying the defunct
pensions :—

" From the minute expenses noticed in the naval estimate, viz. for oiling clocks, killing rats, and keeping cats, I suppose that great care has been taken to have everything correct. It was, therefore, with great surprise that I found the name of my worthy and respected grandmother, the widow of the late Captain Gilchrist of the navy, continuing on the list as receiving 100*l*. per annum, *though she ceased to exist eight years ago!*"

Notwithstanding the unanswerable argument of my grandmother's pension, and the equally unanswerable comparison of sinecures and naval rewards—the Secretary of the Admiralty, Mr. Wellesley Pole, considered that he satisfactorily replied to both, by pronouncing my statements " inaccurate, and my complaints inconsistent! As to the pensions to the children of admirals, Lord Cochrane must know very well that *the widow or children of an admiral were not entitled, strictly speaking, to any pension!*"

In his defence to the sinecures of his own family, Mr. Wellesley Pole was even more infelicitous :—

" Lord Cochrane has thought proper to make an attack on the Wellesley family, of which I am a member. He asserts that the Wellesleys receive from the public no less than 34,000*l*. a year in sinecure places, and then makes a calculation of *the number of arms and legs which that sum would compensate*. In answer to this, I must observe that no member of the Wellesley family, *except the noble lord at the head of it*, possesses any sinecure. That noble lord certainly did, many years ago, receive the *reversion* of a sinecure which had since fallen in, when he was about to go to a distant part of the world, in a most arduous and important public situation. He was at that time in a delicate state of health, and had a large family!"

That is, Mr. Wellesley Pole confirmed my calculation of the arms and legs. Though one sinecure had
"fallen in," he neither said when, nor what other
sinecures had since accrued to the head of the family.
His general reply to the matter is curious even at the
present day. Mr. Wellesley Pole proceeded :—

"There is a considerable degree of eccentricity in the
noble lord's manner, but at the same time he has so much
good British stuff about him, and so much knowledge of his
profession, that he will always be listened to with great respect. It is, therefore, the more to be lamented that he does
not follow the dictates of his own good understanding, instead
of being guided *by the erroneous advice, and adopting the
wild theories of others.* Let me advise him that *adherence
to the pursuits of his profession,* of which he is so great an
ornament, will tend more to his own honour and to the advantage of his country, than a perseverance in *the conduct
which he has of late adopted, conduct which can only lead
him into error,* and make him the dupe of those who use the
authority of his name to advance their own mischievous
purposes."

This overture was unmistakable. If I would quit
Sir Francis Burdett, sell my constituents, and come
over to the ministerial side, the Government would—
despite the affair of Lord Gambier—put me in the way
of advancement. If I did not forsake my party, the
high professional character drawn by Mr. Wellesley
Pole would avail me nothing—not even to get employed again! I need scarcely say that the overture,
—politely insinuating, as it did, that I was to be bought
—was rejected on my part.

The remainder of my speech consisted of a contrast
between this reckless extravagance in pensions and sine-

cures, and the petty saving which rendered the Navy
useless :—

"Such are some of the pretended savings by which, when
any are made, the country is duped. Were there a prospect
of success, I could point out some savings better worthy
attention. By adopting canvass of a better quality, a saving
equal to the additional income-tax imposed by the Whigs
may be made, equal, in fact, to one fourth of the Navy. The
remaining three fourths of the ships will be more effectual
than the whole, as their velocity would be increased by upwards of half a mile in seven, and they would thus be
enabled to capture those vessels which at present escape from
them all. The enemy distinguish our ships of war from
foreign ships by the colour of the wretched canvass, and run
away the moment they perceive our black sails rising above
the horizon, a circumstance to which they owe their safety,
even more than to its open texture. I have observed the
meridian altitude of the sun through the foretopsail, and by
bringing it to the horizon through the foresail, have ascertained the latitude as correctly as I could have done otherwise. The paltry increase of cost will be more than compensated by the superior strength of the canvass, on which
depend the safety of the ship and the preservation of all the
lives on board.

"I shall, no doubt, hear it urged that a remedy is about
to be applied, and so it has ever since I can remember, but
remedies at public boards are sought in vain."

To comprehend the preceding statements, it may be
necessary to observe that we had at that time more
than 1000 ships of war of all classes afloat, and that
from the general bad character of their sailing and
equipment, the enemy, who had little more than a
tenth of the number, fairly laughed at us. Under any
circumstances, the waste of money was deplorable, but
under the corrupt system by which worthless ships

were then introduced into the Navy, to which subject
allusion is made in the first volume, it was utter
paralysation of every natural effort.

The amount of obloquy these efforts to raise the
condition of the naval service brought on me, amongst
persons who held that afloat or ashore the duty of a
naval officer was implicit obedience to the ministry of
the day, will be readily understood.   Reply to my
statements being impossible, the ministerial organs made
me the subject of numerous bad squibs, one of which is
subjoined :—

> " You fight so well and speak so ill,
>   Your case is somewhat odd,
> Fighting abroad you're quite *at home,*
>   Speaking at home — *abroad ;*
>
> Therefore your friends, than hear yourself,
>   Would rather of you hear;
> And that your name in the *Gazette,*
>   Than *Journals,* should appear."

The wit is somewhat obtuse, but the feeling here
expressed was no doubt sincere.   The Ministers
indeed began to suspect that they had committed an
error in preventing me from joining my ship, and
shortly afterwards attempted to repair it by ordering
me immediately to sea !   With what effect will appear
in the next chapter.

To the credit of the present age, wilful corruption
has passed away, but false economy still prevails.   It is
only six years ago that we commenced a war without
a single gun-boat, the only description of vessel that
could operate with effect in the enemy's waters.   The
consequence was that nothing was effected.   At the

close of the war we built gun-boats by the score, but
now that they may be required for the defence of our
own coasts, only to find them so rotten, as to be in
danger of crumbling under the concussion arising from
their own fire.

In the absence of a more assignable reason, it may be
assumed that they have been cheaply built, for it cannot for a moment be supposed that the disaster arose
from want of proper supervision. The subjoined extract from a leading article of the *Times* of April 25th,
1860, will tell the story better than I can, and by that
the public will see that the vice of what may be termed
extravagant saving is not yet extinct :—

"Five years ago we were compelled to denounce the
management of our military and naval establishments. The
public and the Government have long since done us justice
in this matter, the former by demanding that 'the system'
which paralysed the efforts of Englishmen should be at once
reformed, the latter by setting about those reforms with
more or less activity. We have now, most unwillingly, to
return to the charge, and to lay before our readers a sad
history of mismanagement and waste.

"At this time, we are told, there are forty-seven gunboats,
besides mortar vessels, hauled up at Haslar yard. All the
world remembers the pæan which was sung over this minia-
ture fleet. Christened with coquettish little names, the gunboats, built according to the newest model and commanded
by gallant young officers, were the pets and the pride of the
country. It was told how after the war they were all drawn
up ready for use on the shortest notice, how they could be
brought down to the water in less than an hour, and the
enemy confronted in less than a week with an extempore
fleet as formidable as any that could issue from Cherbourg.
Twenty-two, we are told, have been repaired at a great cost,

and, with the exception of coppering, are fit for launching.
Nine vessels are under repair, fourteen are waiting examination.   These repairs began more than three years ago, and
have been continued at intervals to the present time.   It
will appear singular that vessels built only in 1854 and 1855
should so soon require such extensive reconstruction.   Very
quietly do these repairs seem to have been carried on.   The
decay has been attributed to the fact that the gunboats had
been stripped of their copper, and placed high and dry in a
current of air.   But now it is announced that the decay
must be attributed to another cause.   Some gunboats which
had been kept afloat have been hauled up, and have been
found to be ' far more defective than those stored beneath
the sheds, and the only conclusion which can be arrived at is
that the whole of our gunboats afloat are unfit for service.'
They have been constructed with the most reckless disregard
to the quality of the material.   If those which have been
examined are a sample of the whole, we are at this moment
without an efficient gunboat.   Scarcely a sound piece of
wood can be seen about them, every part bearing marks of
' sap,' and some of the ribs are completely enveloped with it;
the pressure of the hand on their frame crumbles it to dust.
Much more to this effect is given in our Naval Intelligence.
The copper bolts, also, which should have gone through and
been clinched on each side, ' were found to have been
changed into short ends of about two inches, driven in on
each side;' a fact which, if correct, convicts either the
builders or their workmen of a deliberate and most disgraceful
fraud.

" It may he that *the Government price was too low, and
it is said that the only two sound vessels were built by a
firm which lost money by their construction.*   But that cannot be an excuse for the others.   The public will demand a
searching and unsparing inquiry into these delinquencies,
and if it should appear that men holding a foremost position
in the community have been guilty of such malpractices,
they should be duly exposed and punished."

CHAP. XXX.

MY PLANS FOR ATTACKING THE FRENCH COAST REFUSED, AND MYSELF SUPERSEDED.

PLANS FOR ATTACKING THE FRENCH COAST SUBMITTED TO THE FIRST LORD, THE RIGHT HONOURABLE CHARLES YORKE. — PEREMPTORILY ORDERED TO JOIN MY SHIP IN AN INFERIOR CAPACITY. — MY REMONSTRANCE. — CONTEMPTUOUS REPLY TO MY LETTER. — THREATENED TO BE SUPERSEDED. — MR. YORKE'S IGNORANCE OF NAVAL AFFAIRS. — RESULT OF HIS ILL-TREATMENT OF ME. — MY REPLY PASSED UNNOTICED, AND MYSELF SUPERSEDED.

It has already been stated that the *Impérieuse* frigate under my command had been placed by the Admiralty under the orders of the Honourable Captain Duncan, son of the distinguished admiral of that name, as act-ing-captain ; but that permission to resume her com-mand in the Scheldt had been refused on my applica-tion to rejoin her ; no doubt with the intention of preventing me from effecting anything more which might become obnoxious to another admiral.

Now that my presence in the House of Commons had become inconvenient, the Admiralty affected to consider that *I was unjustifiably absenting myself from my ship!* and an intimation was given that I must join her *within a week!*

So far from my absence being voluntary, *it had been forced* upon me from the necessity of attending the court-martial and an acting-captain was to be put

in my place.   When I found that this step was determined on, I asked that Captain Duncan might be
appointed, knowing that he would carry out my views
in the management of a crew to which I was attached,
as from long and arduous service they were attached
to me.   But notwithstanding this temporary appointment, I was anxiously urging on the Board of Admiralty
the necessity of further operations in which it was my
earnest wish to bear a part.

The correspondence which took place with the Admiralty will not only show this, but the record may
prove useful in case of future wars.

On the 7th of June, 1810, I transmitted the subjoined letter to the Hon. Charles Yorke, who had
succeeded Lord Mulgrave as First Lord of the
Admiralty :—

" London, 7th June, 1810.

" Sir,—When I had the honour to present myself to you
the other day, I used the freedom to submit to your judgment the mode by which the commerce of the enemy might,
in my humble opinion, be greatly injured, if not completely
ruined, and that such mode, whilst assisting the present,
would be providing for the future, exigencies of the State.
The subject has pressed itself so forcibly on my attention,
that I am induced to address you by letter, which is perhaps
the best means to avoid engaging too much of your time.

" Passing over the points I then noticed as a stimulus to
the Navy, which, unfortunately for this country, though for
the benefit of our inveterate foe, is checked and restrained in
its operations, I shall beg permission to call your attention
to other parts of the subject I had then the honour to
introduce.

" I am the more impelled to the intrusion by the intelligence recently received of the islands of Las Medas on the
coast of Catalonia having been taken by the French, who

were doubtlessly influenced by the motive *that ought to actuate us to possess ourselves of the islands on the coast of France,* or such of them as tend to aid her best interests.

" In the present state of our Navy, the French rest in the fullest confidence of assured security, and are, therefore, entirely at our mercy, as regards the objects in my contemplation.

" In the present state of French security, L'Ile Groa at the mouth of the Loire, and L'Ile Dieu on the coast of Brittany, may be easily seized by 800 men, in defiance of any opposition; and by a *coup de main* a fourth part of that number would be sufficient. These islands would afford safe anchorage to our cruisers, with the wind on shore, and when, in the winter season, it is dangerous to approach them.

" The islands at the entrance of the port of Marseilles could be taken by 100 men, and their importance is demonstrable by their situation. United with the possession of one of the Hières, they would enable us to cut off the communication between that part of France which consumes the commodities of Italy, and thus the trade of Leghorn and Genoa—once of importance to us—would be lost to our enemy, who now exclusively enjoys it.

" The port of Bayonne, whence the French supply their dockyards at Rochefort and Brest with timber, may be rendered useless by sinking a few old vessels laden with stones. In like manner the anchorage of Ile d' Aix might be destroyed — the passages in the entrance of the Garonne rendered impracticable—and that of Mamusson filled up.

" Proceeding on a more extensive scale, Belle Isle offers itself to particular notice, and would be a most valuable acquisition, as it gives shelter at all times to shipping. At Cette—commanding the entrance of the canal through which the whole produce of Italy and the shores of the Mediterranean are transported to the north of the French empire— the locks might be seized on with facility, and held or blown up, in defiance of the whole power of Buonaparte now in France. The island of Elba might be reduced with as little difficulty, and as it contains two excellent harbours, and protects the anchorage in the Piombia passage, it is well calculated to interrupt all intercourse between the Roman, Italian, and Tuscan States. Were it in our hands at this moment, it would be an invaluable depôt for our manufactures, which, on cutting off the trade with France, would be in the greatest demand throughout the whole of Italy. It was given up at the termination of the last war in ignorance —as may be presumed—of the great advantage which it affords in this respect.

"I need not suggest to you, Sir, that if the measures on which I have thus slightly touched were carried into effect, it would—even should the enemy be disposed to disturb us— require a large portion of the force *intended for the subjugation of Spain,* to be diverted from its purpose. If these measures were to be followed up by a flying naval expedition of trifling extent, and with comparatively only a handful of troops, the enemy might be held in check, or at any rate their plans elsewhere would be frustrated in part, and the remainder must become insignificant from perplexity and embarrassment.

"I submit to you, Sir, that were it not for our naval superiority, and a few thousand troops were at Buonaparte's disposal, our coasts would not be safe—the vessels in our ports would be swept away—and very possibly the ports themselves laid in ashes. As we have at least physical powers, and more honourable incitements than Buonaparte to aid our energies and direct our objects, we ought bravely to pursue all that he would dare to attempt.

"If, Sir, these points should appear to interest you, and you should think it necessary to require of me further detail or information, I shall be happy to wait on you for that purpose at any time you may be pleased to name. I had intended to bring this subject before the House, but a variety of obvious reasons showed me the propriety of addressing you in the first instance.

"I have the honour, &c.,

"COCHRANE.

"The Right Hon. Charles Yorke."

In reply to this letter, I was told by Mr. Yorke that the acting-captain had been appointed to the *Impérieuse* for "*my accommodation*" *! !* instead of Captain Duncan having been appointed from the necessity before mentioned! Mr. Yorke concluded his letter with a peremptory order for me to proceed to sea within a week:—

"Admiralty, June 8th, 1810.

"MY LORD,—I had the honour this morning of receiving your Lordship's letter of yesterday, communicating your Lordship's opinions on various points of service connected with operations on the French coast in the Bay as well as in the Mediterranean, which appear to be nearly of the same effect with those which I had the honour of hearing from your Lordship personally some days ago.

"I beg to return you my thanks for this communication of your sentiments, and have now to inform you that as your Lordship's ship, the *Impérieuse*, is now nearly ready for sea, and destined for the Mediterranean, and as *the period of the session of Parliament during which your Lordship has been accommodated with an acting-captain to command the frigate in your absence* (!) *has now nearly reached its close*, I presume that it is your intention to join her without loss of time, and to proceed in her to join Sir Charles Cotton, who will no doubt employ your Lordship in the annoyance of the enemy and in the protection of our Allies in the manner best suited to the exigencies of the service.

"I request that your Lordship will have the goodness to inform me as early as you can *on what day next week it is your intention to join your ship*, as His Majesty's service will not admit of her sailing being much longer postponed.

"I have the honour, &c.,

"Capt. Lord Cochrane."   "C. YORKE.

The assertion that an acting-captain had been appointed to the *Impérieuse* for my accommodation as a member of Parliament was monstrous, for after the court-martial was ended I begged to be allowed to join her; first, soon after the Walcheren expedition sailed, and again when it failed to satisfy the national expectations; even then offering to destroy the enemy's fleet as had been done in Aix Roads. I afterwards asked permission to view the siege of Flushing as a spectator only, and *was refused*, the refusal being fortunately still in my possession :—

"Admiralty, Oct. 11th, 1809.

"MY DEAR LORD,—I have mentioned your request to the Naval Lords at the Board, and find it cannot be complied with.   I am, my dear Lord,

"Your very faithful servant,

"MULGRAVE.

"The Lord Cochrane."

Notwithstanding Mr. Yorke's version of the reason of my absence from the *Impérieuse*, I determined to make one more effort for permission to carry out my plans for harassing the enemy's coast, and thereby preventing them from forwarding troops to Spain. My object was to get two or three frigates and a few troops under my command. Had I been able to accomplish this, what had been effected with the *Impérieuse* alone on the coast of Catalonia will be my excuse for saying, that such a force would have been the most valuable aid to the British army in the Peninsula.

Preferring, therefore, the service which I was desirous to render to my country to my own wounded feelings, I addressed another letter to Mr. Yorke :—

"London, June 11th, 1810.

" SIR,— In acknowledging the receipt of your letter of the
8th I confess much embarrassment. The measures submitted
to your judgment were, in my humble opinion, of great
national importance. They had in view to weaken the hands
of our enemy and strengthen our own. I therefore indulged
in the hope that they would have received your countenance
and support.

" It must have been apparent to you, Sir, that I did not
offer them on light grounds, nor without calculated certainty
of success in the event of their prosecution. I flattered
myself with the hope of being employed in the execution of a
service on which my previous observations would have enabled
me to act with confidence.

" But although, Sir, you are pleased to thank me for my
communication, you pass over in silence the objects it embraced; and do away with even the expressions of courtesy
bestowed on it by asking ' on what day *in this week* it was
my intention to join my ship, as His Majesty's service would
not admit of her sailing being much longer postponed;' thus
leaving me to conclude that in taking the liberty of approaching you I had trespassed too far, and that to prevent
my importunities in future you had deemed it advisable to
order me to join my ship, and further, to join Sir Charles
Cotton, who, you signify, ' would no doubt employ me in
the annoyance of the enemy, and in the protection of our
Allies, in the manner best suited to the exigencies of the
service.'

" I have throughout life been accustomed to do my duty
to the utmost of my power, and my anxiety to render the
performance of it acceptable to my country, whilst it stimu-
lated me to inform myself on the best means for that purpose, may have led me to intrude on those with whom alone
rests the power of encouraging my expectations. Yet I
might have imagined that my motives would sufficiently
plead my excuse. On the present occasion I had an additional inducement in addressing myself in the first instance

to you, Sir, instead of the House of Commons. I felt that
I was paying the respect due to the First Lord of the Admiralty.

" It appears, however, that I have inadvertently offended,
and am sorry for it, as the public interest may be injured by
the step I have taken. I should have been gratified had you
done me the honour to call for details of the sketch which I
laid before you, when I should have been happy to supply a
properly digested plan by which I propose to secure the objects
there shadowed forth.

" Had this plan been brought under your consideration, I
may venture to say that you would have directed it to be
carried into execution; and I should have envied any person
whom you might have honoured with the charge of it, however much I might have regretted the refusal to permit me
to share in it, I should nevertheless have cheerfully rendered
every information required of me, or that I might have
conceived necessary.

" I have now no alternative than to submit to the wisdom
of the House the propositions you have thought proper to
reject, or rather suffer them to die away without further
notice. I do not pride myself on the accuracy of my judgment, but may be allowed to understand those matters that
come under my own immediate observation better than those
who have had no experience in such kind of warfare.

" The capture of Los Medas by the French has confirmed
me in the opinions I gave to Lord Mulgrave on my last *re-
connaissance* of Ile d'Aix, and which I had the honour to
state to you in my last. I again submit that a similar
course pursued by His Majesty's Government towards France
would distract the purposes of Buonaparte, and injure him
infinitely more than any other step likely to be taken. The
capture of even one of the islands enumerated in my former
letter would be felt by him much as we should feel if a French
force were to capture the Isle of Wight.

" In another part of your letter you say that I have been
' *accommodated with an acting-captain to command the*

frigate during my absence.' I have to assure you that it was an accommodation I never solicited, and one which, far from conveying a favour, was extremely painful to my feelings, as it prevented my going on a service which I was extremely desirous of witnessing. I even made an application to Lord Mulgrave for permission to be a spectator only of the scene of Flushing, so as to avail myself of the opportunity to acquire information about the Scheldt and its environs, but was refused, although others not connected with the service obtained leave to proceed there.

"In conclusion, I beg permission to say that I have yet some objects of moment to bring forward in Parliament, and that as there is no enterprise given to the *Impérieuse,* I have no wish that she should be detained for me one moment.

"I have the honour, &c.,

"COCHRANE.

" The Right Hon. Chas. Yorke.

" P.S. Your letter, Sir, is marked 'private,' which I consider as applying solely to the destination of the *Impérieuse,* and, of course, shall be silent on that subject."

The reply of the First Lord was that it was " *neither his duty nor his inclination to enter into controversy with me!* " A proof how the interests of a nation may suffer from the political pique of a single man in power. Not an individual of the Ministry considered me incapable of carrying into execution, even with an insignificant force, the plans foreshadowed; yet they were treated with contemptuous silence, and a command to proceed immediately on a subordinate service.

" Admiralty, June 12th, 1810.

" MY LORD,— I have had the honour this morning of receiving your Lordship's letter of yesterday. *As I do not conceive it either my public duty so it is by no means my*

*private inclination to be drawn into any official controversy
with your Lordship, either in your capacity of captain of
a frigate in His Majesty's service or of a member of
Parliament.*

" For this reason I must beg to decline replying to several
parts of your Lordship's letter, in which you appear to have
much misconceived my meaning, as expressed in my former
letter, or to observe upon the turn and direction which
your Lordship is pleased to endeavour to give to our correspondence.

" I have thought it proper to lay the two letters which I
have received from your Lordship, being on points of service,
before the Board of Admiralty for their consideration; and
have only now to request to be distinctly informed whether
or not it is your Lordship's intention to join your ship, the
Impérieuse, now under orders for foreign service, and nearly
ready for sea, as soon as Parliament shall be prorogued.

" I shall be much pleased to receive an answer in the
affirmative, because I should then entertain hopes that your
activity and gallantry might be made available for the public
service.   I shall be much concerned to receive an answer in
the negative, because in that case I shall feel it to be my
duty to consider it as your Lordship's wish to be superseded
in the command of the *Impérieuse.*

                    " I am, my Lord,
                         " Your most obedient servant,
                                   " C YORKE.
     " Capt. Lord Cochrane."

A more unjust order from a lay Lord of the Admiralty than this, to join the *Impérieuse* and proceed on
foreign service, was never issued from the Admiralty.

As a lay Lord, he was wholly ignorant of naval
affairs, but nevertheless refused *even to listen* to the
advice of an experienced sea-officer, who had at least
seen some service, and was therefore capable of offering

an opinion. In place of this he ordered me to sea, without the semblance of promotion in any shape, or even the offer of a larger ship.

I had nevertheless received the warm thanks of Lord Collingwood for—as his Lordship expressed it—having with a single frigate stopped a French army from penetrating into Eastern Spain. With the same inadequate means I had kept the whole coast of Languedoc in alarm, so as to prevent any combination of troops on the Spanish frontier, this voluntary service being executed in such a way as to induce Lord Collingwood to write to the Admiralty, that " *my resources seemed to have no end.*" Weighed down with fatigue and anxiety I had returned home, in the hope of relaxation, when the Admiralty, even before there had been time to pay off my ship, ordered me to prepare plans for destroying the French fleet in Aix Roads, Lord Gambier having plainly told them that, if he made the attempt, " it must be at *their peril and not his.*" I prepared those plans, with the addition of a novel element in naval warfare, and drove ashore the French fleet, which afterwards became a wreck, in spite of the want of proper co-operation on the part of the Admiral who had hesitated to attack them.

On my return to England I had been offered by Lord Mulgrave the thanks of Parliament in conjunction with the Commander-in-chief, but refused to couple my name with his. After all these services, for which I never received reward nor thanks — except the red ribbon of the Bath from the hands of my sovereign — another First Lord ordered me to proceed to sea *in a week*, and that in a capacity as subordinate as the one occupied before any of these services had been performed! nay, more, in spite of my pointing out to him, how, with a trifling force, I could do far more than I had done—a proposition which he treated with contemptuous silence. There is nothing worse in the records of the Admiralty even at that period.

Nevertheless, this ill-treatment determined me not to shrink from my duty, though I was resolved that Mr. Yorke should neither get an affirmative nor a negative from me as to joining the frigate. If the command of the *Impérieuse*, under the orders of Sir Charles Cotton, were forced upon me I would take it, but of this the Admiralty should be the judges—not I. Had Lord Collingwood lived to reach England the Admiralty would not have ventured to thrust such a command upon me after my services of the previous three years and my plans for future operations, which, as I have once or twice said, would have saved millions spent on prolonged strife in the Peninsula.

In the vain hope that the national welfare would, on calm deliberation, rise superior to petty official spite, I again addressed Mr Yorke as follows :—

" Portman Square, June 14th, 1810.

"Sir,—When I had the honour to present to you in writing those ideas that I had previously communicated verbally, it was far from my views and contrary to my intention to draw you into any unofficial correspondence. My solicitude to see the interests of my country promoted and the power of the enemy reduced were my only objects. I presumed that amidst the pressure of business any hints thrown out in desultory conversation might escape your memory, but that committed to paper they would meet your consideration. This was my chief reason for addressing you by letter.

"As a member of Parliament I never harboured a wish to intrude myself on your notice. I know that as a captain of a frigate I do not possess any consequence, and am conscious that I never assumed any. But, Sir, I submit that if information promising essential benefit to the State is procured, the source from which it flows, however insignificant, is not of the least moment.

"With an impression which I must lament, Sir, that you decline entering on those parts of my letter which alone prevailed with me to trouble you, I regret having done so. I am not in the habit of entreaty, but when the public service is to be advanced entreaty becomes a duty. I trust, therefore, that you will pardon me if I repeat the hope that you will be pleased to regard the subject in a more favourable light, and examine the grounds and principles on which my opinions are founded. I feel convinced that any other officer possessed of the knowledge necessary to form his judgment will tell you that the measures I have proposed may *to a certainty and with great ease be carried into execution;* and that the enemy would, in consequence, be entirely crippled in his best resources.

"Had I been fortunate enough to receive the least encouragement from you I should have brought forward other objects than those noticed. Amongst these is one that has reference to the coast of Catalonia, where the maritime towns are occupied by troops of the enemy just sufficient to keep the peasantry in awe and exact from them provisions. These, by possessing the open batteries, the French convey coastways in fishing boats and small craft to their armies, which, from the scarcity of cattle, fodder, and the state of the roads, they could not obtain by any other means.

"The few troops stationed along the coast for these purposes might be seized and brought off with a trifling force employed in the way I have indicated. As a proof of this, the aid-de-camp of General Lechu, and a whole company were brought off by the marines and crew of the *Impérieuse* alone, to whom they surrendered, well knowing that had they left the battery they would have been put to death in detail by the oppressed and irritated Spaniards.

" I am thankful, Sir, for your kindness in laying my letters before the Lords Commissioners. The flattering terms in which you speak of my humble abilities also demand my acknowledgment ; and, whilst again tendering them to the service of my country, I beg permission to say that it is the first wish of my heart and the highest aim of my ambition to be actively employed in my profession, and that from former associations I prefer the *Impérieuse* to every other frigate in the Navy. But as she is to proceed immediately on foreign service, I fear it is impossible for me to be in readiness to join her within the time specified.

" I have the honour, &c.,

" COCHRANE.

" The Right Hon. Chas. Yorke."

To this letter no reply was vouchsafed, and the Honourable Captain Duncan was confirmed in the command of the *Impérieuse*, which in the *following month* sailed to join Sir Charles Cotton off Toulon.

Parliament being prorogued within a few days after the date of the last letter, I had no opportunity of bringing the subject before the House.

On the publication of the first volume, it was said by some gentlemen of the press, when kindly reviewing its contents, that something more might have been said of that excellent and gallant admiral, Lord Collingwood. This, I admit, would have been an easy task as regards the gossip of others relative to his Lordship, but that is not the principle upon which this work is conducted, every incident therein having befallen myself personally.

The fact was, that though I had the good fortune to serve under Lord Collingwood, it had never been my lot to serve with him. His Lordship's first act on joining him was, as is narrated in the first volume, to appoint me as the successor of the officer in command of the squadron in the Ionian Islands. Shortly after my arrival at Corfu, I fell in—as has also been said in the first volume—during a cruise with a number of enemy's vessels *bearing the commandant's license to trade!* and in spite of the license captured and sent them to Malta for condemnation. The commandant, as shown in the first volume, hereupon denounced me to Lord Collingwood *as an unfit person to command a squadron.* I was immediately afterwards recalled, and, as the reader knows, was subsequently employed in harassing the French and Spanish coasts, without further personal intercourse with his Lordship, except when paying a flying visit to the fleet blockading Toulon.

CHAP. XXXI.

VISIT TO THE ADMIRALTY COURT AT MALTA.

THE MALTESE ADMIRALTY COURT.—ITS EXTORTIONATE FEES, AND CON-
SEQUENT LOSS TO CAPTORS.—MY VISIT TO MALTA.—I POSSESS MYSELF
OF THE COURT TABLE OF FEES.—INEFFECTUAL ATTEMPTS TO ARREST
ME. — I AT LENGTH SUBMIT, AND AM CARRIED TO PRISON.—A MOCK
TRIAL.—MY DEFENCE.—REFUSE TO ANSWER INTERROGATORIES PUT
FOR THE PURPOSE OF GETTING ME TO CRIMINATE MYSELF.—AM
SENT BACK TO PRISON. — AM ASKED TO LEAVE PRISON ON BAIL.—
MY REFUSAL AND ESCAPE.—ARRIVAL IN ENGLAND.

AT the commencement of 1811, finding that, in place
of anything being awarded to the *Impérieuse* for numerous prizes taken in the Mediterranean, the Maltese
Admiralty Court had actually brought me in debt for
vicious condemnation, I determined to go to Malta, and
insist on the fees and charges thereon being taxed according to the scale upon which the authority of the
Court in such matters was based.

It is not my intention to enter generally into the
nature of the demands made by the Maltese Court, but
rather to point out the manner in which, after realisa-
tion of the prize funds, costs were inflicted on the
officers and crews of ships of war, till little or nothing
was left for distribution amongst the captors. This

will give a good idea of the practices which prevailed ; preventing officers from harassing the coasting trade of the enemy, as the expenses of condemning small craft were ruinous, being for the most part the same as those charged by the Court for the condemnation of large vessels.

One of the customs of the Court was as follows : to charge as fees *one fourth* more than the fees of the High Court of Admiralty in England ; this one fourth was practically found to amount in some cases to *one half*, whilst any scale of charges by which the conduct of the Court was guided, remained inaccessible to the captors of prizes.

The principal officer of the Court in this department was a Mr. Jackson, who held the office of Marshal. This officer, however, though resident in Malta, performed his duty of marshal by deputy, for the purpose of enabling him also to exercise the still more profitable office of proctor, the duties of which he performed in person. The consequence was that every prize placed in his hands as proctor had to pass through his hands as marshal ! whilst as proctor it was further in his power to consult himself as marshal as often as he pleased, and to any extent he pleased. The amount of self-consultation may be imagined. Right profitably did Mr. Proctor Jackson perform the duty of attending and consulting himself as Mr. Marshal Jackson !

Subjoined is an extract from the charges of Proctor Jackson for attending himself as Marshal Jackson : —

	Cro.	reals.	sc.
Attending (as proctor) in the registry and bespeaking a monition	2	0	0
Paid (himself as marshal) for said monition under seal, and extracting . . .	9	0	0
Copy of said monition for service . . .	2	0	0
Attending the Marshal! (himself) *and feeing and instructing him to execute the same!*	2	0	0
Paid the Marshal (himself) *for service of said monition!* (on himself)	2	0	0
Certificate of service! (on himself) . .	1	0	0
Drawing and engrossing affidavit of service! (on himself)	2	0	0
Oath thereto, and attendance! (on himself) .	2	2	3

By what ingenious process Marshal Jackson managed to administer the oath to himself as Proctor Jackson I know not, but the above charges are actual copies from a bill in my possession, the said bill containing *many hundred* similar items besides. Some idea of its extent may be formed from the statement that, previously to a debate on the subject, I pasted together an exact copy the different sheets of which the bill of charges was composed, formed them into a huge roll, and, amidst the astonishment and laughter of the House of Commons, one day unrolled it along the floor of the House, when it reached from the Speaker's table to the bar ! !

In addition to this multitude of fees and charges, the Marshal also claimed, and received as his own especial perquisite, *one half per cent* on the inspection of prizes, *one per cent* for their appraisement, and *two and a half per cent* on the sale. This, with *one fourth* added as

aforesaid, made just *five per cent* on all captures for the
Marshal's perquisite alone, irrespective of his other fees;
which, being subjected to no check, were extended according to conscience. So that, for every amount of
prizes to the extent of 100,000*l*. the Marshal's share,
as a matter of course, would be 5000*l*., wholly irrespective of other fees of Court calculated on a similar
scale. When numerous other officials had to be paid
in like manner, also without check on their demands,
it scarcely needs to be said that such prizes as were
usually to be picked up by ships of war on the
Mediterranean coast entailed positive loss on their captors; the result, as has been said, being that officers
avoided taking such prizes, and thus the enemy carried
on his coasting operations with impunity. In other
words, the most important object of war — that of
starving out the enemy's coast garrisons — was suspended by the speculations of a colonial Admiralty
Court !

Foiled in procuring redress in the House of Commons, where my statements were pooh-poohed by the
representatives of the High Court of Admiralty as rash
and without proof, I determined on procuring, by any
means whatever, such proof as should not easily be set
aside.

Embarking, therefore, in my yacht *Julie*, one of the
small French ships of war captured at Caldagues and
afterwards purchased by me, as narrated in the first
volume, I set sail for the Mediterranean.

On arriving at Gibraltar I considered it prudent to
quit my yacht, fearing that so small a vessel might fall

a prey to the French cruisers, and embarked on board a brig-of-war bound to Malta.

My first demand upon the Admiralty Court on arriving at that place was, that the prize accounts of the *Impérieuse* and *Speedy* should be taxed according to the authorised table of fees. This revision was refused.

Entering the Court one day when the Judge was not sitting, I again demanded the table of fees from Dr. Moncrieff, then Judge-Advocate, who denied that he knew anything about them. As by Act of Parliament they ought to have been hung up in the Court, I made careful search for them, but without success. Entering the Judge's robing-room unopposed, I there renewed the search, but with no better result, and was about to return tableless; when, having been directed to a private closet, I examined that also, and there, wafered up behind the door of the Judge's retiring-chamber, was the Admiralty Court table of fees! which I carefully took down, and reentered the Court in the act of folding up the paper, previously to putting it in my pocket.

Dr. Moncrieff instantly saw what I had got, and rose from his seat with the intention of preventing my egress. Reminding him that I had no cause of quarrel with or complaint towards him, I told him that guarding the Judge's water-closet formed no part of his duties as Judge-Advocate; and that it was rather his place to go and tell the Judge that I had taken possession of a public document which ought to have been suspended in Court, but the possession of which had been denied. He seemed of the same opinion, and suffered me to depart with my prize; this in half an hour afterwards being placed in the possession of a brother-officer who was going over to Sicily, and promised to take charge of it till my arrival at Girgenti.

This "Rape of the Table," as it was termed in a poem afterwards written on the occasion by my secretary and friend, Mr. Wm. Jackson, caused great merriment, but the Judge, Dr. Sewell, was furious, not perhaps so much at the invasion of his private closet, as at losing a document which, when laid before the House of Commons in connexion with the fees actually charged, would infallibly betray the practices of the Maltese Court. A peremptory demand was accordingly made of me for the restoration of the table, this being met by my declaration that it was not in my possession. The Judge, believing this to be untrue, though in fact the tables were in Sicily, finally ordered me to be arrested for an insult to the Court!

The duty of arresting me devolved on my friend in duplicate, Mr. Marshal Mr. Proctor Jackson. I reminded him that the Court was not sitting when the alleged offence was committed, and therefore it could be no insult. I further cautioned him that his holding the office of proctor rendered that of marshal illegal, and that if he dared to lay a finger on me, I would treat him as one without authority of any kind, so that he must take the consequences, which might be more serious to himself personally than he imagined.

The proctor-marshal, well knowing the illegality of his double office, which was not known—much less officially confirmed in England—prudently declined the risk, on which the Judge ordered the deputy marshal, a man named Chapman, to arrest me. Upon this I informed Chapman that his appointment was illegal also, first as holding the office of deputy marshal to an illegally constituted person, and secondly, from his also exercising the duplicate office of deputy auctioneer — the auctioneer being a sinecurist resident in London!! So that if, as deputy marshal combined with deputy auctioneer, he ventured to arrest me, he too must put up with the consequences.*

This went on for many days, to the great amusement of the fleet in harbour, no one being willing to incur the risk of arresting me, though I walked about Malta as usual, Chapman following me like a shadow. At length the Judge insisted on the deputy marshal-auctioneer arresting me at all risks, on pain of being himself committed to prison for neglect of carrying out the orders of the Court. Finding himself in this dilemma, Chapman resigned his office.

On this a man named Stevens, unconnected with any other official position, was appointed in a proper manner ; and all the legal formalities being carefully

---

* The Tory organs in England said that I threatened to shoot Chapman. I need hardly say that this was a gratuitous falsehood. With the exception of the silly duel narrated in the first volume, I never either harmed, or intended to harm, a man in my life, otherwise than in action. The fact was, both these Maltese officials were illegally appointed, and they knew it. The officers and crews of the ships of war present had but too much experience of their selfish conduct, and were as well pleased as myself at the success of my method of keeping their natural enemies at bay, so that the *pseudo*-marshals were in reality frightened at their own warrants.

entered into, I no longer resisted, as that would have been resistance to law.

The manner in which the arrest was made showed a spirit of petty malevolence quite in keeping with the dispositions of men who were making enormous fortunes by plundering the officers and crews of His Majesty's ships of war. I was on a visit to Percy Fraser, the naval commissioner, when the newly appointed deputy marshal who had watched me in was announced, and on entering told me he was come to arrest me. On demanding his credentials, I found them to be signed by Mr. Proctor Jackson, and as I wanted this proof of his acting as marshal illegally, admitted myself satisfied with them.

The deputy marshal then requested me to accompany him to an inn, where I might remain on parole. I told him that I would do nothing of the kind, but that if he took me anywhere it must be to the town gaol, to which place he then requested me to accompany him. My reply was :—" No. I will be no party to an illegal imprisonment of myself. If you want me to go to gaol, you must carry me by force, for assuredly I will not walk."

As the room was full of naval officers, all more or less victims of the iniquitous system pursued by the Maltese Court, the scene caused some merriment. Finding me inflexible, the Vice-admiralty official sent— first for a carriage, and then for a piquet of Maltese soldiers, who carried me out of the room on the chair in which I had been sitting. I was then carefully deposited in the carriage, and driven to the town gaol.

The apartments assigned for my use were the best
the place afforded, and were situated on the top story
of the prison, the only material unpleasantness about
them being that the windows were strongly barred.
The gaoler, a simple worthy man, civilly inquired what
I would please to order for dinner.   My reply was :—
" Nothing ! — that, as he was no doubt aware, I had
been placed there on an illegal warrant, and would not
pay for so much as a crust ; so that if I was starved
to death, the Admiralty Court would have to answer
for it."

At this declaration the man stood aghast, and shortly
after quitted the room.   In about an hour he returned
with an order from Mr. Marshal Jackson to a neighbouring hotel-keeper, to supply me with whatever I
chose to order.

Thus armed with *carte-blanche* as to the *cuisine*, I
ordered dinner for six ; under strict injunctions that
whatever was prized in Malta, as well in edibles as in
wines, should be put upon the table.   An intimation to
the gaoler that he would be the richer by the scraps,
and to the hotel master to keep his counsel for the
sake of the profits, had the desired effect ; and that
evening a better-entertained party (naval officers)
never dined within the walls of Malta gaol.

This went on day after day, at what cost to the
Admiralty Court I never learned nor inquired ; but, from
the character of our entertainment, the bill when presented must have been almost as extensive as their
own fees.   All my friends in the squadron present at
Malta were invited by turns, and assuredly had no

ward-room fare. They appeared to enjoy themselves the more heartily, as avenging their own wrongs at the expense of their plunderers.

At length the Admiralty authorities thought it high time to decide what was to be done with me. It was now the beginning of March, and I had been incarcerated from the middle of February without accusation or trial. It was evident that if I were imprisoned much longer, I might complain of being kept out of my place in Parliament, and what the electors of Westminster might say to this, or what the House of Commons itself might say, were questions seriously to be pondered by men whose titles to office were unconfirmed. They had at length discovered that I had committed no offence beyond the fact of having been seen to fold up and put in my pocket a piece of dirty paper, but what that paper might be, or where it was, there was no evidence whatever.

At length they hit upon a notable expedient for getting rid of me, viz. to get His Excellency the Governor to ask me to give up the table of fees. This I declined, telling His Excellency that as I had been incarcerated illegally I would not quit the prison without trial.

It was accordingly determined that I should be put on my trial, the puzzle being as to what offence I should be accused of. The plan, as I afterwards found, was to interrogate me, and thus to entrap me into becoming my own accuser.

On the 2nd of March I was taken to the Court-house, accompanied by the naval commissioner Mr. Fraser,

Captain Rowley the naval officer in command, and nearly all the commanding officers in port.

Two clerks, one a German and the other a Maltese, were said to have deposed to " seeing a person, whom they believed to be Lord Cochrane, with a folded paper." On the strength of this evidence, the following charge was made out : — "That I had entered *the Registry* of the Admiralty Court, and had there taken down the table of charges ; that I had held up the same, so as to cause it to be seen by the King's Advocate, Dr. Moncrieff, and had then put it in my pocket, and walked away." *

To this I replied that " there must be an error, for as the Act of Parliament ordered that the table of charges should be displayed in open Court, it could not possibly have been the paper which I saw in the Judge's water-closet. That the paper showed by me to Dr. Moncrieff was folded up, so that he was necessarily ignorant of

---

* This charge contained a wilful falsehood, viz. that the table of fees was hung in " the Registry ; " the perversion of truth being proved by the remarks in Parliament of the King's Advocate, Sir John Nicholls, on the authority of the Maltese Court, as follows :—

" Lord Cochrane went to the court-room of the Vice-Admiralty, for the purpose of comparing the charges in his bills with the table of established fees, which, according to Act of Parliament, ' should be suspended in some conspicuous part of the Court.' After looking for it in vain in the Court, *and in the Registry*, whither he was first directed by His Majesty's Advocate, he was told that he might see it affixed on a door leading to the adjoining room. The table was certainly not in its place—but it was as certainly not concealed !" (*Speech of Sir J. Nicholls in the House of Commons, June 6th*, 1811.)

It was equally false that the King's Advocate directed me where to look for the table of fees ; the whole affair having taken place as narrated in this chapter.

its purport or contents.   Finally, I denied having taken
down the table of charges, as established by Act of
Parliament, from the Court-room."   After this reply I
demanded to be confronted with my accuser, for the
purpose of cross-examining him.

This the Judge would not allow, but said he should
consider my denial in the light of a plea of "not
guilty."   He then put to me a series of interrogatories,
for the purpose of getting me to criminate myself; but
to these I refused to reply in any way, merely repeating
my assurance that his Honour must have made a mistake, it being highly improbable that the lost table
of fees should have been hung anywhere but in open
Court, as the Act of Geo. II. prescribed, viz. : *in an
open, visible, and accessible place*, which his Honour's
retiring-closet was not.   Dr. Sewell then admitted that
the charges entered on the table of fees *had not been
ratified by the King in Council!* and that he had therefore not caused them to be suspended in open Court,
according to the Act.   On which declaration I protested against the whole proceedings as illegal.

Finding that nothing could be done, the Judge then
asked me to go at large on bail!   This I flatly refused,
alleging myself to be determined to remain where I
was, be the consequence what it might, till the case
should be decided on its merits.   At this unexpected declaration the Court appeared to be taken
aback, but as I refused to be bailed, the Judge had no
alternative but to remand me back to prison.*

---

* As it may be useful to note the despotic practices of our foreign
tribunals in those days, I will transcribe a portion of the Judge's

On arriving there, my friends were of opinion that the affair had been carried far enough, and that I should apologise for taking the table of charges, and send for it to Girgenti. To this counsel I refused to listen, as I wanted the tables for exhibition in the House of Commons, and would in no way compromise the matter.

On this the senior naval officer, Captain Rowley, said to me :—" Lord Cochrane, you must not remain here; the seamen are getting savage, and if you are not out soon they will pull the gaol down, which will get the naval force into a scrape. Have you any objection to making your escape ?"   " Not the least," replied I, " and it may be done ; but I will neither be bailed, nor will I be set at liberty without a proper trial."

In short, it was then arranged that my servant, Richard Carter, should bring me some files and a rope ; that I should cut through the iron bars of the window ;

speech on this occasion, as correctly reported at the time. On my demanding to cross-examine the witnesses against me, Dr. Sewell said :—

" The present course was the one practised on these occasions. He would not allow any but a direct answer to the charge made, and if that contained no crime, he should himself be responsible."

He then said that he must administer to Lord Cochrane certain interrogatories, and on Lord Cochrane persisting in demanding his accuser or accusers, in place of replying to the questions, *the Judge peremptorily required answers.*

In place of giving these, I denied the competence of the Court to take cognizance of a criminal charge, asserting that it was not a Court of Record; and that on a pretended accusation made by witnesses who could not be produced, I had been arrested, imprisoned in the common gaol, and publicly criminated, without being permitted to clear myself by being placed face to face with my accusers, &c. &c.

and that when everything was in readiness, on the first favourable night, a boat should be manned at the sally-port, and that I should be taken across to Sicily, to pick up the table of fees at Girgenti.

Some three or four nights were occupied in cutting through the bars, the marks being concealed in the day-time by filling up the holes with a composition. When all was in readiness, my friends and I held our last *symposium* at the expense of the Admiralty Court. The gaoler was purposely made very tipsy, to which he was nothing loth; and about midnight, having first lowered my bedding into the streets, to be carried off by some seamen under the direction of my servant, I passed a double rope round an iron bar, let myself down from the three-story window, pulled the rope after me, so that nothing might remain to excite suspicion, and bade adieu to the merriest prison in which a seaman was ever incarcerated.

On arriving at the harbour I found the *Eagle's* gig in readiness, and several brother-officers assembled to take leave of me. The night was dark, with the sea smooth as glass, it being a dead calm. When pulling along the island we came up with the English packet, which had sailed from Malta on the previous day, she having been since becalmed. As she was bound to Girgenti, to pick up passengers and letters from Naples, nothing could be more opportune; so, dismissing the gig, I went on board, and was on my way to England, doubtless, before I was missed from my late involuntary domicile at Malta. I had thus a manifest advantage in those days of slow transit, viz. that of arriving in

England a month before news of my escape from Malta
could be sent home by the authorities of the Admiralty
Court.

As I afterwards learned, nothing could exceed the
chagrin of the Admiralty officials at having lost, not
only their table of charges, but their prisoner also. No
one had the slightest suspicion that I had gone to sea,
and that in a man-of-war's boat. Yet nothing could
better show the iniquitous character of the Maltese
Admiralty Court than the fact that my escape was
planned in conjunction with several naval officers present in harbour who lent me a boat and crew, for the purpose ; the whole matter being previously known to half
the naval officers present with the squadron, and, after
my escape, to not a few of the seamen, all of whom must
have been highly amused at the diligent search made
for me the next day throughout Valetta, but still more
at the *reward offered for those who aided me in escaping*.
Yet not a word transpired as to the direction I had
taken, or the time occupied in searching for me on the
island might have been turned to better account by an
endeavour to intercept me at Gibraltar, where I remained long enough to dispose of my yacht, and amuse
the garrison with a narrative of my adventures since I
left the Rock two months before!

CHAP. XXXII.

NAVAL LEGISLATION HALF A CENTURY AGO.

INQUIRY INTO THE STATE OF THE NAVY. — CONDITION OF THE SEAMEN. — THE REAL CAUSE OF THE EVIL. — MOTION RELATIVE TO THE MALTESE COURT. — ITS EXTORTIONATE CHARGES. — MY OWN CASE. — A LENGTHY PROCTOR'S BILL. — EXCEEDS THE VALUE OF THE PRIZE. — OFFICERS OUGHT TO CHOOSE THEIR OWN PROCTORS. — PAPERS MOVED FOR. — MR. YORKE'S OPINION. — SIR FRANCIS BURDETT'S. — MY REPLY. — MOTION AGREED TO. — CAPTAIN BRENTON'S TESTIMONY. — FRENCH PRISONERS. — THEIR TREATMENT. — MINISTERS REFUSE TO INQUIRE INTO IT. — MOTION ON MY ARREST. — CIRCUMSTANCES ATTENDING IT. — MY RIGHT TO DEMAND TAXATION. — THE MALTESE JUDGE REFUSES TO NOTICE MY COMMUNICATIONS. — AFRAID OF HIS OWN ACTS. — PROCEEDINGS OF HIS OFFICERS ILLEGAL. — TESTIMONY OF EMINENT NAVAL OFFICERS. — PROCLAMATION ON MY ESCAPE. — OPINION OF THE SPEAKER ADVERSE. — MR. STEPHEN'S ERRONEOUS STATEMENT. — MOTION OBJECTED TO BY THE FIRST LORD. — MY REPLY.

ON my return from the Mediterranean, having no prospect of employment, I devoted myself assiduously in Parliament to the course I had marked out for myself, viz. the amelioration of the condition of the naval service; whether by originating such measures of my own accord, or assisting others who had the same object in view.

At this period it was the custom to compel naval officers on foreign stations, in whatever part of the world located, to draw bills for their pay. The consequence was that the bills had to be sold at a discount some-

times amounting to 35 and 40 per cent, the whole of
the loss falling on the officers negotiating the bills.

A motion to place officers of the navy upon the
same footing as officers of the army was made by
Captain Bennet, and strenuously opposed by the First
Lord of the Admiralty, Mr. Yorke, as an innovation on
old rules and customs, which, when once sanctioned, no
one could tell where it might stop.

Upon this I inquired " what greater difficulty there
could be in paying officers of the navy abroad than in
paying officers of the army? There were consuls at
all the foreign stations, who could certify what the rate
of exchange really was. Under the present system, to
my own knowledge, officers on the Gibraltar station were
25 per cent, or a fourth of their scanty pay, out of
pocket, and it was with great difficulty that they could
provide themselves with proper necessaries."

The effect of these remarks was, that Sir C. Pole
moved as an amendment that a Committee should be
appointed to inquire into the state of the navy generally, and this was seconded by Admiral Harvey.

The debate having taken this turn gave me the opportunity of entering more minutely into particulars. I will
transcribe my remarks from the reports of the time : —

" LORD COCHRANE said an increase of pay to the seamen in
the navy would be of little advantage to them, so long as the
present system continued. He had in his hands a list of
ships of war in the East Indies. The *Centurion* had been
there eleven years—the *Rattlesnake*, fourteen years, came
home the other day, with only one man of the first crew—
the *Fox* frigate, under the command of his brother, had been
there fifteen years—the *Sceptre* eight years—the *Albatross*
twelve, &c. Not one farthing of pay had been given all

that period to all those men. He had made a calculation on the *Fox* frigate, and supposing only one hundred of the men returned, there would be due to the crew 25,000*l.*, not including the officers. What became of these sums all the while? The interest ought to be accounted for to Government or to the seamen themselves. The *Wilhelmina* had been ten years, the *Russell* seven years, the *Drake* six years, of which the men would be exiles from England for ever, and another vessel four years. Nothing would be of greater service than the frequently changing the stations of ships, which might be done without any inconvenience, and even with much advantage to the East-India Company's ships.

" The seamen, said Lord Cochrane, from the want of their pay, had no means of getting many necessaries of the utmost consequence to their health and comfort. They drew less prize-money under the existing acts than formerly. He instanced a vessel, the proceeds of which came to 355*l.*; by the present mode of distribution the seaman would receive 13*s.* 5½*d.*, whilst by the old mode he would have received 15*s.* 1½*d.* From the officers' share there was deducted in all 75 *per cent*, allowing only 10 per cent for the prize courts.

" The Minister had exultingly asked, what had become of the commerce of France? But he would undertake to show him, before he was 48 hours on the coast of France, at least 200 sail of the enemy's vessels. If they were to pay more liberally the Judges of the Admiralty Courts, and operate a proper reformation in them, he would undertake to say that they might score off at least one third of the present ships of the navy. Ministers said there were no vessels on the coast of France, but he said there were ; and, if they would go with him, he would show them how they could be got at.

" He rather thought that the inattention of Government to the profligate waste of the public money, arose from their unwillingness to believe anything contrary to their own crude notions on these subjects. He stated, and he begged the House to attend to it, for it was as important as the subject

of Mrs. Clarke, that in the reign of James the Second the pay
of a captain of a first-rate was 80*l*. more than at present.
King William, when he came over with his Dutch troops,
whom he was much more anxious to attend to than he was
to attend to his subjects here, took up his pen and cut off
one half of the pay.   So much for foreign troops; but still,
taking the advance of prices into view, King William left it
far better than it is now.   His Lordship then again called the
attention of the House to the extent to which the French
coasting trade was carried on, and observed that it could not
be checked, unless greater encouragement were given to the
captains.   If he commanded a ship on the French coast, by
keeping at a good distance he might go to sleep, but in order
to intercept those coasting vessels the captain must be on
deck watching all night.   It was impossible officers would
do this merely to put money into the pockets of those who
practised in the Admiralty Courts.

" Mr. Yorke said that at this late period of the session it
would be impossible to enter upon a subject of such detail.
As to ships being detained so long upon foreign and distant
stations, it was much to be regretted, but it was often unavoidable."

These were singular reasons for not entertaining a
subject of such importance.   According to Mr. Yorke,
it was too late in the session to conduct the war successfully, whilst the other evil complained of could only
be " regretted ! "

For want of better argument, I was accused of insinuating that without the chance of prize-money
officers would lose a great incentive to duty.   I only
took human nature as I found it, and it is not in human
nature to exercise unremitting vigilance and exertion
without the hope of reward ; much less that unceasing
vigilance, by night as well as day, requiring almost
constant presence on deck to intercept an enemy's

coasting trade, carried on almost solely in the night, when the enemy felt secure of our vessels being run out to sea, from want of motive to remain in shore.

On the 6th of June I entered on the subject of the Maltese Court of Admiralty. As the debate in the House is sufficiently explicit, previous comment is unnecessary.

" Vice-Admiralty Court of Malta.

" Lord Cochrane rose to make the motion of which he had given notice. The noble lord began by stating that he had before had occasion to trouble the House on this subject, but he then failed in his attempt to obtain justice, on the ground that there was not sufficient evidence of the facts stated to warrant the House in entertaining his motion.   He had since, however, personally been at Malta, and had procured such a chain of evidence, that if the House should now be pleased to entertain his motion, he had no doubt but he should be able to lay before them such a connected string of evidence of flagrant abuses in the Vice-Admiralty Court at that island, as would astonish all who heard it.

" He would undertake to prove that, if the Court of Admiralty at home would do their duty, one third of the naval force now employed in the Mediterranean would be sufficient for all purposes for which it was employed there, and that a saving might be made in the naval service alone of at least five millions sterling a year.   If the Committee for which he moved last year had been granted, the evidence to prove this might now have been before the House."

There was no question at the time, and many naval officers are yet living to confirm the assertion, that the rapacity of the Admiralty Courts and their extravagant charges for adjudication and condemning prizes did prevent the interception and capture of the majority of the numerous small vessels employed in the coasting trade of the enemy, this forming to him the most vital consideration, as the means of provisioning his armies. At the commencement of the war, the capture of large vessels coming from distant parts with valuable cargoes gave so much prize-money as to render both officers and crews careless about a little exertion more or less, but when the enemy's foreign trade was destroyed nothing remained to be looked after but small craft, and as the Admiralty Court charges had increased in an inverse ratio to the worthlessness of small craft, few would run the risk of looking after them, with the certainty of small gain, and the more than probability of being brought in debt for their pains. The consequence was, that little or no destruction was offered to the enemy's coasting trade, which, important as it was to him for subsistence, ought to have been far more so to us, as its destruction would have deprived him of the means of subsistence.

Between the years 1803 and 1807, the naval establishment was increased from 200 to 600 vessels of war, notwithstanding which the coasting commerce of the enemy still went on, and it should have been obvious that when the navy was increased to upwards of 1000 ships, *nothing more was done.* The amusement of cutting out coasting vessels when under the protection of batteries ceased to operate as an incentive. The logs of frigates showed that their commanders avoided the risk of keeping their ships in contiguity with the shore *at night,* and secured a good night's rest for their men by running into the offing. Hence the enemy's coasting convoys proceeded by night, and in the day ran into some port or other place of protection. The result in the frigates' daily journal,—" Employed *as usual*," was no less true than comprehensive.

For telling such truths as these, an outcry was raised against me for depreciating the character of officers ! The case was my own. I took prizes in the Mediterranean and elsewhere by dozens, for which neither my officers nor crews got anything, the proceeds being swallowed up by the Admiralty Courts. I then turned to harassing the coast armies and forts of the enemy, without hope of reward, deeming this kind of employment the most honourable to myself, and the most advantageous to my country. So far from my pointing out the effect on the mind of officers in general being a reflection on their honour, it was only creditable to their common sense. They could not reasonably be expected to sacrifice their rest and that of their crews, or to run their ships into danger and themselves into debt, for the exclusive emolument of the Courts of Admiralty ! I have no hesitation in asserting that had the Ministry diminished the navy one half, and given the whole cost of the other half to the Admiralty Court officials in lieu of their charges, the remaining ships would of themselves have turned the course of the war, and their commanders would have reaped fortunes. *

These remarks will enable the naval reader to comprehend what follows. They are not intended so much for a history of past maladministration as a beacon for the future.

* In February, 1811, I pointed out to the House of Commons the monstrous fact that 107 ships of the line were in commission to watch 23 ! (Hansard, vol. xv.)

"The noble lord then read a letter from a captain of a vessel at the Cape of Good Hope, complaining 'that the officers of ships of war were so pillaged by those of the Vice-Admiralty Courts, that he wished to know how they could be relieved; whether they could be allowed the liberty to send their prizes home, and how far the jurisdiction of the Vice-Admiralty Court extended; for that the charges of that court were so exorbitant, it required the whole amount of the value of a good prize to satisfy them. In the case of one vessel that was sold for 11,000 rupees, the charges amounted to more than 10,000. This was the case at Penang, Malacca, and other places, as well as at the Cape.' He would not, however, wish to dwell on this, but put it to the feelings of the House, whether naval officers had any stimulus to do even their duty, when the prizes they took would not pay the fees of the Vice-Admiralty Courts merely for condemning them? It had been stated the other day at some meeting or dinner by a very grave personage, the Lord Chancellor, that the ships of France were only to be found in our ports. If that statement were believed by Ministers, he should be glad to know why we at this moment kept up 140 sail of the line, and frigates and sloops of war in proportion to that number."

What follows is very curious, as establishing the magnitude of the charges for adjudication in the Vice-Admiralty Courts. The bill for the condemnation of the *King George* privateer, the first vessel taken by the *Impérieuse*, had brought me 600 crowns in debt, and was of such magnitude that I had an exact copy made of it, and pasted continuously together. The result will be gathered from what follows.

"His Lordship then produced the copy of a Proctor's Bill in the island of Malta, which he said measured six fathoms and a quarter, and contained many curious charges. [*The unrolling this copy caused a general laugh, as it appeared long enough*

to reach from one end of the house to the other.] This Proctor,
the noble lord said, acted in the double capacity of Proctor
and Marshal; and in the former capacity feed himself for
consulting and instructing himself as counsel, jury, and
judge, which he himself represented in the character of
Marshal; so that all those fees were for himself in the one
character, and paid to the same himself in the other. He
then read several of the fees, which ran thus:—for attending
the Marshal (himself) 2 crowns, 2 scudi, and 2 reals; and
so on, in several other capacities in which he attended, consulted, and instructed himself, were charged several fees to
the same amount. An hon. member, not then in the house,
had last year opposed the motion he had brought forward,
for a Committee to inquire into this subject; but, on seeing
these articles of this his own Proctor's bill, his Lordship
flattered himself that the hon. member would now join in
the support of the present motion. The noble lord said he
had produced the copy of the bill to show the length of it.
He then showed the original; and to show the equity and
moderation of the Vice-Admiralty Court, he read one article
where, on the taxation of a bill, the Court, for deducting
fifty crowns, charged thirty-five crowns for the trouble in
doing it. A vessel was valued at 8608 crowns, the Marshal
received one per cent for delivering her, and in the end
the net proceeds amounted to no more than 1900 crowns
out of 8608—all the rest had been embezzled and swallowed
up in the Prize Court. He was sorry, he said, to trespass on
the time of the House, on a day when another matter of
importance was to come before them. He pledged himself,
however, that no subject could be introduced more highly
deserving their serious attention and consideration."

I am not sure that by late treaties prize-money in
future wars is not in effect abolished, though how treaties
can exist during war I am not aware. If this be so, or
anything like the spirit of such an arrangement, certain
I am that the prestige of our navy is gone till the old
system is restored. The United States Government has,

I am told, had the good sense not to conform to any arrangement of the kind. If my life be longer spared I may in a future volume revert to this subject.

However, even as the matter now stands, something must be captured, and I would suggest as a remedy for this enormous Admiralty Court evil to assimilate the regulations of those courts to the courts of law. Pay the judges and officials as other judges and officials are paid. Permit officers of the navy to choose their own proctors, as suitors in other courts choose their own attorneys. It is not honourable to the Government nor just to those serving under its authority, to compel officers to place the litigation of all prizes — even detained neutrals — in the hands of one individual, who, under the name of proctor, may have hundreds of causes in hand at the same time. The detention of a neutral may compromise a captain's fortune in the event of an unfavourable or hurried decision, for in such cases the liability to damages falls exclusively on captains, the admirals and crews having no responsibility. For my own part, as it was neither my bounden public duty, nor safe to my personal interests, to interfere with neutrals, I avoided their detention, however apparently flagrant the violation of their nominal neutrality.

" He (Lord C.) would not trouble them with anything concerning himself, because he trusted he had a remedy elsewhere. The noble lord then stated that altering or regulating the fees established by the King in council, for the island of Malta, was contrary to Act of Parliament, that when he went to Malta five years ago he found the fees very exorbitant; and, in order to prove to the House that the fees demanded now were fees which had been altered since the table of fees was sent out, the noble lord mentioned an instance of thirteen small vessels which had been taken by the gallant Captain Brenton, who lately lost his arm in the service, being brought into the Vice-Admiralty Court for condemnation ; the charge made for doing that act (which must be done before the prizes could be sold) was 3767 crowns ; but on a severe remonstrance from Captain Brenton, the Judge deducted 3504 crowns, and was glad to accept 263 crowns instead of 3767, rather than have a noise made about it in England.

" He (Lord C.) could assure the House the subject was well worthy their attention ; and, if the Lords of the Admiralty knew all the circumstances, he was confident that, instead of opposing, they would support his motion. He meant to accuse the Judge, the Marshal, and the Registrar of the Court with abuse of their offices, and concluded by moving, ' That there be laid before this House, 1. Copy of the Commission or Appointment of Dr. Sewell to officiate as Judge of the Vice-Admiralty Court of Malta. 2. Copy of the Commission or Appointment of Mr. John Jackson to the office of Marshal to the said Court. 3. List of the Proctors officiating in the said Court, with the dates of their admission. 4. Copy of the Appointment of Mr. Locker to execute the office of Registrar of the said Court. 5. Copies of the several deputations given by the Registrar and the Marshal of the said Court to their respective deputies to the end of February last ; together with the notifications of those appointments to the High Court of Admiralty, or the Board of Admiralty, with the reasons assigned for such nominations or appointments. 6. Copies of any representations made to the Lords Commissioners of the Admiralty regarding the incompatibility of the situations of Proctor and Marshal, united at Malta in the person of Mr. Jackson, and the consequent correspondence with the Court of Admiralty, or the Judge of the Court of Admiralty, on that subject. 7. Copy of any Table of Fees established by His Majesty in Council, and furnished to the Courts of Vice-Admiralty under the Act of 45 Geo. III. c. 72, or any other Act of Parliament. 8.

Copy of the Table of Fees by which the charges were made
on the suitors in the Court at Malta. 9. Copy of the Authority by virtue of which the Judges of the Vice-Admiralty
Courts are empowered to alter or amend the Table aforesaid ;
or to make any other Table of Fees, to regulate the charges
incurred by the suitors in that Court. 10. Copies of Official
Demands made, or Official Correspondence which has taken
place, between the Judge of the Vice-Admiralty Court at
Gibraltar, or at Malta, and the High Court of Admiralty,
or the Judge of the High Court of Admiralty, requiring
or regarding a Table of Fees to be sent for the guidance of
those Courts, or either of them. 11. List of the number of
vessels that have been prosecuted in the Court of Vice-Admiralty at Malta, and which have been liberated on payment
of costs and damages or otherwise. 12. Copies of the Appointments which —— Wood, Esq., late Secretary to Lord
Viscount Castlereagh, holds in the island of Malta.'

" MR. YORKE said that he did not mean to object to the
production of the greater part of the papers moved for by
the noble lord. His motion seemed to charge with extortion
the persons connected with the Admiralty Court at Malta ;
and certainly the *prima facies* appeared to justify it, and
some reform might be necessary in some of the departments,
which induced him to acquiesce in the general features of
the noble lord's motion ; but some difficulty might exist in
the production of one or two of the papers he moved for, as
they possibly implicated some private correspondence which
it would be improper to produce. Many of the papers moved
for must be brought from Malta, and therefore it would be
impossible that the investigation could take place this session;
and he hoped the noble lord would, on examination, if he
found just ground, persevere in his motion, as it was certainly
highly improper for the dignity of the House and the due
management of the affairs of the country that a remedy
should not be applied to those evils, if they existed.

" SIR JOHN NICHOLL (King's Advocate), while he admitted
with the First Lord of the Admiralty, that the case, as it stood

at present, called for inquiry, thought proper at the same time to state, in the absence of his learned friend (Sir W. Scott), that he had no control over the Vice-Admiralty Court of Malta in matters of prize. The appeal lay to the King in Council, and his learned friend was not in the smallest degree responsible. If the abuses charged by the noble lord existed, they ought to be corrected; but his doubt was as to the means. His Majesty in Council had authority to correct abuses as to fees, &c.; but no application, as far as he knew, had been made in that quarter. It was the fashion now to come to Parliament in such cases. As to the character of the Judge of the Prize Court at Malta, he not having been in the habit of corresponding with him could not undertake to speak positively to that point. Having practised with him for some time at the same bar, he had every reason to believe that he was a man of talent and integrity, and the noble lord knew that he was not wanting in spirit to execute what he thought right. He was absent, and he was a Judge — and no prejudices ought to be admitted against him till he had an opportunity of being heard in his defence. He hoped the noble lord was under a misapprehension. The regulation of the fees had been probably left to the Judge because he himself could hardly have any interest in augmenting them. They could hardly fall below 2000*l.*, to which sum only he was entitled out of them. From the failure of the noble lord in substantiating charges made by him on former occasions, it might be fairly inferred that accusations preferred by him might possibly turn out to be unfounded.

"Sir Francis Burdett said he should have made no observation on the subject, after having seconded the motion, but from what had fallen from the right hon. gentleman who had just sat down, that his noble colleague had not substantiated the charges he formerly brought forward. The reason of this was obvious; the noble lord had never had an opportunity given him to substantiate his charges. He had pledged himself to prove them at the bar of the House, but his motion for a committee was negatived.

" MR. ROSE said that when abuses in the Vice-Admiralty Courts abroad were detected, measures were always taken to rectify them, and proceedings were at present pending *against three of those courts.* But he defied the noble lord to point out any impropriety in the Admiralty Courts at home. After the minutest investigation, he could not find a single ground of complaint against the officers of that Court. The proctor for the navy was remarkable for his attention and integrity, and his charges were more moderate than those of any other proctor. The interests of the officers of the navy were as well attended to as those of any individual. The noble lord had failed in two charges on former occasions. He had brought charges against the Admiralty Court, and against the Government for the treatment of the prisoners of war. Both were utterly unfounded. The prisoners, as had been found on inquiry, were even more healthy than our militia regiments.

" MR. LYTTLETON said the right honourable gentleman who had spoken last *allowed abuses existed ;* he did not know whether it was so or not, but he knew several officers of the navy of the highest character who complained loudly that there were, and this was in his opinion good ground for granting the present motion.

" LORD COCHRANE stated that, having complained to the Admiralty here of a grievance in being obliged to submit to exorbitant charges in the prosecution of a prize cause at Malta, the opinions of the Attorney and Solicitor-General, and other lawyers, had been put into his hands, purporting that his plan was to apply to the Judge at Malta. He wrote to the Judge accordingly, who referred him to the Proctor, as he did not choose to enter into private correspondence with suitors in causes before him. He then wrote to the Proctor, who sent for answer that it was unprecedented to demand a bill to be taxed that had been paid so long ago as 1808 ; so that he thought his having got the money a good reason for not parting with it. He then wrote to the Judge but got no answer, and this was the redress he got in the quarter where the crown law officers had advised him to apply. The noble lord further observed, that in opposition to the act of the 45th of the King, the Judge at Malta had not only established but altered the table of fees. An allusion was made to the spirited conduct of the Judge; but he had affidavits of Captain Maxwell and others, who were present, that the Judge had admitted that he had no proof of the crime for which he (Lord C.) had been sent to gaol. Against him, however, he would proceed in another way, unless he should find it necessary to call for the interference of the House to bring this Judge home. He had consulted lawyers, and understood that he could not proceed against him till he came to this country. As to his former charges, he had been denied the opportunity of proving them. He concluded by repeating his charges of extortion, &c., against the Judge and Marshal.

" Mr. Whitbread said that if the official correspondence did not clear up the case, he would move for further papers if no one else did.

" Some alterations were then made in the motion, in consequence of a difference of opinion as to the construction of the 45th of the King, relative to the establishment of tables of fees in the Prize Courts, after which they were all carried."

Notwithstanding the admission of the First Lord of the Admiralty that the papers were necessary, and that they were produced, it is scarcely creditable that the Government subsequently refused to act in the matter, thus turning a deaf ear to proofs that the enactments of the Legislature were defeated by the rapacity of distant Admiralty Courts, which continued to impound without scruple the rewards which the Legislature had decreed for effective exertion.

The naval reader who may wish to know more respecting the extortionate fees of these courts may refer

generally to Capt. Brenton's "Life of Lord St. Vincent."
I will extract one passage. He says (vol. ii. p. 166) :—
"Lord Cochrane made a statement of some facts to this
effect in the House of Commons, but he might have
gone much further. The proctor's bill for a prize taken
by the *Spartan*, when my brother commanded her, was
1025*l.*, which, when refused payment and taxed, *was
reduced to* 285*l. !* "

Capt. Brenton thought "I might have gone much
further." So I might, but with as little effect. Even
the facts I did state were impudently denied or shamelessly defended.

On the 14th of June an attack was made upon me by
the Secretary of the Treasury, on account of some
remarks which I had deemed it my duty to make on
the condition of the French prisoners at Dartmoor.
In consequence of circumstances which had come to
my knowledge, I visited that prison and *was refused
admittance* the moment my name was announced. This
did not, however, prevent my surveying the prison from
an eminence on the exterior: this cursory inspection
confirmed the information I had received.

"MR. ROSE observed that it would appear from these
documents that the total number of French prisoners remaining in England amounted to 45,939, and that the
returns of the sick were 321. The number on parole were
2710; and the sick 165. This statement, he conceived, would
be a sufficient answer to the imputations of negligence upon
the part of the Government which had been thrown out by a
noble lord.

"LORD COCHRANE referred to the manner in which he had
been reproached by Mr. Rose's pointed address, and thought

it incumbent upon him, considering the repeated assertions
of that hon. member, that he was unable to prove facts which
he had stated to the House, to justify his conduct in having
given notice of a motion relative to the prison in Dartmoor ;
but in which he did not persevere, for reasons very different
from those assigned by the right hon. gentleman. His Lordship had never asserted that which he could not establish.
The time that had elapsed would sufficiently evidence his reluctance to bring the matter to the knowledge of the public,
fearing that a disclosure might add to the misfortunes of his
countrymen in France.

" Having received many letters stating the condition of
the prisoners of war at Dartmoor to be truly deplorable,
he determined to investigate the subject ; and, having had
occasion to go to Exeter, he proceeded to Launceston and
other depôts, whence he obtained the intelligence, and, being
satisfied that the complaints had some foundation, he went
to Dartmoor ; but was refused admittance, even in his capacity as a member of Parliament (a laugh). Though members
might laugh, he thought members of Parliament should
be entitled to admission there, or to any other prison in the
kingdom. Having contributed to place many individuals there,
he applied for permission to see the interior, but was refused
leave, except to look through a grating into the outer court-
yard. He found the climate of the prison accurately and
faithfully described, and he was the more anxious to see the
interior, owing to the refusal directly given him. He inquired the reason for building a depôt in such a barren,
elevated, and extraordinary situation, and was told that it
was for the purpose of attracting inhabitants. He proceeded
to Plymouth, where he obtained a plan of the prison, which
fully corroborated one complaint, that the health of the prisoners had suffered by exposure to heavy rains whilst standing in an open space for several hours receiving provisions
issued at a single door ; the cooking-room being several
hundred feet from the prison, which then contained six
thousand prisoners, divided into messes of six ; consequently

one thousand were soaked through in the morning attending
for their breakfast, and one thousand more at dinner.   Thus
a third were constantly wet, many without a change of
clothes.   He was told, however, that they gambled or sold
them.   On his second visit to Dartmoor his Lordship, being
again refused admittance, began to explore the exterior, and
found, by a very peculiar coincidence, that the manure from
this prison had been placed on the only spot in Devon
whence the stercoraceous matter of the depôt could descend
on a neighbouring and elevated estate belonging to the
Secretary of His Royal Highness the Prince Regent (Mr.
Tyrwhitt).   Had such a circumstance happened in the island
of Walcheren to an estate of the Secretary of Louis Napoleon,
he would not have been surprised.   The prison of Dartmoor
was built in the most inclement part of all England, on the
top of the highest mountain in Devonshire, involved in perpetual rains and eternal fog.   That the prison was not built
there on a principle of economy might be seen by inspecting
the contracts for provisions, coals, and necessaries furnished
at Dartmoor and at Plymouth.   He thought he calculated a
difference of more than seven thousand pounds a year on
the provisions alone.   It might be very proper, he imagined,
that prisoners should not be collected in great numbers at
Plymouth, but he asserted that Dartmoor depôt ought not to
have been placed upon the top of the highest and most
barren range of mountains in Devonshire, where it is involved in constant fog, and deluged with perpetual rain.
He had relinquished his intention of entering into the
matter, because he received assurances that the situation of
the prisoners would be immediately attended to.   He would
abstain from remarking upon the manner in which Mr. Rose
had taken him by surprise, and wrested from him those facts
in his own defence.   Had he brought that matter forward
voluntarily, his Lordship would have cleared the House, to
prevent publicity."

Capt. Brenton, in his " Life of Lord St. Vincent," when

speaking of the treatment of our prisoners of war, bore testimony to the truth of my representations, which Mr. Rose had so emphatically denied :—

"The charge of sick and wounded prisoners of war fell into the hands of a set of villains, whose seared consciences were proof against the silent but eloquent pleading of their fellow-creatures — sick and imprisoned for no crime, in a foreign land, far away from their friends and relations." (Vol. ii. p. 165.)

No one supposed the Government to be guilty of the matters complained of, but they refused to inquire into the conduct of those who were, thereby protecting them in their iniquity.   I saw at Dartmoor old and *recently mutilated* bulls, covered with dust and gore, driven along the road towards the prison, leaving tracks of blood behind!   Thus the contract for supplying the prisoners with *ox beef* was fulfilled by some partisan of the government, who had *sublet* his contract to a Devon butcher.   It was not always in those days that a contract was given to the tradesman who fulfilled it.

On the 18th of July I brought forward a motion on the subject of my arrest at Malta :—

"*Conduct of the Vice-Admiralty Court at Malta. — Arrest of Lord Cochrane.*

" LORD COCHRANE rose and said :—

" SIR,—The delay that has taken place since my return to England, and the legal authorities that I have consulted, will, I trust, evidence that I trespass on your attention with reluctance, relative to the conduct of the Judge and members of the Court of Vice-Admiralty at Malta; partly from a desire to avoid the possibility of private motives being imputed to

me, but chiefly from a conviction that Parliament should not
interfere in matters cognisable in the courts of justice.

" How far, under the last impression, I am warranted in
calling upon this House to exercise an authority in the present instance, will appear by the opinions of Sir A. Piggott,
Mr. Holroyd, Mr. Leach, and of another learned gentleman
who is not now in his place. 'Process of the Courts,' says
Sir A. Piggott, 'does not extend to Malta : there is no mode
whilst they are abroad to compel appearance to actions here.'
The answers of the other learned gentlemen being the same
in substance, I need not detain you by reading them.

" Three years have passed since I memorialised the Admiralty on this subject ; it cannot therefore be said that I
have acted with precipitation. Indeed, I have had time
enough to reflect, and I do assure you that I am fully aware
of the responsibility which I shall incur if I fail in establishing whatever accusations I bring against a judge presiding in
one of His Majesty's courts, and against those acting under
his authority ; but furnished as I am with original documents, having the signatures of the judge and members of
the Court, I am not inclined to shrink from the task of
proving their violation of the Acts on your table, especially of
the 37th, 38th, 39th, and 41st sects. of the 45th of his
present Majesty, c. 72. The first of which empowers the
King in Council alone to make or alter a table of fees to
regulate the charges in Courts of Vice-Admiralty, and yet
'the members of the Court of Malta fabricated one for themselves, which the judge subsequently altered by affixing a
note in his own hand, abolishing the table *in toto*, except by
reference to certain unascertained charges made in a distant
court, which were not set forth. This note is as follows :
' At a meeting of all the members of the court shortly after
its arrival, for the purpose of settling what should be considered as reasonable fees, it was agreed, that in no instance
they should exceed the proportion of one third more than
those paid for similar services in the High Court of Admiralty in England,' signed ' J. Sewell ;' who thus assumed

the authority of the King in Council, in open violation of
the 37th, and in contempt and defiance of the penalties
enacted by the 38th and 39th sections, which declare that
' receiving or taking any fee or fees beyond those specified in
the table aforesaid,' that is, the table authorised by the King
in Council, shall be punished by the loss of office; and
further, ' demanding or receiving any sum or sums of money
other than the fees aforesaid shall be deemed and taken to
be extortion and a misdemeanour at law, and shall be
punished under and by virtue of this Act.' Words cannot
convey a more distinct prohibition, and yet I hold in my
hand demonstration of an opposite line of conduct being
pursued by the Court. This is not all; the law directs that
the ' Table of Fees, authorised as aforesaid, shall be suspended in some conspicuous part of the Court in which the
several judges of the Vice-Admiralty Court shall hold their
courts.' At Malta, however, it was concealed, first, during
five years in a drawer, and when taken therefrom in consequence of loud complaints on the subject of their charges,
it was affixed, not ' in some conspicuous part of the Court,'
not in the Court at all, but on the door of a private room
behind the Registry, where suitors could have no access to it.

"Sir, The fabricating, altering, and concealing the table
of fees is, perhaps, the least profligate part of their conduct.
What will the House think when they find that John
Jackson the marshal, who, to the knowledge of the judge,
acts also as proctor in defiance of the law, is in the constant
habit of charging his clients of the navy for attending, feeing, consulting, instructing, and admonishing himself, and
this in the very teeth of the 41st section, which enacts that
' No registrar or deputy-registrar, marshal or deputy-marshal, of or belonging to any of His Majesty's Courts of Vice-
Admiralty, shall, either directly or indirectly, or himself or
themselves, or by any agent or agents, or any person or
persons whomsoever, act or be concerned in any manner
whatsoever, either as an advocate or proctor.' Mr. Jackson's
charges are so ingenious that I must beg leave to read a few

of them. 'Attending in the Registry and bespeaking a monition, two crowns; paid for the said monition, under seal and extracting, nine crowns; copy of the said monition for service, two crowns; attending the marshal (himself, observe) and instructing him to serve the same, two crowns; paid the marshal for service of said monition, two crowns; certificate of service, one crown; drawing and engrossing an affidavit of service, two crowns; oath thereto and attendance, two crowns, two reals, and three scudi.' How exact! ten shillings and two-pence three farthings for an oath that he had attended on himself with a monition! One of these bills was taxed by the deputy registrar, who admitted these iniquitous charges. Yes, Sir, they were allowed and admitted by Stevens, the deputy registrar, who treats his friends with Burgundy and Champagne out of the proceeds of captures made by the navy, from which fund, John Locker, the sinecure registrar, like the sinecure registrar at home, also derives his unmerited emoluments. I ask, is it fit that the reward granted by His Majesty and the legislature to the navy, for the toil and risk which they undergo in making captures from the enemy, should be thus appropriated?

"That I had a right to demand the taxation of such a bill as that which I have shown there can be no doubt, even if I could not produce the opinion of His Majesty's Attorney-General to that effect. Yes, the opinion of Sir V. Gibbs, and of the Solicitor-General, signed also Charles Robinson, William Battine, T. Jarvis, to all of whom the memorial which I presented to the Admiralty was referred in April, 1809. 'The expenses,' say these learned gentlemen, 'in this case do not appear to have been brought to the knowledge of the Court so as to have given the judge an opportunity of exercising his judgment upon them; that would be the proper mode of redress for grievances of this description.'

"Thus instructed, I addressed the judge on my return to Malta, in February last, soliciting that he would be pleased to direct my bill to be taxed, to which he returned the following answer, addressed on His Majesty's service:—'My Lord, In reply to your letter of yesterday's date, I beg leave to refer you to your proctor for the information you are desirous of, it not being the practice of the Vice-Admiralty Court here, any more than the Court of King's Bench in England, to enter into private correspondence with suitors on the subject of their suits or of any matters connected with them. Signed J. Sewell.'

"It appeared extraordinary that I should be referred to the person complained of, as judge in his own cause. Still, however, in compliance with Dr. Sewell's advice, I directed my agent to make the application, and the following, as might have been anticipated, was the ingenious gentleman's reply :—' Sir, My bill in this case having been delivered to you so long ago as the 8th of August 1808, and having been paid by you soon after, I was a good deal surprised at your note, received yesterday, informing me that Lord Cochrane wishes to have the said bill taxed, and therefore I beg that you will apprise his Lordship that it is a thing quite unprecedented to tax a bill which is paid. I should have supposed that the advice I gave his Lordship, not to proceed in this cause, would have exempted me from the suspicion of having made unwarrantable charges. Signed John Jackson.' As the unwarrantableness of the charges did not rest on suspicion, I wrote to Mr. Jackson myself, who answered :—' I humbly conceive that your Lordship is not now entitled to demand a copy of your account, and therefore I beg that you will excuse me from complying with such demand.' I next required him to submit my account for taxation, this he also declined as follows :—' My Lord, In reply to your letter of this day, I have to inform you that I cannot consent to open an account that was closed two years ago, and that is my only objection to my bill in the cause of King George being taxed, which I hope your Lordship, on reflection, will see to be a reasonable objection.' I confess I did not consider the lapse of two years to be any objection at all, particularly as I was absent from Malta when the bill was paid, and no earlier opportunity had offered to call for a revision of the charges; for this reason, and fortified with the opinion of the learned gentleman opposite (Sir V. Gibbs) about a month afterwards, I again addressed Dr. Sewell on the subject, who, so far from ' exercising his judgment' on the marshal's iniquitous bill of costs, did not condescend to take the slightest notice of my communication, though furnishing him with extracts from Mr. Jackson's written refusals. Neither did the judge reply to a note delivered to him on the following day.

" Being thus excluded from the ' proper mode of redress for grievances of this description,' I proceeded to the court-room of the Vice-Admiralty for the purpose of comparing the charges contained in numerous bills in my possession with the established fees, which I was instructed by the Acts of Parliament, ' should be suspended in some conspicuous part of the Court,' every part of which I searched in vain ; neither was the table in the Registry, where His Majesty's Advocate directed me to look for it, who, on my returning into Court again, to make further inquiry, said that I would find it affixed on a door leading to the adjoining room.

" That mutilated paper, concealed contrary to law, I was accused of having taken down and carried away from a place where it could not have been affixed, except in defiance of these statutes, and in contempt of justice. That, Sir, was the paper for which I was followed through the streets of Malta for the space of a week by the deputy auctioneer, styled in the judge's warrant and attachments by the title of ' deputy marshal,' but who, in fact, never had an authority from the marshal ; perhaps, because the marshal was conscious of having vitiated his powers by the illegal acts of which he was guilty, and thus thought to escape the consequences which might arise from the acts of his nominal deputy. So loosely are things conducted in that Court ! Surely no reasonable man can blame me for refusing to be taken to gaol by the deputy auctioneer. Indeed, Chapman admits, in his affidavit of the 24th of February, that my objection was to his want of authority ; for, I naturally concluded that unless he was an officer of the Court his acts might be disowned, and thereby the guilty would escape punishment.

"That this was the view which I took of the case, will appear by my offering no resistance to James Houghton Stevens, who was appointed on Chapman's nominal resignation; I say, Sir, that I offered no resistance, for, by refusing to walk to gaol, I did no more than decline, by an act of my own, to contribute to illegal proceedings.

"It is not my intention to trouble the House at length relative to this affair, which is of trifling importance compared with the mischiefs that arise from the system of plunder and abuse practised in the Courts of Vice-Admiralty. However, it may not be improper to mention that I was conducted by the keeper of the gaol to a place with a broken window barred with iron, furnished with an old chair, and a close-stool in the corner. From this, however, I was removed, as the judge began to fear the consequences of his illegal acts; and on the third day, being brought from the keeper's room to the Court of Vice-Admiralty, there, without an accuser, except the judge, that learned and worshipful gentleman attempted in the absence of proof to administer a long string of interrogatories, which I, of course, refused to answer, and thereby furnished what might be construed by him into evidence of my having taken away his illegal table. Being further pressed and threatened, I delivered a protest in writing, ' against the illegal warrant issued by William Stevens, an examiner and interpreter to the Vice-Admiralty Court of Malta, registered merchant, commission broker, and notary public, calling himself deputy registrar of the Court, and professing to act under an appointment of John Locker, sinecure registrar, and further against the illegal endeavours to execute the warrant by John Chapman, deputy auctioneer, acting for and on behalf of — Wood, late private secretary to Lord Castlereagh, a non-resident, enjoying an income of about seven thousand pounds sterling per annum, derived from the sale of prizes and the goods of merchants trading to Malta, but calling himself deputy marshal of the Vice-Admiralty Court, and professing to act under an appointment from John Jackson, proctor and marshal, contrary to law; and farther against all acts of the said John Jackson, in the capacity of marshal, by himself or his deputy, and against John Locker, sinecure registrar, and William Stephens, calling himself deputy registrar; John Locker having, under the signature of William Stephens, taxed bills of fees and expenses of the Court of Vice-Admiralty, wherein the fees of the said John Locker and William Stephens in their capacity of registrar, deputy registrar, examiner, interpreter, &c. &c. &c., are made and examined by themselves, and in which various illegal charges were allowed and suffered to be made by John Jackson, as proctor, for attending, feeing, consulting, and instructing himself as marshal; in which double capacity he acts, in defiance of the 41st and of the 45th Geo. III. chapter 72.' And further, I solemnly protested John Sewell, styling himself judge of the aforesaid Court, for refusing, by letter dated the 13th January, 1811, to order satisfaction to be given by the said John Jackson, referring to him a judge in his own cause; and likewise for not having given any answers to official letters delivered to him, bearing date the 19th and 20th of February, 1811, on the same subject. And further, I protested against the said John Sewell, for not complying with the Act of Parliament, which directs that ' a table of fees shall be suspended in some conspicuous part of the Court, in which the several judges of the Court of Vice-Admiralty hold their sittings.'

" Sir, The judge at first refused to receive any protest, but afterwards did so; and afterwards I was re-committed to prison, not for contempt of court, but for the old accusation of not having complied with certain warrants addressed to a person styled deputy marshal, who never had an authority to act as such. That no proof existed of my having taken the table of fees will appear from the following affidavit of Commodore Rowley, Commissioner Fraser, and Captain Murray Maxwell, of the navy:—

" Be it known to all persons whomsoever it may concern,

that on the 2nd day of March, in the year of our Lord 1811, personally came and appeared before me the undersigned notary-public Percy Fraser, commissioner of His Majesty's navy, resident in the island of Malta, Charles Rowley, Esq., captain of His Majesty's ship *Eagle*, and Murray Maxwell, Esq., captain of His Majesty's ship *Alceste*, and solemnly made oath that on the aforesaid 2nd day of March, whilst the Court of Vice-Admiralty of the said island of Malta was sitting, they severally and distinctly heard John Sewell, LL.D. the judge thereof, and whilst sitting in his judicial chair, admit in open Court, and in the presence of divers persons there assembled, to the Right Honourable Lord Cochrane, that there existed no proof in the aforesaid court of his said Lordship's having taken down the paper in question, by the judge aforesaid called the table of fees.

(Signed)   Percy Fraser, C. Rowley, Murray Maxwell.'

' On the second day of August, 1811, the aforegoing attestation was duly sworn at Malta, where stamps are not used, before me, Chas. Edw. Fenton, Notary-Public.'

" Notwithstanding the confession of the judge in open Court thus attested, I remained unnoticed three days longer in the public gaol, where I now clearly saw that it was the intention of the judge to detain me until the packet had sailed for England, and probably until she returned to Malta with instructions. I therefore wrote to the Governor, who, having consulted Messieurs Moncreiff, Forrest, and Bowdler, three gentlemen of the law, sent me their opinion, that His Excellency should not interfere with a Court, acting, as they were pleased to call it, under His Majesty's authority, although in violation of the law. I addressed the President also, who said, that the Courts of Malta could not interpose. Indeed, had it been otherwise, little good could have been expected from an appeal to these Courts, which are still governed by the iniquitious and oppressive code of Rhoan, to the disgrace of all the ministers who have ruled since the surrender of the island to England. Sir, The Maltese stipulated then that a constitution securing property and rights should be granted, and trial by jury; but these have been denied, and examinations are still taken, and sentence pronounced, with shut doors, by their judges, whose appointments are during pleasure. I do not impute blame to His Excellency the Governor, for whom I have a high respect, yet I must say that the system of blending the military and civil authority cannot fail to become oppressive. Ministers have no better excuse for this union of power contrary to the express stipulations of the inhabitants of the island, than a despicable petition signed by the dependents on Government, and shamelessly transmitted and received as the voice of the people! Being furnished with an affidavit that the judge did not intend to proceed in the matter on the next Court day, I resolved, as the door was locked and guarded, to get out by the window, which I according effected; and the following proclamation was issued for my apprehension, in which I am designated by as many names as if I had been a notorious thief:—

"' Escape of Lord Cochrane.

"'Whereas, the Honourable Thomas Cochrane, esquire, otherwise the Honourable Sir Thomas Cochrane, Knight Companion of the most Honourable Order of the Bath, commonly called Lord Cochrane, escaped out of the custody of James Houghton Stevens, the Deputy Marshal of the Vice-Admiralty Court of this Island, from the prison of the Castellanea during the course of last night. This is to give notice, that whoever will apprehend or cause to be apprehended the said Lord Cochrane, and deliver him into the custody of the said Deputy Marshal, shall receive a reward of Two Thousand Scudis currency of Malta, and that whoever will give such information as may lead to the apprehension of any person, or persons, who was or were aiding and assisting the said Lord Cochrane in such his escape, shall receive upon such conviction, if only one person was so aiding and assisting, the sum of One Thousand Scudis, or if more persons than one were so aiding and assisting, then upon the conviction of each of such persons the sum of Five Hundred Scudis, notwithstanding that in such latter case the person so giving information shall himself have been aiding and assisting to the said escape. Witness my hand, this sixth day of March, 1811. — Jas. H. Stevens, Deputy-Marshal. No. 188 Strada Stretta.'

"Now, Sir, although the treatment which I received is altogether foreign to the main point, yet I am desirous to learn from you as Speaker of this House, whether my imprisonment was or was not a breach of the privilege of parliament?"

The Speaker.—I do not know whether the House expects me to reply to the questions which the noble lord has put to me, perfectly new as one appears to be; but, as far as my information goes, I will give it, if the House thinks fit that I should do so. (Hear, hear!) With respect to the privileges of the House, I know of no means of enforcing its privileges, but in the usual way, from time imemorial, by its own officers; and I never knew one instance of any officer having been sent across the seas at the instance of any member, on a complaint of insult offered to him personally. (Hear, hear!) So much for the question of privilege. In the next place I never knew an instance in which any member of parliament, properly before a court of justice, was at liberty to treat with impunity the proceedings of that court, or to say that what was done in respect to himself was done in contempt, or that could authorise him to say that the privileges of parliament were infringed in his person for such conduct.

Lord Cochrane.— Sir: It was at first my intention, to have moved an address to the Prince Regent, to recall the judge, registrar, and marshal, to answer for their conduct and proceedings, contrary to the express words of acts of parliament; but on consideration, and in compliance with the suggestion of the First Lord of the Admiralty, I have thought it better to move, " That a committee be appointed to examine into the conduct of the judge, registrar, and marshal, and their deputies, of the Court of Vice-Admiralty at Malta, for the violation of the 37th, 38th, 39th, and 41st sections of the 45th, Geo. 3, cap. 72."

MR. P. MOORE seconded the motion, not from any knowledge of its merits, but thinking that if the matter of charge was not inquired into it would reflect upon the House.

MR. STEPHEN could not avoid applauding the benevolent motive of the honourable gentleman who had seconded the poor outcast of the noble lord. With respect to the conduct of the learned judge alluded to, he was satisfied it was the opinion of the House that he had done nothing amiss — that the dignity of his office required that he should exert his authority after the direct insult that the noble lord had offered to the court. The charge against the noble lord was for taking down the public document of the court, a charge which he had not denied, nay, indeed, the noble lord had exhibited what he termed a fac-simile of the table of fees, and so closely imitated, that the very impression of the wafers — the document itself, and its smoke-dried appearance, seemed to proclaim its originality. The conduct of the noble lord, when required to answer for this contempt, was not merely that he refused to obey the monition, but that he pulled out a pistol, and threatened to shoot any man who attempted to execute it upon him. Chapman, the officer, therefore (and the fact was confirmed by two witnesses), thought it not prudent to execute a warrant at the point of a pistol, and had not the courage to act. The noble lord had stated that he refused to answer interrogatories, and that he made a protest against the proceedings of the court. It was not regular for the court to receive protest arraigning its proceedings, and upon the inquiry it did not think there was sufficient grounds for discharging the noble lord from his arrest. If, however, he was aggrieved, there was a channel through which he might have had redress, without coming to the House, by appearing before the Privy Council, and stating his charges against Dr. Sewell, who would, if proved, be removed. But should there not have existed, in th⁝ executive government, a disposition to redress the noble lord's grievances, then it would have been open for him to appeal to the House, but to come at the end of the session was not very regular.   Dr. Sewell was a person of correct conduct, and unlikely to act with injustice to any individual.

MR. YORKE objected to the motion on three grounds : first, because the case was one of the *most frivolous* ones he had ever met with ; secondly, because the noble lord, if he had just cause for complaint, should have made it at the Admiralty, and that Board would have investigated the complaint ; and thirdly, because the complaint, instead of being made by the noble lord, was by his own showing a complaint against himself.   He had this to state to the noble lord, that if he had not been an officer on half-pay he would have heard from the Board of Admiralty in a different way.   With respect to the marshal exercising the office of proctor, in conjunction, he would recommend an inquiry to be made, as it was contrary to the express provisions of the Act of Parliament.   But with respect to the noble lord's case it was, he must repeat it, one of the most frivolous cases ever brought before Parliament.*

" Mr. Rose," said his lordship in reply, " has expressed his persuasion that the interests of the navy are best protected by being in the care of the king's proctor ; that is," continued his lordship, " under the absolute control of one man, who, in addition to the management of his majesty's business in two courts, and the monopoly of libelling and prosecuting to condemnation all the captures made by the navy, possesses also the exclusive privilege of conducting the numerous and intricate litigations which have arisen of late years out of the seizure of neutrals ; causes in which not only the property detained is at stake, but all that a captor possesses is answerable for the costs of suit and demurrage, which, if he is unable to pay, he may be thrown into gaol, not for errors or misconduct of his own, but owing to neglect arising from confusion in an office where there have formerly been from

* That is, the First Lord agreed with my statements, but objected to inquiry because I moved for it !

1800 to 2000 causes in progress at one and the same time;
an evil which, unfortunately for the country, is working its
remedy in a way highly prejudicial to its best interests. Let
me ask, would the right honourable gentlemen opposite exert
themselves with zeal, if every motion they made subjected
them to risk of costs, damages, and imprisonment? They
would not sit on these soft cushions unless they were amply
paid, although it is easier to do so than to make captures on
the enemy's coast. How would they like to be compelled, as
the navy is, to employ one attorney to conduct all their
affairs, even if he had not their opponent's interests also to
promote, as is the case with the procurator-general? Will
such management of their affairs encourage the navy to
impede suspicious commerce in neutral bottoms? And if
the condemnation of a boat costs as much as the condemnation
of a ship, is not the capture of the enemy's coasting commerce
virtually discouraged?

"Nothing," he continued, "can better demonstrate the
effect which the dread of fraud and neglect in the procurator's
office has on the exertions of the navy, than an account
before the House, by which it appears, that the numbers of
causes belonging to the whole navy amounted only to ninety-
two, including droits of the Admiralty and Crown; while
about three dozen privateers, possessing the inestimable privilege of employing counsel of their own choice, had actually
110,—not injudicious captures, but such as had been sanctioned by the decisions of the lower courts. The navy are
told, by a public minute in the procurator-general's office,
'that it is the king's proctor's particular desire, in respect to
his bills, first, that in all successful cases they should be made
out moderately; secondly, that in unsuccessful cases they
should contain those fees only which are allowed on taxation.'
Permit me," said Lord Cochrane, to ask what fees he is
entitled to that are disallowed on taxation; and permit me to
ask the treasurer, who is desirous to remove the misconception
that prevails in the navy, if he thinks that were the commanding officers all compelled to employ one tailor, (the

chancellor's for instance,) that it would be quite satisfactory to learn, whilst there was a certainty of their cloth being damaged, that being cut and sewed by old women it was made up cheaper, as might be ascertained by a minute behind the shop-board; 'that it was the master tailor's particular desire, in respect to his bills, first, that the old ladies should be moderate in their cabbaging if the coat fitted; and secondly, if spoilt, that they should take only what they could get,' would not persons thus restricted, and desirous of expedition or care, stimulate the old ladies by a dram; and would not they quit one job and take up another? Would the interests of all be best protected thus?"

Lord Cochrane instanced a case of capture, wherein the captor had a balance of 11*l*. 14*s*. against him in the prize courts, after the prizes were condemned. He stated a case wherein 63*l*. were deducted from a bill upon taxation, and the same sum to a farthing charged for taxing it; and he asked the attorney-general, whether he did, or did not, receive twenty-two guineas out of the pockets of the navy for every cause which came before the Court of Appeals, though he had attended but once there since the court commenced sitting in November. " Is this," said he, " one of the law charges which the treasurer has no occasion to disapprove of? And does he think it right that the procurator, the boasted guardian of the interests of the navy, should not only pay the attorney-general for staying away, but fee another for coming to court, and performing his duty? I have passed nearly twenty years in the navy. Having been constantly employed until lately, I have had full opportunity to be acquainted with the feelings of those with whom I have mixed, and I believe that, unless the laws and regulations made to guide the Courts of Admiralty are reformed, captures will soon cease to be made. Were that done, the enemy would then suffer the loss of all the trade which is of such importance to France and her dependent states. Two thirds of our present naval establishment would be quite sufficient for the purposes of blockade, and all others; nay, I am clearly of opinion, that if the courts were reformed, it would be a benefit to our country if one third of our ships were converted into fire-wood. I am sure that the First Lord of the Admiralty would not vote against the production of papers and full investigation, if he knew the extent of the evil. He has, however, no means personally to become acquainted with the facts, and there are but few who will venture to inform him."

The motion was negatived without a division.

CHAP. XXXIII.

OPENING OF PARLIAMENT, 1812.

THE opening of the session of 1812 was in many ways
remarkable. The speech of the Prince Regent, read
by the Lords Commissioners, made everything *couleur
de rose*, both as regarded our foreign wars and domestic
policy. Notwithstanding that we were on the brink of
war with America, both Houses were assured that the
affair of the *Chesapeake* had been " finally adjusted,
though other discussions were not yet brought to a
close." The finances were represented as being in a
flourishing condition, and His Royal Highness had no
doubt of the liberal disposition of Parliament " to
sustain the country in the great contest in which it
was engaged."

The hollowness of these representations was met by
Lord Grenville, who contrasted it with the " critical
circumstances of the times, and the present alarming
state of the country. The framers of the speech, said

his Lordship, were the very men who by their obstinate
blindness had brought the country to the brink of ruin,
but who, in the midst of the distresses they had
themselves occasioned, still held forth the same flattering and fallacious language. He would protest
against a continuance of those measures which had
brought such calamities upon the country. People
might choose to close their eyes, but the force of truth
must dispel the wilful blindness."

Lord Grey similarly denounced the policy which
was "the source of present and impending calamities.
Yet these very complications were brought forward in
assertion that the system of the government had contributed to the security, prosperity and honour of the
country!" &c. &c.

In the House of Commons an unusual circumstance
occurred. After the speech had been read by the
Speaker, Lord Jocelyn was rising to move the usual
complimentary address, but Sir Francis Burdett, having risen at the same time, first caught the eye of the
Speaker, who decided that Sir Francis was in possession
of the House.

One of the honourable baronet's cutting speeches
followed, in which he denounced the Ministers as an
"oligarchy of rotten-boroughmongers" — who alike
imposed upon the people and the Prince Regent. "A
system of taxation had been created which ruined
many and oppressed all. This fiscal tyranny being
carried to its height, the lower orders had been reduced
to a state of pauperism — whilst the desperate resistance which such pauperism was calculated to pro-

duce was kept down by the terrors of a military force. Depôts, barracks, and fortifications had been established in all quarters, and foreign mercenaries, who had been unable to defend their own country, had been brought over to protect the native land of courage and patriotism, or rather to protect its rulers against an indignant and oppressed people, and to support the scandalous invasions of the liberty of the press, and the severe punishments with which those who ventured to express popular opinions were visited by the courts of justice."

This interruption by Sir Francis took the House by surprise, but still greater was its astonishment when the honourable baronet proposed, in place of the ordinary address to the Prince Regent, a memorial of remonstrance, laying before his Royal Highness all the instances of misgovernment and oppression—of infringement of the public liberty, and accumulation of abuses, which had been characteristic of the system pursued by Government for many years past.

As a matter of course, the address proposed by Sir Francis was read by the Speaker, amidst the ill-concealed dismay of those most affected by it. I then rose to second the address, denouncing the impolicy of the war, and more still the way in which it was conducted, so far as the policy of ministers was concerned. The subjoined is from the usual reports of the period.

" LORD COCHRANE rose for the purpose of seconding the address of the honourable baronet. He agreed with the speech delivered in the name of the Prince Regent, that a high tribute was due to the bravery of our army in Portugal, and to the conduct of the Commander-in-Chief, but he would deny that the war in the Peninsula would come to speedy or successful conclusion. The forces of Great Britain there were insufficient to cope with those Buonaparte could bring against us as soon as he had completed the subjugation of Spain and obtained command of its resources. Of this, we were quiet spectators. To what was our army indebted for its success and for maintaining itself in Portugal, but to the unproductiveness of that country. Every credit was due to Lord Wellington for his conduct of affairs, but even his lordship expected little from the Portuguese, who were dragged to the army more like slaves than soldiers, to support, they did not know what. At Peniche he had seen ten thousand of them collected, almost naked, and in want of every necessary

" The Portuguese were themselves despots. The dungeons of the Inquisition were full of victims, and the British minister, who formed part of the Regency, was lately under the necessity of retiring from Lisbon that he might not appear to countenance arrests and imprisonments which he could not approve. He would not scruple to assert that the Portuguese government was obnoxious to every class of society in that country. Nay, farther, that both in Sicily and in Portugal the British name was detested, because of the support which this country gave to the respective governments of each with all their oppressive abuses.

" With regard to Sicily, he thought that the real purpose of ministers was not so much to keep the French out of that island as to keep the people subject to one of the most despotic governments in existence. With regard to Portugal, which was considered of such importance, he would ask, How long would our army defend that country ? Only till the French had made themselves masters of Spain, and then it would be compelled to retire within its fortified lines, the whole extent of which could not afford grass enough to feed bullocks for six weeks' subsistence of the troops alone. He would assert, as a fact, extraordinary as it might appear, that even at present the bullocks and flour for the supply of Lord

Wellington's troops passed through the French army with licenses from the interior of Spain. This was a notorious fact, and he would leave the House to make reflections upon it.

" The noble lord then adverted to that part of the honourable baronet's proposed address, which referred to the internal state of the country, and professed his concurrence with the greater portion of the sentiments therein contained. All must own that the freedom of the people had been greatly encroached upon, particularly by the oppressive mode of levying taxes, the produce of which, he regretted to say, was grossly misapplied. No part of a man's house was free from the visits of the tax-gatherer, and a man could not remove articles that had paid duty on importation, without a permit, even so much as a dozen of wine. The noble lord trusted that a committee would be appointed to take both the conduct of the war, and the state of the nation into consideration.

" Lord Cochrane then adverted to that part of the speech which referred to the naval defences of the country, and maintained that our naval force was not rendered efficient in annoying the enemy. Commanding the seas, as this country did, our navy ought to be employed in threatening the coast of France in all directions, by which means Buonaparte would be compelled to keep his armies at home, instead of sending them to be *fed, clothed, and paid by our allies!* for the purpose of their own subjugation. Were the gigantic naval force of England used as it ought to be, *the whole force of France, vast as it was, would prove inadequate to the defence of its widely extended shores.* Perhaps demonstrations of attack might prove sufficient. If the enemy despised these, it would *then* be, as at this moment *it was,* easy to destroy everything on the French coasts, for England could, in spite of all the efforts of the enemy, being a force to any given point far superior to anything the enemy could assemble for our annoyance, and thus we might effect most powerful diversions."

The address proposed by Sir Francis and seconded by myself was, of course, unsuccessful. The mover of the address originally intended was Lord Jocelyn, who, when I had concluded, made not a word of allusion to any part of the speeches of Sir Francis or myself, beyond stating that "*he wholly disapproved of all we had said.*" Such was legislation in those days, that the arguments of those who did not belong to the ruling faction were not listended to, much less answered. Lord Jocelyn's address, which was only an echo of the Lords Commissioners' speech, had, however, to be proposed as *an amendment* to that of Sir Francis, and was carried without a division.

The feeling towards myself for having — as was said — "thought fit to countenance Sir Francis" — needs not be animadverted on. Yet I had given some good advice as to the way in which our naval power was frittered away to no purpose. English historians, by their silence on this point, appear to have little conception as to the extent of the evil.

As in seconding the address of Sir Francis Burdett, I had mentioned Sicily, I will give a remarkable example of the way in which war was carried on in that quarter *against the French!* The reader may deduce from that why I was not permitted to put my plans of harassing the French coast into execution.

The following letter is from Captain Robert Hall, commanding what was singularly enough called the "*army flotilla*" at Messina. The document is a curious one, and may do something towards enlightening future English historians :—

"Messina, Jan. 14, 1812.

"MY DEAR LORD,—It is so long since I heard of you, and being disappointed at not seeing you in this country, as the papers gave us reason to believe, that I must take the liberty of asking you how you are. We were led to expect you in the Mediterranean with a flying squadron, but I am sorry to see there is *now* no probability of it.

"I am serving here in an *amphibious* kind of way — having the rank of brigadier to command an "*army flotilla!*" but why it should be an "army" one I cannot find out, though I have well considered the matter *for the last eighteen months.*

"There is *an immense naval establishment here of a hundred and forty vessels of different descriptions quite independent of the Admiral!* * These are maintained by the British Government, at an expense of at least 140,000*l.* per annum. I have, in fact, lessened its expense by 60,000*l.* a year, merely by reducing the pay of the seamen to the standard of our own, though they have been paid at double the rate of English sailors, whilst the *padrones* of gunboats, taken from the streets, *are paid more than our lieutenants.*

"It is a singular thing that this establishment cannot be thrown into its proper channel — the navy. The island of Zante has another flotilla of 60,000 dollars a month to protect it, and the commandant of the barren rock of Lissa — not content with his gunboats — sent in, the other day, a serious memorial, stating the necessity of defending his island, by placing gunboats *all round it,* wherever there were no guns on shore ! If this flotilla mania should reach our West India Islands, what will be the consequence ? At least, I should think as army matters are conducted, an expense equal to one half that of the whole navy ! It is the duty of officers to serve where they are ordered, but this

---

* I had only asked for three or four handy frigates to carry out my plans, and indeed, could not have employed more with effect, as being under my entire supervision.

mixture of services is, I believe, altogether new, and may, if followed up, be fatal to the independent spirit of the navy. If that spirit perishes all ardour is gone, and we shall be like some foreign countries where the services are mixed—neither the one thing nor the other.

"My Lord, I believe you know me. You may therefore guess my feelings, after *eighteen years' service*, to be ordered to serve under a person *who is a perfect stranger to the service to which I belong.* What do you think of an order to make a passage to Zante in the dead of winter by *sailing close to the land in the Gulf of Tarento?* It is too ridiculous — and really deserves the consideration of the Admiralty.

" If we can combine our naval and military tactics, it will be a greater effort of human ingenuity than has hitherto been devised. We may then dispense with the rapidity of our manœuvres and *" march in ordinary time."* Figure to yourself *eighteen subalterns of different regiments commanding divisions of the flotilla!* When I took it out to sea, they were all sea-sick, and —— about the decks! Each of these subalterns received *seventeen and sixpence a day for this extraordinary and fatiguing service;* — nearly three times as much as a lieutenant in the navy!

"Endeavour, my Lord, to reconcile the meaning of such an establishment, glancing your eye at the same moment on the manner of conducting the flotilla establishment at Cadiz. We have at this moment *more troops on the Faroe line, than the French have in both Calabrias* — independent of those which, under our nautico-military chief, sacrificed our friends in Catalonia.

Yet there is a sad outcry here. We tell the Sicilians that they mean to murder us all, and there is no doubt their will is good enough.* Numerous are the remonstrances against sending a single soldier out of the island. The firm and

---

* See my speech on the address of Sir Francis Burdett.

manly mind of Lord William Bentinck was proof to this outcry, and it is to be regretted that circumstances did not admit
of this zealous and active officer accompanying the expedition
himself. Nothing can equal my respect for Lord William
Bentinck as a soldier and a gentleman, but I must say with
old Neptune, when jealous of the interference of some "*long
shore*" *Deity,*

> 'Non illi imperium pelagi sævumque tridentem
> Sed mihi — sorte datum est.'

What end, what purpose, can it answer, to put a naval establishment under the command of a person who acknow-
ledges that he does not know how to use it? As it was formed
under the auspices of my Lord Mulgrave, this arrangement
may probably have been made with a view of simplifying
naval matters. For example, my Lord, the long sentence
of "*back the main topsail,*" might be more readily expressed
by the short word "*halt!*" "Filling and making sail," according to the strength of wind, might be called "*marching
in quick or ordinary time!*" Instead of boatswain's mates
to "*march off*" the different "*detachments*" of the watch,
it would, according to our present system, be more regular to
"*march them off with corporals!*" though in squally
weather this might be inconvenient. In short, there might
be many improvements. The *army officer* appointed to
command one of our vessels mislaid what he called the
"*route given him by the Quarter-Master-General!*" "*lost
his way,*" as he expressed it, and got ashore in the Gulf of
Squillace. On his exchange he reported to me that "the
night was *so dark, he could not see the rock on which the
vessel ran!*" and that when fast, "*a board broke in her
bottom,* so that the water ran in so fast, he could not *scoop
it out* again! Thus it is, that Mr. Bull is humbugged. For
my part, I have remonstrated repeatedly on the folly of this
establishment, and it only remains with me to serve where I
am ordered.

"Of the politics of this country the public journals will have informed your Lordship. We are certainly doing nothing in the way of amelioration, and all parties seem discontented. The newfangled constitution strikes too much home to be popular amongst those who profited by the old system. Our views are certainly for the prosperity of Sicily, yet no Sicilian thinks so. They dislike us, and I believe they know not why. Some of the knowing ones appear apprehensive of our assuming the government altogether; and urge their fears of our treating them as we do the Irish Catholics! The French partisans, of course, make the most of this state of things.

"It is to be hoped that Buonaparte's failure in Russia will blast his other prospects, or Sicily will be his in a short time, if we do not oblige the Government to adopt some energetic measures. If they would only put the troops we have here on shore in Calabria, there would be no necessity for gunboats. They would excite an immediate insurrection, and would throw plenty of grain, of which we are in want, into Sicily. But if the Sicilian troops should intend running away on the approach of a French regiment — as they did formerly — we had better remain and *colonise* at Messina.

"Your Lordship's faithful servant,

"ROBERT HALL.

"The Lord Cochrane."

The above will show the useless manner in which our best naval force and officers were employed — no less than their testimony to their own uselessness. Yet with upwards of a thousand ships in commission, we had no naval enemy to oppose, and persisted in employing our seamen anywhere but on the enemy's coast! For simply urging the common sense employment of our numerous navy, and a proper investigation into the minor details which crippled its action, I was regarded as a common disturber of the ministerial peace.

Yet it had not been my intention to throw blame on the Admiralty, but simply on *the system* under which they continued to act, but which, for all practical purposes, had become obsolete. The Admiralty, whatever might be its wish, was unable to do its work for want of some one of high professional skill and resolute character, whose business it should be authoritatively to investigate the efficiency of naval establishments, and personally to superintend investigation alike into inefficiency and suggested improvements. Had this been done, many evils, hidden from the knowledge of successive Admiralties, would be perceived and remedied.

The Admiralty, even as at present constituted, is not sufficiently numerous to execute so many and such varied duties, even though the ability of the members comprised all professional knowledge, and that their industry was indefatigable. The overwhelming pressure of detail renders inquiry into, and deliberation on, important matters impracticable, whilst on minor matters it is prohibitory, and thus abuses remain unremedied, because unperceived.

The Board, at all times within my recollection, has been one of reference to persons in inferior departments. These persons pronounce *an unquestioned verdict* on all matters referred to them ; their reports remaining concealed under a rule adopted to avoid trouble or correspondence, the framers of the rule not anticipating that such concealment may be fraught with the most injurious consequences to the navy, whilst it may shield from exposure the most self-interested and flagrant impositions.

This, however, is not the place to enter on a subject, the ramifications of which have penetrated into every department, till beyond the control of the most patriotic and unflinching ; who, with all their pains, can only arrive at the one fact, that the whole system requires renovation, which, as it is nobody's business, is never undertaken.

So long, however, as such a system exists, so long shall we be in danger of being taken unawares by powers fully alive to the importance of unity of purpose and action. To such a system we have nothing to oppose in case of emergency but our own embarrassment.

CHAP. XXXIV.

MY SECRET PLANS.

SOON after my return from the Mediterranean, I had
the honour of laying before His Royal Highness the
Prince Regent, a new and most formidable method of
attacking and destroying an enemy's fleet, and of performing other warlike operations on a large scale. His
Royal Highness was pleased to refer the plans laid
before him to a Secret Committee, consisting of the
late Duke of York, as president, Lord Keith, Lord
Exmouth, and the two Congreves, one of whom, Sir
William, was the celebrated inventor of the rocket
which bears his name.

These officers — as stated to me in a private letter
from Lord Keith, who took a warm interest in the matter
—gave it as their opinion that under the circumstances

detailed in my explanatory paper, such a mode of attack would be irresistible, and the effect of the power and means proposed, infallible; adding, however, that if the plan was divulged, it might become perilous to our Colonial possessions; an observation marked by no little foresight, *for had the same plan been known to the rebels in the late Indian mutiny, not a European in India would have escaped.*

The Prince Regent and the Duke of York fully concurred with the Committee in the destructive character of the plans submitted, for their consideration as well as in the danger of divulging them. His Royal Highness sending for me to Carlton House, commanded secresy on my part. I told His Royal Highness that my plans were only known to Sir Alexander Cochrane, and to my uncle, Mr. Cochrane Johnstone, who had, in fact written out for me the papers which had been laid before His Royal Highness, but that I would obey his injunctions, and had no fear of my relatives disclosing so important a secret. The investigation being secret, of course no official report was made on the subject.

Not long after this interview Lord Melville signified to me his intention to put in execution *a portion* of my plans, and requested my attendance at the Admiralty for the purpose of conferring on the subject. To this partial execution of the project I of course demurred, as unfair to the invention and necessarily incomplete in operation, whilst development of a portion might give the enemy such an insight of the whole as would enable him to turn it against ourselves on a large scale; his lordship, nevertheless, did not seem inclined to give way, and I quitted the Admiralty without having been enabled to arrive at any satisfactory conclusion.

Lord Melville having mentioned to Lord Keith the result of our interview, Lord Keith urged me to acquiesce in the First Lord's views, adding, that he was too well acquainted with the soundness of my plans to doubt the practicability of destroying with a portion only the enemy's ships in Genoa harbour and the outer roads of Toulon. His lordship further urged that a success once achieved, the popular voice would place it in my power to enforce the execution of the more destructive portion of the invention within the enemy's inner harbours.

In deference to Lord Keith's opinion I at once prepared a plan of attack on the outer roads of Toulon, in accordance with the views of Lord Melville. That communication, omitting the essential parts of the plan, I now subjoin.

" 12 Portman Square, May 12th, 1812.

"MY LORD,—In consequence of the conversation I had the honour of holding with your Lordship yesterday, and of your desire that I should state what force would be required for carrying into execution the plan submitted for the destruction of the Toulon fleet, I beg to submit the following arrangements as applicable *to this particular object.**

" One seventy-four.

" Two 38-gun frigates.

" Two 18-gun brigs.

" Two cutters or schooners.

" The above force is requisite as an escort, and to protect the boats.

* Viz. as not having reference to the execution of the whole.

˙ " In order to ensure success, although one-half will probably be sufficient, the subjoined will be necessary.

[Here follow particulars.]

" As your Lordship permitted me to recommend such
officers as I thought best calculated for this service, I beg
leave to name the following : —

" Captain Robert Baine.

" Sir Thomas Staines, now of the *Hamadryad*.

" Captain Johnstone, now commanding the *Avenger*, if he
has not sailed ; and if he has —

" Captain Hall, now commanding the gunboats at Messina,
and lastly

" The Honourable Lieutenant Napier, now in the Mediterranean.

" My late first Lieutenant, Travers, now in the *Impérieuse*,
to be first of whatever ship your Lordship may be pleased to
assign to me, which, in order further to conceal the enterprise, may, if your Lordship should think proper, be placed
under the command of my brother Captain Archibald Cochrane, late of the *Fox* frigate. I can furnish him confiden-
tially with all the necessary instructions, so that I might at
once proceed to Lisbon, apparently in a private capacity, so
as to disarm suspicion.

" I have taken the liberty of submitting the names of the
above officers to your Lordship, because I am well acquainted
with their characters and zeal for the service, and am sure
that whatever is undertaken by them will first be well
weighed, and then executed with determination.

" The above operation is calculated *without the assistance
of troops*, but if your Lordship wish to *secure* the ships, instead of *destroying* them, 4000 troops should be embarked at
Messina * as though under the destination of Catalonia, and
having been shifted into the ships of war now blockading
Toulon, should be held in readiness to be disembarked in the

* How well these could have been spared is evident from Capt.
Hall's letter, see page 221.

peninsula of Cape Cepet, the heights of which may be held,
although not yet fortified, against any force that may be
brought against them.   When I was last there, with Lord
Collingwood's fleet, I stood particularly close in, within point
blank range of shot, and there were not sufficient men in any
of the batteries to train more than one gun at a time —
indeed, they appeared merely to be stationed there to take
charge of the stores.   There was neither smoke in the
chimneys of the barrack-rooms, nor was there a door or
window open, though the weather was extremely hot.

"If the operations are to be extended along the coasts,
your Lordship will see the propriety of embarking 300
marines on board the seventy-four, and 100 in each of the
frigates.

"The expense of the expedition will be *within three
months' cost of that of the blockading force,* and half the
stores enumerated may accomplish the service.

"I have, &c. &c.
"COCHRANE.
"The Right Honourable Lord Melville, &c. &c."

Inconsiderable as was the expense, in comparison
with other armaments producing little or no result,
Lord Melville hesitated to incur it; or rather, as I
have reason to believe, his lordship was overruled by
the ill-feeling against me at the Admiralty, as the concurrence of the Board would have placed me in command of a squadron, with my flag flying in a line-of-
battle ship.   This was evidently considered too high a
position for one who had been for three years kept
unemployed from political and personal dislike, was
evidently not to be thought of, and the project after
long fruitless expectation was dropped.

I then proposed to conduct a similar expedition
against Flushing, but this also was declined.   As,

however, public dissatisfaction began to manifest itself,
Lord Melville informed me that I might make
an attempt on Toulon *on a small scale!* In other
words, that I might, " on a small scale," show the
enemy how to put my plans in operation against
ourselves *on a large scale!* The permission was so
preposterous, besides being not altogether free from the
suspicion that failure would be more acceptable than
success, I declined it, notwithstanding the renewed
recommendation of Lord Keith to close with Lord
Melville's offer. As at this time only a few sail of the
line remained at Toulon, I hesitated to comply, considering that the result of destroying these would have
been badly compensated by the disclosure of the means
whereby their destruction had been effected.

Soon after the accession of William IV. I submitted
my plans to His Majesty's consideration, and being
himself a practical seaman, His Majesty at once admitted their importance and honoured me with personal
interviews on the subject, at which I explained my
methods of putting them in execution under various
circumstances. His Majesty was further pleased to
observe that I ought to be rewarded as well for the
plans as for the secrecy which had been observed, yet
not the slightest reward did I ever reap for the invention
or for having kept my secret out of pure love to my
country, a motive which will be better appreciated
when subsequent temptations to divulge it come to be
shown.

An incontrovertible proof of the efficiency of the
plans submitted by me to various ministries is on

record in the shape of a report *from a comparatively recent commission*, one of the commissioners — who ranks amongst the highest in his profession — *being still living*. As from the non-employment of those plans on any occasion, an opinion may have gone abroad that their destructive character is illusory, I feel myself justified in dispelling the illusion by subjoining the report.

Towards the close of 1846, when the late Lord Auckland was at the Admiralty, suspicion being excited as to the motives and intentions of the then French government, another commission was appointed, to decide upon a mode of trying my inventions in a way to satisfy the public as to their efficacy, and at the same time to preserve secresy. This being found impracticable, the trial was never made, but the commission proceeded to report on the plans. The members were Sir Thomas Hastings, Sir J. F. Burgoyne, and Lieut.-Col. Colquhoun.

The subjoined is their report, addressed to the then Master of the Ordnance and forwarded to me by Lord Auckland.

"Ordnance Office, Jan. 16, 1847.

" MY LORD,— In conformity with your Lordship's instructions, we, the undersigned, have met to consider and report on the secret war plans of Vice-Admiral the Earl of Dundonald, transmitted to us by the First Lord of the Admiralty, the Earl of Auckland.

" These plans may be classed under three heads :—

" 1st. One, on which an opinion may be formed without experiment, for concealing or making offensive warlike operations ; and we consider that, under many particular circumstances this method of his Lordship may be made available as well by land as by sea, and we therefore suggest that a record of this part of Lord Dundonald's plans should be deposited with the Admiralty, to be made use of when in the judgment of their Lordships the opportunity of employing it may occur.

" 2nd. One on which experiments would be required before a satisfactory conclusion could be arrived at.

" 3rd. Nos. 1 and 2 continued for the purpose of hostile operations.

" After mature consideration, we have resolved that it is not desirable that any experiments should be made. We assume it to be possible that the plan *contains power for producing the sweeping destruction the inventor ascribes to it ;* but it is clear this power could not be retained exclusively by this country, because its first employment would develope its principle and application. The last observation applies equally to plan No. 1.

" We considered in the next place, how far the adoption of the proposed secret plans would accord with the feelings and principles of civilised warfare. We are of unanimous opinion that plans Nos. 2 and 3, would do so.

" We therefore recommend that, as hitherto, plans Nos. 2 and 3 *should remain concealed.* We feel that *great credit is due to Lord Dundonald for the right feelings which prompted him not to disclose his secret plans when serving in war as naval Commander-in-Chief of the forces of other nations, under very trying circumstances, in the conviction that those plans might eventually be of the highest importance to his own country.*

" We have only to add that we have sealed up, under one cover all the papers which have been submitted to our consideration by the First Lord of the Admiralty and the Earl of Dundonald, and our correspondence with the latter in another — both of which we have marked ' secret.'

" With regard to the disposal and future custody of these papers, we await instructions from your Lordship, or the Earl

of Auckland, to whom we propose this letter should — after
your Lordship has perused it — be transmitted.

> " We have the honour to be,
>> " Your Lordship's obedient servants,
>>> " THOMAS HASTINGS, Capt. R. N., and
>>>> Principal Storekeeper.
>> " J. F. BURGOYNE.
>> " J. S. COLQUHOUN, Lieut.-Col. R. A.

" To the Marquis of Anglesey, K.G. and K.C.B."

Let the public now judge of the nature and value
of those plans—of the merit of never having disclosed
them, though exposed to severely trying circumstances,
and also whether they are impracticable.

I have been told, on indubitable authority that
during the late war with Russia an interchange of
warlike plans took place between the English and
French Governments.   It was further pointed out
to me but the other day, that a French journal of high
authority had remarked to this effect, " *should a war
arise between England and France, the latter power
would bring warlike engines into play to which rifled
cannon were a trifle.*"   From this I make little doubt
but that my plans *are* known to the French Government, and if so, whenever they are applied, the people
of this country will find them no " trifle " — for as
the report just adduced infers, no power on earth
can stand against them.   It is one of my most bitter
reflections that such plans have been utterly thrown
away as regards our own nation, and that from the
imprudence of Governments they may one day be
turned against my own country.

In the late war with Russia, I twice offered these plans to the Government. The first time they were declared " *inexpedient !* " The second time I offered to *conduct them myself*, either against Cronstadt or Sebastopol — old as I was — the forts of Cronstadt being especially open to their application. As regarded Sebastopol, the question was put to me whether I would instruct two engineer officers in applying them? My answer was, " No, I have offered to risk my own life and reputation on their efficacy, but will not impart my mode of applying them to others, who may not, either from preconceived notions or professional jealousy of naval inventions, comprehend them."

Had I not adduced the report of the last committees appointed to examine the plans, this might be thought the bombast of an old admiral whose physical vigour had outlived his judgment. I flatter myself, however, that more years of sharp experience than usually falls to the lot, even of admirals, has fixed my judgment of warlike operations too firmly to be shaken even by age. I repeat that should those plans ever be turned against ourselves, the English public will be in a condition to pronounce an opinion on that point.

The report of the committee gives me great credit for *not having made use of those plans elsewhere*. As before stated, I promised the Prince Regent never to divulge them except for the honour and advantage of my own country, and although driven from the profession of my choice I did not forget my promise.

It may be permitted me to add that when, in 1820, I came with four ships before the Castles of Callao, it was perfectly well known to me that money and property considerably exceeding in value a million sterling, besides all the plate in Lima, had been sent to these castles for security. I could, with the aid of a small portion of my plans only, and in spite of opposition, have possessed myself of this treasure in an hour, and my share could not have been less than half a million sterling.

Let posterity judge of my conduct, as compared with the blind enmity of those who persecuted me wrongfully. Yet there was every inducement to employ my own plans for my own benefit. When I entered the service of the South American States, my private income, never large, and entirely of my own creation, had been wholly wasted by the expenses consequent on forced litigation and in defending myself from an iniquitous prosecution. For more than four years I had been deprived of my professional income, and at forty years of age found myself thrown on the world to seek the means of making provision for myself and an increasing family.

Had I been indifferent to the welfare of my own country, my position, as Commander-in-Chief of the squadrons of Chili and Peru, and afterwards of the Brazilian squadron, would have enabled me to amass an immense fortune, by putting an early end to the wars of those countries through the adoption of secret plans, as the Governments of those states expected. For not having done so, they manifested their displeasure and declined to pay me the stipulated rewards for what I effected towards their liberation.

It was forcibly urged upon me by the South American governments that the unjust deprivation of rank and honour in my own country released me from any obligation to obey the injunction of secresy which had been imposed upon me, and that I ought to profit from my own discovery, by applying it to the ample opportunities before me. I can safely say, that love of country, alone restrained me from listening to their temptations, and that I did not yield to the great necessities of my position is now one of the proudest consolations of my life.

Yet I repeat — and the assertion will one day be confirmed—that these plans afford the infallible means of securing at one blow our maritime superiority and of thereafter maintaining it in perpetuity — of at once commencing and terminating war by one conclusive victory. A hundred millions employed in war could not complete the ruin of our maritime opponents so effectually as could be done by the simple methods indicated in my plans; and that too in spite of the apparently formidable fortifications and other defences of ports and roadsteads. The expenditure of millions in the construction of such works on the coasts of any country would be in vain, when any hostile power in possession of the knowledge of such means of attack, could at a trifling cost and with the utmost facility accomplish in a few hours any assignable amount of destruction without impediment from such costly but really impotent safeguards. Still more easily might this country protect itself by destroying at one blow the marine of an enemy, and that by a process which our most eminent engineer officers —as has been seen —have pronounced infallible.

It is somewhat singular — that, notwithstanding my admitted experience, as demonstrated by the acts and success of my early life, and notwithstanding the destructive character of my plans as certified by committees of the most eminent men to be found in both services, *I have never, throughout my whole life, been officially consulted on the means of defence of this country !*

This cannot have been accidental. It is not probable that any prime minister should consider himself so well up in naval matters as to despise my experience. Nor is it probable that he should prefer consulting officers who never saw a shot fired in actual warfare, — as was frequently the case previous to the Russian war,— to the opinions of one whom committees of the highest professional character had declared to be the inventor of plans which would totally change the aspect of war, and supersede every known system of warlike operations.

When the dominion of the sea, the existence of our mercantile marine, and the peace of Europe were — *as they are at this moment* — in question, it is nevertheless difficult to conceive this extraordinary inconsistency. Still there is the fact. None to whom my plans have been submitted, have ever pretended to throw doubt on their efficacy. Some, it is true, have said, "For heaven's sake, don't encourage such plans, — what is to become of us ?" What ? Universal peace : for after their disclosure not a man would be found to engage in war except for defence of his country, when, as was said of the cholera by an eminent French surgeon, " *Il cadavreisera le monde.*"

What can have been the cause of such neglect and contumely as I have suffered, under the full knowledge that such a secret was in my power? There can only have been two causes, — unmerited personal aversion without reason, or want of political courage to put my plans in execution. Whether of the two causes be accepted, they form the highest compliment which was ever paid to man, viz. *that no amount of neglect or persecution could induce me to betray my country.* The report of the committee paid me the compliment which is at least my right, and how great a compliment it is, futurity may one day unexpectedly have to decide.

No doubt to use such powers for ambitious purposes would be wicked; but what guarantee have we that if in the possession of ambitious nations, they may not be turned against us. To use them in the defence of order and civilisation would be praiseworthy, but to let the world know that we are at all times prepared to use them against aggression, would be a protection of the best interests of mankind no less than of our own. Such knowledge can only be dangerous to those who have cause to fear it, but to those possessing it it is power, strength, and safety.

The public is now in possession of all material circumstances connected with the subject, except the plans themselves, which, for obvious reasons, are, it is to be hoped, *still secret.*

I am not certain whether — were the plans disclosed — the advantage would not be in favour of publicity. Such disclosure would demonstrate that there could be no security in coast defences and other stationary asylums, on the construction of which it is now proposed to expend so many millions of the public money. It would show the inexpediency of an expenditure of ten — which may mean twenty — millions for the construction of forts and harbours, instead of applying half the amount to remodel and renovate the navy. The disclosure might have the effect of preventing useless expenditure, and of averting the danger of future parsimonious naval administration, by leading to the adoption of essential measures of nautical improvement, by which alone the safety of the country can be preserved.

The disclosure of these plans would also have the effect of binding over nations to keep the peace. Still less would the English public countenance the extravagant and inefficient projects devised for the protection of their insular position, open at all points, and only to be protected by a superior naval force, which shall avert danger on the first menace.

As the subject of fortifications is now uppermost in every man's mind, I will venture a few remarks on my experience of this mode of defence.

A story is told of the Duke of Wellington which embraces the whole subject. On his appointment as Warden of the Cinque Ports, the inhabitants of Dover, well known for their keen scent of a profitable job, applied to the Duke for an increase of their fortifications, already a stupendous monument to the folly of those who have added to them.

The Duke's reply was the perfection of military wisdom. "*The fortifications of Dover would be, no doubt, very useful if an enemy came in that way, but I don't think he would! They might also be very useful if an enemy went out that way, but I don't think he would!*" In that sentence is comprised the whole subject of fortifications, unless erected specifically for the defence of a dockyard or an arsenal, as at Portsmouth, Plymouth, &c. It is true that in his last years the Duke retracted his opinion in some degree, but I could never learn the reasons he assigned for so doing.

Why should an enemy go to a coast fortification when he can land miles away from it? I will take the instance of the Dover fortifications, which are amongst the most stupendous in this country. What is there to prevent an enemy from landing at Walmer, where there is nothing to oppose him but the six popguns in the flower garden of the Castle? He may effect a debarkation there at all times of the tide, in any wind and almost in any weather. The distance from the fortifications of Dover is little short of seven miles. By making a strong feint by sea on Dover, the garrison could not quit their works to prevent the disembarkation at Walmer, for if they did the feint would be turned into a real attack. Neither, when the disembarkation had been effected, would they be likely to quit their works for the purpose of harassing the invaders, for so surely as they marched out for this purpose a sufficient portion of the enemy would march in. The whole would simply amount to this, that the garrison, say 10,000 or 20,000, would be cut off from communication with the army elsewhere, and would thus be completely neutralised. Lastly, when disembarked at Walmer, the fortifications of Dover could not in the slightest degree interrupt the enemy's communications by sea. Nothing but an efficient navy could do that; and with an efficient navy the disembarkation at Walmer would never be attempted. All this is plain enough; for, after all, military tactics are founded on common sense, and the amount of common sense decides their superiority.

Where fortifications are the key to a province, frequently advisable to capture them, and this may be an easier matter than military men in general are willing to admit. Of course, if they sit down before fortifications *secundum artem*, the matter is one merely of time and calculation, as we have learned at Sebastopol.

When on the coast of Chili I captured a province with 120 men only, and that by storming its fortifications. These were thirteen in number, and were garrisoned by 2000 men. I was accused of rashness for the attempt; yet no more doubted the fact of my success than I doubted the reality of the attack. It was simply a matter of well matured deliberation and calculation, in which, of course, the panic of the enemy formed an important item. The result was that I did not lose a man, whilst the enemy's killed and wounded amounted

to more in number *than my whole force!* With this
in addition to my former experience it perhaps will not
be wondered at that my respect for fortifications is by
no means great, though my respect for an efficient navy
is excessive.

Full discussion of this matter would, however, require more space than can here be devoted to it, and
should my life be spared I will on a future occasion
enter more extensively into this and other cognate
subjects. Were I now to do so, I am afraid public
faith in some of its newly cherished fortifications would
be materially shaken, and will therefore refrain from so
doing, in the hope that improvements in our navy, the
only true basis of national safety, will render such
remarks unnecessary.

In short, immovable stations of defence as a protection against invasion, are not only costly and of
doubtful utility, but a *reliance on them* is, in my mind,
an indication of a declining state. It is little short of
national imbecility to suppose that because we erect
imposing fortifications an enemy *will come to them!*
when he can operate elsewhere without the slightest
regard to them ; and the more so, as the common experience of warfare will tell him that numerous fortifications are in the highest degree national weakness,
by splitting up into detail the army which ought to be
in the field against him, but who are compelled to
remain and take care of their fortifications. Yet *half
the sum* required for fortifications as defences in case
of war, would suffice to place the navy in a condition

of affording far more effectual protection.   There is
no security equal to that which may be obtained *by
putting it out of the power of an enemy to execute
hostile intentions.*   This can never be effected by forts,
but may be accomplished by the adoption of proper
measures, which I shall at present refrain from commenting on.

CHAP. XXXV.

NAVAL AND OTHER DISCUSSIONS IN PARLIAMENT.

SINECURES.—ADMIRALTY EXPENSES ILL DIRECTED.—WHAT MIGHT BE DONE WITH SMALL MEANS.—FLOGGING IN THE ARMY AND NAVY ATTRIBUTABLE TO A BAD SYSTEM : NEVERTHELESS, INDISPENSABLE.— NATIONAL MEANS WRONGLY APPLIED.—INJURIOUS CONCESSIONS TO THE FRENCH.—DENIED BY THE GOVERNMENT.—EXPLANATIONS OF MY PARLIAMENTARY CONDUCT ON THE DISSOLUTION OF PARLIAMENT.— LETTER TO MY CONSTITUENTS.—APPOINTMENT OF OFFICERS BY MERIT INSTEAD OF POLITICAL INFLUENCE THE TRUE STRENGTH OF THE NAVY.—MY RE-ELECTION FOR WESTMINSTER. — ADDRESS TO THE ELECTORS.—MINISTERIAL VIEWS.—TREATMENT OF AN OFFICER.—MY INTERFERENCE.

AT the commencement of the session of 1812, it became known that His Royal Highness the late Duke of Cambridge had voluntarily given up a military emolument of nearly 5000*l.* a-year. The patriotism which moved His Royal Highness to relinquish a lucrative command which had dwindled into a sinecure, was too conspicuous to be lost sight of, not only on account of his disinterestedness, but because there was hope this practical specimen of reform, proceeding from so high a quarter, might be brought to bear on others in such a way as to induce them to emulate the example.

On the 23rd of January, I therefore moved for a copy of His Royal Highness's letter of resignation, for the purpose of grounding thereon a resolution expressive of the opinion of the House on the subject, at the same time intimating to sinecure-holders in general the desirableness of imitating the magnanimity of the royal duke. The effort was, however, in vain.

On the 23rd of February, a question was raised by Mr. Bankes respecting the payment of 2790*l.* a-year to the Secretary of the Prince of Wales, as paymaster of widows' pensions. A former report on a committee of the House had pronounced this office a perfect sinecure, of no public utility whatever, and that the office of deputy-paymaster was little better, the whole business being transacted by a clerk in the War Office at a salary of 100*l.* a-year. The reply of Mr. Perceval (then Prime Minister) to this statement was " that there was more danger to the country *from declamations against sinecures than from the sinecures themselves!* "

On this occasion I supported the *retention* of the sine-cure, on the ground that the abolition of so insignificant a sum might *deceive the public into a belief that their interests were watched in that House.* The House had suffered the reports of various committees on the subject to lie dormant for thirty years, and now wished to abolish *three only* out of the long list of sinecures, which their committees had declared to be useless and burdensome to the country. It was the bounden duty of the House to have pronounced *on the whole class*, and not par-tially. They ought to have enumerated the sinecures to be abolished, and thus put it out of the power of ministers to exercise any discretion on the subject; instead of singling out a comparatively insignificant place from a long list of enormous sinecures, upon which the House had not so much as expressed an opinion, notwithstanding the numerous representations of its committees.

On the motion of the First Lord (the Right Hon. C. Yorke) that a sum of upwards a million should be granted for the contingent expences of the Admiralty, I spoke as follows:—

" LORD COCHRANE hoped, that, as a deviation from mere detail was allowed when the army estimates were in a committee, it would not be entirely out of course to offer a few general remarks while the supply of the navy was before the House; not with a view to oppose the supply for the ordinary establishment of the navy, but as to the proper application of the enormous sums granted for that service generally.

" To this nothing could, in his opinion, contribute more than that the Board of Admiralty should not be considered as a *mere appendage to the minister of the day, and be displaced by every agitation of the political system* — whereby misapplication of means was rendered perpetual; for, just as the members acquired some knowledge of their complicated duties, and of the powers they ought to direct against the enemy, they were then displaced, to make room for others of *no experience.*

" The observations which he had to address to the chairman related chiefly to the means of annoying the enemy, which means the Government possessed in a right disposal of the naval force of the country. This was at present totally useless, except for the purpose of passive blockades. Had 5000 men, with attendant naval transports, been kept in readiness in such a central situation as Minorca, for instance, it would have been impossible for the French to have made any progress on the eastern side of the Peninsula; for no sooner should the enemy have laid siege to Tarragona, Valencia, Alicant, or any other place on the Mediterranean coast of Spain, than their affairs might have been reversed at the other extremity. Rosas, for instance, was within *twelve hours' sail* of Minorca, and about eighteen from

Alicant, whereas on the other hand it was *twenty-five days'
march* at least from Alicant to Rosas.

" Comparing the respective populations of Britain and
France, it was impossible to think of carrying on an equal
warfare in the Peninsula. A greater number of men than
all the British who were at present there, must perish before
it could be possible to drive out the French. The desultory
nature of naval warfare was, in his opinion, the best calculated for that purpose, and for this we had the highest
authorities in ancient and modern times. If the French,
with a contemptible flotilla, could keep this country in alarm,
what was our gigantic navy not capable of doing ? The
whole of France lay at the mercy of the British ministry.
Had the enemy a naval superiority, and only 10,000 disposable troops, on what part of the shores of England could
people repose in tranquillity ?

" The war as at present conducted could not possibly have
a successful termination. It was a great misfortune that the
House of Commons listened to nothing which was beyond
the sphere of their own knowledge ; and when any professional man, like himself, rose up to give information, *party*
was immediately thrown in his teeth ; *factious motives* were
instantly imputed, however pure his wishes for the good of
his country. He put it to the committee, whether the whole
force of this country was not on the alert, and almost concentrated on the coasts of Kent and Sussex, when an invasion
was threatened by a contemptible flotilla of the enemy ; and
if so, what might not be done, if the gigantic naval power
of England was to threaten the enemy's shores ? It was his
sincere opinion, that the whole coast of France was completely at the mercy of His Majesty's ministers.

" The noble lord next adverted to the coasting trade carried
on by France, and which it was in our power to destroy.
That trade existed to an extent almost incredible. It was in
our power to dismantle their batteries, — to blow up their
towers,—and, above all, to destroy that chain of signal-posts,
by which a telegraphic communication was kept up from

Flushing to Bayonne, and from the south-east point of Spain to Venice.   Each of those signal-posts could be successfully attacked by ten men, as, except in a few situations, they were exposed, and seldom had above two or three maimed soldiers to conduct them.   He had no interest whatever in forcing those observations on the attention of the committee, and he hoped the right hon. gentleman would not think them altogether unworthy of his consideration.   He should not, he said, at that time attempt to say more; but he trusted that members who were far more capable to do justice to the subject than he could pretend to be, would turn it in their minds, and bring the subject forward, or that His Majesty's ministers would investigate the truth and act accordingly.   In either case he was certain attention to the hints he had thus thrown out could not fail of being attended by the most beneficial results to the country.   He did not think ministers, in not having attended to the subject, were so much to blame as the House itself, for they were, or ought to be, the guardians of the public purse; but he was sorry to say, the practice of the House was *to vote estimates to a very great amount, without at all troubling themselves to inquire how those estimates were applied.*

"Besides the signal-posts he had mentioned, there were placed along the whole coast of Spain many small parties of soldiers in churches, convents, and other buildings, for the purpose of keeping the people of the maritime towns in awe, and passing along supplies to the armies, which supplies it was in our power to intercept, as the only practicable military road was within a pistol-shot of the margin of the sea.   The smallest assistance would encourage the people to rise upon them; but without such assistance they are afraid to do so, knowing that the French would burn their houses, violate their wives, and murder themselves.   This he had seen them do.

"During all the time he was off Catalonia, the French had barely sufficient force to defend themselves against the natives, and in every enterprise which they undertook they were foiled. It was notorious, however, to all the world, that the attention of ministers was always engaged exclusively on one or two objects, and that they never took an extended view of things. If our commander on that coast had had discretionary powers to supply Figueras, which was the key of Catalonia, with provisions, it could not have been taken by force, for it was impregnable. If Government would only act in a proper way, it was impossible that Buonaparte could go on a twelvemonth longer.

"The noble lord then referred to the American war: had ministers during that war, instead of marching large armies through the country, only transported 10,000 men from one place to another, they would soon have laid waste the whole sea-coast, and the country must have submitted.

"MR. HUTCHINSON deprecated the species of warfare recommended by the noble lord, which he thought would not be productive of the effects he expected.

"LORD COCHRANE, in explanation, defended the system which he had recommended, as peculiarly calculated to injure the enemy's coasting trade, which was the great nursery of his seamen.

"After a few questions from Admiral Markham and Mr. Tierney, as to the decrease in the estimates, and replies from Mr. Yorke, the resolution was agreed to, as were also the other usual annual resolutions relating to the navy."

As the subject of flogging in the army and navy forms a prominent subject in the present day, I may be pardoned for putting my own views, then and now, on record. On the 13th of March, on the motion for the third reading of the Mutiny Bill, Sir Francis Burdett, in a speech distinguished for humanity and eloquence, animadverted on the punishment of flogging in the army and navy, as a system derogatory to our country, where the principles of liberty, of humanity, and of civilisation were better understood and practised than in any other country.

On this occasion, I delivered my sentiments as follows :—

"Lord COCHRANE hoped that, by degrees, this punishment might in due time be abolished, but declared that it was impracticable to govern any large body of men without having the power of recourse to it. He believed, however, that much of the mischief which arose from the punishment of flogging, especially in the navy, had been caused by the influence of that House. Great parliamentary interest had enabled the first families in the kingdom to force their children into the service, when too young to understand the nature of the authority entrusted to them. Many of them insisted on their decks being as clean and as shining as the floor of a drawing-room, and that their kitchen utensils should be scoured as bright as silver, with a variety of other useless and fantastic commands; and if such commands were not obeyed, they flogged severely those who had those articles in charge.

"The discipline of the navy depended on the commanding officer of each ship; and if they continued to flog for such offences, the navy must suffer. Gentlemen might think otherwise, but he knew it to be true, and he was afraid they would be convinced of it too soon. The family interest he had alluded to prevailed also, to such a degree, that even the Lords of the Admiralty had lists made out, and when an officer went to offer his services, or to solicit promotion for services performed, he was asked — 'Are you recommended by my Lady this, or Miss that, or Madam t'other?' and if he was not, he might as well have stayed at home.

"He could not, however, vote for the motion. It would be better to look to those to whom power was entrusted, than to take away the power of punishing altogether. If it were so taken away, it would ruin the service. The best seamen in the navy would say so, and if put to the vote among the sailors, he was sure the decision would be in favour of the present mode of punishment; but they would at the same time tell the Lords Commissioners of the Admiralty that they ought to be commanded by persons of experience, and not by young men appointed by parliamentary or any other influence. He hoped he should see the practice of flogging abolished, while the power of inflicting it was suffered to remain."

Good seamen are thoroughly aware that they have nothing to fear from a judicious and well-regulated captain, a man of sense, who knows his duty and that of those under him. Such captains have indeed no difficulty in manning their ships, whilst those in whom the men have no confidence find difficulty. Good men on board ship stand as little in awe of the cat as do the good people ashore — who make so much fuss about what they cannot possibly understand. Amongst many hundreds of men there are always some vagabonds, who, were it not for the fear of punishment, would throw their whole work on the hands of others. On such men reasoning has no effect, nor have good seamen any sympathy with them. On the contrary, they would rather see them compelled to do their duty by the dread, or even the application of the lash, than be obliged to do the work of lazy men in addition to their own.

Landsmen also forget that a naval officer cannot get rid of a worthless vagabond. He has to account for him to the Admiralty. Were it possible to give an officer power to turn such over the side, as a landsman can turn away an unprofitable servant, and he would have no occasion for the lash. But so long as he is obliged to retain such men, he must secure their obedience by the only means which will control them.

On the 16th of March came on one of those questions which added so materially to our national debt. Lord Castlereagh proposed a sum of two millions sterling as a subsidy to Portugal. He declared that the circumstances of Portugal were so much improved, and her troops exhibited so much valour, that he did not expect any opposition to the measure. This was, however, opposed by several members, on the ground of impoverishing ourselves by a system which did not produce the results the nation had a right to expect. By myself it was not opposed, but I embraced the opportunity of giving my opinion to the following effect :—

" LORD COCHRANE considered Portugal to be defensible against the French arms chiefly at the lines of Torres Vedras, which were so strong as not to require so great an army as we had there, and which gave us a free communication with the sea; whereas our operations were conducted on a much more extensive scale between Ciudad Rodrigo and Badajoz,—places which, if we got possession of them both, were not tenable unless we had a force perfectly capable of coping with the French forces in the open field. Both these places stood on plains, and the French, it should be recollected, were much superior to us in the number of their cavalry, and had often brought a much larger general force into the field.

" The war would be much less expensive, were the lines of Torres Vedras considered as the true defence of Portugal; by which means, instead of our keeping 60,000 or 70,000 men in Portugal, comparatively idle, or, at least, not in a state of military activity, we might detach just now, as we might have done before, a portion of our army to Cadiz, and raise the blockade of that city. A small portion of our army might also be sent to Catalonia, where they might reverse all the success of the enemy; and we might act all along the margin of the Mediterranean with the best effect. There were numerous small forts on the coast which we might get possession of, and thereby command all the neighbouring country. We might have done much on the whole eastern side of Spain — at Valencia particularly, and might probably retake Barcelona. All this was not only useful, but practicable at a much smaller expense than our present system. Thus we might have constantly checked and counteracted the objects of the French.

"This suggestion he did not make as his own. It had been the recommendation of others as well as his, and seemed obvious to anybody. For the principles on which it was founded he had the advantage of great authority, which he quoted. He declared that he saw nothing in the war to occasion our despair, if we conducted it on principles by which we might be enabled entirely to clear the sea-coast, and have, at the same time, a large proportion of our army, now in Portugal, disposable at home or elsewhere, for such objects as we desired to obtain. The vote for the two millions might, if applicable to these views, prove very beneficial; for no service could be more important than to sweep the French, as we might do with one effort, from the neighbourhood of Cadiz, and clear the whole Mediterranean coast from their intrusion.

"The resolution was then put and carried."

On the 4th of May, I gave notice of a motion for an account of the quantity of French silks imported into this country under licence. The effect of this system has on one or two occasions been brought under the notice of the reader, as encouraging the French Navy, by encouraging their shipping whilst our own laboured under every species of discouragement.

On the statement of Mr. Rose, Vice-President of the Board of Trade, that he had no objection to the motion,

I then said that, if agreeable to the House, I would at once proceed with it, and adverted to the fact that large quantities of French silks were openly exposed for sale in this country to the prejudice of our manufacturers, to whom not the slightest concession was offered in return. Whether rightly or wrongly, it was the established policy of the legislature to prevent the importation of French manufactured goods, but the licence to do so to a small extent had been construed into a licence to import to any amount, and that without the necessary introduction through the Customhouse. I had been credibly informed that silks, to the value of several hundred thousand pounds, were at that moment lying in the river, whilst the only clause in the licences under which these goods were suffered to be imported, and which went to secure any reciprocity whatever to this country, was one requiring that sugar or coffee, to the value of 5*l.* per ton burden, should be exported in lieu of these rich manufactured goods of the enemy. If this were the policy of our ministry at the present period of unexampled distress to the manufacturing interests, the great dissatisfaction of the manufacturers was by no means surprising.

The correctness of the statement being denied by Mr. Rose, I remarked that if no silk goods had really been imported, the return would effectually show this, and as effectually calm any dissatisfaction that might prevail. After some further unimportant discussion, the motion was agreed to.

On the order of the day for the third reading of the Sinecure Offices Bill (June 15th), I expressed my conviction of the propriety of abolishing all unnecessary offices during the present state of the country, feeling persuaded that sinecures were the bond of union which held parties together in that House, and that if sinecures did not exist, much more attention would be paid to public expenditure.   I did not so much object to the expense which necessarily devolved on the public, as to the influence which the power of giving sinecures gave to the ministry for the time being.

The Parliament being shortly afterwards dissolved, my explanations, to the electors of Westminster relative to the conduct I had deemed right to pursue in Parliament were comprised in the following letters : —

"Portman Square, 28th September, 1812.

"GENTLEMEN,—Being conscious that I have not used the trust reposed in me to my private advantage, or to promote the interests of those with whom I am connected by the bonds of consanguinity or friendship, and that I have no personal object to attain, I shall venture to submit my conduct to the scrutiny it must undergo, on presenting myself with a view of again becoming one of the representatives of this great city ; an honour which I do not aspire to from a vain notion that I possess the qualifications requisite to perform its duties, otherwise than by acting uniformly according to the best of my judgment, uninfluenced by considerations of a personal nature.   Should it appear, however, that I have erred, I am ready to assign the reasons which have determined my vote on every occasion.

" It is unnecessary to apprise you, Gentlemen, who are so well acquainted with the fact, that it is impossible for an individual, unconnected with either party, to succeed in any measure which has for its object a diminution of the means of corruption, or, in other words, the power of rewarding those who are base enough to support men in office, regardless of their measures. Had the list of places and pensions, possessed by the members of the House of Commons and their relations, been granted, which list I moved for shortly after my return to Parliament, the public would long ago have been convinced that sinecures ought not to be considered, as they generally are, a burden of a known amount. It has ever been my opinion that their abolition alone would relieve the Crown from the thraldom in which it is held ; and restore the depreciating currency, by promoting the proper inquiry into the general application of the public money, particularly as to the sums demanded for our enormous and disproportionate military establishment.

"I have frequently stated, without avail, that simply by enforcing the acts relative to prize concerns, two-thirds of the navy now employed would be more efficient than the whole is, under the mortification of finding the fruits of their toil, and often more, taken for the mere condemnation of legal captures ! History shows, without the example of the House of Commons, that this is not the way to stimulate men to undergo fatigue, and encounter that kind of danger, from which no honour is to be derived. On this subject I have not been able to induce the House to look at the proofs which I held in my hand, and offered to produce. I am averse to trespass on your time, though I feel that I have material points to explain ; but these I shall defer to a more fit opportunity.

"I am, however, anxious to add, that my absence lately, on occasions when you have had a right to expect my attendance, has been occasioned solely by ill health, and not by a disposition to tamper with ministers for employment, even in the execution of important plans which I had suggested ; and which, if prosecuted on a fit scale, would afford France full employment in her own defence, instead of suffering her troops to employ themselves in the subjugation of our allies, by whom they are paid and maintained !

"Whether I am returned to Parliament or not, as soon as I shall have tried every means to promote measures which, if disclosed at present, would prove highly prejudicial to the public interests, I pledge myself to prove to the country, that ten millions sterling may annually be saved, and that the relative military force of England will be increased.

" Viewing your exertions in the cause of freedom and the purity of election with that admiration which they so justly deserve,

" I have the honour to be, Gentlemen,

" Respectively, your obedient servant,

" COCHRANE.'

" Portman Square, Sept. 30, 1812.

" GENTLEMEN,— Since I had the honour of addressing you, by letter, at your last meeting, I have been informed by the public prints and otherwise that some gentlemen deemed it a material omission that I had neglected to state my opinions therein relative to Parliamentary Reform,—a course which I adopted, perhaps erroneously, as most respectful to the Committee for promoting the Purity of Election ; under the conviction that they would judge of the future by the past, and not by professions. Now, however, to clear up this doubt, if any, after reflection, remains on their minds, I hereby pledge myself to vote on all occasions for Reform, from a persuasion that the ruin of the country can be averted by that means only. I will likewise support every measure for the abolition of sinecures, which form the bond of union in the House of Commons against the interests of the people. Indeed, reflection impresses this fact so strongly on my mind, that I am disposed to think, if the advocates for Parliamentary Reform were to direct their efforts first against these glaring evils, that an efficient Reform would not be so far distant as the difference of sentiments amongst its advocates unhappily indicates.

" As to the Catholic Question, Gentlemen, it is proper to inform you that so long as its inquisitorial auricular confession and its principles so favourable to despotism prevailed on the Continent, I was hostile to it ; but that I am now inclined to grant the claims of the Catholics of Ireland, provided that they are content to receive the privileges of Englishmen, and to relinquish their predilection in favour of the jurisdiction of the Pope, which, however, they seem anxious to establish in that part of these kingdoms.

" Having said thus much on the most important questions that occur to me, I have only to add, relative to the objection made to a naval officer being a representative for Westminster (which I conclude is meant to extend to all other parts of the kingdom) that one half of the taxes levied on the people of England is disbursed on the navy— for objects which the ability of all the civil members of Parliament cannot detect to be erroneous from the inspection of accounts. Neither are they judges of the means best calculated to give protection to trade, and annoy the enemy by that mode of warfare to which England must at last resort.

" I had nearly omitted to notice that I am no advocate for flogging ; although I maintain, from a knowledge of fact, that your fleets could not be governed at present if the power did not exist,— a power which will cease to be abused when Parliamentary influence shall cease to place incompetent persons in command, and that in a great measure depends upon your exertions.

" I have the honour to be,

" Gentlemen,

" Your most humble obedient servant,

" Cochrane."

The concluding paragraph of this letter will bear comment, even in our day. The appointment of officers to commands ought to be regulated less by interest than *desert*. The truth of this is now practically admitted in other departments of the State, but unhappily the Admiralty, to which is confided our only protection from invasion, is, to a great extent, looked upon as a ministerial patronage preserve, and to this supposed necessity the national safety may one day be sacrificed. It has been urged, in defence of the system, that it is a matter of little consequence, for that steam having bridged the Channel, invasion is only a question of a few hours, whoever may be in command of our ships. This I deny. If our ships are in a fit condition, and properly commanded, it is as easy to destroy the enemy's "bridge" as ever it was, and we shall be as much at liberty to use our own bridge as in former days.

If the Admiralty could be freed from its political trammels, there is no question but that those who direct its affairs would be generally guided in their appointments *by merit alone.* That it is not so, is a proof that, under the unfortunate prevalence of political influence and patronage, no fair and well-understood system of promotion can be established. Hence boys and subordinate officers, if destitute of influence, have no stimulus to acquiring a knowledge of their profession. Far otherwise, for whatever may be their proficiency or services, the only certainty they have is that some one with more influence and perhaps inferior claims may be promoted over their heads. It is not reasonable to suppose that such a system can produce energetic captains or admirals, except by accident.

As one ship well officered and manned is more effective than two of an opposite description, a defined and well-regulated system of promotion upon which all can rely will cost less to the nation, and become the most economical as well as the most effective. The true strength of the navy is not in the multitude of ships, but in the energies and alacrity of officers and crews ; and the repression of these qualities by a false system of political influence, renders a double force requisite for the accomplishment of the vital objects of the naval service.   This is as much a waste of power as the system itself is *want of power*.

The necessity of wholesome stimulating encouragement was deeply felt in the wars consequent on the French Revolution, and it will be felt in future wars whenever they arise.   No one unacquainted with the matter can imagine how much was lost during those wars from a total disregard of the fitness of individuals appointed by political influence.   The subordinate officers appointed to ships of war were frequently so incompetent as to paralyse the exertions even of the most able commanders, who could not be expected to sustain the fatigue of being always on deck.   For my own part, I was so annoyed by the description of persons attempted to be palmed upon me, that, as I have somewhere else said, I preferred going to sea with midshipmen of my own training, making them perform the duties of lieutenants, rather than run the risk of receiving such lieutenants as were frequently appointed to situations in active frigates, through aristocratic or political influence. I am sorry the names of my midshipmen have for the most part escaped my memory, but I may point to three of my own making — the late Lord Napier, Captain Marryat, and the present gallant Admiral Sir Houston Stewart.   These were my officers in Basque Roads, where I had only one lieutenant.   On quitting Plymouth in the *Impérieuse* to undertake that perilous duty, I sailed with *one lieutenant only*, to avoid the encumbrance of persons in whom I feared to repose confidence.

To return to my subject. On my re-election for Westminster, I published a long address to my constituents. From this I shall only adduce the following extracts :—

" GENTLEMEN, — Being unable to convey in words the sensations I experience in reflecting on the manner in which you have returned me to Parliament, I shall leave it to you, who are capable of such acts, to estimate my feelings.

" Gentlemen, no part of the cant of the times seems to me more hypocritical than the declamation by party-men against what they term the ' overwhelming influence of the Crown ; ' when the fact is notorious to us all that the ruling faction in Parliament seize the offices of state and share them amongst themselves. If a doubt as to this truth exist in the mind of any one, let him reflect on the language of the parties themselves, ' Such an administration cannot stand.' And why, Gentlemen ?—not because the royal protection has been withdrawn, but because a sufficient number do not agree as to the division of the spoil. Our liberties in these days are not in danger from violent and open exercise of regal authority ; such acts, being free from the deception practised by the mock representatives of the people, would not be tolerated for an instant. No, Gentlemen, it is by the House of Commons alone that the Constitution is subverted, the prerogatives of the Crown usurped, the rights of the people trampled upon.

" Gentlemen, I shall not attempt to enumerate the decisions of the late House of Commons, — these stamp little credit on the memory of the principal actors, who cannot escape from the contempt of posterity, as may, from their insignificance, the nameless individuals who composed their corrupt majorities. The *effects*, however, of this system of corruption may be thus briefly stated; the prolongation of war, the increase of the national debt, the depreciation of our currency, the disappearance of our coin, the stagnation of our commerce, and the consequent unexampled embarrassment of our manufactures.

" Hurtful, however, as the measures pursued have been, our total neglect of others has proved still more prejudicial; for whilst France has inflicted on us the evils of war, intimidating surrounding states into compliance with her views, we, who have possessed facilities to direct every portion of our force to unknown points within the extensive range of 2000 miles of unprotected shore, have never even made a demonstration with intention to disturb the enemy's projects and force him to keep his legions at home, but have left him at full liberty to prosecute his plans at the expense of our allies, or in the way most conducive to his interests; and, surely, none could suit him better than to fix the little army of England in the centre of the Peninsula, where its movements are not of a desultory nature, and where, admitting the great ability of its commander, a comparatively small portion of the enemy's force is fully adequate to counteract its *known movements!* What part of these kingdoms would be secure from attack if the French possessed a naval superiority, with only 20,000 troops at their disposal? It is obvious that there must be in every district a force equal to that which the enemy could bring against it.

" Gentlemen, I cannot avoid stating a fact to you which I have often offered to prove at the bar of the late House of Commons, namely, that whilst our commerce has decreased, that kind of trade which is most beneficial to a state has augmented on the shores of the enemy, in a prodigious ratio; and the produce of the northern and southern provinces is freely interchanged under the protection of the abuses of our Admiralty Courts, which afford better security than all the batteries of France. The plain reason for this is, that each of the numerous coasting vessels must, for the benefit of the court, be separately condemned, at an expense greater than was formerly demanded for the adjudication of an Indiaman! Gentlemen, the rapacity of these courts is frequently not satisfied by appropriating the *whole* proceeds to themselves, but the captors are compelled *to pay* an additional sum for thus performing a service to their country. Gentlemen, that you may have a correct notion of a proctor's bill, I take the liberty of inclosing one for your inspection, which, I assure you, may be considered very moderate, being only six fathoms and a quarter long, or thirty-seven feet six inches, whereas I now possess others that extend to fifty feet; but I prefer sending this to your committee, as it is the one produced by myself in the House of Commons, and by the venerable Earl of Suffolk in the House of Lords; the exhibition of which was pronounced by the present Lord Chancellor Eldon (the brother of the judge of the Admiralty Court) to be a species of *mummery* never before witnessed within those walls, and altogether unbecoming the gravity of that branch of the legislature.

"The example of the industrious bee demonstrates by the laws of nature that the drone is not to live at the expense of the community, notwithstanding what the Whigs have said of sinecures being held by tenure equal to that of freehold property."

From the preceding incomplete enumeration of my parliamentary efforts, it will be apparent that as regarded my profession I had not been idle; but every step I took appeared to remove me farther from my chance of being again employed. Notwithstanding that in those days the language of members frequently passed those bounds which the modern practice of the House of Commons has prescribed, in no instance, that I am aware of, could I be accused of intemperate treatment of any subject under discussion. Independently of the sore point of Lord Gambier's court-martial,

which was no act of mine — my offending could have
been none other than the one of attempting to rouse
the authorities to an effort for the amelioration of the
navy, for objects which under the old system were
notoriously not achieved, viz. *crippling the energies of
the enemy.* It was in the circle of my political opponents considered that as member for Westminster I had
no right to interfere with naval matters — *because I
was a post-captain!*

It is, nevertheless, a singular fact — and one which
cannot be said of any other officer of my then standing as a post-captain — that from 1801 to 1812, — on
no occasion, not even for a single day was any vessel
of war — save the one in which my pennant flew —
once placed under my command, or once offered to
me, with the single exception of the affair of Basque
Roads, when I was for a few days appointed to or-
ganise and make use of a flotilla of explosion and
fireships, the command of which *had been declined
by several other officers to whom it had been proposed,*
and then thrust on me contrary to my inclination.

That one cause of my being thus passed over was
my unceasing advocacy of the navy, admits of no doubt.
It must be apparent that my motions relative to the
Courts of Admiralty raised the enmity of all who profited
by their abuses, and these were neither few nor unin-
fluential, — that my repeated invectives against sinecures
and pensions arrayed against me all who benefited by
them—whether personally or through their connections.
It is, indeed, not too much to say, that those interested
in sinecures and pensions comprised in those days a

majority of the House of Commons, who stood up for their own interest at the national expense as for a right.

My motion respecting the treatment of French prisoners, and especially my declaration of the probable motive for erecting the prison of Dartmoor in a dreary, desolate, and unhealthy position, such as ought not to have been selected for convicts, served to increase the ministerial anger. Nor was the evil abated. On a second visit to the place, I encountered a spectacle which made me ashamed of my country.

The reader will remember the action between the *Pallas* and *Minerve* in Basque Roads, as narrated in the first volume. My gallant adversary in that frigate was Captain Collett, who kept the deck after every one of his crew had been driven below by our fire, which, as the *Minerve* had taken the ground, swept her decks. My gallant opponent, however, kept the deck, or rather stood on a gun, with as much *sang-froid* as though we had been firing a salute. On our becoming entangled with the *Minerve's* rigging, he raised his hat, with all the politeness of a Frenchman of the old school, and bowed to me, a compliment which I returned. Judge of my surprise, when refused admission into the prison at Dartmoor, and prowling about its out-offices, at finding my gallant enemy *located in the stall of a stable*, he having been recently made prisoner. I promised to use my best endeavour to get him removed, and on my arrival in London did so. I believe with effect, but to what other locality has passed from my memory.

There is no necessity to enumerate other matters already familiar to the reader in order to show the estimation in which I must have been held by those who opposed what they considered innovations, though they must have been as well aware of the evils of a rotten system as myself.

CHAP. XXXVI.

MY MARRIAGE.

ROMANTIC CHARACTER OF MY MARRIAGE.—UNFORESEEN DIFFICULTIES.—
FAMILY RESULTS.

THE event recorded in this chapter is the most important and the happiest of my life, in its results, — the " silver lining " to the " cloud," viz. my marriage with the Countess of Dundonald. It has been said by a Scottish writer that " the Cochranes have long been noted for an original and dashing turn of mind, which was sometimes called genius—sometimes eccentricity." How far this may be true of my ancestors, I shall not stay to inquire. Laying no claim to the genius, I however dispute the eccentricity in my own case, notwithstanding that appearances, so far as relates to my past life, may be somewhat against me. Without a particle of romance in my composition, my life has been one of the most romantic on record, and the circumstances of my marriage are not the least so.

Early in the year 1812, it was my good fortune to make the acquaintance of the orphan daughter of a family of honourable standing in the Midland Counties, Miss Katherine Corbett Barnes. In consequence of the loss of her parents, the lady had been placed during her minority under the guardianship of her first cousin, Mr. John Simpson of Portland Place and also of Fairlorn House, in the county of Kent, of which county he was then High Sheriff. The story is the old one. Shortly after my introduction to this lady I made proposals of marriage, and was accepted.

But here an unexpected difficulty arose. I was at that time residing with my uncle, the Hon. Basil Cochrane, who had realised a large fortune in the East Indies. My attachment — though not my engagement — to my *fiancée* had by some means reached him, and he at once attempted to divert my purpose by proposing to me a marriage with the only daughter of an Admiralty Court official who had realised a very large fortune by the practices which have already been made familiar to the reader.

I cannot describe the repugnance which I felt even to the proposition, and pointed out to my uncle the impossibility of marrying the daughter of one of those persons whom I had so severely denounced; adding that not only would such a step be a deviation from those principles which ought to guide a well-regulated mind in the selection of a wife, but must be destructive of my public character, which would be so clearly sacrificed for money, that it would render me contemptible to my constituents, and would prevent my again meriting public confidence. His reply was brief and caustic. "Please yourself: nevertheless, my fortune and the money of the wife I have chosen for you, would go far towards reinstating future Earls of Dundonald in their ancient position as regards wealth."

This conversation was communicated to the lady to whom I was affianced, on whom I urged a consent to a secret marriage, — a proposition in which she refused to acquiesce. My uncle, however, continuing firm in his resolves, I at length prevailed upon her to overcome her repugnance, and we were, on the 8th of August 1812, married at Annan in Scotland.

On my return my uncle again renewed the subject, and one morning, during our walk he informed me that he had made his will, leaving me one half his fortune. He, however declared, that compliance with his wish as to my marriage with the heiress of the Admiralty Court official was essential to its eventual confirmation. On arguing this, on the same grounds as before, he observed that some other person of wealth must be sought for, as his object was to retrieve the family fortnne. Meanwhile he required my assurance that I would not marry without his sanction. Compliance with this was declined for the best of all reasons, that I was already married.

The fact of our marriage was not long concealed, and I did not inherit a shilling of my uncle's wealth, for which loss however, I had a rich equivalent in the acquisition of a wife whom no amount of wealth could have purchased. A yet more singular sequel has to be told. On the discovery of the marriage, my uncle, though then an old man, also married, and was easily made to believe that non-payment of a large sum due to him from Government, on account of some contracts undertaken before he quitted India, had been delayed on account of my parliamentary opposition to the Ministry. This may or may not have been the case, but it induced my uncle to request that our future association might be less frequent. An intimation followed by the still more questionable course of his requesting an interview with Lord Liverpool, for the purpose of informing his lordship of the step he had taken with regard to myself, and assuring him that he had never countenanced my conduct in Parliament. Singularly enough, my uncle's demands upon the Government were soon afterwards settled.

It was my wish here to have spoken of my wife's devotedness to me amidst the many trying circumstances in which, I have been placed. They do not however, come within the scope of this volume, as regards their chronological order, I therefore postpone their narration.

CHAP. XXXVII.

NAVAL ABUSES.

Soon after the commencement of the session of 1813, I made an attempt to direct the attention of Parliament to the administration of the funds of Greenwich Hospital, in the hope of restoring them to their legitimate purpose of rewards for wounds and long service in the navy. At this period their perversion had become notorious. In place of old retired seamen, not a few of the wards were occupied, and pensions enjoyed, by men who had never been in the navy at all, but were thus provided for, to the exclusion of worn-out sailors, by the influence of patrons upon whose political interest they had a claim.

As the only way to arrive at the full extent of the

evil, in the absence of definite knowledge as to the specific documents required, I moved in the House of Commons, on the 11th of March 1813, for *all papers* relative to the chest at Greenwich.

The motion was met by a suggestion from the Speaker—that " if those papers *had been* laid on the table during the present session there would be no difficulty in granting them, but that if not, I must *specify* the particular papers required." This, of course, I was unable to do, but gave my reason for the motion as follows.

" Lord Cochrane then proceeded to express his wish that the state of the funds in Greenwich Hospital should be known, in order to ascertain whether they were sufficient to make provision for that great body of seamen and petty officers who would be entitled to be placed on the establishment at the conclusion of the present war. The House, he was satisfied, could have no objection to this information being laid before them. One of his reasons for moving for it now was, the fact of his having learned that it was in contemplation to devote the Droits of the Admiralty to the current services of the year. The noble lord concluded by moving, ' That there be laid before this House an account showing the revenues of Greenwich Hospital and the sources whence they are derived, also the disbursements for management and the number of pensioners in each class; distinguishing those maintained within the hospital from the out-pensioners; also an account of the number admitted in each year since 1800, and the amount of the pensioners at that time maintained within and without the hospital.'

" Lord A. Hamilton seconded the motion.

" The Chancellor of the Exchequer said it was perfectly new to him that there was any intention to devote the Droits of Admiralty in the manner stated by the noble lord. He knew of no right which existed in His Majesty's Government to make such an application of those Droits, and if they were so applied, it must be considered entirely as arising from an act of royal bounty. The noble lord had adduced no reasonable ground for the production of the papers for which he had moved. Whether they were of an objectionable description or not he was unable to judge; but he could not see why the table of the House was to be crowded with useless and unnecessary documents. He should, therefore, move the previous question."

It was true that my having heard of the intention of the Government with relation to the Droits of Admiralty might not be a parliamentary ground for their production, but it was a ground for asking the question. Had I, however, stated my real motives, the only effect would have been prompt denial of the fact by all interested in the continuance of the abuse, which could only be proved by the papers themselves. I therefore endeavoured to procure them on other grounds.

" Lord Cochrane persisted in the propriety of the House having before them the information for which he had moved. There never was a period at which it was more desirable that some steps should be adopted to ameliorate the situation of His Majesty's navy. Those brave men of which it was composed were subject to the most heartrending oppressions; and, in his opinion, had every cause to complain of their situations. After having been released from the labours of a long and arduous service, they were not, as they richly deserved, suffered to return to the bosoms of their families, but were kept almost to the last hour of their existence in a constant and unremitting state of servitude, unless where they determined to sacrifice that reward which their country had provided for them as a consolation for the buffeting they had undergone to purchase their discharge.

" This had frequently been the case ; and he had received

constant applications complaining of this species of hardship. Two men had lately applied to him, who, after a service of seventeen years and a half, as petty officers, had been sent to perform that most scandalous of all duties — harbour duty; where there was no distinction whatever between petty officers and private men; and, who, rather than submit to be longer disgraced, had expended 80*l.* or 90*l.* each, to obtain their discharge. These men were entitled to pensions of 12*l.* or 14*l.*, a year; and he was convinced that there was not an insurance office in town that would not have given, at their age, for the sums they had paid for their discharge, annuities equal to their pensions. Instead of Greenwich being a source of advantage and reward to aged seamen it was made a means of recruiting for the navy.

" Unless some alteration was made in this system he should feel it his duty to move for leave to bring in a bill to limit the service of the navy. The House, he was convinced, would see the necessity of pointing out some term at which a seaman's service was to be brought to a conclusion, and at which he might have some hope of resting his frame, after an arduous and gallant service, in the lap of domestic happiness and retirement. In consequence of the present arrangements, men were employed who were absolutely incapable of performing their duty, and in his own ship he had found men who, if he had the power, he would much rather have discharged than have suffered to remain on board. In other instances he knew men, who had been invalided three times and sent into harbour duty, volunteer into active service three times, in order to avoid that disgrace, and finally die amidst the roar of battle, when their tottering limbs were scarce able to support them to their quarters.

" Mr. Rose could not see that any grounds whatever had been laid for the noble lord's motion. The statement into which he had entered tended to censure the practice that at present existed with respect to the discharge of seamen. He recollected that this subject had been before under discussion in the House, and that it was then stated that the present practice had been introduced in order to exempt the men from the necessity of finding two substitutes, under which they before laboured. This question, however, had no connection with the motion, which referred entirely to the management of Greenwich Hospital. He believed that the affairs of that department were as well and regularly conducted as any other branch of the public service.

"Lord A. Hamilton said he understood the noble lord complained of the present system by which the allowance received by seamen from Greenwich Hospital was rendered useless to them, in consequence of the large sums which they were compelled to pay for their release.

"Mr. Wynn confessed he could see no connection between the matter of the speech and the motion itself of the noble lord. As the case, however, to which he had called the attention of the House, was undoubtedly hard, it was very desirable that information should be communicated in some mode.

"The previous question was then put and carried, when Lord Cochrane immediately gave notice that he would, that day month, move for leave to bring in a bill to limit the service of the navy."

There was not, in fact, much apparent connection between my speech and the motion, because the Speaker had prohibited me from making the motion in such a way as would establish the connection. Nevertheless, that both the House and the Ministry well understood my aim, was evident from the fact, that the Secretary of the Treasury was sufficiently alarmed by the attempt which had been made, to induce him to come down to the House *after 1 had quitted it*, and at the last moment of its sitting, in order to defend the Admiralty from the effects of a motion which had been refused !

" MR. CROKER, before the House adjourned, rose to make
a few observations upon what had fallen from the noble lord
in the early part of the evening, when he did not happen to
be present. If, however, he had correctly understood what
had fallen from that noble lord, he begged leave to say, that
the noble lord had been wholly misinformed with respect to
the sums of money taken instead of substitutes for the navy.
The fact was, that the grossest frauds having been practised
upon the poor men under pretence of providing substitutes
for them, the Admiralty had come to the resolution of receiving a certain sum of money from them, and to find substitutes."

Notwithstanding the want of connection, Mr. Croker
perfectly understood the point to which I was coming
in the end, and hence his taking the course of flatly
contradicting the premises after I had quitted the
House. My early connection with this gentleman has
been stated in the first volume*, as well as the fact,
that believing in his sincerity as an ardent opponent of
administrative abuses of all kinds, I had, during our
acquaintance, without reserve, and in the belief that I
had an able coadjutor, unbosomed to him my views
with regard to the abuses of naval administration. Now
that he was in an official position which required him
to defend *all abuses*, and considering that I stood
almost alone in exposing them, he was in possession
of all my plans of action ! There can, however,
be no better proof of the soundness of my views,
than the fact, that although he had previously been
made well aware of my line of argument, he never
attempted to meet me by argument, but always by

* Page 209.

flat contradiction of my facts. We shall presently come to some remarkable instances of this nature.

On the 2nd of June I presented to the House a petition from the inhabitants of Manchester, a petition complaining of ill usage, false imprisonment, and malicious prosecution, whilst peaceably assembled to petition Parliament for a reform. It is unnecessary to advert to these allegations, as they are now an historical record, but that the people of Manchester should have selected me as the exponent of their grievances, only added to the ministerial aversion with which I was regarded.

On this occasion, an attempt was made by Mr. Bathurst to procure the rejection of the petition, on the ground that the petitioners, if aggrieved, *" could seek redress in a court of law, but that the House could not afford them relief !"* There was something so heartless in such an attempt that it called up some members by no means hearty in the popular cause.

" MR. WHITBREAD supported the motion, contending that to men in the circumstances of the petitioners (some of them being now prisoners for debt), it was a mere mockery and taunt to tell them that the courts of law were open to them, where they might bring actions for malicious prosecutions It reminded him of a saying of the late Mr. Horne Tooke, who, on being told that the courts were open to all classes, replied, " Yes, and so is the London Tavern, if you have money enough." As the petition was couched in respectful terms, he thought it would be setting a bad precedent to reject it; it was usual, even though Parliament could not interfere, to see the magistrates did not exceed the bounds of their jurisdiction.

" MR. WYNN observed that the House had been at all times peculiarly jealous that no obstructions should be given to the exercise of the right of petitioning; and as the present complaint related to an alleged obstruction of that nature, it ought to be received.

" The petition was ordered to lie on the table.

The circumstances which brought upon me the subsequent vengeance of the Admiralty will be found in two debates which took place in the House of Commons shortly before its prorogation — the one on the 5th, and the other on the 8th of July 1813.

As the subject matter of these debates possesses great naval interest, and as the causes which led to them are not wholly inoperative in our day, I shall adduce them at some length, not so much for my own vindication, as in the light of history teaching by example.

The subject matter of the debates being sufficiently included in the reports of the time, very little comment will suffice.

" LORD COCHRANE rose, pursuant to notice, to bring forward his motion for increasing the remuneration and limiting the service of seamen. He thought it was his duty to lay before the House the reasons why our seamen preferred the *merchant foreign service* * to that of their own country, to enter which they discovered a very great reluctance.

" The facts by which he meant to prove this he had compressed into one resolution ; as he was anxious that when the members of that House retired from their Parliamentary duties, they might consider these facts at their leisure, and satisfy themselves as to the correctness of the statement, in order that when they met again they might have no hesitation in adopting such propositions, the object of which would

* The American merchant service.

be the redress of those grievances which were the subject of it. As he did not conceive that any objection could be made to the mode of proceeding he had adopted, he would not occupy the time of the House any longer than by reading the resolution. The noble lord then read the following resolution :—

" ' That the honour of His Majesty's Crown, the glory and safety of the country, do, in a great degree, depend on the maintenance, especially in time of war, *of an efficient naval establishment:*

" ' That during the late and present war with France, splendid victories have been gained by His Majesty's fleets and vessels of war, over a vast superiority in the number of guns and men, and in the weight of metal :

" ' That these victories thus obtained were acquired by the skill and intrepidity of the officers, and by the energy, zeal, and valour of the crews :

" ' That during the present war with the United States of America, His Majesty's naval service has, in several instances, experienced defeat, in a manner and to a degree unexpected by this House, by the Admiralty, and by the country at large :

" ' That the cause of this lamentable effect is not any superiority possessed by the enemy, either in skill, valour, nor the well-known difference in the weight of metal, which heretofore has been deemed unimportant; but arises chiefly from the decay and heartless state of the crews of His Majesty's ships of war compared with their former energy and zeal; and compared, on the other hand, with the freshness and vigour of the crews of the enemy :

" ' That it is an indisputable fact, that long and unlimited confinement to a ship, as well as to any other particular spot, and especially when accompanied with the diet necessarily that of ships of war, and a deprivation of the usual recreations of men, seldom fails to produce a rapid decay of the physical powers, the natural parent, in such cases, of despondency of mind :

" ' That the late and present war against France (including a short interval of peace, in which the navy was not paid off) have lasted upwards of twenty years, and that a new naval war has recently commenced :

" ' That the duration of the term of service in His Majesty's navy is absolutely without any limitation, and that there is no mode provided for by law for the fair and impartial discharging of men therefrom; and that, according to the present practice decay, disease, incurable wounds, or death, can alone procure the release of any seaman of whatever age or whatever length of service :

" ' That seamen who have become wholly unfit for active service are, in place of being discharged and rewarded according to their merits and their sufferings, transferred to ships on harbour duty, where they are placed under officers wholly unacquainted with their character and former conduct, who have no other means to estimate them but on the scale of their remaining activity and bodily strength ; where there is no distinction made between the former petty officer and common seamen, between youth and age, and where those worn-out and wounded seamen who have spent the best part of their lives, or have lost their health in the service of their country, have to perform a duty more laborious than that of the convict felons in the dockyards — and with this remarkable distinction, that the labours of the latter have a known termination :

" ' That though the seamen thus transferred and thus employed have all been invalided, they are permitted to re-enter ships of war on actual service; and that such is the nature of the harbour duty, that many, in order to escape from it, do so re-enter—there being no limitation as to the number of times of their being invalided, or that of their re-entering :

" ' That to obtain a discharge from the navy by purchase, the sum of 80l. sterling is required by the Admiralty, which, together with other expenses, amounts to twenty times the original bounty, and is equal to all that

a seaman can save with the most rigid economy during the
average period in which he is capable of service; that this
sum is demanded alike from men of all ages and of all lengths
of servitude—from those pensioned for wounds, and also from
those invalided for harbour duty; thus converting the funds
of Greenwich, and the reward of former services, into a
means of recruiting the navy:

" 'That such is the horror which seamen have of this
useless prolongation of their captivity, that those who are
able, in order to escape from it, actually return into the
hands of Government all those fruits of their toil which
formerly they looked to as the means of some little comfort
in their old age:

" 'That, besides these capital grievances—tending to perpetuate the impress service, there are others worthy the
serious attention of this House; that the petty officers and
seamen on board of His Majesty's ships and vessels of war
though absent on foreign stations for many years, receive no
wages until their return home, and are, of course, deprived
of the comforts which those wages, paid at short intervals,
would procure them; that this is now very severely felt,
owing to the recent practice of postponing declarations of
war until long after the war has been actually begun, by
which means the navy is deprived, under the name of Droits,
of the first fruits and greatest proportions of the prize-money
to which they have heretofore been entitled; and thus, and
by the exactions of the Courts of Admiralty, the proportion
of captures which at last devolves to the navy is much too
small to produce those effects which formerly were so beneficial to the country:

" 'That while their wages are withheld from them abroad,
when paid at home, which, to prevent desertion, usually
takes place on the day before they sail out again, having no
opportunity to go on shore, they are compelled to buy slops
of Jews on board, or to receive them from Government at
fifteen per cent. higher than their acknowledged value; and
being paid in bank-notes they are naturally induced to

exchange them for money current in other countries, and which, it is notorious, they do at an enormous loss:

" ' That the recovery of the pay and prize-money by the widows, children, or relatives of seamen is rendered as difficult as possible ; and, finally, the regulations with regard to passing of the examination requisite previous to an admission to the benefits of Greenwich Hospital, subject the disabled seaman to so many difficulties, and to such long delays, that, in numerous cases, he is compelled to beg his way in the pursuit of a boon, the amount of which, even in the event of loss of both eyes or both arms, does not equal that of the common board-wages of a footman:

" ' That one of the best and strongest motives to meritorious conduct in military and naval men is the prospect of promotion ; while such promotion is, at the same time, free of additional expense to the nation; but that in the British naval service this powerful and honourable incitement has ceased to exist, seeing that the means of rewarding merit has been almost wholly withdrawn from naval commanders-in-chief under whose inspection services are performed ; in fact it is a matter of perfect notoriety that it has become next to impossible for a meritorious subordinate petty officer or seaman to rise to the rank of lieutenant ; that in scarcely any instance promotion or employment is now to be obtained in the navy through any other means than what is called parliamentary interest, that is to say,—the corrupt influence of boroughs:

" ' That owing to these causes chiefly the crews of his Majesty's ships of war have in general become in a very considerable degree worn out and disheartened and inadequate to the performance, with their wonted energy and effect, of those arduous duties which belong to the naval service ; and that hence has arisen, by slow and imperceptible degrees, the enormous augmentation of our ships and men, while the naval force of our enemies is actually much less than in former years:

" ' That, as a remedy for this alarming national evil, it is absolutely necessary that the grievances of the navy, some of which only have been recited above, should be redressed; that a limitation of the duration of service should be adopted, accompanied with the certainty of a suitable reward, not subject to any of the effects of partiality; and that measures should be taken to cause the comfortable situations in the ordinary of the dockyards, the places of porters, messengers, &c. &c., in and about the offices belonging to the sea service, the under-wardens of the naval forests, &c., to be bestowed on meritorious decayed petty officers and seamen, instead of being, as they now generally are, the wages of corruption in borough elections:

" ' That this House, convinced that a decrease of energy of character cannot be compensated by an augmentation of the number of ships, guns, and men, which is, at the same time a grievous pecuniary burden to the country, will, at an early period next session, institute an inquiry, by special committee or otherwise, into the matters above stated, and particularly with a view to dispensing suitable rewards to seamen; that they will investigate the state of the fund of Greenwich Hospital, and ascertain whether it is necessary to apply the Droits of the Admiralty and the Droits of the Crown as the natural first means of compensation to those who have acquired them by their valour, their privations, and their sufferings.' "

" SIR FRANCIS BURDETT seconded the resolution."

" MR. CROKER thought that, when the noble lord had adopted his present method of proceeding, he would have acted only consistent with the courtesy of Parliament had he *given notice* * of his intention to those persons whose duty it might be to take part in any discussion. The honourable member said he would have felt obliged by any information the noble lord might have imparted; but though wanting such, he had come unprepared into the House to meet the noble lord's resolution. He should be wanting in his duty if he did not state most positively, that, excepting the tribute of

---

* I had given notice.

just praise, which, in the commencement of his resolution, the noble lord had paid to the gallantry and heroism of our own seamen, *every other part of it was liable to the charge of being wholly unfounded in fact*, or very much indeed exaggerated. The statements those resolutions contained were so astonishing — true it was *less astonishing when coming from the noble lord than from any other person* — but still even from him they were so astonishing, that surely they ought not to have been so suddenly, and with so little preparation, brought under the consideration of that House. There was no one but the noble lord who conceived that the disasters which we had experienced in the course of the present war with the United States were not to be attributed to a superior force on the part of the enemy, but to a decay of all ardour in our seamen in the defence of their country. Was the crew of the *Java* then, who had maintained so stubborn a conquest, dispirited? Was the crew of the *Macedonian* disheartened and reduced by hard-usage to imbecility and cowardice? So far was that from being the fact, that it was in the latter part of the action the spirit of the crew of the *Macedonian* was most conspicuous, that the spirit of her officers and her brave commander was most conspicuous. So little broken was the spirit of that crew which the noble lord had described as utterly heartless and imbecile, that till the very last they met the attacks of the enemy with loud and repeated cheers.

"Now for another fact on which the noble lord had formed his resolution. He had stated that seamen were obliged to purchase their discharge by no less a sum than 80*l.*, no matter what was the condition of the individual. Now he had to state most positively that this was not the case.* The sum specified might, indeed, be *required from able seamen* who wished for their discharge; but the sum of 40*l.* only was required from ordinary seamen; from ordinary seamen transferred to harbour duty, only 30*l.*; from persons who were originally landsmen, not more than 20*l.* And he had to state

* The truth of the matter will appear in the second debate.

further that many persons transferred to harbour duty, and considered unfit for service, were discharged without any consideration whatsoever. The noble lord had stated formerly in the House the case of a harbour duty man who had been obliged to pay 80*l.* for his discharge.

" When the noble lord had thought proper to make that statement, he had answered in his place that he could not take upon him to vouch for the individual case. He had, however, subsequently been at considerable pains to discover the particular case alluded to by the noble lord, and had examined every document in which he thought it could be traced — but in vain — he could find nothing of the kind ; he had then applied to the member for Bedford to procure for him the name of the man from the noble lord, but this had not been done, and he had never had the pleasure of seeing the noble lord since. Now he thought that under such circumstances the noble lord should have abstained from receiving the statement unless he was disposed to give the name of the individual, and thus supply the means of confuting it.

" Our seamen, said the noble lord, were heart-broken ; they would indeed be heart-broken had they heard his resolutions ; that was provided always, though, he retained so much authority with them, as would impart to his unjust assertions, with respect to them, the power of inflicting pain which they would once unquestionably have possessed. They would be heart-broken if the House passed a resolution which constituted the grossest libel that was ever put forth against them. Formerly, said the noble lord, they were full of vigour and life under a better system ; now they were deprived of every comfort, penned up on board of ships which were rendered prisons to them, and their health injured by defective sustenance.

" Now he had to state an improvement in the condition of those men whose hardships the noble lord had deplored, which would enable them to form fair conjectures as to the justice of his statement in general. A practice had been adopted

within these few years of granting seamen leave of absence
on a plan more liberal and better adapted to promote their
comfort than any that had been previously thought of. When
a ship returned from a foreign station, all the men who had
three years pay due to them got leave of absence for three
months, for the purpose of enabling them to visit their
friends; if the individuals were Scotch or Irish the time was
prolonged. This practice was now so well understood, that
every ship's company looked upon it as a matter of right,
and he was ready to say that though ill effects had been expected to result from it, the expectation had been found
delusive. Several officers had anticipated desertion, others a
relaxation of discipline; but, he was happy to have to state,
that so far from their expectations being answered, the men
returned to their duty with their minds refreshed — new
strung, and better fitted for the toils imposed on them by
their duty; and much fewer desertions took place since the
adoption of such a system of indulgence than before it. He
stated this to show what a tissue of false promises, as well as
false inferences, were contained in the resolution of the noble
lord.

"The noble lord's resolution asserted that there was no fair
system of promotion in the navy; that everything was conducted upon a principle of corruption. Was, then, the
commission of the noble lord himself given him upon such a
principle? Did he obtain the red ribbon, which was before
him never given to an individual of his rank, through corruption? Was it through corruption that a relative of the
noble lord's had made his way to the top of his profession,
and had been appointed governor of Guadaloupe? Was it
through corruption that the influence of the noble lord had
had considerable weight in effecting the promotion of those
persons on whose behalf he had used it? He was aware that
an answer to this last question in the affirmative might be
grounded upon the assumption that the naval acquaintance
of the noble lord were persons of little worth, and such as
could owe their promotion to nothing but corruption. But

he who well knew the reverse would not allow him even this miserable refuge. Was the promotion of Captain Duncan the effect of corruption? Were the honours which that gallant officer's father had obtained the result of corruption? The friends of the noble lord had felt the benefit of his interference, and much was it to be wished that it had been confined to promote their wishes, and through them the interest of the country, and had never been mischievously exercised on such occasions as the present. Did not the noble lord recollect, when he had left his ship, that he had been consulted as to who was the fittest to succeed him, and that his recommendation had been acted upon? * If indeed he had never left that ship it would have been well for his own reputation, as it would have been well for the interests of his country. Most heartily did he wish the noble lord had stayed in her to be serviceable to the public instead of coming here to be the reverse. The noble lord loved to deal in generals. He talked loud about corruption, but he wished him to state who paid and who received the wages of corruption.

" He was conscious that he had spoken with much heat, and hoped for the indulgence of the House; but he could not say that he had not meant to reprehend, and that with as much severity as he could use, the conduct of the noble lord; that he did not mean to set in as strong a light as possible the futility of those labours for six months' duration, which had so engrossed the noble lord, that he had been unable to attend his parliamentary duties; and which he now imagined would enable him to call out in triumph to his constituents, 'Behold, if I have appeared to desert my duty, I have only appeared to do so; I have not spent my time in idleness. Here are the fruits of my industry; here is the operose conclusion of my labours, and the debt you, my constituents, suppose me to have contracted, you now find fully liquidated.'

" Now, I beg the House to recollect that these accusations of the noble lord have not been couched in fleeting and evanes-

* For a refutation of this see chap. vii.

cent speech, but have been regularly arranged in a written
document, which it is the wish of the noble lord should be
studied by every member in the leisure which the cessation
of parliamentary duty will allow him. The noble lord, I
contend, has taken a very unfair method of conveying his
opinion; he would have acted more fairly in making them
the subject of a pamphlet. If he had done so, I certainly
have not much time for writing, but out of respect for the
noble lord, I should certainly have answered him, and I
should have been glad of the opportunity of answering him
when I could have used freely those terms which he had deserved should be applied to him. I must express my sanguine
hope that the house will not, by adopting such motions as those
moved by the noble lord, sanction the gross libel which they
contain against the navy, against parliament, and against the
country. I wish to lay aside all little considerations to suppose that the resolutions are not meant to apply more to the
persons now engaged in the management of our naval affairs
than their predecessors; but if it be otherwise, still I wish to
sink any feeling that might be supposed to arise in my mind
in consequence, and to answer the noble lord only as the
defender of that gallant body of men who have stood so long
forward as our firmest bulwark against the vileness of our
foe, and who are well entitled to the warmest feeling of gratitude we can cherish towards them. I hope, therefore, that
if the noble lord does dare to push the House to a division,
that he will be left in a minority such as will not merely
mark their sense, but also their indignation."

The reader will not fail to observe the way in which
the resolution was met by the Secretary of the Admiralty, Mr. Croker. In defiance of the fact that the
notice required by the regulations of the House *had*
been given, Mr. Croker openly accused me of dis-
courtesy for *not having given proper notice !* He then
stated that he was "*unprepared*" to meet the resolu-

tion ; whilst his next words in the same sentence were, that the facts set forth in the resolutions were *positive falsehoods*, " *wholly unfounded in fact !* " This being the mode in which Mr. Croker now chose to meet all unpleasant resolutions relating to the navy when originating with myself, well knowing that *they could neither be contradicted nor controverted !*

In order to show the efficiency of our navy, Mr. Croker then instanced two of our ships, the *Java* and the *Macedonian,* both of which were in a high state of discipline ; but he did not notice the fact of one of those which had been defeated by the enemy from the inefficient state of their crews and the inadequacy of their equipment, to both which facts numbers of officers now living can testify. I do not know whether I am justified in bringing forward an anecdote which I have heard from Sir Charles Napier, who had the misfortune to command one of these miserable craft ; viz. that expecting shortly to engage a United States frigate which bore down upon him, he sat down and wrote a letter to the Admiralty in case of his capture or death, informing their lordships that his frigate had been lost from inefficiency of her crew and equipment, when, to his surprise, the American sheered off, and he was in no condition to follow. I have no doubt the gallant admiral will repeat the anecdote to any one whom it may interest.

Mr. Croker stated, that so far from the Admiralty demanding 80*l.* for the discharge of a seaman, they only demanded 40*l.*, and sometimes not more than 20*l.* In the course of the debates it will be shown that in some cases the seamen in reality paid 90*l.* The man who made the former statements should not have asserted that mine were *false.* Even the stale trick of "virtuous indignation," the invariable resort of a practised orator when he has nothing better to say, was here out of place, otherwise than to indicate to the partisans of the Government the course to be pursued.

Further, Mr. Croker himself admitted the bad condition of the navy by saying, now that it suited his purpose, " *he had to state an improvement in the condition of the men.*" The instances which he adduced in proof were unfounded in fact or practice, so that my only way to meet Mr. Croker's assertions was of necessity to imitate his example when commenting on mine, viz. to deny them *in toto.*

Mr. Croker's allusion to my own career as an instance of promotion apart from political corruption, was amusing ; the inference being that nothing but actual deeds could possibly command promotion ! His adducing the case of promotion by the exercise of my influence, was pure invention, the rule of the Admiralty being that *no man, whatever his deserts, should be promoted on my recommendation.* In the first volume I gave the instances of Lieut. Parker, my first lieutenant in the *Speedy,* and Lieut. Haswell in the *Pallas* *, for neither of whom could I obtain promotion till, from my presence in the House of Commons, it was no longer deemed politic to withhold it. Even then, in the case of poor Parker, a mock promotion was given which proved his ruin and that of his

* See vol. i. p. 150.

family, who were afterwards plunged in the lowest depths of poverty.

Claptrap of this nature was considered a sufficient reply to my resolutions, which embraced the whole subject of the abuses of naval administration. The object was to mislead the House, ignorant as it was of facts, and to throw doubt on my statements, though these had been carefully based on the clearest evidence.

The oratorical display of Mr. Croker was met by my excellent colleague Sir Francis Burdett. As no opportunity has occurred in the course of this work whereby the reader may judge of the comprehensive nature of his parliamentary efforts over any to which I could make pretension, I will adduce the speech of the honourable baronet on this occasion.

"SIR FRANCIS BURDETT said that the honourable secretary had indulged in a warmth and severity of animadversion which the occasion by no means justified. His noble friend had asserted much, and the honourable gentleman had *denied* much, and that on a very important subject; *but it remained to be seen who was in error.* He was willing to admit that the late period of the session rendered the motion inexpedient; but he conceived that if his noble friend was induced to withdraw it, he would feel himself in duty bound to bring it forward at an early period of the ensuing session, when, of course, the present strong objections to it would be removed.

" The honourable member had taxed his noble friend with exaggeration, but it was impossible to conceive anything more exaggerated *than the whole of the honourable gentleman's speech.* He had stated his noble friend to have described our seamen as having wholly lost the energy and

valour which had once distinguished them. Now, his noble
friend had never so described them. He had stated that
their spirits were *depressed* by longc onfinement and various
other hardships, but he had never stated that their hearts
were subdued, or that when brought into action they did not
forget everything, but that they had their own character and
the character of their country to support.

" The honourable baronet then proceeded to contend that
as it was not denied that in some cases the sum of 80*l.* was
taken for the discharge of a seaman, his noble friend's assertion on that head *had not been refuted,* and went on to
remark on the impropriety of the harbour-duty men being
mixed with convicts (" No, no," from the Treasury benches).
He knew nothing of the matter, and therefore would support
the inquiry, because the facts stated were of the last importance, and it ought to be generally known whether they were
correct or incorrect. He hoped his noble friend would not
withdraw his resolutions without giving notice that he would
bring them again under the consideration of the House at an
early period of next session."

" LORD COCHRANE replied. He said he was not displeased
at the warmth with which his proposition had been met. It
certainly would be injurious to no one except to the feelings
of certain members of that House. The honourable secretary had met his statements with individual instances of
gallantry. The existence of these he had not denied. But
he asserted that the physical power of our seamen was
decreasing partly from the length of the war and partly
from the system of harbour-duty established in 1803, from
which service decayed seamen re-entered the navy. He had
heard that the system was about to be changed; and he
should be happy to learn from the honourable secretary that
such was the fact.

" The honourable secretary had challenged him to show
him an instance of a petty officer having purchased his discharge from such service. He would name a William Ford,
who had served with him in the *Impérieuse,* who had done

so, Nelson, his coxswain, and a person of the name of Farley, who had been returned to him and died on board completely worn out in the service. These were facts which he was prepared to prove at the bar, as he was all those which had been denied with so much warmth by the honourable secretary.

"To show further that the crews of British ships of war were unequal to themselves heretofore, he would relate what was the opinion of a person not at all likely to be disaffected to the order of things — he was the son of a bishop, who had taken an American privateer, the crew of which consisted of only 130 men; and he had declared publicly, that *he would rather have them than the whole of his own crew, consisting of* 240. If the honourable secretary doubted this fact, he might inquire, and he would easily verify it. The noble lord had heard that the sailors taken prisoners by the Americans had been found running away into the back settlements; that forty of them had been brought back by force, and that from the manifestations of this propensity the exchange of prisoners had been broken off.

"The lateness of the period at which he had brought forward his resolution had been complained of. He did intend to bring in a bill to limit the term of service, but circumstances had prevented him; but he would carry his intention into effect in the next session. With respect to parliamentary influence, the honourable secretary had asked whether *he had found it of service to himself in his profession?* He certainly had not, because *he had never prostituted his vote for that purpose; but he knew others who had found that influence of great avail!!* When he again brought forward the subject he should prove all the facts he had adduced, and he hoped so much ignorance of important facts would not then be found to prevail. He had chosen the present form of his motion in order to put his statements on record in a way not susceptible of misrepresentation."

"Mr. Croker replied that the Government had at all times been very watchful over the harbour-duty, but that it had

not taken *any new steps** since the suggestions of the noble
lord. He had never heard of any disposition in the seamen,
taken by the Americans, to run away to the back settlements;
nor of forty men being brought back by force. The exchange of prisoners was broken off in consequence of some
wrong done to the British seamen, and not in consequence
of any fault of theirs."

The resolution was then negatived without a division.

Astonished at the result of the debate, which, by
negativing my resolutions without a division, amounted
to a decision of the House that the naval administration
of the country required neither amendment nor even
investigation, and that the platitudes of the Secretary
of the Admiralty formed a sufficient answer to the
subjects sought to be inquired into, it was determined
by the few independent members of the House that
the subject should be renewed during the present session, notwithstanding that the prorogation of Parliament
was at hand.

Accordingly, Sir Francis Burdett gave notice of a
motion respecting seamen's wages and prize money,
this being the form in which the renewed debate, on
the 8th of July, took place.

" SIR FRANCIS BURDETT called the attention of the House
to the motion, of which he had yesterday given notice,
respecting the difficulties which presented themselves to
the obtaining by the relatives of deceased seamen and
marines the proper information and the means of recovering the wages and prize-money due to them on the
ships' books. The bonds required of the clerks in the navy
pay office, to prevent them from giving the necessary infor-

---

* He had just said there was a great improvement in the condition of the seamen.

mation, which might be applied for, were, in his opinion, more calculated to produce fraud and mischief than to be of any real utility. They would, in fact, be subject to become the instruments of collusion between the persons in possession of the means and information, and persons desirous of converting those means to their own fraudulent views and emolument.

" If these bonds were of real benefit, and operated, as it had been represented, to prevent imposition, he would ask, why were they not introduced into other branches of the navy department where the clerks were as well acquainted with the sums respectively due as in the pay-office? He could not discover any satisfactory or solid reason for continuing the practice or confining it to one particular office. It seemed to him that the best mode both of preventing frauds and of giving to the relatives of deceased seamen fair and easy opportunities of ascertaining the amount of what was due to them on the ships' books, would be to publish the names of such seamen and marines every six months in the *Gazette*, with the sums due to them respectively at the time of their death. He concluded with moving ' That every six calendar months a list be published in the *Gazette* of the unclaimed wages and prize-money due to deceased seamen and marines upon the books of His Majesty's ships of war, expressing the places where they were born.' "

" MR. CROKER said that the honourable baronet had made no statement to justify the House in agreeing either to the propositions he had advanced in his speech, or to the motion which he had made. He could not perceive any ground stated by the honourable baronet for convincing the House that the practice of which he complained ought to be altered, and a new system introduced. Was it not right that the lower clerks should be prevented from disclosing that information which was in other places *at all times to be had?* Was the Treasurer of the Navy, the Secretary of the Admiralty, or the Comptroller of the Navy more obscure than any one of the petty clerks who had entered into the bonds of which the noble lord had complained? Was it not their duty to supply the information when duly applied for ; and was there any charge preferred, or any case made out, of their having refused to do so?"

This mode of meeting the case showed, beyond a doubt, the justice of the complaint and the necessity for the acquiescence of the House in the motion of the honourable baronet. Sir Francis complained that bonds were taken of the clerks, subjecting their securities to penalties and themselves to dismissal if they gave information of any matters within their respective departments. Mr. Croker not only admitted but justified this, on the ground that it was the duty of the Secretary of the Admiralty and the Comptroller of the Navy to supply the information " *when duly applied for.*"

Before commencing his attack on me, Mr. Croker curtly informed Sir Francis that " if he wished to know what became of the wages and prize-money which remained due to the seamen, he would tell him. It was *carried to the chest at Greenwich.* The interest was employed in paying the pensions of meritorious seamen, and the capital was preserved untouched for the claimants whenever they might appear."

Had this been in reality the case, Mr. Croker would *gladly have proved the fact to the House*, as an answer to my previous motion for all papers relating to Greenwich. In place of so doing, he made it convenient — as has been shown in a former chapter — to stay away from the House during the debate on that motion, which it was " his duty " to meet. After I had quitted the House, he then appeared in his place and

said that my statements were without any foundation
in fact, though he had not listened to them! and could
only have heard them at second-hand from those
whose interest it was to misrepresent what I had said.
Imagine a secretary of the treasury pursuing the same
course and adopting the same language in the present
day, and the reader will have little difficulty in arriving
at the motives or the accuracy of Mr. Croker's imaginary statements, in reply to one who made the Navy his
entire study, and was practically acquainted with everything relating to its administration.

The preceding reply was all that was vouchsafed to
the honourable baronet, Mr. Croker converting the
subject into a lengthened attack on me, a course which
the House permitted without question. As the speech
of the Secretary of the Navy admitted of easy refutation, and as—amongst civilised persons in modern times
—it tells far more against himself than against me, Mr.
Croker shall enjoy the benefit of it with posterity.

" He was happy to see the noble lord opposite in his place
(Lord Cochrane), as he would give him the opportunity of
making amends for the mis-statement of which he had been
guilty on a former evening. He could now flatly contradict
the noble lord's assertions in point of fact, as he had before
contradicted them in point of principle. The first case was
that of William Ford. The noble lord had stated that William Ford had paid 80*l.* for his discharge from harbour-duty.
He had not paid 80*l.* nor any other sum for his discharge.
The fact was directly contrary. William Ford was an able
seaman on board the *Impérieuse*, the very ship commanded
by, and which exposed the ignorance of, the noble lord.
Ford's wife wrote a letter to him requesting her husband's

release on providing proper substitutes. It was attended to by the Admiralty and Ford was discharged, having never been invalided, and having been favoured by those very arrangements on which the noble lord had founded this charge.

" The next case stated by the noble lord was that of J. Milton, his coxswain. The assertion made by the noble lord was, that John Milton, after being invalided for harbour-duty, and a Greenwich pensioner, had also paid 80*l.* for his discharge.

" Now, what would the House think of the veracity of the noble lord when he could prove beyond a possibility of doubt that J. Milton was neither a harbour-duty man nor a Greenwich pensioner? He had also received a letter from J. Milton's wife requesting the Board to discharge her husband upon the usual provision of substitutes being made. A compliance with the prayer of the letter took place, and her husband was discharged. He surely, after such misrepresentations, would not be thought to go too far in maintaining that the noble lord's assertions should have little or no weight, since it was so very clearly proved that he was ignorant of what passed in his own ship. John Milton, however, after having been discharged, contrived, through the means of Gawler, whose frauds he himself had detected, to obtain upon a false certificate *a pension of* 12*l. a year from Greenwich.* The fraud was discovered, and the pension was withdrawn.

" But the noble lord did not seem satisfied with exposing his own ignorance, where he had the best opportunities of being informed; he went much farther, he exposed his own faults and condemned himself. The noble lord declared he had discharged sixty men belonging to the *Pallas* in consequence of their incapacity, and risked all the responsibility of the measure at the hazard of a court-martial. If the noble lord did so, he would tell the noble lord he had done that which he ought not to have done — he had falsified the books of the ship entrusted to his honour and care. (Hear, hear.) For the books which he had signed with his own

hand contradicted his positive assertion. The fact was, that
fifteen men only were discharged from the *Pallas* within the
period mentioned by the noble lord; no such entry there
appeared; and he could not have exchanged them for supernumeraries, because from these books it was seen that only
twenty-nine supernumeraries had been taken on board."

When I said that Ford had been obliged to pay 80*l.*
for his discharge, instead of the representation being
false the amount was much *understated*. He had been
compelled to find *four substitutes, which cost ninety
pounds !* and was then, as a matter of course, discharged
without further personal payment. The case of Milton
was a matter of veracity between myself and Mr.
Croker. I offered to prove to the House that Milton
had paid nearly 100*l.* for *substitutes*, which Mr. Croker
construed into paying *nothing*, for his discharge, an
offer which Mr. Croker did not accept, though he
admitted the substitutes! which had been provided—
a fact which he did not attempt to disprove otherwise
than by his own perverted statements. As Mr. Croker
himself said " *he had contradicted* my main assertion;
how *did I get rid of that?* " Not anticipating an
attack on myself, I had not come to the House
prepared with documents, so that the only way in
which I could possibly have got rid of Mr. Croker s
" *contradictions* " would have been to imitate his example, viz. to convert myself into a bully for the sake
of outbullying him, a resource from which I was, as a
gentleman, averse. My reply, presently to be adduced,
will, I have no doubt, be sufficiently satisfactory to the
reader.

Again, Mr. Croker appealed to the House whether

my veracity was to be depended upon, for having stated
that Milton was a Greenwich pensioner, and in the
same breath himself stated that *he was one!* though
through, as he alleged, a false certificate obtained from
another man, about which, if true, I could have known
nothing except from Admiralty investigations, which
were kept secret. All I could have known was, that
when Milton's case was brought under my notice he
was a Greenwich pensioner, which Mr. Croker, when
appealing to the House not to trust my veracity, confirmed by stating " that he *had a pension of* 12*l. a year
from Greenwich!* "

Mr. Croker's explanation with regard to Farley was
even less to his credit. My complaint to the House
had been that Farley, a man useless from hard service,
had been returned to me on board the *Impérieuse*, and
that he had died completely worn out. As an instance
of my want of veracity, Mr. Croker assured the House
that " he was not invalided for harbour-duty, neither
died in the service." The fact was, that the man was
not invalided at all till within a few days of his death,
when, unable to return to his friends, I retained him
on board from a motive of humanity after his discharge, and he *died on board the Impérieuse.* Mr.
Croker spoke truth when he said he " was not invalided
for harbour-duty, and that he did not die in the service ; " but he most unwarrantably concealed truth when
he suppressed the circumstances under which the man
really died, which were more disgraceful to the nation
than invaliding a worn out man for harbour-duty.

Unworthy as was this course, it was as nothing com-

pared with what fell from the lips of Mr. Croker in the
subsequent portion of his address to the House; in
which address he asserted that my resolutions were
"gross and scandalous libels against the honour, the
valour, and the character of the British navy"—accused
me of having traduced the commander of the *Java* and
Macedonian, though the names of either ships or their
commanders had never passed my lips, nor were in my
thoughts — and wound up by asserting that I had
grossly libelled Captain Broke of the Shannon frigate!!!
though I had never mentioned the name of one or the
other in the House, and only regarded them either in
or out of the House with the highest admiration!

As this would be incredible were I not to introduce
Mr. Croker's own words I, shall do so without abridg-
ment.   1st, to show the impudence of the falsehood,
and 2ndly, as a really clever tribute to the gallant
Captain Broke, had it been uttered in common honesty
and not to get rid of Sir Francis Burdett's motion; which
was thus converted into a pretext of vilifying me in
such language as no modern House of Commons would
for a moment tolerate.

"Having shown, he trusted, to the satisfaction of the
House, the ignorance and unfounded statement of the noble
lord, he could not suffer the present opportunity to pass by
without also showing that the resolutions lately proposed by
his Lordship were gross and scandalous libels against the
honour, the valour, and the character of the British navy.
The noble lord appeared to be peculiarly and most unseason-
ably unfortunate both in his mis-statements and libels. It was
not necessary for him to tell either the noble lord or the House
that he alluded to the gallant action fought by the *Shannon*
frigate with the *Chesapeake* American frigate.   The com-

munication which he was about to make to the House had
not been sought for or prepared by him. It had presented
itself to him as if from a divinity to confute and confound
the noble lord's misrepresentations and libels, and rescue the
honour of the British navy from unfounded aspersions, and
raise the glory of the British flag still higher than ever.   As
*he was coming to the House the official information of that
glorious engagement was put into his hands!!* He should not
trouble the House at any length with the character of Captain
Broke, who commanded the *Shannon*. It would be sufficient for him to say that Captain Broke was an officer no less
distinguished for his indefatigable activity and unwearied
enterprise than for his skill and valour. With many occasions of making and preserving the valuable prizes which
must have materially contributed to increase his private
fortune, he had uniformly preferred the cause of his country
and the good of the service to his own interests. Cases had
even occurred, when, although he might have fairly preserved
his prizes, he rather chose to send them, with all they contained, to the bottom of the sea than let any opportunity
slip in which his exertions and co-operation could be useful
in another quarter. The action which he fought with the *Chesapeake* was in every respect unexampled.   It was not—and he
knew it was a bold assertion which he made — to be surpassed
by any engagement which graced the annals of Great Britain ;
the enemy's ship was superior in size, superior in weight of
metal, superior in numbers. She entered into the contest
with the previous conviction of all her superior advantages,
and with a confirmed confidence of victory resulting from
that conviction. All this superiority served but to heighten
the brilliancy of Captain Broke's achievement. What,
continued Mr. Croker, will, or rather what can, the
noble lord say now ? Will he persist in still maintaining
that the captures made by the Americans have been caused
by the decayed and disheartened state of our seamen, and
not by the enemy's superiority in numbers and weight of
metal ? He begged leave to assure the House, that he had

not introduced the account of the glorious victory gained by
Captain Broke as a single instance of the success of one
of our frigates; but it had come so opportunely to confound the noble lord's statement and confute his misrepresentations, that he felt he would be doing an act of injustice
to our gallant officers and seamen, to the House, and to the
country at large were he to pass it over unnoticed, at a
moment so peculiarly fitted and seasonable for its introduction. It was not, he knew, the day or the hour which could
enhance the value and glory of Captain Broke's great achievement, nor had he any occasion to strengthen by its effects his
arguments and statements against the noble lord, for he
sincerely believed there could not be any day or hour in the
course of the year in which he would not have more than
ample means of contradicting and disproving such assertions
as the noble lord had made on this occasion. Mr. Croker
concluded with observing that he trusted he had shown not
only the impropriety, but the danger of adopting the motion
proposed by the honourable baronet."

The reader may possibly inquire what this tirade
could possibly have to do with Sir Francis Burdett's
motion? or with anything that I had said? He
may wonder too that the House should have patiently
listened for an hour to an imaginary charge against
me *for what I had never said!* and the Secretary
of the Navy's refutation of a charge *which his own
ingenuity had trumped up!* In our day it could not
be that gentlemen by birth or education should
have endured such claptrap, when its object was to
malign one of their own body without a shadow of
foundation for the malice displayed. The history of
the period, however, so fully details the reasons
for all this, that I may be spared the trouble of recapitulating them.

Unpractised in oratorical arts, whether professionally or as the hired advocate of a faction, my reply may appear tame; yet what it lacked in eloquence it made up by facts which had been *contradicted*, because they could not be *impugned*.

"LORD COCHRANE admitted all that could be said of the gallantry of our seamen; but maintained that a great and a rapid decay had been produced in their physical powers by the cause to which he had felt it his duty to call the attention of the House. He was pleased that he had done so in the form of a resolution which could neither be misrepresented or misquoted without detection. It was in the recollection of the House that he had not cast the slightest reflection either on officers or men, collectively or individually, although the honourable secretary had chosen to defend them in both cases. Such a line of conduct might be best calculated to excite a feeling of disapprobation towards him (Lord Cochrane) in the minds of those who had not attended to the subject, but it was not an honourable or a candid mode of proceeding to put *words into his mouth and then argue to refute them*. He had never mentioned the name of Captain Broke or alluded to him in the slightest degree, although the secretary had spared no pains to defend him. Captain Broke had done his duty; his men proved adequate to the task he had imposed upon them; but, if his information was correct, the *Shannon* was the only frigate on the American station in which the captain would have been justified in trusting to the physical strength of his crew.

"The honourable secretary seemed to flatter himself, from the exulting manner in which he had delivered his speech, that he had also *refuted* those facts, which he (Lord Cochrane) did state. 'Ford,' says he, 'did not pay 80*l*. for his discharge, or any other sum.' But does not the honourable secretary know that this man raised *four substitutes*, and that he (W. Ford) could not procure them otherwise than by money?* Was not the difficluty of getting seamen such that the Admiralty demanded four men for the discharge of one? Under such circumstances it was obvious that the navy was manned not by the national bounty or the prospect of reward from the service, but out of the funds of those who had long served their country. The noble lord pledged himself to establish at the bar of the House every circumstance stated in the resolutions which he had moved on a former evening. Ford, he repeated, paid 90*l.* for his discharge — a sum equal to all that he could have saved during eighteen years' service! No man of feeling could justify the continuance of such a practice.

" As to the case of Farley, the honourable secretary assured the House that he was not invalided for harbour-duty, neither had he died in the service — facts which will not be deemed important when it is known (and it can be proved) that this respectable petty officer, who had been in thirteen general actions, and thirty-two years in the navy, was not invalided until within a few days of his death; and that, unable to return to his friends, he died on board the *Impérieuse.* Ought not seamen to be entitled to their discharge before they are reduced to this state? Can ships be efficient whilst men so debilitated form part of their crews?

" It is impossible. The honourable secretary laid particular emphasis on the case of Milton, as above all the most unfounded of his (Lord Cochrane's) unfounded assertions. He had discovered that Milton had received his pension through Gawler, perhaps this was the easiest way; but he (Lord Cochrane) knew that Milton deserved that pension, having been wounded under his command. He was the first man who boarded the *Tapageuse* in the river of Bordeaux, when that ship's corvette was captured by the boats of the *Pallas* alone. This led him to observe that the lieutenant of the *Pallas,* who executed this service was not promoted by the Admiralty until Sir Samuel Hood's first lieutenant had brought out

* He had paid 90*l.* for them, as I had asserted.

another sloop, long afterwards, from the same place with the boats of a whole squadron — nor, is it probable that he ever would have obtained the reward of his gallant conduct, unless the Admiralty had felt that the one could not longer be neglected if the other was promoted. So much for impartiality! He pledged himself to prove to the House the literal fact that Milton *had* served seventeen years, and *had paid* nearly 100*l.* for his discharge. Surely such length of service should entitle seamen to some deduction from so oppressive an expense! This was not the case, however; neither was there any period fixed to which they could look forward as the termination of their compulsory confinement.

" He (Lord Cochrane) did not accuse the present Admiralty of originating these abuses; possibly they were even ignorant of their existence. Boards never listen to individuals, and therefore he had adopted the present mode of calling the attention of parliament and of the country to the state of the navy. Could any person have believed that the Admiralty, instead of *decreasing* the sum to be paid by meritorious seamen after long service, actually *increase* the amount? He wished that the present first lord would look into his father's papers, who had it in contemplation to have made many alterations and improvements in naval affairs, with which he was well acquainted. Probably had he remained in office the seamen would have had no cause now to lament the continuance of those evils of which he (Lord Cochrane) was desirous to inform the House, with a view that they might investigate the subject.

" Here the noble lord read an extract from a letter he had received that morning from a seaman's wife, the mother of a family, and whose husband was compelled to pay 60*l.* for a discharge, which left their children without bread. She owed 7*l.* to her doctor, who had written to Mr. Croker, stating her extraordinary exertions for her family's support as the cause of her illness. The husband after a long service had but 17*l.* remaining; and he was obliged to go down to Plymouth before he could get his discharge. Was this the situation in which British sailors should be placed? He was in the judgment of the whole navy, and he would prove his facts at the bar. If the honourable secretary had any feelings they ought to wring his breast, and prevent him from daring to defend such abuses. He would not detain the House longer than to say that the army was now a model on which to form the navy — so much had circumstances changed. Their service was limited, and officers who did gallant acts were rewarded by promotion and brevet. He named Lieutenant Johnson, who served under his command in the Basque Roads, as an instance to prove the unwillingness of the Admiralty to do justice unless by favour."

" MR. CROKER would not permit the noble lord to *lead the House away!* by stating that his material facts had not been *disproved.* He (Mr. Croker) had *contradicted* his main assertions. The noble lord had not got *rid of that;* and if he would give him further opportunities he would give him *an equally satisfactory answer!*

" LORD COCHRANE admitted that the honourable secretary had *contradicted* his assertions, but he defied him to *disprove one word* contained in his resolution. As the feelings of his brother officers might be excited by the statement of the honourable secretary who had stood forward in their defence, though they had not been attacked, he would again add, that he had not even thought disrespectfully of any individual to whom the honourable secretary had alluded. He admired the gallant conduct of Captain Broke, and asserted that if the Admiralty did their duty no 38-gun frigate of ours need shrink from a contest with the Americans.

" LORD COCHRANE repelled with scorn the accusation made against him of endeavouring to excite dissatisfaction in the navy."

The end of Mr. Croker's attack on me was fully answered, viz. that of averting the attention of the House from Sir Francis Burdett's motion, which fell to the ground.

So far I have vindicated myself, I will now appeal to authorities far more reliable than Mr. Croker.

" You may guess my surprise and disappointment on viewing forty-five of the most filthy creatures that ever were embarked, sent as part of our complement."—(*Letter of Lord St. Vincent to Admiral Markham, quoted by Brenton.*)

If such men were sent as part of the complement of the ship of the commander-in-chief, the public may judge of the description furnished to private ships of war. Captain Brenton when confirming the above opinion of Lord St. Vincent, shall describe them.

"I can vouch for the correctness of the above picture of the men who used to infest our ships. Their personal appearance, in spite of every attention, was most miserable, particularly the importations at Plymouth. I remember being ordered on a survey of *some of them in* 1811 ; and so truly wretched and unlike men did they appear, that I took portraits of them, which I gave to Captain Nash, of the *Salvador del Mundo. My wonder is that more of our ships were not taken by the Americans in the late struggle, when it is considered how shamefully they were manned*"!!— (*Brenton's St. Vincent,* vol. ii. p. 246.)

Yet for speaking of them in 1813, after our ships were everywhere beaten by the Americans, I was denounced by Mr. Croker as wanting in veracity! My arguments all pointed to the reorganisation of a noble service whose cause of failure was solely attributable to a want of proper ships, well-trained men, and an armament capable of contending with a nation which, in this respect, had gone ahead of us.

This is not the place to enter into a description of

our disasters in the American war, or it would be easy for me to show their origin in the abuses embodied in my resolutions.   Nor is it to be wondered at that seamen who were so ill treated, and who suffered so much in former wars, should have recounted their sufferings to their descendants, now arrived at manhood.   Which of them, who could obtain a better livelihood, would be likely, after such a description of the miseries of naval life, to enter on board an English man-of-war?   It was no wonder they preferred the American service.

Had Mr. Croker been candid, he would, when speaking of the victory of the *Shannon*, have adduced the fact, which must have been known to the Admiralty that one-third of the *Chesapeake's* crew *were British seamen*, driven from their own national service by ill-treatment.   A man in Captain Broke's frigate found his own brother amongst the enemy's wounded !

I will adduce the following extracts from Brenton.

" Sir Sidney Smith never spared himself.   He was ever present in danger, and the last to retreat from it.   He was equally gallant and enterprising with his contemporary, Cochrane, but less cautious and less of a sailor.   Both these valuable officers were latterly lost to the service, because the Admiralty would not, *when they might have done it*, give them sufficient employment at sea to keep them at work." (p. 461.)

" Vernon owed much of his celebrity to his manly and straightforward dealing in the House of Commons." (p. 347.)

" The services of the gallant Vernon were rewarded by his *being struck out of the list by a weak and wicked govern-*

ment. Vernon was supposed to have been the author of two
pamphlets, reflecting on the conduct of the Admiralty, and
the gallant Admiral very shortly afterwards received a letter
from Mr. Corbett, the secretary, announcing that His Majesty
had been pleased to direct their Lordships *to strike his name
off the list of flag officers."* (p. 345.)

" If we would have good and faithful seamen to man our
ships, we must give them full and ample remuneration for
their services, *with security from want and penury in old
age.* I most earnestly pray God that the next parliament may
have sense and influence enough to listen to men belonging
to our profession who will fearlessly advocate the cause of
our sailors."—(*Brenton.*)

It would not be difficult to multiply these extracts by
dozens from naval writers of this and a subsequent
period. These, however, being well known to students
of naval history, need not be recapitulated. The following extract from a letter of Lord Collingwood,
quoted by Brenton, vol. i. p. 436, embraces the whole
subject.

" What day is there that I do not lament the continuance
of the war ? Nothing good can happen to us short of peace.
Every officer and man of the fleet is impatient for release
from a situation which daily becomes more irksome to all.
I see disgust growing around me very fast."

The debates in parliament sealed my fate.

It is, however a remarkable fact, that, notwithstanding my resolutions respecting the navy were thrown
out without a division — that everything I advanced for
the good of the navy was pooh-poohed — and that
every fact I brought forward was flatly denied by Mr.
Croker, in his position as Secretary of the Admiralty—
the Government secretly proceeded to adopt nearly

every one of the *reforms which had been originated and advanced by myself.* Thus instead of *my plans,* my efforts for the removal of naval abuses became *their plans!*

This would certainly never have been known to me, but for the recent publication of the " Diaries and Correspondence of the Right Hon. George Rose," the Treasurer to the Navy. From this work I will cull a few extracts. Mr. Rose thus writes:—

" I dined at Lord Mulgrave's with the Board of Admiralty, to discuss some points respecting *my plan* for *ensuring regular* adjudication and speedy distribution of the proceeds of prizes. . . . At the Levee to day, Mr. Wellesly Pole kissed hands as principal Secretary for Ireland, and Mr. Croker as his successor as Secretary to the Admiralty. *I continue to think this last appointment, without any impeachment of the gentleman's character,* VERY MUCH TO BE REGRETTED." (Vol. ii. p. 411.)

Nothing of the kind, Mr. Rose, Mr. Croker was the only man who could be found to contradict my facts, and then induce his superiors to act upon them — to ridicule my plans, and then adopt them. So far from being out of his place, he was a necessity, since being thoroughly acquainted with all my plans and aspirations in our days of friendship, he could effectively defeat my efforts in the House of Commons and profit by them in Whitehall. Mr. Rose possibly did not suspect the causes for Mr. Croker's appointment.

At page 503 of the same work, is an intimation from Mr. Perceval to Lord Bathurst of " *some future arrangement of the interests of Greenwich Hospital in*

prize-money;" the very subject I had for the first time
introduced into the House under the disadvantage of
not knowing what papers to call for! My motions
for the *proper payment of seamen*, though repudiated
in the House, were completely successful in the Administration, as is shown by the subjoined correspondence
between Lord Melville and Mr. Rose on the subject : —

"Admiralty, September 15th, 1814.

"DEAR ROSE, — I do not trouble you with the inclosed
from any special consideration of the particular case, but as
a specimen of a considerable and increased number which I
have of late received. The circumstance may be accidental,
and I have little doubt that the several instances may be
satisfactorily accounted for. . . . I have no doubt that
real neglect does not occur, but it is very desirable that there
should not be even the appearance of it. On your return to
town, you will probably examine into the subject, with a view
to ascertain whether in the inferior branches of the Pay
Office, the business is conducted to your satisfaction.

"Believe me, &c. &c.

" MELVILLE."

The business was not conducted to Mr. Rose's satisfaction, for in his reply to Lord Melville, he says: —

" I gave the most positive orders, accompanied by strong
assurances of my severe displeasure if they should not be
complied with, for insuring early answers to all applications,
and, *finding these ineffectual*, from not knowing on whom
individually to fix blame, where there was an appearance of
neglect, I divided the alphabet amongst the clerks in the
inspection branch, assigning to each certain letters in it, that
I might know with whom the responsibility rested, who
should not perform his duty. That has been followed up by
mulcts and reprimands. At one time I had the whole branch
into my room, and stated to them in the most impressive

terms, my fixed determination to dismiss the first person against whom a well founded complaint should be made ; on which I had *remonstrances for having disgraced the branch!*

*   *   *   *   *

" My servants have general orders, never, under any pressure of business, to refuse admittance to seamen or their relations, or, indeed, to any poor inquiring person. I have sometimes picked up stragglers in the country and maintained them till I could ascertain whether I could be useful to them, *either in getting their prize-money, or obtaining for them admission to Greenwich Hospital !* . . . I have by the aid of a law I brought in, punished *frauds of every description practised upon the seamen,* even in cases where *only larger prices have been exacted than ought to have been paid for articles sold to them.*"

Formidable admissions, truly, despite the virtuous indignation of Mr. Croker on the supposition that anything could be wrong at the Admiralty. Yet here, after my attempts at remedying abuses, the Treasurer to the Navy testifies to the difficulty of seamen obtaining access to the Admiralty — to their begging about the country in the character of common tramps for want of their prize-money, whilst even the wounded and aged required Mr. Rose's humane intervention to get them a chance of Greenwich Hospital—to the fact, that frauds of all kinds were practised upon them — whilst the " *branch which was disgraced,*" by merely being told of its misconduct, was in the habit of charging to the seamen " *larger prices than ought to have been paid for articles sold to them ! !*"

I had brought nothing before the House half so bad as this testimony of the Treasurer of the Navy. Yet for bringing forward what I did on behalf of the navy, I was, as will presently be seen, hunted on a false accusation into prison, whilst those who marked me down were quietly adopting as their own the reforms I had advocated!!

CHAP. XXXVIII.

THE STOCK EXCHANGE TRIAL.

NECESSITY FOR ENTERING ON THE SUBJECT.—LORD CAMPBELL'S OPINION
RESPECTING IT.—LORD BROUGHAM'S OPINION.—HIS LATE MAJESTY'S.
—MY RESTORATION TO RANK.—REFUSAL TO REINVESTIGATE MY CASE.
— THE REASONS GIVEN. —EXTRACT FROM LORD BROUGHAM'S WORKS.
—MY FIRST KNOWLEDGE OF DE BERANGER.—HOW BROUGHT ABOUT.—
THE STOCK EXCHANGE HOAX. — RUMOURS IMPLICATING ME IN IT. —
I RETURN TO TOWN IN CONSEQUENCE. — MY AFFIDAVIT. — ITS
NATURE. — IMPROBABILITY OF MY CONFEDERACY.—MY CARELESSNESS
OF THE MATTER.—DE BERENGER'S DENIAL OF MY PARTICIPATION.—
REMARKS THEREON.—SIGNIFICANT FACTS.—REMARKS ON THE ALLEGED
HOAX COMMON ON THE STOCK EXCHANGE.

I NOW approach a period of my life in which occurred
circumstances beyond all others painful to the feelings
of an honourable man. Neglect I was accustomed to.
Despite my efforts to rise superior to the jealousies
of others, it has followed me through life. Exclusion
from professional activity at a period when opportunity for distinction lay before me, was hard to bear;
but I had the consolation of exerting myself ashore
for the benefit of the noble service, in the active duties
of which I was not permitted to participate. But
when an alleged offence was laid to my charge in 1814,
in which, on the honour of a man now on the brink
of the grave, I had not the slightest participation, and
from which I never benefited, nor thought to benefit

one farthing, and when this allegation was, by political, rancour and legal chicanery, consummated in an unmerited conviction and an outrageous sentence, my heart for the first time sank within me, as conscious of a blow, the effect of which it has required all my energies to sustain. It has been said that truth comes sooner or later. But it seldom comes before the mind, passing from agony to contempt, has grown callous to man's judgment. To this principle, I am thankful to say, I have never subscribed, but have to this hour remained firm in the hope and confidence that by the mercy of God I shall not die till full and ample justice of my fellow-men has been freely rendered me.

It may be thought that after the restoration to rank and honours by my late and present Sovereigns—after promotion to the command of a fleet when I had no enemy to confront — and after enjoyment of the sympathy and friendship of those whom the nation delights to honour, — I might safely pass over that day of deep humiliation. Not so. It is true that I have received those marks of my Sovereign's favour, and it is true that from that day to the present I have enjoyed the uninterrupted friendship of those who were then convinced, and are still convinced of my innocence; but *that unjust public sentence has never been publicly reversed, nor the equally unjust fine inflicted on me remitted;* so that if I would, it is not in my power to remain silent and be just to my posterity. The Government of my country has, though often invoked, refused to re-investigate my case, as impossible in form, and from fear of creating a precedent. Nevertheless, I will, repugnant as is the subject, re-state the facts, and, posterity being my judge, have no fear as to the verdict.   The coronet of my ancestors, and the honour of my family, which will, in the course of nature ere long be committed to the keeping of a devoted and sensitively honourable son, demand no less at my hands.

It must not, however, be imagined that the recital of leading facts, is for the first time adopted in pursuance of the dictates of family duty and affection. Neither would it have been possible to write my autobiography without entering on this most important and painful portion of my life, because such an omission would be fatal to my reputation, as it might be construed into an admission of my culpability.

At a period before the experience of the present generation, the circumstances about to be recorded were over and over again submitted to public judgment, but at a time when the rod of justice was suspended *in terrorem* over the public press, which did not venture openly to espouse my cause on its own merits.   Yet even then my efforts were not in vain. The press, instead of being, as in those days it was, the organ of ill-concealed public dissatisfaction, has now become the exponent of the public voice; which, through its medium, is heard and felt throughout the length and breadth of the land.   Though approaching the subject with distaste, I do so with confidence that my unvarnished tale will not be told in vain.

For the more ready appreciation of the reader in the

present day, as regards facts, the details of which the lapse of half a century has nearly obliterated, I may be permitted to introduce the subject by extracts from the works of two of the most learned and distinguished lawyers and statesmen of the age in which we live— two noblemen, of whose learning, of whose judgment and integrity it is unnecessary for me to say one word, because they are much above my praise, and therefore can receive no addition from it — viz. Lord Brougham, formerly our Lord High Chancellor, and Lord Campbell, the present Lord High Chancellor of England. I will take those of Lord Campbell first, because they embrace points into which Lord Brougham does not enter, and also because Lord Campbell, in addition to the dignity which he now adorns, for many years occupied the same high position as did Lord Ellenborough, when he presided at the trial to which the reader's attention is now directed.

Lord Campbell, at page 218, vol. iii. in his valuable work, entitled "The Lives of the Chief-Justices of England," says :—

" I have now only to mention some criminal cases which arose before Lord Ellenborough in later years. Of these, the most remarkable was Lord Cochrane's, as this drew upon the Chief-Justice a considerable degree of public obloquy, and, *causing very uneasy reflections in his own mind, was supposed to have hastened his end.*"

" Lord Cochrane (since Earl of Dundonald) was one of the most gallant officers in the English navy, and had gained the most brilliant reputation in a succession of naval engagements against the French. Unfortunately for him, he likewise wished to distinguish himself in politics, and taking the Radical line, he was returned to Parliament for the city of Westminster. He was a determined opponent of Lord Liverpool's Administration ; and at popular meetings was in the habit of delivering harangues of rather a seditious aspect, which induced Lord Ellenborough to believe that he seriously meant to abet rebellion, and that he was a dangerous character. But the gallant officer was really a loyal subject, as well as enthusiastically zealous for the glory of his country. He had an uncle, named Cochrane, a merchant *, and a very unprincipled man, who, towards the end of the war, in concert with De Berenger, a foreigner, wickedly devised a scheme by which they were to make an immense fortune by a speculation on the Stock Exchange."

"For this purpose they were to cause a sudden rise in the funds, by spreading false intelligence that a preliminary treaty of peace had actually been signed between England and France. Everything succeeded to their wishes ; the intelligence was believed, the funds rose, and they sold on time bargains many hundred thousand pounds of 3 per cents. before the truth was discovered."

" It so happened that Lord Cochrane was then in London, was living in his uncle's house †, and was much in his company, but there is now good reason to believe that he was not at all implicated in the nefarious scheme. However, when the fraud was detected, — partly from a belief in his complicity, and partly *from political spite*, — he was included in the indictment preferred for the conspiracy to defraud the Stock Exchange."

" The trial coming on before Lord Ellenborough, the noble and learned Judge, being himself persuaded of the guilt of all the defendants, used his best endeavours that they should all be convicted. He refused to adjourn the trial at the close of the prosecutor's case, about nine in the

---

* This is an error. My uncle, an East India merchant, was the Hon. Basil Cochrane, a highly honourable man, not the one alluded to by Lord Campbell.

† It was my uncle Basil with whom I for a time resided.

evening, when the trial had lasted twelve hours, and the jury, as well as the defendants' counsel, were all completely exhausted and all prayed for an adjournment.   The following day, in summing up, prompted, no doubt, by the conclusion of his own mind, he laid *special emphasis on every circumstance which might raise a suspicion against Lord Cochrane,* and ELABORATELY EXPLAINED AWAY WHATEVER AT FIRST SIGHT MIGHT SEEM FAVOURABLE to the gallant officer.   In consequence the jury found a verdict of GUILTY against *all* the defendants."

"Next term, Lord Cochrane presented himself in Court to move for a new trial, but the other defendants convicted along with him did not attend.   He said truly that he had no power or influence to obtain their attendance, and urged that his application was founded on circumstances peculiar to his own case.   But Lord Ellenborough would not hear him, because the other defendants were not present.   Such a rule had before been laid down *, *but it is palpably contrary to the first principles of justice, and ought immediately to have been reversed."*

"Lord Cochrane was thus deprived of all opportunity of showing that the verdict against him was wrong, and in addition to fine and imprisonment, he was sentenced to stand in the pillory.†   Although as yet he was generally believed to be guilty, the award of this degrading and infamous punishment upon a young nobleman, a member of the House of Commons, and a distinguished naval officer, raised universal sympathy in his favour.   The judge was proportionably blamed, not only by the vulgar, but by men of education on

* On one special occasion only.

† This vindictive sentence the Government did not dare carry out.   My high-minded colleague, Sir Francis Burdett, told the Government that if the sentence was carried into effect, he would stand in the pillory beside me, when they must look to the consequences.   What these might have been, in the then excited state of the public mind, as regarded my treatment, the reader may guess.

both sides in politics, and he found upon entering society and appearing in the House of Lords *that he was looked upon coldly.*

"*Having now some misgivings himself as to the propriety of his conduct in this affair, he became very wretched.* Nor was the agitation allowed to drop during the remainder of Lord Ellenborough's life, for Lord Cochrane being expelled the House of Commons, *was immediately re-elected for Westminster.* Having escaped from the prison in which he was confined under his sentence, he appeared in the House of Commons. In obedience to the public voice, the part of his sentence by which he was to stand in the pillory was remitted by the Crown, and a bill was introduced into Parliament altogether to abolish the pillory as a punishment, *on account of the manner in which the power of inflicting it had been recently abused. It was said that these matters preyed deeply on Lord Ellenborough's mind and affected his health. Thenceforth he certainly seemed to have lost the gaiety of heart for which he had been formerly remarkable.*" (Lord Campbell's " Lives of the Chief-Justices," vol. iii. pp. 218, 219, 220.)

Such are the recorded opinions of one of the most learned and acute men of the age, one who now does honour to the judgment-seat of the highest tribunal of our country ; and who, at the time those opinions were given to the world, held the scarcely less dignified position of Chief-Justice of England, sitting in the very court in which that cruel sentence — the unmerited cause of so much misery to me — was pronounced. From such an authority — as much judicial as historic — may the reader form his own conclusions.

It is with no less satisfaction that I add the opinions of another learned and highly gifted peer of the realm,

who has also adorned the dignified office of Lord High
Chancellor of England, viz. my friend Lord Brougham,
to whose name, as the untiring advocate of everything
nationally progressive and socially expansive, no testimony of mine could add weight.

In the year 1844, when I submitted to Her Majesty's
Government how incomplete I considered the restoration of my honours, I wrote to Lord Brougham, ever my
constant and steadfast friend, to ask his opinion of the
step I was taking. The subjoined was Lord Brougham's
reply :—

> " Grafton Street, March 29th, 1844.

" MY DEAR LORD D.—I think, upon the whole, the time
is favourable.

" I have well considered the matter as of importance, and
have read the papers through. I don't think the best way of
bringing the subject before the Duke is to send that correspondence, but rather to make a statement, and I authorise
you distinctly to add to it these two important facts.

" First, that William IV. only objected to the Bath being
restored *at the same time* with your rank, and not absolutely
at all times.

" Secondly, that your counsel were clearly of opinion that
the verdict as *concerned you was erroneous*, and I always
concluded that you had sacrificed yourself out of delicacy to
your uncle, the person really guilty.

" The restoring you to rank without your honours is too
absurd and unfair. It means ' we will take all we can get
from you in service, and give you nothing.'

> " Yours ever truly,
> " H. BROUGHAM."

No one knew better than His late Majesty, King
William the Fourth, the injustice under which I had
laboured, and the causes of the political spite which
had been directed against me. Before His Majesty

came to the throne he warmly interested himself in my behalf, and intimated to Sir Francis Burdett, that if I were to memorialise the Government, he would use his influence to procure my restoration. This was accordingly done, but in vain, His Royal Highness's influence *then* proving insufficient for the purpose, but not so after His Majesty's accession to the throne.

The following extract of a letter from Sir Francis Burdett, coming shortly before my restoration to rank, will show the continued interest taken by His late Majesty and those near him to remove unmerited obloquy from a brother sailor, notwithstanding the failure of His Majesty's previous effort when Duke of Clarence. The same intimation to Sir Francis Burdett being made, a similar memorial was laid before His Majesty in Council; this time with effect.

"MY DEAR LORD DUNDONALD, — I went to the Levee on Wednesday to give your memorial to Greville, the Clerk of the Council, to present — but the King returned to Windsor immediately after the Levee and no council was held. Had it been, I can entertain no doubt that your memorial would have been presented and granted.

"I went to see Greville about it the next day — he was so kind and so desirous of doing everything in his power to expedite it, even proposing to take it out of its usual turn, that I cannot but feel quite satisfied and assured that there will be not a moment's unnecessary delay. A little patience and all will be right. I should like to see you for a day or two, and perhaps may.

"Yours sincerely,
"F. BURDETT."

My restoration not long afterwards followed, and no one knew better than His Majesty the justice of reversing the unjust sentence which had so long and so undeservedly excluded me from a service which from my youth upwards had been my pride.

I shall ever consider this inteference on my behalf as a testimonial from His late Majesty not only to my innocence, but also to my unjustifiable persecution, for had he not believed me innocent, His Majesty would have been the last person to interfere so pertinaciously. Still less when, on coming to the throne, his former influence had become authority.

I was not restored to my honours till the reign of Her present Most Gracious Majesty, and on this restoration being made, I again requested of Her Majesty's Ministers a reinvestigation into the causes which led to my unjust conviction, alleging that my restoration to rank and honour might be construed into an act of mercy, were not my innocence of the Stock Exchange hoax fully established. In this sense I addressed the late Duke of Wellington and Sir Robert Peel. The following was his Grace's reply.

" Walmer Castle, Sept. 12th, 1844.

" MY LORD,—I have just received the package from your Lordship, containing your Lordship's letter to myself of the 10th inst. and other papers, which I will peruse with attention according to the desire and for the purpose expressed in your Lordship's letter.

" I have the honour to be, &c.

" WELLINGTON.

" Admiral the Earl of Dundonald, &c."

The reply of Sir Robert Peel was more explicit, and

gave as a reason why my request could not be complied with, that just, or unjust, it was not, from lapse of time, in the power of the Government to attempt to reverse a decision in a court of law.

"Whitehall, Nov. 7th, 1844.

"My Lord,—Her Majesty's servants have had under their consideration the letter I received from your Lordship, bearing date the 10th of September 1844, together with the documents by which that letter was accompanied.

"On reference to the proceedings which were adopted in the year 1832 *, it appears that previously to the restoration of your Lordship to your rank in the navy a free pardon under the great seal was granted to your Lordship, and, adverting to that circumstance, and to the fact that thirty years have elapsed since the charges to which the free pardon had reference were the subject of investigation before the proper judicial tribunal of the country, Her Majesty's servants cannot consistently with their sense of public duty advise the Queen to re-open an inquiry into those charges.

"I beg leave to refer your Lordship to the letter which the Earl of Haddington, the First Lord of the Admiralty, addressed to your Lordship in the year 1842 — as I am not enabled to make any communication to your Lordship on the part of Her Majesty's Government differing in purport from that letter.

"I have the honour, &c.,
"ROBERT PEEL.

"Admiral the Earl of Dundonald, &c."

Here was the whole secret why I had never been able to obtain an investigation of my case, and why the Admiralty, which deprived me of rank and honour, declined to investigate it, notwithstanding that an appeal from the verdict had been refused by the Court

* My restoration to rank.

of King's Bench, though I had then in court such additional evidence as must have set aside the verdict, which evidence will shortly be laid before the reader who will now be in a condition to understand the following explanation of Lord Brougham, given, under the article " Ellenborough," in his " Historic Sketches of British Statesmen in the time of George the Third."

" On the bench, it is not to be denied that Lord Ellenborough occasionally suffered the strength of his political feelings to break forth and to influence the tone and temper of his observations. That he ever, upon any one occasion, knowingly deviated one hair's breadth in the discharge of his office is wholly untrue. The case which gave rise to the greatest comment, and even led to a senseless show of impeachment was Lord Cochrane's. * * * I must, however, be here distinctly understood *to deny the accuracy of the opinion which Lord Ellenborough appears to have formed in this case, and deeply to lament the verdict of guilty which the jury returned, after three hours' consultation and hesitation.*

" If Lord Cochrane was at all aware of his uncle Mr. Cochrane Johnstone's proceedings, it was the whole extent of his privity to the fact. Having been one of the counsel engaged in the cause I can speak with some confidence respecting it, and I take upon me to assert that Lord Cochrane's conviction was mainly owing to the extreme repugnance which he felt to giving up his uncle, or taking those precautions for his own safety which would have operated against that near relation. Even when he, the real criminal, had confessed his guilt, by taking to flight, and the other defendants were brought up for judgment, we, the counsel, could not persuade Lord Cochrane to shake himself loose from the contamination by abandoning him.

" Our only complaint against Lord Ellenborough was his

Lordship's refusal to adjourn after the prosecutor's case closed, and his requiring us to enter upon our defence at so late an hour—past nine o'clock—that the adjournment took place at midnight, and before we called our witnesses. Of course, I speak of the trial at Guildhall only. Lord Ellenborough was equally to blame with his brethern in the Court of King's Bench for that most cruel and unjustifiable sentence, which at once secured Lord Cochrane's re-election for Westminister when the House of Commons expelled him upon his conviction.

" In 1833, the Government of which I was a member restored this great warrior to his rank of Admiral in our navy. The country, therefore, in the event of hostilities, would now have the inestimable benefit of his services, whom none perhaps ever equalled in heroic courage, and whose fertility of resources, military as well as naval, place him high amongst the very first of commanders. That his honours of knighthood, so gloriously won, should still be withholden is a stain, *not upon him,* but upon the councils of his country; and after his restoration to the service, it is as inconsistent and incomprehensible as cruel and unjust." (Lord Brougham's " Historic Sketches.")

A brief outline of the circumstances which led to the trial will enable the reader to comprehend the grounds upon which the opinions just quoted were based.

At the commencement of 1814 I was appointed by my uncle, Sir Alexander Cochrane, then commanding the British fleet on the North American station, as his flag-captain; and in the month of February was busily engaged in getting the *Tonnant* line-of-battle-ship, then fitting at Chatham as my uncle's flag-ship, ready for sea. The presence of Sir Alexander being imperatively required upon the station, he had previously quitted

England in a frigate; and it had been understood between my uncle and myself that, on joining him with the *Tonnant*, the most efficient measures should be adopted to compensate for our late defeats with the better manned and equipped vessels of the United States.

Previous to my uncle's departure at the latter end of 1813, he had, in pursuance of this object, repeatedly though unsuccessfully applied to the Admiralty for permission to engage an officer in the Duke of Cumberland's regiment of Sharpshooters, as having a reputation not only for skill in teaching rifle practice, but also for his pyrotechnic acquirements, as an engineer officer; this proficiency having become known to Sir Alexander through his brother, who, strongly urged the employment of the person alluded to, a Captain De Berenger, with whom Mr. Cochrane Johnstone had been for some time acquainted. It was thus that I was subsequently brought in contact with a man who eventually proved my ruin, by involving me in an appearance of complicity in an attempt to raise the public funds by the dissemination of groundless news to the prejudice of the Stock Exchange speculators, one of those common deceptions which, I am told, were then, as now, practised by parties connected with the transactions of the Stock Exchange.

In the month of January Mr. Cochrane Johnstone invited De Berenger to a dinner, at which I was present. Towards the close of the evening this person asked me to step aside with him for the purpose of con-

versation. His object was to request me to take him on
board the *Tonnant* in any capacity, for having failed
to obtain the consent of the Admiralty he would be
happy to trust to Sir Alexander's generosity to employ him in any situation for which he was qualified.
With this view he begged me to peruse his testimonials as Adjutant of the Duke of Cumberland's rifle
regiment, as well as other documents of a similar
character.

Finding the testimonials satisfactory, I expressed my
regret at not being able to take him in the *Tonnant*
without an appointment, or at least an order, from
the Board of Admiralty; adding, that no person
could possibly have less influence with their Lordships
than myself, and that therefore it was useless for me to
apply to them on his behalf, especially as they had
refused the application of Sir Alexander Cochrane.
Knowing, however, that it was the wish of Sir Alexander that De Berenger should go if possible, I recommended him to exert himself to secure the influence
of those under whom he appeared to have served
so satisfactorily; adding that, if he succeeded, 1
should have great pleasure in taking him in the
Tonnant.

With these prefatory remarks the reader will readily
comprehend what follows : —

About midnight on the 20th of February, according
to the current report of the transactions hereafter to be
named, a person calling himself Colonel de Bourg, aide-
de-camp to Lord Cathcart, presented himself at the
Ship Hotel at Dover, representing that he was the

bearer of intelligence from Paris, to the effect that
Buonaparte had been killed by the Cossacks — that the
allied armies were in full march for Paris — and that
immediate peace was certain. After this announcement
he forwarded similar intelligence by letter to the Port-
Admiral at Deal, with a view — as was supposed — of
its being forwarded to London by telegraph; thus
making the Port-Admiral the medium of communication with the Government.

This person, as was afterwards known to the Stock
Exchange only *through my instrumentality*, was the
before-named De Berenger. The intelligence was false,
having been concocted for the purpose of causing a
rise in the public funds.

On the 7th of March, the Committee of the Stock
Exchange published an advertisement offering a reward
of two hundred and fifty guineas for the discovery of
the person who had perpetrated the hoax; a report
being at the same time current that the pretended Du
Bourg had, on the morning of the 21st of February,
been *traced to my house in Green Street.*

At this time I had joined the *Tonnant* at Chatham,
and was preparing to sail for the North American
station, but on learning the injurious report above
mentioned, and being aware from the ordinary channels
of public intelligence of the nature of the transaction — being moreover indignant that the perpetrator
of the deception should have dared to visit me, I
determined to denounce him, in order that if he
were really the guilty person, his name should be
made public at the earliest possible moment, so that

no time might be lost in bringing the matter home to him.

In pursuance of this determination I obtained leave of absence from the ship. On my return to town, I found that although the authorities were ignorant of the name of the person who came to my house on the 21st of February, public rumour did not hesitate to impute to me complicity in his transactions, simply from the fact of the suspected person, whoever he might be, having been there.

To rebut these insinuations was of the first importance. Accordingly I immediately consulted my legal advisers.

The result was that an affidavit was prepared and submitted to an eminent barrister, Mr. Gurney, to whom I disclosed every particular relative to the visit of De Berenger, as well as to my own previous, though very unimportant transactions, in the public funds. I was advised by him and my own solicitors to confine myself simply to supplying the authorities with the name of De Berenger as the person seen in uniform at my house on the 21st ultimo.

With this suggestion, wisely or unwisely — but certainly in all honesty, I refused to comply, expressing my determination to account *for all my acts* on the 21st of February, even to the entire occupation of my whole time on that day. Finding me firm on this point, the affidavit was settled by Mr. Gurney, and sworn to, the name of De Berenger for the first time thus becoming known to those who were in quest of him. (See Appendix.)

A circumstance may here be mentioned which has an important bearing on the subject. My letter to the Admiralty, giving my reasons for asking leave of absence for the purpose of rebutting the insinuations against my character, contained most material matter for my exculpation. It was written to Mr. Secretary Croker, but when I afterwards moved for and obtained from the House of Commons an order for the production of my correspondence with the Admiralty, *this letter was not to be found, though all others asked for were!!* Had the letter been produced, it must have had great weight with the House, the adverse decision of which I mainly ascribe to its nonproduction. Unfortunately, in the haste of the application, no copy was taken.

I have been particular in recording dates, because it has been insinuated to my injury that I *had been tardy* in giving the information in my power. It is hence my desire to put on record that *the moment* the necessity for vindicating myself arose not an hour was lost by me in giving the Stock Exchange a clue to the offender, if such De Berenger should turn out to have been.

I will here notice another circumstance, viz. that the very Mr. Gurney who had advised me in the matter of my affidavit, and to whom I had unreservedly communicated every circumstance connected with my private affairs, as well as those connected with the visit of De Berenger, was afterwards chosen by Mr. Lavie, the *solicitor to the committee, as the leading counsel for the Stock Exchange at the subsequent trial against me!* I simply relate the fact, without comment.

It is not necessary here to weary the reader by the insertion of a lengthy affidavit, which accounted for every act of mine on the day of the alleged hoax. The main facts, as relating to the visit of De Berenger, are these. That early on the morning in question I had gone to a lamp manufactory in the city, for the purpose of superintending the progress of some lamps patented by me, and ordered for the use of the convoy of which I was about to take charge on their voyage to North America. Whilst thus engaged, my servant came to me with a note, which had been given to him by a military officer, who was waiting at my house to see me. Not being able to make out the name, from the scrawling style in which the note was written, and supposing it to have come from a messenger from my brother, who was then dangerously ill with the army of the Peninsula, and of whose death we were in daily expectation of hearing, I threw down the note, and replied, that I would come as soon as possible ; and, having completed my arrangements at the lamp manufactory, arrived at home about two hours afterwards, when, to my surprise, I found De Berenger in place of the expected messenger from my brother. The reader may gather from my affidavit what occurred at this interview. (See Appendix.)

The comprehensiveness of the voluntary disclosure contained in the affidavit has been termed indiscreet, and may have been so, as entering on much that might be deemed unnecessary. But I had nothing to

conceal, believing it could in no way affect me — nor
would it have done so but for the trickery subsequently
resorted to.   There was nothing extraordinary in the
document.   A poor but talented man — a prisoner
within the Rules of the King's Bench — came to me in
the hope that I would extricate him from his difficulties
by taking him to America in the *Tonnant.*   After my
renewed refusal, on professional grounds, De Berenger
represented that he could not return to the Rules in
his uniform without exciting suspicion of his absence.
The room happened at the time to be strewed with
clothes, in process of examination, for the purpose of
being sent on board the *Tonnant,* those rejected being
thrown aside;   and at his urgent request I lent, or
rather gave, him a civilian's hat and coat to enable
him to return to his lodgings in ordinary costume.
This simple act constituted my offence, and was construed by the Court into complicity in his fraudulent
conduct!   though under ordinary circumstances, and
I was aware of no other, it was simply an act of com-
passionate good nature.

A very remarkable circumstance connected with this
affidavit, and afterwards proved on the trial, was this—
that on De Berenger's arrival in town from Dover, he
neither went to the Stock Exchange, nor to his employers, whoever they might be, nor did he take any
steps on his arrival in town to *spread the false intelligence which he had originated.*   He was proved on the
trial to have dismissed his post-chaise at Lambeth —
to have taken a hackney-coach — and to have proceeded
straight to my house.   The inference is plain, that the

man was frightened at the nature of the mission he had undertaken, and declined to go through with it, preferring to try once more whether he could not prevail on me to take him on board the *Tonnant*, where he might remain till the ship sailed for North America.

Had I been his confederate, it is not within the bounds of credibility that he would have come in the first instance to my house, and waited two hours for my return home, in place of carrying out the plot he had undertaken, or that I should have been occupied in perfecting my lamp invention for the use of the convoy of which I was in a few days to take charge, instead of being on *the only spot* where any advantage to be derived from the Stock Exchange hoax could be realised, had I been a participator in it.   Such advantage must have been immediate, before the truth came out, and to have reaped it, had I been guilty, it was necessary that I should not lose a moment.   It is still more improbable, that being aware of the hoax, I should not have speculated largely for the special risk of that day.

Neither, had I been his confederate, is it more probable that I should have declined to take him on board the *Tonnant*, when, by so doing, I could have effectually concealed him under another name, together with every trace of the plot, and could have either taken him with me, or have shipped him in safety to the Continent.

I will here repeat what has been previously stated, that before my affidavit the committee of the Stock Exchange was ignorant even of the name of *any* person,

that my affidavit alone disclosed the necessary information. In other words, *I voluntarily gave the only information upon which the subsequent trial was based,
and this disclosure was so complete as to leave the Stock
Exchange nothing to do but to prosecute De Berenger.*

Let me ask the common-sense question, whether this
was the act of a guilty person, who by concealing
his knowledge could have effectually prevented all
further investigation?   Or, to put the question in
another form — would it not have been the act
of an insane person, if guilty, to have denounced
another to his own conviction, when by holding his
peace both would have been safe from detection?
To have done such an uncalled-for act, would have
been little in accordance with the *acumen* for which
the public had for many years given me credit. In
one respect, my affidavit might have been an error,
but it was not the *error of a guilty man;* viz. in not
deferring to the opinion of my legal advisers, who
wished me to confine myself to the single fact that the
pretended Du Bourg had been traced to my house, and
that I suspected De Berenger to be the person.

My fault was, that being conscious — till too late —
that nothing in the whole affair could in any way concern me — I was careless about my defence — had nothing to do with the brief beyond a few rough notes (see
Appendix) — and never even read it after it was finally
prepared for counsel. This was not the act of a guilty
man. Yet, had I been guilty, I should have had every
chance in my favour of acquittal ; first, by concealing
the fact that De Berenger was the stranger who

came to my house on the 21st of February, in military uniform — and, without this voluntary information on my part, the case must have disappeared; secondly, had I really been guilty, my chance of acquittal would have been greater than if innocent — because the knowledge of facts which I must have possessed if guilty, and *could not have possessed* if innocent, would have enabled me to make an effectual defence in place of the aimless defence which was made.

If proof of my non-participation in the hoax were required, it existed, so far as the statement of such a person was credible, in the handwriting of De Berenger himself, immediately after my affidavit disclosing his name in furtherance of the purposes of justice; a proceeding on my part which might naturally be supposed to embitter him against me. So far from this being the case, an innate sense of justice on the part of De Berenger led him to admit even the truth of the declaration contained in the affidavit as regarded himself.

> "13, Green Street, April 27th, 1814.
>
> "Sir,—Having, I trust, given ample time and opportunity to those who have endeavoured to asperse my character to learn from your own mouth the circumstances which induced you to call upon me on the 21st of February last, I feel it now due to myself no longer to delay this my earnest request, that you will afford me that explanation.
>
> > "I am, Sir, your obedient Servant,
> > (Signed) "Cochrane.
>
> "Baron de Berenger."

[De Berenger to Lord Cochrane:—]

> "King Street, Westminster, April 27th, 1814.
>
> "My Lord,—I have the honour of acknowledging the

receipt of your Lordship's favour, which has this moment been delivered.

" Rest assured, my Lord, that nothing could exceed the pain I felt when I perceived how cruelly, how unfairly my unfortunate visit of the 21st of February was interpreted (*which, with its object, is so correctly detailed in your affidavit*); but my agony is augmented, when I reflect that acts of generosity and goodness towards an unfortunate man have been, and continue to be, the accidental cause of much mortification to you : a fear of increasing the imaginary grounds of accusation caused me to refrain from addressing you.

" I have the honour, &c.,

" CHAS. RANDOM DE BERENGER."

The tone of this letter, which, without answering in express terms my query as to the object of his visit on the 21st of February, declares the truth of my affidavit as to the same, and also to what occurred during the short time he remained there.* This indisposed me for further communication with the writer, who, finding such to be the case, commenced a series of vituperative epistles, the object of which was evidently the extortion of money. The whole of these letters were transmitted by me to the public press, without reply or comment, and were so published at the time.

A no less important admission emanated from De Berenger. The press had by some means or other got hold of the fact that this man, whom I had denounced to the Stock Exchange, was *in communication with certain members of the Government for the purpose of implicating me!* The communication does not appear

---

* See my affidavit in the Appendix.

to have resulted in anything further than was known from my affidavit, and I have reason to know that from fear of the man's character, the Government abstained from committing themselves with him.

" King's Bench, July 19th, 1814.

"Whereas several newspapers have asserted that I have written to Lord Sidmouth, whilst others state that I have addressed the committee of the Stock Exchange, &c. disclosing particulars to prove Lord Cochrane's guilt, I feel justified thus solemnly, publicly, and positively to declare, That, *since my confinement here*, I have neither written, or otherwise applied, directly or indirectly, to any of the offices of Government for the purpose of disclosure. That I have not written to any one on the subject of the 21st of February last, *since the* 11*th instant* (July), excepting one private letter to Lord Cochrane. That the assertions in the newspapers are totally false, &c. &c.

" CHARLES RANDOM DE BERENGER."

The plain inference is, that De Berenger did so *before the trial*, and whilst he was writing to me that the contents of my affidavit, as regarded himself, contained the exact truth. That he had such communication with both Government and Stock Exchange, before the trial, is beyond doubt, and part of the reasons which warrant my assertion, that a higher authority than the Stock Exchange was at the bottom of my prosecution. Deeply degraded as was the man, he affords the strongest *presumptive* evidence of my non-participation in the hoax. In the next chapter I trust to adduce such *positive* evidence as shall place the matter beyond doubt.

I do not blame the Judge for not taking these matters into account, for, confident in my entire innocence, I could not see their importance or bearing, and did not even communicate them to my solicitor till too late.

Bitter after-knowledge has however convinced me of the error of carelessness—even from a consciousness of innocence — when once entangled in the meshes of law—a word by no means synonymous with justice.

Of the subject of the prosecution itself, I will here say one word. It was that of one set of stock-jobbers and their confederates trying — by means of false intelligence—to raise the price of " *time bargains*" at the expense of another set of stock-jobbers, the losers being naturally indignant at the successful hoax. The wrong was not then, and still is not, on the statute-book. Such a case had never been tried before, nor has it since — and was termed a " conspiracy ;" or rather, by charging the several defendants—of most of whom I had never before heard — in one indictment, it was brought under the designation of a " conspiracy." The " conspiracy " — such as it was — was nevertheless one, which, as competent persons inform me, has been the practice in all countries ever since stock-jobbing began, and is in the present day constantly practised, but I have never heard mention of the energy of the Stock Exchange even to detect the practice.

I do not make these remarks to palliate deception, even at the expense of Stock Exchange speculators. My object is, that the present generation, knowing that in my early life I was imprisoned and fined 1000*l.* for an alleged offence against the Stock Exchange fraternity, may understand the exact character of the accusation. It is clear that the influence and vindictive-

ness with which this most unjustifiable prosecution was
carried out as against me, arose from motives far deeper
than the vindication of stock-jobbing purity, viz. from
a desire in more influential quarters to silence, if
possible, an obnoxious political adversary; the visit of
De Berenger to my house, as disclosed by myself, and
his acquaintance with my uncle as before stated,
affording a basis for the accomplishment of this object.

Happily, Providence has implanted in the breast of
man an amount of moral and physical energy pro-
portioned to the wrongs and inflictions he may be
called upon to bear, and, even in my eighty-fifth year,
I am still left sound in mind, and with a heart unbroken,
to tell my own story.

CHAP. XXXIX.

HAD I been aware of a very curious coincidence connected with the trial which followed, my confidence,
arising from consciousness of innocence, would have
vanished in an instant; so that instead of indifference
about the result, I should have seen the necessity of
meeting every accusation with the most deliberate
caution, supporting the same by every attainable evidence, in place of no evidence at all.

The fact alluded to is this — that the same Mr. Lavie
who had displayed so much tact on Lord Gambier's
court-martial *was selected as solicitor to the prosecution
in the present case*, to the exclusion of the appointed
solicitor to the Committee of the Stock Exchange!
The fact was significant, as affording additional sus-

picion that an influence other and higher than that of the Committee was at work.

As in various publications connected with Lord Gambier's trial I had spoken very freely of Mr. Lavie as regarded the fabricated charts, exposed at the commencement of this volume, there could be no doubt of his not unreasonable personal animosity towards myself. But when, *after the trial*, I became for the first time aware that he had been employed to conduct it, the enigma was solved as to how I, from having voluntarily given the only information upon which the case could have originated at all, came to be mixed up in one common accusation with a number of persons, of most of whose very names I had never before heard.

More than this, it then became but too apparent that from the selection of Mr. Lavie as prosecuting attorney, I was not so much the subject of a Stock Exchange prosecution as of the political vindictiveness of which I have spoken, and which had gone out of the usual course to secure his services. That there was collusion between a high official at the Admiralty and the Committee of the Stock Exchange on this point, I do not hesitate for one moment to assert; nor do I think, from previous revelations in this work, that many of my readers will be inclined to differ with me.

I will not, however, dwell upon this matter. Whoever selected Mr. Lavie had a perfect right so to do, as Mr. Lavie had to accept the conduct of the case; the result of which is attributable to my being so satisfied of my own innocence as to decide that an accusation which so little concerned me ought not to take me from the more important duties in which I was employed. Had I been aware at the time of Mr. Lavie's appointment, I should have known its meaning, and prepared accordingly.

The principal circumstance which was held to have implicated me in the hoax practised on the Stock Exchange was this : — That (as gathered from my own voluntary information) De Berenger came to my house on the 21st February ; but that instead of being dressed in a green uniform, as set forth in my affidavit, he was in scarlet uniform, that being the alleged costume in which he had disseminated the false intelligence at Dover. If this point could be proved, it was inferred that I must have had a motive in wrongly describing the uniform in my affidavit, and that motive could be none other than my own knowledge of the hoax which had been perpetrated. How this inference was arrived at will appear in the sequel.

The main question relied on by the prosecution related to the colour of De Berenger's coat, whether *scarlet* or *green :* the point held by the Court being, that if *scarlet*, I must have made a false declaration in my affidavit as to its colour, and therefore must have at least known how De Berenger had been engaged. A *non sequitur* truly, but nevertheless the one relied on for my conviction as one of the conspirators.

The evidence was this — that when De Berenger arrived from Dover at the Marsh Gate, Lambeth, he exchanged the post-chaise in which he had been travelling for a hackney coach, in which he drove to my house,—which was true enough. The waterman on the stand was called as the first link in the chain ; but as he said " he did not see that he could recollect De Berenger, having only seen him for half a minute," (*Report*, p. 120,) this evidence is not worth commenting on, unless to remark that, failing to recognise De Berenger in court, the extraordinary course was taken of pointing him out, and then asking the witness if " he *thought* he *was like* the man who got into the coach ?" The reply was " he *thought* he was, but he only saw him for half a minute."—(*Ibid.*)

The next witness brought forward was a man named Crane — the hackney coachman who drove De Berenger. In his examination, Crane did not say a word about the colour of De Berenger's coat, but in his cross-examination swore that he had on a "red coat underneath his great coat " (*Report*, p. 124). At the same time he stated that De Berenger had with him " *a portmanteau big enough to wrap a coat in.*" Other witnesses proved that he had drawn down the sun blinds in the vehicle, so that he had abundant opportunity to exchange his red coat in which he appeared at Dover, for the green sharpshooter's uniform, and this no doubt he had done. The person of whom the red uniform had been purchased also deposed, that he had carried it away from his shop in a portmanteau, so that there was no doubt of the capacity of the latter to contain the coat. In short, he left London in the uniform of the rifles, and put on the scarlet uniform at Dover, to assume the pretended rank of a staff officer. On his return to London he in like manner, no doubt, changed his uniform by the way.

It has been shown that the waterman who opened the coach-door for De Berenger refused to identify him, but swore that the person alluded to had a red coat beneath his military coat. It is also remarkable that the hackney coachman, Crane, could not be got to identify him, though, like the waterman, he swore to the red coat. The subjoined is Crane's evidence on the subject :—

Mr. ADOLPHUS.—" Have you seen that person since that you drove that morning ? "

CRANE.—" Yes; I saw him in King Street, Westminster." (At the messenger's house, where Crane was taken by Mr. Lavie for the purpose of being identified by this witness.)

Mr. ADOLPHUS.—" Do you see him in court ? "

CRANE.—" I *think* this is the gentleman here."

Mr. ADOLPHUS.—" Were you of the same opinion when you saw him in King Street ? "

CRANE.—" When I came down stairs he looked very hard at me."

Mr. ADOLPHUS.—" Did you know him then ? "

CRANE.—" Yes : it was *something of the same appearance,* but he had altered himself very much by his dress."

Mr. RICHARDSON.—" He was pointed out there as being the person in custody ? "

CRANE.—" No : I walked down stairs, and met the gentleman coming up stairs."

Mr. RICHARDSON.—" You thought you saw a resemblance?"

CRANE.—" Yes, I thought he was *something like* the same gentleman that I had carried."

Mr. RICHARDSON.—" You do not pretend to recollect every person you carry in your hackney coach every day ? "

CRANE.—" *No,* but this gentleman that I took from a post chaise and four : when he got out at Green Street, I saw that he had a red coat underneath his great coat. "

Thus, neither the waterman nor the hackney coachman would swear to *the man*, but to a red coat only. I have no hesitation in saying, that in a court of justice in the present day no weight whatever would have been attached to such evidence. I will, however, assume that the evidence was such as to carry weight, and that it was in every respect unexceptionable, because I shall shortly come to the reason why they swore to the coat, but not to the man who wore it.

The case against me then stood thus. *One* witness (the waterman), but no more, swore to the under coat of a person whom he had seen step from one vehicle into another; and *one* witness, but no more (the hackney coachman) swore to the person whom he brought to my house, as having on a red coat beneath his military coat, but would not swear positively to the wearer. It was, however, to support this extraordinary evidence that my voluntary declaration in my affidavit, of lending De Berenger an old hat and coat, because he alleged that he could not return to his lodgings in the King's Bench in uniform, without exciting suspicion of his absence from the rules, and thus endangering his securities — was charged against me as involving confederacy.

On the evidence here adduced — and there was not a tittle beyond it, on the subject of the coat — the point was held by Lord Ellenborough to be established that De Berenger stripped off the red coat in my house! and as it was afterwards found in the river, his lordship charged the jury in a way which bore the construction of my having been also a participator in

that act, though there was not a particle of evidence
on the trial which could give even the shadow of
such a conclusion, nor was there even a pretence on
the part of the prosecution that such was the case.
His Lordship's address to the jury on this head is
amongst the most remarkable that ever fell from the
lips of an English judge.

" Now, gentlemen, he (*De Berenger*) is brought to the
house of Lord Cochrane; *further evidence afterwards arises
upon the subject of his being there.* We will at present
follow the dress to its conclusion. George Odell, a fisher-
man, says, ' In the month of March, just above Old Swan
Stairs, off against the Iron Wharfs, when I was dredging for
coals, I picked up a bundle which was tied with either a
piece of chimney line or window line in the cover of a chair
bottom ; there were two slips of a coat, embroidery, a star,
and a piece of silver, with two figures upon it; it had been
sunk with three pieces of lead and some bits of coal ; I gave
that which I found to Mr. Wade, the Secretary of the Stock
Exchange ; it was picked up on the Wednesday, and carried
there on the Saturday. I picked this up on the 24th of
March.' *You have before had the animal hunted home,
and now you have his skin,* found and produced as it was
taken out of the river, cut to pieces ; the sinking it could
have been with no other view than that of suppressing *this
piece of evidence*, and preventing the discovery which it
might otherwise occasion ; this makes it the more material to
attend *to the stripping off the clothes which took place in
Lord Cochrane's house.*"—(*Report*, p. 478.)

That this unwarrantable assumption, based on no
evidence whatever, of De Berenger's stripping off his
clothes at my house, could have anything to do with
a coat found in the river, was positively absurd, and
was not supported by a particle of evidence. Besides

which, I had some reputation for shrewdness, and should not have been likely to tie up the coat "in an old chair cover, with three pieces of lead and some lumps of coal!" when the winter's fire in my grate would in five minutes have destroyed the coat and its evidence together, had it been "stripped off" in my house, or had I been a party to its destruction. The position in which the coat was found, showed where it came from, viz. from the Southwark side of the river, where De Berenger's lodgings were.

The Judge thus proceeded : —

"De Berenger must have had that dress with him, whatever it was in which he had come in the coach, and *it does not appear that he had any means of shifting himself*. If he had on an aide-de-camp's uniform with a star, and so presented himself to Lord C., how could Lord C. reconcile it to the duties he owed to society, to government, and to his character as a gentleman, to give him the means of exchanging it? It must be put on for some dishonest purpose.

"It is for you, gentlemen, to say whether it is possible he should not know that a man coming so disguised and so habited, — *if he appeared before him so habited*, — came upon some dishonest errand, and whether it is to be conceived a person should so present himself to a person who did not know what that dishonest errand was, and that it was the very dishonest errand upon which he had so recently been engaged, and which he is found to be executing in the spreading of false intelligence for the purpose of elevating the funds. If he actually appeared to Lord Cochrane stripped of his coat, and with that red coat and aide-de-camp's uniform, star and order, which have been represented to you, he appeared before him rather in the habit of a mountebank than in his proper uniform of a sharpshooter. This seems wholly inconsistent with the conduct of an innocent and honest man; for if he appeared in such an habit, he must have appeared to any rational person fully blazoned in the costume of that or some other crime." (*Report*, pp. 484, 485, 486.)

The preceding quotations from his Lordship's address to the jury are taken from the " *revised* " report of the trial. They will appear still more extraordinary as quoted from the report of the *Times* newspaper, taken *verbatim* at the time. Of this no one acquainted even with ordinary newspaper reports will doubt the accuracy, and after having perused it, there will be as little doubt but that the " *revised* " report was subsequently altered from what really occurred in Court.

The subjoined is the *Times* report of the Judge's speech : —

" *Having hunted down the game,* the prosecutors showed *what became of his skin,* and it was a very material *fact* that the defendant De Berenger *stripped himself at Lord Cochrane's.* HE PULLED HIS SCARLET UNIFORM OFF THERE, and if the circumstance of its not being green did not excite Lord Cochrane's suspicion, what did he think of the star and medal ? It became him on discovering these, as an officer and a gentleman, to communicate his suspicions of these circumstances. Did he not ask De Berenger where he had been in this masquerade dress? It was for the jury to say whether Lord Cochrane did not know where he had been. This was not the dress of a sharpshooter, but of a mountebank. HE CAME BEFORE LORD COCHRANE FULLY BLAZONED IN THE COSTUME OF HIS CRIME ! ! "

The reader will not fail to perceive that in the *Times* verbatim report, which is no doubt correct, the Court in every sentence affirms my *positive guilt.* In the " *revised* " report, his Lordship is made to go throughout on the hypothetical " if," whilst in the revised report

of the trial,—which revised report, I affirm, was made
up for the occasion, — I am represented to have been
treated with all proper fairness! Every evil which followed afterwards was inflicted on the strength of this
revised report, and not on the actual transactions at the
trial, as reported in the daily papers.

This "revised" report was, indeed, a very serious
matter for me. From the reports in the daily papers,
which were unquestionably accurate, the public mind was
in a state of great ferment at the unfairness of the trial
as regarded myself, and therefore the prosecution got up
the "revised" report. On its appearance, the Attorney-
General said in the House of Commons (July 20th)
" He was glad the period had arrived when the trial
could be read at length, and thus *do away the effect of
those imperfect statements* (the reports of the daily
papers) which *misled the public mind.*" The Solicitor-
General, on the same date, went farther, and accused
me of having in my defence *misrepresented and misquoted the Judge*, because I had quoted the reports of
the daily papers, not having in fact any other to quote.
On the testimony of that " revised " report further investigation was declined by the Admiralty, and I was
dismissed from the naval service.

On the strength of Crane's evidence, the Court had
held that " *De Berenger appeared before me blazoned in
the costume of his crime — that he pulled off his scarlet
uniform in my presence — and that, if the circumstance of its not being green did not excite my suspicion,
what did I think of the star and medal?*" It is
certain, that, even in the " revised " report of the trial,

these unqualified assertions, which, put as they were to the jury, were sufficient for my conviction, *are not supported by one particle of evidence!!*

But more has yet to be said of Crane's evidence, which led to these expressions on the part of the Judge. It will admit of little doubt that a man who would swear to the colour of a coat, and would not swear positively (by the " revised " report) to the identity of the person who wore it, must have had cogent reasons for a course so extraordinary.

I will now adduce those reasons :—

It has been stated, that, conscious of my innocence, I took no personal steps for my defence, beyond forwarding a general statement of a few lines to my solicitors (see Appendix), that I never even read the completed brief which they drew up for the guidance of my counsel, nor was I present in court to suggest questions in cross-examination. After my conviction, however, it became necessary to seek additional evidence to support an appeal from the conviction, or an application for a new trial as against myself.

Lord Ellenborough refused the application, *because all the persons tried were not present to concur in it*, though the law gave me no power to compel their attendance. The evidence on which it was grounded, however, is none the less conclusive because Lord Ellenborough and his colleagues declined to receive it, or even *to hear it!!* but in place of so doing, at once delivered their outrageous sentence against me.

This appeal was grounded on the evidence of several respectable tradesmen, residing in the neighbourhood of Crane, the hackney coachman, they voluntarily and unsolicited by me, but as an act of public justice, going before the Lord Mayor, and making the affidavits from which the subjoined extracts are taken. Not one of these tradesmen was even known to me or my solicitors:—

JAMES MILLER, butcher, of Marsh Gate, Lambeth, made affidavit that he saw De Berenger "get out of the chaise into a hackney coach—that he was *dressed in green*, with a grey great coat, and that *there was no red on any part of his dress.*"

JOSEPH RAIMENT, fishmonger, Westminster Bridge Road, made affidavit that he saw De Berenger "get out of the chaise into the hackney coach—that his great coat was partly open, and that *the under dress was dark green, like that of the sharpshooters.*"

CHARLES KING, stable-keeper, Westminster Bridge Road, made affidavit that he met William Crane accidentally, and asked him what he had been doing with Sayer?* He answered, that "he had been to see De Berenger, in order to identify him, but *he could not swear to him, as many faces were alike.*" But he said, using a protestation in the most horrible language, too gross to repeat — "he would have a hackney coach *out of them*," meaning, as deponent believed, the prosecutors. During this conversation, a person passed dressed in a grey great coat, which Crane said was just like De Berenger's, and that he (Crane) did not see De Berenger's under-dress, *as his coat was closely buttoned up.*

" Deponent further saith, that after the trial he saw Crane's father, who told him that 'he was *going after the money*' (meaning the reward), adding that '*his son was considered a first-rate witness!*' On this deponent asked Crane the elder 'how he could consider his son in that light, as he knew very well that had he (deponent) been examined, he must have

* A messenger of the Court.

beat him out of Court.' To this Crane's father replied, 'that if he had appeared, there was the place where the clothes were bought, and the post-boy.' On deponent being severe in his remarks, the father said, 'I don't know what they did with the boy, *they had him two days locked up in the police officer's house, that he might not be tampered with.'* * Deponent asked him if there had been any advances by the opposite party. He said, 'None.'

"Deponent further saith, that he has seen William Crane since the trial, and on deponent accusing him of going too far with his evidence, he said, '*he would swear black was white, or anything else, if he was paid for it!*'

"Deponent further saith, that before the trial, the said William Crane's coach and horses *were of a most miserable description, but that since the trial he has purchased a hackney coach and horses of the best description!*

"Deponent further saith, that the said William Crane's general character *is most infamous*, and his mode of expressing himself *so obscene and blasphemous* as to preclude deponent from stating the exact words made use of by the said William Crane. This deponent further saith, that Mr. Keir, and the groom of Colonel Taylor, were present when Crane said that '*he would swear black was white, or anything else, if he was well paid for it.*'"

RICHARD BALDWIN, servant to Mr. Keir, made affidavit "that, on the 2nd of July, he was present at a conversation between Charles King and William Crane, when he heard Crane, in reply to King, who had accused him of having gone too far in his evidence, say that '*he would be damned if he would not swear black was white, or anything else, if any one would pay him for it.*'"

THOMAS CRITCHFIELD, Westminster Bridge Road, coachmaker, made affidavit "that he knew William Crane, and that he heard him say, previously to the said trial, when

---

* The post-boy admitted on the trial that he had several previous examinations, and that he *received 52l. for his evidence!*

speaking of his father, that ' *he did not care a damn for his father*, that he was twenty-one years of age, *and should soon have more money than ever his father had.*'

" Deponent further said that *since* the trial the said William Crane has been enabled *to purchase a very good hackney coach, with horses and harness*, though *previous* to the trial his coach and horses were of the most miserable description. Deponent lastly saith, that the said William Crane *is a man of the most infamous character, and this deponent positively declares that he would not believe him on his oath.*"

JAMES YEOWELL, of Silver Street, Falcon Square, ticket porter, made affidavit "that *a few days after the* 21st *of February*, William Crane told him that the person whom he took from a post-chaise and four at the Marsh Gate, was NO OTHER THAN LORD COCHRANE HIMSELF ! that he knew Lord Cochrane as well as he knew him (deponent). That he *had driven Lord Cochrane from the Opera House, and other places of amusement twenty times*, and described Lord Cochrane as a tall man, with a long face and red whiskers.

" Deponent further saith, that after the trial he (deponent) accused the said William Crane *of perjury*, in having sworn to De Berenger as the man taken up by him at the Marsh Gate, whereas he had *previously declared* before the Stock Exchange Committee that LORD COCHRANE WAS THE PERSON ! Whereupon Crane refused to converse with him further on the subject.

" This deponent further saith, that having on the same day again met William Crane, he inquired if he had received the reward offered by the Stock Exchange Committee, when he, the said William Crane, admitted that *he had received a part, and expected more.*"

JAMES LOVEMORE, of Clement's Lane, made affidavit "that he heard the said James Yeowell interrogate William Crane as to the person of Lord Cochrane, and that Crane said he knew Lord Cochrane as well as he did him (Yeowell), and that he had driven Lord Cochrane from the Opera House and other places of amusement, *twenty times,* and Crane further declared that *it was Lord Cochrane* whom he drove from the post-chaise and four at the Marsh Gate, Lambeth, and described his Lordship as a tall man with a long face and red whiskers."

Such was a portion only of the facts which I was prepared with in my appeal to Lord Ellenborough and his colleagues.   But, as before said, the same judge refused to listen to the appeal, not on the ground of my having no evidence to rebut the perjury of Crane, but because *all the persons convicted were not present in Court to join in the appeal.*   It was the rule of Court, which I had no power to alter, though, as has been seen in a recent chapter, Lord Campbell, in his "Lives of the Chief Justices," states, that such a case had *only been ruled once, and that in this case it ought to have been overruled.*

In the two affidavits last adduced there is abundant proof that if the resource of the *red coat* had not been adopted, Crane was prepared to swear that *it was I whom he had driven from the Marsh Gate to my own house!* the conclusion being that I was the pretended De Berenger.   Crane evidently knew my personal appearance, as did most persons in London, and said, further, that he knew me from having driven me *twenty times to the Opera;* the fact being that I was never at the Opera but twice in my life, and once in the vestibule, when I was refused admittance from not being in full evening dress, the deficiency consisting in wearing white pantaloons on a very hot day.

It should be remembered, that Crane stated this

before the Committee of the Stock Exchange *soon
after the* 21*st of February*, i. e., *before* I had given
the clue to De Berenger in my affidavit as the person
who visited my house on the morning of that day.
After I had thus disclosed the name of De Berenger,
the project of proving by the perjury of Crane that *I
was the pretended Du Bourg*, was given up by the
prosecution,— from the dissimilarity of his personal appearance to mine ; and then — *but not till then* — was
the equally atrocious perjury of the *red coat* resorted to.

Upon the evidence of such a man as Crane was I
convicted, and refused an appeal from the conviction,
or a new trial because the defendants to the indictment
were not all in Court !! It was " *a rule of Court,*"
which, as Lord Campbell says, ought to have been in
my case overruled, but Lord Ellenborough refused to
hear a word of the abundant evidence *then in my
hand* and available for my exculpation. Crane's evidence that De Berenger had on a red coat, was relied
on, but the far more reliable evidence that the coat was
" *green,*" as I had stated, was repudiated. Crane had
boasted that " *he would swear black was white, if well
paid for it*"— and I held in my hand the most reliable
evidence that from the money he had been paid for
his perjury, he had bought " *a new coach, horses, and
harness.*" None of these circumstances were allowed
to be received in Court, or even listened to, because
all the persons included in the indictment were not
present, though, as Lord Campbell has well said, the
rule of Court in my case ought, under the peculiar circumstances, to have been overruled.

A few more particulars relative to this *convict*, Crane,
— for such was his subsequent fate,— are necessary to
enable the reader to judge of my prosecution and those
who selected this man as their chief witness.

Not long after the trial, the solicitor of Mr. Cochrane Johnstone wrote me to the following effect relative to a discovery made when too late as to Crane's
character : —

" This fellow has lately been prosecuted by Mr. Dawson,
before the Commissioners of the Hackney Coach Office, for
brutality and general misconduct.   This offence was so flagrant that the *severest punishment* was inflicted, and at
present he is under a long suspension.   He is a worthless
rascal, and if Mr. D. can do your Lordship any service, you
have only to command it."

Enclosed in the above communication was the following extract from the *Times* newspaper of May 25th,
1814 :—

" On Friday last, William Crane, driver of the hackney
coach No. 782, was summoned before the Commissioners on
a charge of cruelty to his horses, and for abuse to a gentleman who noticed his conduct.   The circumstances detailed
were so shocking as to induce the Commissioners to observe
that they never *heard a more atrocious case*.   They would
have inflicted a pecuniary penalty, but as it must necessarily
be paid by his father, they ordered him instead to be suspended from driving any hackney coach for three months."

The trial, which resulted in my conviction, *on this
very man's evidence*, took place on the 8th of June,
1814, *only a fortnight after his conviction of the atrocity
just quoted!* so that at the moment of giving his evi-

dence this man was himself under punishment for an offence pronounced by the Commissioners to be "*so shocking that they never heard of a more atrocious case*"*!!!* Had this information been available at the trial, the jury would have paid but small attention to Crane's evidence.

Crane was convicted of stealing twenty sovereigns and other property under circumstances no less atrocious. He was sentenced to transportation for seven years, but at the expiration of three years *received a free pardon from the Government on his own petition.*

The subjoined certificate from the officials of Newgate, however, place his conviction and premature pardon by the Secretary of State in 1830 beyond doubt :—

" Office, Newgate, 23rd October, 1830.

" I do hereby certify that William Crane (aged 33) was committed to this gaol on the 17th of February, 1826, by J. C. Conant, Esq., for ' stealing a box, a pair of scissors, and twenty sovereigns, the property and moneys of William Bucknall ; ' tried before Mr. Sergeant Arabin on the 20th of February, convicted and sentenced to transportation for seven years, and that he was removed on the 23rd of March following, on board the *Justitia* hulk at Woolwich."

Endorsement at the back of this certificate :—

" William Crane has been discharged from the hulks *on petition to the Secretary of State,* and is now again driving the coach No. 781, belonging to his father ! Crane's discharge took place Thursday before last.

" 13th November, 1830."

(No signature, but evidently a police memorandum.)

These facts will be sufficient to convince the reader

of my innocence as regarded the evidence of Crane, the hackney coachman. Yet his evidence was laid before the jury as of the highest reliable kind, whilst the very facts relative to his character, even to his being under conviction whilst giving his evidence, Lord Ellenborough and his colleagues refused to hear, because all the parties convicted were not present in Court. It is scarcely possible to imagine greater injustice and folly, even in that day.

So little apparent danger was there of the possibility of my being declared implicated in this hoax, that even my solicitors had not taken the precaution of summoning my servants to give evidence as to the kind of dress worn by De Berenger; though during the period he remained in my house, previous to my arrival from the lamp-maker's, where, on receiving his letter, I was busily engaged, and amidst the busy operations of packing my clothes, and other effects, to be sent on board the *Tonnant*, he had been seen by nearly all my servants, the selection of clothing being carried on in the very room in which he was waiting my return for nearly two hours.

On my appeal to the Court of King's Bench, I provided myself with the following affidavits from such of my servants as had come in contact with De Berenger, whilst waiting at my house :—

" THOMAS DEWMAN, servant to Lord Cochrane, maketh oath, and saith, that he, this deponent, has lived with branches of Lord Cochrane's family for nearly twenty years; that he attended Lord Cochrane last year to take letters and go on errands, and that he has been in the habit of going to Mr. King's manufactory almost every day; that this deponent was in Lord Cochrane's house, in Green Street, Grosvenor Square, on the 21st day of February last, when an officer came in a hackney-coach, about ten o'clock in the morning; that this deponent opened the door and spoke to the officer in the coach, who asked if Lord Cochrane was at home; that this deponent replied he was not, upon which the officer asked the deponent, if he knew where Lord Cochrane was gone to, which deponent answered that he believed his Lordship was gone to breakfast with his uncle in Cumberland Street; that the officer then asked him if he could let him have a slip of paper and a pen and ink, which this deponent said he could; that this deponent then opened the coach door, and the officer came into the house, and went into the parlour, where this deponent gave him a small slip of paper, upon which he wrote a few lines by way of note, and desired this deponent to take the same to Lord Cochrane in Cumberland Street; that this deponent went immediately into Cumberland Street, but finding that Lord Cochrane was gone, he returned with the note to the officer in Green Street; that on his return the officer asked deponent if he knew where he could find him, that deponent then told the officer he had been ordered by Lord Cochrane to follow him to Mr. King's manufactory with a glass globe, and thought it probable he might meet with his Lordship there, and if he did not, he would then go to the Admiralty, where he understood his Lordship was to go that day; that the officer then took back the note from this deponent, opened it, and wrote a line or two more, and then re-sealed it and gave it to deponent, requesting him to take it immediately to Mr. King's manufactory, and that if he did not meet with Lord Cochrane there, he would take the note to the Admiralty, and if his Lordship had not been at the Admiralty, to leave it there; that on the officer's requesting deponent to go to Mr. King's manufactory, he told the deponent that his finding Lord Cochrane was of consequence, and therefore begged deponent to be as expeditious as he could, and, if necessary, to take a coach; that this deponent did not take a coach, but went instantly to Mr. King's manufactory, where he met Lord Cochrane, and delivered him the note, which he opened in deponent's presence; that upon opening the note, Lord Cochrane asked deponent several times if he knew who the gentleman was that had written it, and upon deponent's informing him that he did not, Lord Cochrane made several inquiries as to his appearance and dress, observing that he could not make out the whole of the note, or who it came from; to this deponent answered, that he was an army officer; upon which Lord Cochrane having torn the note, threw it down, and then said, ' Very well, Thomas, I'll go back;' that from Lord Cochrane's manner and appearance, and the questions he put to deponent, on his delivering the note, this deponent verily believes that his Lordship did not know from whom it came. And this deponent further saith, that when the officer came into Green Street, as above stated, he *was dressed in a great grey coat, such as the Guards wear, which was buttoned very close round the body up to the breast, and that such part of the under coat as he could see was of a dark-green colour*; that upon the officer's coming out of the coach into Lord Cochrane's house, he brought with him a sword, and a small leather clothes-bag or portmanteau, which deponent believes might have held a change of clothes. That this deponent further saith, that he was hired by his Lordship at Christmas last to go into the country, and relieve Richard Carter, his Lordship's sea-steward; that this deponent left London about the 25th day of February, and Richard Carter, the sea-steward, then came to town, for the purpose of accompanying Lord Cochrane to his ship.

" THOMAS DEWMAN.

" Sworn in Court, June 14th,
    " 1814. By the Court."

" MARY TURPIN, cook-maid to Lord Cochrane, maketh oath and saith, that she went into his Lordship's service on the 18th day of February last, and that she was in the house on the 21st day of February, when an officer came there, and that she was in the kitchen at the time the coach drove to the door ; that she saw an officer alight from the coach and come into the house ; that he arrived a little before nine o'clock ; that this deponent went twice into the parlour while the officer was there, and doth most positively swear, *that he wore a great grey coat, buttoned up, with a dark-green collar or facing under it.* That the officer had with him a dark military cap with a gold band round it, and also a sword, and a small portmanteau.

" MARY TURPIN.

" Sworn in Court, June 14th,
" 1814. By the Court."

" SARAH BUST, of No. 4, Great Marylebone Street, in the county of Middlesex, spinster, maketh oath and saith, that she lived a servant to Lord Cochrane for nearly twelve months, and that she quitted his service on the evening of the 21st of February last ; that she well remembers an officer coming to his Lordship's house in Green Street, on the morning of that day ; that the officer sent the man-servant out ; that the officer *had on a grey great coat, which was buttoned up to the breast,* and that the neck of his under coat or such part as she could see, was a *dark green,* and he had also with him a military cap.

" SARAH BUST.

" Sworn at my Chambers,
" June 13th, 1814. Before me,
" S. LE BLANC."

To this I will append my second affidavit :—

" Sir THOMAS COCHRANE, commonly called Lord Cochrane, one of the above-named defendants, maketh oath and saith, that the several facts and circumstances stated in his affidavit, sworn on the 11th day of March last, before Mr. Graham the Magistrate, are true. And this deponent further saith, that in addition to the several facts and circumstances stated in his said affidavit, he deposeth as follows ; that is to say: That he had not, directly or indirectly, any concern whatever in the formation, or any knowledge of the existence, of an intention to form the plot charged in the indictment, or any other scheme or design for affecting the public funds. That the sale of the pretended omnium, on the 21st day of February, was made in pursuance of orders given to his broker at the time of the purchase thereof, on or about the 14th of that month, to sell the same whenever a profit of one per cent. could be realised: and that those directions were given, and the sale thereof took place, without any knowledge, information, hint, or surmise, on the part of this deponent, of any concern or attempt whatever, to alter the price of the funds; and the said sale on the 21st took place entirely without this deponent's knowledge. That when this deponent returned home from Mr. King's manufactory on the 21st of February, which he did directly after the receipt of a note, he fully expected to have met an officer from abroad, with intelligence of his brother, who had, by letter to this deponent, received on the Friday before, communicated his being confined to his bed, and severely afflicted by a dangerous illness, and about whom this deponent was extremely anxious; but this deponent found Capt. De Berenger at his house, in a *grey* great coat, and a *green* jacket. That this deponent never saw the defendants Ralph Sandom, Alex. M'Rae, John Peter Holloway, and Henry Lyte, or any or either of them, nor ever had any communication or correspondence with them, or any or either of them, directly or indirectly. That this deponent, in pursuance of directions from the Admiralty, proceeded to Chatham, to join His Majesty's ship the *Tonnant*, to which he had been appointed on the 8th day of February last. That the ship was then lying at Chatham. That, previous to the 8th day of February, this deponent applied to the Admiralty for leave of absence, which was refused, until this deponent had joined the said ship, and had removed her down to Long Reach; that this deponent, in pursuance of those directions, removed the said ship from Chatham to Long Reach, and after that was done,

viz. on Saturday the 12th day of the said month, this deponent wrote to the Admiralty to apply for leave of absence
for a fortnight, for the purpose of lodging a specification for a
patent, as had been previously communicated by this deponent
to their Lordships; that leave of absence was accordingly
granted for fourteen days, commencing on the 14th of the
said month; that this deponent was engaged in London,
expecting the said specification, till the 28th of the said
month, when the said specification was completed, and this
deponent left town about one o'clock on the morning of the
1st of March, and arrived at Chatham about daylight on
the same morning: that on the 8th or 9th of the same month
of March, this deponent received an intimation that placards
were posted in several of the streets, stating that a pretended
Colonel De Bourg had gone to this deponent's house in
Green Street; that at the time this deponent received this
intimation, he was on board the said ship at Long Reach,
and in consequence went to Admiral Surridge, the Port
Admiral at Chatham, to obtain leave of absence, which was
granted; previous to the receipt of the leave forwarded by
the Lords Commissioners of the Admiralty, this deponent
arrived in London, on the 10th of that month, to the best of
his belief; and that after his trial, he himself, conscious of
his own innocence, and fearing no consequences from a development of his own conduct, and desiring only to rescue
his character from erroneous impressions, made by misrepresentations in the public prints, he, without any communication whatever with any other person, and without any
assistance, on the impulse of the moment, prepared the
before-mentioned affidavit, which he swore before Mr. Graham, the Magistrate, on the 11th; that at the time he made
such affidavit, he had not seen or heard the contents of the
Report published by the Committee of the Stock Exchange,
except partial extracts in the newspapers; that when the deponent understood that the prosecution was to be instituted
against him, he wrote to Admiral Fleming, in whose service
Isaac Davis, formerly this deponent's servant, then was, under

cover to Admiral Bickerton, at Portsmouth, and that Admiral
Bickerton returned the letter, saying that Admiral Fleming
had sailed for Gibraltar; that this deponent sent his servants, Thomas Dewman, Sarah Bust, and Mary Turpin, on
the trial of his indictment, to prove that an officer came
to this deponent's house on the morning of the said 21st of
February, and to prove the dress that he came in; but that
the said Thomas Dewman only was called, and, as this deponent has been informed, he was not interrogated as to the
dress in which the said officer came to his house; and this
deponent further saith, that had the said witnesses been examined according to the directions of this deponent, and who
were in attendance on the Court for that express purpose,
they would, as he verily believes, have removed every unfavourable conclusion respecting this deponent's conduct,
drawn from the supposed dress in which the said De Berenger appeared before the deponent on the 21st of February,
and on which circumstances much stress was laid in the
charge to the jury, the said De Berenger's dress being exactly as stated in this said deponent's former affidavit hereinbefore mentioned: and this deponent solemnly and positively
denies, that he ever saw the said De Berenger in a scarlet
uniform, decorated by medals, or other insignia; and he had
not the least suspicion of the said De Berenger being engaged in any plot respecting the funds, but merely believed
he wished, for the reasons stated in deponent's former affidavit, to go on board this deponent's ship, with a view to
obtain some military employment in America; and this deponent declined complying with his request to send him on
board his ship without permission, or an order from the
Admiralty: and this deponent further saith, that he was in
no degree intimate with the said De Berenger; that he had
no personal knowledge of his private or public character;
that he never asked the said De Berenger to his house, nor
did he ever breakfast or dine with this deponent therein, on
any occasion whatsoever; and further, this deponent saith,
that he had been informed, and verily believes, that the jury

who tried the said indictment, and the counsel for the defence, were so completely exhausted and worn out by extreme fatigue, owing to the Court having continued the trial without intermission for many hours beyond that time which nature is capable of sustaining herself without refection and repose, that justice could not be done to this deponent."

" COCHRANE.

" Sworn in Court, June 14, 1814.
        By the Court."

With such documents in my hand I was refused a new trial, for reasons hereafter to be adduced. Of the vindictiveness with which I was pursued, there can be no better proof than that the other parties convicted on clear evidence were let off with imprisonment and half the fine inflicted on myself and Mr. Butt ; whilst we, who had nothing to do with the matter, were fined 1,000*l.* and in addition sentenced to the barbarous punishment of the pillory. I advisedly say "we," for I will here put on record my conscientious belief that Mr. Butt had no more to do with the hoax than myself. I give this testimony to the memory of a truly excellent man, whose misfortune it was to have become the dupe of others, without the least hope of benefit to himself.

It is impossible in an autobiography like the present to go into the entire case *seriatim*, as it would be easy to bring forward other proofs as clear as those now adduced. The evidence of Crane was, however, the important point. I have now laid before the reader the documents which the Court of King's Bench declined to entertain, and have no doubt as to what his decision

must be. Whether was it the more probable, that a
man in my position, with nothing to gain by it,
should, in order to commit a fraud, conspire with
several other persons of whose names he had never
before heard, and then swear that I did not commit
it — or, that such a man as Crane, at the moment of
giving his evidence, himself under conviction and sentence for a heinous offence, should swear falsely to
the colour of a coat for a pecuniary reward? I, to
whom the public voice, and the rewards of my sovereign, had elevated to an honourable rank in my
profession, or a hackney coachman, under conviction
at the moment of giving his evidence, and known in
his own line of life to have been the most depraved of
one of the most depraved classes of society?

My conviction was followed by expulsion from the
House of Commons, and was voted by a majority of
140 to 44. But that in a House like the one with
which the reader is now well acquainted, *forty-four*
independent gentlemen should be found to believe in
my innocence, in the teeth of the ministers of the day,
of whom Lord Ellenborough was one, the same mi-
mistry being, as personified in Lord Castlereagh and
Mr. Croker, is perhaps as good proof of innocence as
could be desired, — certainly as great as could be
expected.

It is with no small pride that I publish the names
of the minority. There are those amongst them whose
testimony will weigh with posterity :—

"LIST OF THE MINORITY

WHO VOTED AGAINST THE EXPULSION OF LORD COCHRANE.

Allan, G.

Atherley, A.

Barham, S.

Bennet, Hon. H.

Brand, Hon. T.

Brown, D.

Brydges, Sir E.

Burdett, Sir F.

Burrel, Hon. P.

Butterworth, Jos.

Challoner, R.

Ebrington, Visc.

Flood, Sir F.

Gaskell, B.

Grant, Ch., sen.

Grant, J. P.

Hughes, W.

Lambton, J.

Lloyd, H.

Macginnis, —

Maddox, Wm.

Martin, J

Mildmay, Sir H.

Mills, Rt.

Montgomery, Sir H.

Moore, P.

Newman, Rt.

Nugent, Lord.

Ossulston, Lord.

Ponsonby, Rt. Hon.
     G.

Power, R.

Rancliff, Lord.

Rashleigh, Wm.

Richards, Rt.

Ridley, Sir M.

Russell, Lord Wm.

Simpson, G.

Smith, W.

Tavistock, Marq. of

Western, C.

Whitbread, S.

Williams, Sir R.

Wortley, J.

TELLERS.

Lord A. Hamilton.

A. Brown."

CHAP. XL.

IF such evidence as has been exposed in the last chapter was unreliable, the use made of it by the Bench was unjustifiable. Crane deposed to De Berenger's having with him "a portmanteau big enough to wrap a coat in." The person of whom the coat was bought deposed to his taking it away in this portmanteau, yet the judge—despite the obvious consideration, that De Berenger could not have gone to Dover in this splendid and ornamented dress, but must have had some other dress for his journey— charged the jury that " it did not appear that De Berenger *had the means of shifting himself!*" He had the means of putting on the red coat at or near Dover, and what doubt could there be that his portmanteau supplied the means of again shifting it after his return? The evidence on the trial showed that shortly before reaching London he *drew down* the sun-blinds of the chaise, when there can be no reasonable doubt that he changed it for the green one in which he went to Dover, and which had been temporarily placed in the portmanteau. Crane, as has been shown by his own words, gave his evidence *under the expectation of reward*, and had no doubt been instructed that a *red coat was the very thing wanted.*

On the evidence of this man Crane, the jury was further charged that De Berenger not only entered my house in a red uniform, but that it was also decorated *with a star and medal!* There was nothing in the testimony of Crane or the waterman, which even related to a star and medal. They never gave the slightest intimation of De Berenger's wearing any such ornaments ; but as he appeared to have worn some ornaments of the kind at Dover, this is *prima facie* proof that he *had changed* his coat on his return, otherwise both Crane and the waterman must have seen ornaments so conspicuous.

Still a star, like a red coat, was wanted to convict me, and a leading question to the postboy — who admitted that, *previous* to the trial, *he had received* 52*l. !!!* was, whether he had seen a star? His reply was that he had seen something of the kind, but that " *he could not swear what it was.*" He nevertheless said that he had " opened the chaise-door," and therefore must have been within a yard of the star, if star there were, so that his refusal to swear to it is palpable proof that De Berenger *wore no star on his return*, this being no doubt on the red coat in the portmanteau. Yet, said Lord Ellenborough to the jury, "HE PULLED OFF HIS SCARLET UNIFORM AT LORD COCHRANE'S HOUSE. HE CAME TO LORD COCHRANE FULLY BLAZONED IN THE COSTUME OF HIS CRIME." (*Times' report of the trial.*)

The fact that De Berenger had with him, according to Crane's evidence, "a portmanteau big enough to wrap a coat in," was not laid before the jury, nor the obvious inference, that he must, beyond doubt, have conveyed his scarlet coat to Dover in that portmanteau, because a man whom the Solicitor-General said "*was no fool,*" would not have committed such an act of folly as *prematurely* to array himself in so remarkable a dress, intended for so criminal a purpose.

A circumstance strongly inferential, occurred which went far to prove that De Berenger *had changed* his dress before coming to my house. On the first part of the journey he was proved to have worn a sword, unquestionably as essential to his assumed character. But before he came to my house, he had disengaged himself from the sword, for Crane swore that on entering, he "took out of the chaise a portmanteau and a *sword*, and went in." So that, according to the evidence of Crane himself, the chief witness for the prosecution, *he had made one material alteration in his appearance.* Why should De Berenger have worn his sword up to the last stage from Dover, during which he "pulled down the sunblinds," and then have taken it off, but for the plain reason that he could not change his scarlet coat for his green uniform without first taking off his sword, which he had not replaced, but laid it on the chaise-seat during the operation. Not a word of this was allowed to go to the jury, though if — as Lord Ellenborough argued — he had been regardless of exhibiting himself to me in the false character of a military officer, he *would hardly have taken off his sword!* These facts were not only proofs that a partial change of dress had been made, but that an entire change had been effected, to which the removal of the sword was absolutely necessary. Had my servants been called upon the trial, their testimony, as seen in their affidavits contained in the previous chapter, must have been decisive.

It has been stated, that at the instance of Mr. Cochrane Johnstone, Sir Alexander Cochrane applied to the Admiralty for permission to engage De Berenger, and the records of the Admiralty would then, as no doubt they will now, prove the fact. There was not a word passed on the subject at the trial, nor any witness brought from the Admiralty to decide the point. Yet Lord Ellenborough put it to the jury as beyond doubt, *that it was I or Mr. Cochrane Johnstone, who was also a defendant in the same prosecution, who applied to Sir Alexander for his engagement!* — thus making this unfounded but important fact part of his direction to the jury. Here are the judge's words:—

" There is no doubt that Sir Alexander Cochrane had, on some application from Mr. Cochrane Johnstone, *or Lord Cochrane,* applied for him." (*Report,* p. 483.)

It is difficult to account for the judge's motive in making such a statement, wholly unsupported by evidence. Neither was there even an attempt to show that I had ever interfered or even interested myself in any application on De Berenger's behalf. The fact of Sir Alexander Cochrane having made the application was most important for my defence, because it added greatly to the probability of my statement in my affidavit, and accounted for the conduct of De Berenger in presuming to call on me to request a passage to America. This Lord Ellenborough completely neutralised by telling the jury that *it was I* who applied to Sir Alexander for his employment; the impression made on the minds of the jury being, that notwithstanding I disclaimed all knowledge of the man, I had been on terms of intimacy with him before the application was made!

The judge then declared as follows :— "But it does not rest there ; for he himself lends to this person the immediate means of concealment,— he lets him have a hat *instead of his laced cap ; and what had such a cap to do with a sharpshooter's uniform?"* (*Report*, p. 485.) I had never said a word about a "laced cap," nor had I ever seen De Berenger's cap, for, as one of my servants testified, it lay in the hall. After this direction to the jury and my consequent conviction, I made it my business to ascertain what kind of cap was worn by the adjutant of Lord Yarmouth's rifle-*corps*, and, to my great surprise and indignation, discovered that the regimental head-dress of De Berenger was a black cap *with a spacious gold band upon it, a long gold tassel pendant, and a death's head and marrow-bones in bronze !* — so that sharpshooters *had* something to do with laced caps.

Still more extraordinary was the judge's observation

to the jury :—" The uniform of the rifle-corps is of a bottle-green colour, made to resemble the colour of trees, that those who wear it may hide themselves in woods, and escape discovery there." (*Report*, p. 478.) This was in direct opposition to the evidence, for Lord Yarmouth had actually testified in Court that the uniform of the corps was " waistcoat-green, with *a crimson cape !* "

MR. PARK.—" What is the uniform of your *corps?* "

LORD YARMOUTH. — " The uniform is the waistcoat-green, with a *crimson cape.*"

MR. PARK.—" A bottle-green, is it not? "

LORD YARMOUTH.—" Some have got it a little darker than others, but it should be a deep bottle-green, with a *crimson collar.*"

I have merely taken these instances at random, and without comment further than necessary to enable the reader to comprehend them. As my judge is no longer here to reply to me, I abstain from comment, however much it might tend, now that the party spirit which ruined me has died out, to establish my innocence. Still I cannot refrain from adducing a few extracts from Lord Campbell's work, relative to the trials of politically obnoxious persons.

Lord Ellenborough's efforts to convict Leigh Hunt of libel, and the verdict of " Not Guilty " pronounced by an indignant jury, are matters within the memory of many now living. " Such scandal," says Lord Campbell, " was excited by the mode in which Government prosecutions for libel were now instituted and conducted, that Lord Holland brought the subject before the House of Lords. The violence of Lord Ellenborough when opposing Lord Holland's motion, is foreign to the subject of the present work.   Sir James Mackintosh, who heard it, expressed himself ' disgusted with its dogmatism.' " (*Lord Campbell*, vol. iii. p. 205.)

The subjoined are Lord Campbell's remarks when introducing the subject :—

" He did his best to convict Leigh Hunt, then the editor of the *Examiner*, upon an *ex officio* information for publishing an article against the excess to which the punishment of flagellation had been carried in the army.

" ' Gentlemen,' said he to the jury, ' we are placed in a most anxious and awful situation.   The liberty of the country — everything we enjoy — not only the independence of the nation, but whatever each individual amongst us prizes in private life, depends upon our fortunate resistance to the arms of Buonaparte and the force of France, which I may say is the force of all Europe, combined under that formidable foe.   It becomes us, therefore, to see that there is not, in addition to the prostrate thrones of Europe, an auxiliary within this country, and that he has not the aid for the furtherance of his object *of a British press.*' "

*   *   *   *   *

" ' This publication is not to draw the attention of the legislature or of persons in authority *with a view to a remedy*, but seems intended to induce the military to consider themselves as more degraded than any other soldiers in the world, and to make them less ready at this awful crisis to render the country that assistance without which we are collectively and individually undone.   *I have no doubt but that this libel has been published with the intention imputed to it, and that it is entitled to the character given to it in the information.*'

" Nevertheless, to the unspeakable mortification of the noble judge, the jury found a verdict of *Not Guilty.*" (Lord Campbell's *Lives of the Chief Justices*, vol. iii. pp. 201 –203.)

The following are Lord Campbell's remarks on the verdict in the seven days' trial of Dr. Watson on a charge of high treason. After charging the jury,

"He asked them whether they would take some refreshment before they left the bar, when the foreman, in a tone which made the *Chief Justice's countenance visibly collapse*, said, 'My Lord, we shall not be long.' Accordingly, after going through the form of withdrawing and consulting together, they returned and pronounced their verdict, to which they had long made up their minds — *Not Guilty*." — (Vol. iii. p. 222.)

The case of Hone, in 1817, is another in point. I know nothing of Hone's works, nor of the libels of which he was accused, but Lord Campbell says, that "he defended himself with extraordinary skill and tact, and at the end of the first day's trial was *acquitted*."

"This being related to the enfeebled Chief Justice, his energy was revived, and *he swore that, at whatever cost, he would preside in Court himself, so that conviction might be certain !*" (He did so, and thus charged the jury:) "'I will deliver to you my solemn opinion, *as I am required by Act of Parliament to do;* under the authority of that Act, and still more, in obedience to my conscience and my God, I pronounce it to be a MOST IMPIOUS AND PROFANE LIBEL.* Hoping and believing that you are Christians, I doubt not but that your opinion is the same.'"

The jury almost immediately pronounced a verdict of "NOT GUILTY."

"Still," says Lord Campbell, " the Chief Justice was undismayed, and declared that he would next day proceed with the indictment. This was a most indiscreet

* The italics and capitals are Lord Campbell's.

resolution. The whole of Hone's third trial was a triumph, the jury plainly intimating their determination to find a verdict in his favour. * * * * After a similar summing up as on the preceding day, there was *the like verdict.* * * * * The popular opinion was, that Lord Ellenborough was killed by Hone's trial, and he certainly never held up his head in public after." (*Lord Campbell*, vol. iii. p. 225.)

These facts prove, that *subsequently to my trial,* whenever Lord Ellenborough, in a popular case, charged the jury to bring in the defendant " GUILTY," the jury made a point of finding " NOT GUILTY." It was unfortunate for me that such a course was not previously adopted, but, perhaps, it may be said, that my case brought about this result.

One most material point connected with the trial cannot be overlooked; one, in fact, which not only concerned the liberties of obnoxious persons like myself, but also the liberties of every man in the country. At the period of my trial, Lord Ellenborough was not only Chief Justice of the King's Bench, BUT AT THE SAME TIME A CABINET MINISTER ! ! ! This terrible combination of incompatible offices was for the first time under constitutional government effected in the person of Lord Ellenborough, and, to the credit of subsequent administrations, for the last time also. No other Chief Justice ever came hot-foot from a Cabinet Council to decide the fate of an accused person, politically obnoxious to the Cabinet; the trial going on from day to day, so as to become open no less to Cabinet than to forensic discussion.

The thing was monstrous, and could only have been acted on in this instance for the purpose of suppressing, by the expedient just shown, the rising spirit of public liberty, which the Government was ever on the watch to keep down.   The *Quarterly Review*, when commenting on the " Life and Correspondence " of Sir Samuel Romilly, thus treats the matter   (No. 132, 1840, page 612) :—

" The Whigs, by way of including *all the talents*, had given the Chief Justice of the King's Bench (Lord Ellenborough) *a seat in the Cabinet*, and upon this before unheard-of combination of the judicial and ministerial characters, this *monstrous attempt to tinge the ermine of justice with the colour of party ! !* "

The chance I had may be readily estimated *with a Cabinet minister for my judge*, and the Cabinet of which he was a member composed of ministers to whom I had become deeply obnoxious by determined opposition to their measures ; having, in fact, given them more trouble than any other of my party, because my knowledge of naval abuses and profligate expenditure enabled me to expose both.   It might, with one of my most bitter opponents for a judge, have been a still greater marvel had I been acquitted, than that I was convicted without and in opposition to evidence.   Had Lord Ellenborough possessed a true sense of delicacy, he would never have presided at that trial.   Still less would he have refused me a new trial when more perfectly prepared ; a proceeding no doubt adopted as the best means of silencing further discussion, which had begun to harass him personally, and to cause uneasiness to the ministry.   The shortest course, if not the justest, was to screen himself and them by *immediately* crushing his adversary.   But the injury went farther than my conviction in the Court of King's Bench.   After my subsequent expulsion from the House, which, as Lord Brougham rightly says, " *secured my re-election for Westminster*," on its adverse note *hung the fate of the ministry*.   Had that vote been in my favour, the Chief Justice could not have held his seat in the Cabinet, and his evacuation could scarcely have been otherwise than followed by that of the whole ministry.   Of this, however, there was little danger, the great bond of adhesion to the Ministry, as has been fully shown in the course of this work, being the pensions and sinecures so freely distributed amongst an unreformed House of Commons.

The question, however, became thus one of ministerial existence.   Had the House, as it ought to have done, irrespective of me or my case, repudiated the anomaly of a Chief Justice holding a seat in the Cabinet, the retirement of Lord Ellenborough must have been indispensable and *immediate*.   He could not have maintained his political office for an hour.   In place of an individual member being heard in his own defence, the question really was the right of a Chief Justice to hold a seat in the Cabinet, or in legal phrase, the issue was, Lord Cochrane *versus* Lord Ellenborough, the Admiralty, and the Cabinet.   In the unreformed House of Commons Lord Cochrane, as a matter of course, went to the wall, no one expecting otherwise.

Of the guilt or innocence of the other parties convicted I know nothing, but this I will say, that, if guilty, there was nothing in their guilt half so bad as the deli-

berate malice which on two occasions had conspired to
ruin me.   My appointment as flag captain to my uncle
was gall and wormwood to those who, for opposing a
vote of thanks to Lord Gambier, had condemned me
to five years' deprivation of employment, at a time
when my services would have been honourable to
myself and beneficial to my country.   I had gained
employment in a way beyond their control, and my
unjust conviction of having participated in a trumpery
hoax, which common sense might have convinced them
was beneath my notice, was converted into the means
of preventing the future exercise of my abilities as a
naval officer.

I have to apologise to Lord Campbell for the freedom with which I have used his great work, but though
an unjustly maligned man, my reputation is as dear to
me as though no spot had ever rested upon it, and I
have adduced these extracts to show that Lord Ellenborough, in his zeal for justice, might have possibly
mistaken my case.   His biographers ascribe to him
pure motives, and I am bound not to set my opinions
against those of his biographers, nor have I done so.
But for forty-six years I have been vainly endeavouring
to *get my case reheard*, and much allowance should
be accorded me.   I would not ask for mercy, if guilty,
but for increased severity of punishment, as I should
most richly deserve.   To demand a hearing of my case
was my first public act after my trial.   It shall be my
last.   That public act was a letter to Lord Ebrington,
deprecating his Lordship's interference for a mitigation
of my outrageous sentence.   The following is a copy of
this letter:—

"King's Bench, July 13th, 1814.

"My Lord, — Although I claim no right to interfere with the Parliamentary conduct of any member, or to interfere with the motions which he may judge proper to originate, yet I owe a duty to myself which demands that I should apprise your Lordship that the motion of which you have given notice respecting me, has a tendency to bring down upon me a greater indignity than any which has been offered to me by my enemies. I had flattered myself, from a recent note of your Lordship, that, in your mind, I stood wholly acquitted; and I did not expect to be treated by your Lordship as an object of mercy, on the grounds of past services, or severity of sentence. I cannot allow myself to be indebted to that tenderness of disposition, which has led your Lordship to form an erroneous estimate of the amount of punishment due to the crimes of which I have been accused; nor can I for a moment consent, that any past services of mine should be prostituted to the purpose of protecting me from any part of the vengeance of the laws against which I, if at all, have grossly offended. *If I am guilty, I richly merit the whole of the sentence which has been passed upon me. If innocent, one penalty cannot be inflicted with more justice than another.* If your Lordship shall judge proper to persist in the motion of which you have given notice, I hope you will do me the justice to read this letter to the House.

"I have, &c.

"Cochrane.

"The Lord Ebrington."

Independently, however, of these or any other considerations, I might point to my previous general services as a naval officer, for which I had not received public reward of any kind; — to my refusal of a squadron of frigates, and Lord Mulgrave's own regiment, if I would consent to a vote of thanks to Lord Gambier conjointly with myself, — an offer which, had it been accepted, would have been tantamount to the acquisition of half a million of prize-money ; — to my unceasing opposition in Parliament to the abuses of the Admiralty Courts and naval administration in general, in direct opposition to my own pecuniary interests ; — to my rejection of the openly-expressed proposal of the Secretary to the Admiralty to quit the Radical party, and come over to that of the Government ; — to my anticipated employment on the coasts of the United States, and the great pecuniary proceeds which there was every reason to expect as the result of putting my previous experience in practice. I would then put it to the common sense of the reader, whether the acquisition of a few paltry hundred pounds — by means of the imputed frauds on the Stock Exchange, was a likely motive to actuate me in joining a conspiracy with persons, some of whom I never knew nor heard of, which, if detected, must have destroyed my future prospects, when on the eve of an expedition calculated in all human probability to have raised me above all political enmity ? The reply is self-evident.

I would again ask, whether, with a guilty knowledge of the act in which De Berenger had been engaged, I should have perpetrated the consummate folly of voluntarily disclosing all that took place on unexpectedly finding him at my house ; this voluntary information on my part affording the only clue to the case, which could otherwise never have been developed.

If guilty, such disclosure on my part would have been an act of absolute insanity. Had I been aware that his asking me for the means of concealing his uniform, — first, on his representation that, not being a drill day, he could not appear in it before his colonel, Lord Yarmouth ; and secondly, that he could not return in it to the rules of the King's Bench without exciting suspicion that he had been violating the rules,— is it likely that I should have voluntarily become my own accuser, when there existed no necessity for me to say a single word on the subject Should I not rather, if guilty, have given him the order to go on board the *Tonnant*, and thus place both him and myself beyond the reach of danger?

In place, however, of further vindication of my character as having had any participation in this wretched hoax, I will, in addition to the legal opinions already adduced, bring forward others since pronounced by men in whom the public repose the most implicit confidence.

And first the voluntary statement of a gallant General, who had been equally ill used with myself, and by the same political adversaries and clique who persecuted me. I mean Sir Robert Wilson, who happily survived his persecution, was reinstated in his military rank and honours, and died honoured and lamented.

"Regent Street, 14th March, 1823.

"MY DEAR LORD, — It has been mentioned to me that a memorandum I once held with the late Mr. Whitbread on the subject of your persecution, and which I have frequently repeated, might be a document of some utility; my compliance with the expressed wish is not an act of friendship, but of duty and justice to all parties.

"I therefore do affirm, upon my honour, to the accurate

truth of the following statement, being ready, if required, to give it any legal character of which it may be susceptible : —

" Being at Southall Park in the year 1814, I took an opportunity of asking Mr. Whitbread for his opinion on the subject of Lord Cochrane's trial and sentence, stating to him that as I had been out of England at the time, I was very imperfectly acquainted with the proceedings; but feeling much interested about the character of an officer so eminently distinguished, I was desirous to pin my faith upon his (Mr. Whitbread's) judgment; but if, from any political or personal consideration, he could only give me a partial or half compliance, I begged him to be silent altogether, as my object was to know the whole truth, and to be put in possession, for my future guidance, of his most secret feelings on the transaction.

" Mr. Whitbread replied, that he had no hesitation to acquiesce with my wish ; that there never was a case to which he had given more attention, or which had caused him more sleepless nights, as he had been resolved to probe the matter to the bottom, if possible, and come to a just conclusion. That he had formed his conclusion ; and, if they were the last words he had to utter before appearance in the presence of the Creator, he should say that *he was convinced that Lord Cochrane was totally and entirely innocent of the whole or any part of the offence laid to his charge,—that he felt certain that Lord Cochrane was in no way privy to the proceedings so far as they related to any imposition.*

" Mr. Whitbread added, ' My family know this to be my conscientious opinion, and *I am persuaded that time will prove it to be the correct one* * ;' but, in any case, you have it

---

* Not if the " *revised* " report of the trial is consulted ; for the studied appearance of fairness which is there put on might mislead the reader.   But if the *verbatim* reports of the trial are consulted, as they appear in the *Times* and other daily papers, I have no fear of any amount of criticism, or that anything but my entire innocence will be made manifest.   The *animus* against me is there so clear, that the reader would hardly be induced to inquire further.

from a man who has endeavoured to form it honestly, and also, for that purpose, divested his mind, as much as possible, of every bias.

" I remain, my dear Lord,

" With much regard, yours,

" R. WILSON."

The following warm-hearted letter was written me by the late Duke of Hamilton on my appointment to the command of the West India fleet : —

"Hamilton Palace, Jan. 6, 1848.

" MY DEAR LORD,—Your letter of yesterday has awakened the liveliest sensibilities of my heart. If I ask myself whether they proceed from the love of justice, or the love of a friend, my reply is, from both.

" The communication you have just made to me is most gratifying ; and the First Lord of the Admiralty has done himself immortal honour in appointing that naval officer Commander in one hemisphere who had previously illustrated his name by his most brilliant exploits in the other. Everything, I think, has now been done to undo the foul aspersions with which you have been assailed, and I am sure everything will be now done that will most serve to establish the ability of the officer and the delicacy of the gentleman.

" I congratulate you most sincerely upon your appointment, and hope you will meet with difficulties when you arrive at your destination. Don't be surprised at my wish. It proceeds from knowing the ample resources of my friend to overcome them, and his constant desire to sacrifice everything to duty and honour.

" My good wishes will follow you across the ocean, and reside with you in your future destinies. Let me have the satisfaction of hearing from you, and with every sentiment of affectionate regard, believe me to be, my dear lord, your truly attached friend and cousin,

" C. H. AND B."

Without multiplying communications of a similar kind, I will merely adduce a portion of a letter written to me by a gentleman, in whose opinions and sterling honesty the public has been accustomed to repose the highest confidence, viz. the late Joseph Hume. The occasion of the letter was my having consulted him in an attempt to obtain a re-investigation of my case so late as 1852 :--

"Bryanstone Square, May 10, 1852.

*   *   *   *   *   *

"I knew at the time the alleged offence was committed, Mr. Cochrane Johnstone, and my conviction at the time was, and still is, that you were the dupe of his cupidity, and suffered from his act. With David Ricardo, who was the prosecutor on the part of the Stock Exchange on that occasion, I have often conversed on the subject*.

"I considered that you were incapable of taking the means resorted to, and for which you suffered, and was pleased to learn that you had been restored to your rank. I considered *that act* a proof that the Government which had restored you to the rank and honour of your profession, and had afterwards appointed you to the command in the West Indies, must have come to the same conclusion; and until the perusal of your draft petition, I concluded that *you had had all your arrears paid to you as a tardy, though inadequate, return* to your Lordship, whose early exploits did honour to yourself, and gave additional lustre to the naval service of your country.

"Sir Robert Wilson, acting with me as a friend of the late Queen Caroline, in our desire to see justice done to her, was,

---

* Mr. Hume's statement that David Ricardo was the prosecutor on the part of the Stock Exchange throws additional light on the selection of Mr. Lavie, as the *acting prosecutor* on the trial. As Mr. Ricardo was selected to manage the prosecution, the transference of his duties to *a known Admiralty solicitor,* who had once before been successfully employed against me, requires no comment.

by *a secret and most unjust decision of the Government of the day, under Lord Liverpool and Lord Castlereagh,* dismissed from the military service, of which he had been a distinguished ornament, and had all his honours taken away. The honour he had received from the Court of Vienna, for the preservation of the life of a member of that family (in a river in Flanders) under Colonel, afterwards Lord, Lake, was also taken from him ! !

" The offence of Sir Robert Wilson was his supposed interfe-- rence in obstructing the funeral *cortége* of the late Queen Caroline in its progress towards the City. The progress was ordered by the Government to have been by the New Road to Essex. The people obliged Sir Robert Baker, then at the head of the police and in charge of the escort, to proceed through the City of London, contrary to the express order of the King (George the Fourth), and under that suspicion Sir Robert Wilson was dismissed and unjustly treated.

" I knew that Sir Robert Wilson had arrived from France in company with Mr. Edward Ellice, and did not reach the house of Mr. Alderman (the name is illegible) where I was until eight or nine o'clock of the evening before the funeral. His offence was his accompanying the funeral along with Sir John Hobhouse, myself, and others; and when the troops fired on the people at Hyde Park, Sir Robert Wilson endeavoured to prevent bloodshed. I was present, and heard and saw everything that passed. For that supposed offence he was cashiered, and remained for years, as your lordship did, under the disgrace.

" His Majesty, King William, was satisfied of the innocence of Sir Robert Wilson of the offence charged against him, and he was restored to the service, and I understood was paid all the arrears of pay and allowance during his suspension, and afterwards appointed to the command at Gibraltar. I was pleased at the result, and it would give me equal pleasure to learn that your application to her Majesty should be attended with an act of justice to you equally merited.

" I think other instances of restoration to rank, accom-

panied with payment of arrears of pay and restoration to all
military honours, will be found if you should adopt the same
course to seek justice.

" I remain, &c.

" JOSEPH HUME.

" The Right Hon. the Earl of Dundonald."

This letter narrates the arbitrary and unjust dismissal
of an eminent officer without trial, without accusation,
and without having in any way rendered himself politically obnoxious, otherwise than to stop the indiscri-
minate slaughter of an unarmed people. The act of his
dismissal was one of pure despotism, committed by a
ministerial faction, of which history affords scarcely a
redeeming feature. It is not surprising that I, of all
others in the House of Commons the most politically
obnoxious to the same faction, should have been for
years selected as the mark for their unscrupulous
hatred. Still less is it probable that men who regarded
and defended place, pensions, and sinecures as a right,
would stick at the practices which have been laid bare
in this work, when a political adversary who exposed
their greediness for national plunder could be crushed.
To say more of them, than that they were the men who
crushed Sir Robert Wilson, would be superfluous.

I will add yet one more illustration. At my re-
election for Westminster — the consequence, as Lord
Brougham has well said, of the outrageous treatment
to which I had been subjected — an incident occurred
with which my wrongs became indirectly mixed up.
Whilst the electors of Westminster were securing the
triumphant return of one who was in durance, under

an infamous sentence, the daughter of the Prince Regent was flying from Court tyranny.

On the day preceding my re-election, the greatly beloved Princess Charlotte, then under age, escaped from her father's protection, and, having called a hackney coach from the stand at Charing Cross, fled to her mother's residence in Connaught Place. The public mind was at the time in a state of great excitement on account of the vindictive sentence passed upon me, and the electors of Westminster having determined to sustain me, every precaution was taken by their leaders to keep alive the public sentiment.

In the midst of this excitement the flight of the princess became known, together with the fact that she had been treated by her father with an amount of unbecoming violence and coercion, and through some of his acquiescent ministers outraged by an injudicious pressure, the object of which was to force upon her a marriage to which she had not only a personal objection, but towards which she had publicly expressed a decided and insuperable aversion.

Notwithstanding this, the Regent, regardless of his daughter's feelings, insisted on proceeding without loss of time with the preparations for her marriage; and it was on repeating his fixed determination as regarded her fate, that she took the step of placing herself under her mother's protection, the terror inspired by the interview with her father being such that, without bonnet or shawl, she ran down the back staircase of Warwick House, and escaped by the servants' *entrée*.

Not many hours elapsed before the fact of her

flight and its cause became publicly known.   This act of political tyranny towards a princess, who, though so young, had, by her powers of mind and engaging manners from her childhood, secured the universal affection of the people, created an amount of sympathy which, coupled with the excitement and irritation at my outrageous treatment, almost amounted to public frenzy.

The Government became alarmed.   Crowds beset the house of her late Majesty Queen Caroline, where their favourite was safely sheltered.   The carriages of the Royal family and of the ministers, including those of the Lord Chancellor, Lord Ellenborough, and the Law Officers of the Crown, were all in attendance, their occupants having been sent to use their influence with Her Royal Highness to induce her to return, but in vain.   She even refused to see any of the royal family except the Duke of Sussex, for whom she had sent, as well as for Mr. Brougham, the latter to advise her in the difficult position in which she had been compelled to place herself.   The advice was to return ; but she declared in strong terms that she could not overcome her repugnance to the violent treatment she had received, or to the attempt to force her into a marriage which she held in aversion.

The day following this scene was the day of my re-election for Westminster.   The same overtures were repeated to the princess, but without making the slightest impression on her wounded feelings.   At length the Duke of Sussex took his niece to the window of the drawing-room, and drew her attention to the angry multitude assembled before the house, explaining to her that such was the public sympathy in her favour, and such the interest the people took in her happiness, that they would form a shield for her protection against which her oppressors would scarcely venture to array themselves.

Still the princess remained inexorable, till the danger of continued public excitement was pointed out to her. She was told by the Duke of Sussex, that the irritation was twofold, for *that very day was appointed for the re-election of Lord Cochrane for Westminster, after the unjust sentence which had been passed upon him, and which also formed another great cause of public excitement, whilst the two causes combined* might lead to a popular outbreak, which it was to be feared would end in bloodshed, and perhaps in the destruction of Carlton House itself. It was further urged, that in case of mischief, no small portion might be laid by ministers to the account of Her Royal Highness.

These considerations sensibly affected the princess, who was moved to tears, and exclaimed : " POOR LORD COCHRANE ! I HEARD THAT HE HAD BEEN VERY ILL USED BY THEM (meaning her father's ministers) ; SHOULD IT EVER BE IN MY POWER, I WILL UNDO THE WRONG."

With a magnanimity which her persecutors could neither feel nor comprehend, the princess then declared her perfect readiness to render herself a self-sacrifice, in order to prevent the dreadful result which she felt might be possible ; and shortly afterwards returned to Warwick House, accompanied by her uncle the Duke of York. Her courage and firmness relieved her from further importunity from her father and his ministers on the subject of the hateful marriage, which was broken off, and this noble-minded woman afterwards contracted with the present King of the Belgians a marriage of affection, approved by the whole country.

Such instances of tyrannical oppression as these will be read with amazement by the present generation, though there are those yet living who can corroborate their recital. When even a princess of the blood royal, the idol of the whole nation, was not exempt from persecution, what hope had I of escaping ministerial vengeance, backed by a House of Commons, the majority of which consisted of sinecurists and placemen, whose fortunes *in esse* and *in posse* depended on their subservience to the place-givers?

It is true, I had with me the sympathy of the public, and this alone sustained me under such an accumulation of injury. Men do not become popular for nothing; but I have no hesitation in saying, to the honour of my constituents, that the injustice done to me by an adverse ministry gave me far greater popularity than anything I had accomplished in my professional capacity. For five years my adversaries had taken care that no fresh achievements in war should be added to my professional reputation; and it was only when, by my uncle's favour, I had once more an opportunity of distinguishing myself in spite of the Admiralty, that the concentrated malice of the faction I had offended by my pertinacious opposition in parliament burst on my head in the shape of a prosecution, in which my judge was a member of the very cabinet to which I was politically and personally obnoxious.

In a general point of view, there can be no two opinions on the impropriety of a Cabinet Minister occupying the bench of the highest law court of the realm.   In all State prosecutions — and mine *was* one — it would fall to his lot to decide in the Cabinet as to their commencement, though in my case this was apparently avoided, by the law officers of the Crown keeping aloof from the proceedings ; care, however, being taken to employ as my prosecutor an attorney of tried shrewdness, having a personal dislike to myself. A judge thus politically connected had to leave the Cabinet in order to carry out its decisions, himself presiding at all trials which might result, adjudging and sentencing the unlucky offenders; of which mode of prosecution the instances of Leigh Hunt, Dr. Watson, and Mr. Hone are cases in point, the parties accused being only saved by the indignant firmness of the juries.   Happily, no such combination of political and judicial offices has occurred since Lord Ellenborough's time, nor can it occur, unless some retrograde spirit of despotism shall again — to use the significant language before quoted from the *Quarterly Review* — " *tinge the ermine of justice with the colour of party.*"

A few words in addition are necessary.   In Mr. Hume's letter before quoted was an enclosure which he had, in his anxiety to procure full justice for my sufferings, with great difficulty obtained.   It is an enumeration of the tardy steps taken to reinstate Sir Robert Wilson in the rank, honours, and emoluments of which for eleven years he had been unjustly deprived by the mere caprice of a political faction.

" 30th October, 1830.—Restoration of his rank submitted to the King.

" 22nd August, 1832.—Sir Robert Wilson claimed the pay of a General Officer from 27th May, 1825, the time when his commission states his rank is to be considered as bearing date.

" 8th October, 1832.—Letter of Secretary at War to the Hon. J. Stewart, recommending Sir Robert Wilson's claim of pay to the Treasury *as a special case, considering the act of Royal favour to extend to pay as well as rank.* The letter also refers to Sir Robert Wilson's signal services *hitherto unrewarded*, and adverts to the fact, that even should the request be granted he will have suffered a considerable pecuniary penalty in the loss of pay from 1821 to 1825, although no military tribunal has tried his conduct.

" 16th November, 1832.—Letter of Mr. Stewart, announcing *the concurrence of the Treasury*, but desiring the opinion of the Commander-in-Chief to be taken.

" 19th November, 1832.—Letter from Secretary at War to Lord Hill, acquainting him that he had, in consequence of a communication from Sir R. Wilson, recommended to the Treasury that *the arrear of back pay from the date of his restored rank of Lieut.-General should be allowed**, and that the Treasury was inclined to acquiesce in this recommendation, but requested his Lordship's concurrence in the first instance.

" 22nd November, 1832.—Lord Hill's concurrence.

" 21st December, 1832.—Treasury sanctions the amount of Sir Robert Wilson's unattached pay as a general officer from the date of his commission being included in the estimates of 1833."

It has been said that Sir Robert Wilson's dismissal from the service differed from mine, inasmuch as his was a consequence of ministerial displeasure, whilst

---

* The italics in this document are Mr. Hume's.

mine arose from the verdict of a court of law. How that verdict was procured, I trust has been satisfactorily shown, and if so, both Sir Robert Wilson and myself were sufferers from ministerial displeasure. On the word of a man about (at no distant date) to give an account to his Maker, I was no more guilty of the act attributed to me, than Sir Robert Wilson was of the disloyalty attributed to him.

Sir Robert Wilson claimed his back pay as a right consequent on his unjust deprivation, and obtained it. I have unceasingly done the same, not from the pecuniary value of the amount due, but from the consideration that its being withheld still operates as a stigma on my character and family, which is inconsistent with any restoration to the service. My efforts have been hitherto without success.

Sir Robert Wilson's application was recommended to the Treasury as a " *special case.*" My applications have not been so regarded.

Sir Robert Wilson's application was further recommended on account of " *services hitherto unrewarded.*" I will here repeat what has been stated in a previous chapter, in reply to writers who have assumed that I had been handsomely rewarded — that on no occasion did I ever receive the reward of a single shilling for any services which it was my good fortune to render to my country, beyond the ordinary pay of my rank, and the good service pension of 300*l.* a-year, conferred upon me by Sir James Graham, in 1844. Yet Lord Collingwood testified that with a single frigate I had done the work of an army, by keeping a French army from overrunning the Mediterranean coast of Spain. Neither for this nor the destruction of the enemy's ships in Aix Roads, did I ever receive reward or thanks.

The reader, who is now well acquainted with my services, can pursue the subject for himself. With the exception of the Red Ribbon of the Bath, which as the gift of my sovereign I highly prize, my reward has been a life of unmerited suffering. Even the stipulations of the South American Governments, to whom I gave freedom, are violated to this day, from a conviction that no sympathy will be accorded by the Government of my own country.

These are the requitals for my "*hitherto unrewarded services.*"

Amongst the curiosities shown to visitors of the Bank of England, there was, and no doubt is still, a thousand pound bank-note, No. 8202, dated 26th June, 1815, on the back of which are endorsed the following words :—

" MY HEALTH HAVING SUFFERED BY LONG AND CLOSE CON-FINEMENT, AND MY OPPRESSORS BEING RESOLVED TO DEPRIVE ME OF PROPERTY OR LIFE, I SUBMIT TO ROBBERY TO PROTECT MYSELF FROM MURDER, IN THE HOPE THAT I SHALL LIVE TO BRING THE DELINQUENTS TO JUSTICE.

(Signed) " COCHRANE.

"King's Bench Prison, July 3rd, 1815."

There is the reward bestowed on me by a ministerial faction, memorable only for its political corruption. With that protest I close the book.

APPENDICES

APPENDIX I.

LORD GAMBIER'S FIRST DESPATCH, GIVING ME CREDIT
FOR THE CONDUCT OF THE ATTACK IN AIX ROADS.

Caledonia, at anchor in Basque Roads,
April 14th, 1809.

SIR, — The Almighty's favour to His Majesty and the
nation has been strongly marked in the success He has been
pleased to give to the operations of His Majesty's fleet under
my command ; and I have the satisfaction to acquaint you,
for the information of the Lords Commissioners of the
Admiralty, that the four ships of the enemy, named in the
margin*, have been destroyed at their anchorage, and several
others, from getting on shore, if not rendered altogether
unserviceable, are at least disabled for a considerable time.

The arrangement of the firevessels, placed under the
direction of Captain the Right Honourable Lord Cochrane,
was made as fully as the state of the weather would admit,
according to his Lordship's plan, on the evening of the 11th
instant; and at eight o'clock on the same night they proceeded
to the attack under a favourable strong wind from the northward, and flood tide, preceded by some vessels filled with
powder and shells, as proposed by his Lordship, with a view
to explosion, and led on in the most undaunted and determined manner by Capt. Wooldridge, in the *Mediator* fireship, the others following in succession ; but owing to the
darkness of the night, several mistook their course, and failed.

On their approach to the enemy's ships, it was discovered
that a boom was placed in front of their line for a defence.
This, however, the weight of the *Mediator* soon broke, and

---

* *Ville de Varsovie,* of 80 guns ; *Tonnerre,* of 74 guns ; *Aquilon,* of 74
guns; and *Calcutta,* of 56 guns.

the usual intrepidity and bravery of British seamen overcame all difficulties, advancing under a heavy fire from the forts in the Isle of Aix, as well as from the enemy's ships, most of which cut or slipt their cables, and from the confined anchorage got on shore, and thus avoided taking fire.

At daylight the following morning, Lord Cochrane communicated to me, by telegraph, that seven of the enemy's ships were on shore, and might be destroyed. I immediately made the signal for the fleet to unmoor and weigh, intending to proceed with it to effect their destruction. The wind, however, being fresh from the northward, and the flood-tide running, rendered it too hazardous to run into Aix Roads (from its shallow water), I therefore anchored again at the distance of about three miles from the forts on the island.

As the tide suited, the enemy evinced great activity in endeavouring to warp their ships (which had grounded) into deep water, and succeeded in getting all but five of the line towards the entrance of the Charente before it became practicable to attack them.

I gave orders to Capt. Bligh, of the *Valiant*, to proceed with that ship, the *Revenge*, frigates, bombs, and small vessels, named in the margin,* to anchor near the Boyart Shoal, in readiness for the attack. At twenty minutes past two P.M. Lord Cochrane advanced in the *Impérieuse*, with his accustomed gallantry and spirit, and opened a well-directed fire upon the *Calcutta*, which struck her colours to the *Impérieuse;* the ships and vessels above-mentioned soon after joined in the attack upon the *Ville de Varsovie* and *Aquilon,* and obliged them, before five o'clock, after sustaining a heavy cannonade, to strike their colours, when they were taken possession of by the boats of the advanced squadron. As soon as the prisoners were removed they were set on fire, as was also the *Tonnerre*, a short time after by the enemy.

I afterwards detached Rear-Admiral the Hon. Robert Stopford, in the *Cæsar*, with the *Theseus*, three additional fire-

* *Indefatigable, Unicorn, Aigle, Emerald, Pallas, Beagle, Etna* bomb, *Insolent* gun-brig, *Conflict, Encounter, Fervent,* and *Growler.*

ships (which were hastily prepared in the course of the day), and all the boats of the fleet, with Mr. Congreve's rockets, to conduct the further operations of the night against any of the ships which lay exposed to an attack. On the morning of the 13th, the Rear-Admiral reported to me, that as the *Cæsar* and other line-of-battle ships had grounded, and were in a dangerous situation, he thought it advisable to order them all out, particularly as the remaining part of the service could be performed by frigates and small vessels only; and I was happy to find that they were extricated from their perilous situation.

Captain Bligh has since informed me that it was found impracticable to destroy the three-decked ship, and the others, which were lying near the entrance of the Charente, as the former, being the outer one, was protected by three lines of boats placed in advance from her.

This ship and all the others, except four of the line and a frigate, have now moved up the Charente. If any further attempt to destroy them is practicable, I shall not fail to use every means in my power to accomplish it.

I have great satisfaction in stating to their Lordships how much I feel obliged to the zealous co-operation of Rear-Admiral Stopford, under whose arrangement the boats of the fleet were placed; and I must also express to their Lordships the high sense I have of the assistance I received from the abilities and unremitted attention of Sir Harry Neale, Bart. the Captain of the Fleet, as well as of the animated exertions of the captains, officers, seamen, and marines under my command, and their forwardness to volunteer upon any service that might be allotted to them; particularly the zeal and activity shown by the captains of line-of-battle ships in preparing the firevessels.

I cannot speak in sufficient terms of admiration and applause of the vigorous and gallant attack made by Lord Cochrane upon the French line-of-battle ships which were on shore, as well as of his judicious manner of approaching them, and placing his ship in a position most advantageous to annoy the enemy and preserve his own ship; which could not be exceeded by any feat of valour hitherto achieved by the British navy.

It is due to Rear-Admiral Stopford and Sir Harry Neale, that I should here take the opportunity of acquainting their Lordships of the handsome and earnest manner in which both these meritorious officers had volunteered their services before the arrival of Lord Cochrane to undertake an attack upon the enemy with fireships; and that, had not their Lordships fixed upon him to conduct the enterprise, I have full confidence that the result of their efforts would have been highly creditable to them.

Not having had it in my power, as yet, to ascertain the conduct of the officers commanding the fireships, except that of the *Mediator*, I am under the necessity of deferring to state how far they fulfilled their duty on this hazardous service in which they were engaged.

I should feel that I did not do justice to the services of Capt. Godfrey, of the *Etna*, in bombarding the enemy's ships on the 12th, and nearly all the day of the 13th, if I did not recommend him to their Lordships' notice; and I cannot omit bearing due testimony to the anxious desire expressed by Mr. Congreve to be employed wherever I might conceive his services in the management of his rockets would be useful; some of them were placed in the fireships with effect, and I have every reason to be satisfied with the artillerymen and others who had the management of them, under Mr. Congreve's direction.

I send herewith a return of the killed, wounded, and missing of the fleet, which, I am happy to observe, is comparatively small. I have not yet received the returns of the number of prisoners taken, but I conceive they amount to between 400 and 500. I have charged Sir Harry Neale with this despatch by the *Impérieuse*, and I beg leave to refer their Lordships to him, as also to Lord Cochrane, for any further particulars of which they may wish to be informed.

I have the honour to be, &c.,

(Signed)   GAMBIER.

April 15th. — P.S. This morning three of the enemy's line-of-battle ships are observed to be still on shore under Fouras, and one of them is in a dangerous situation. One of these frigates (*L'Indienne*) also on shore, has fallen over, and they are now dismantling her. As the tides will be off in a day or two, there is every probability that she will be destroyed.

Since writing the foregoing, I have learned that the Hon. Lieut.-Colonel Cochrane (Lord Cochrane's brother), and Lieut. Bisset, of the navy, were volunteers in the *Impérieuse,* and rendered themselves extremely useful, the former by commanding some of her guns on the main-deck, and the latter in conducting one of the explosion vessels.

APPENDIX II.

LORD GAMBIER'S SECOND DESPATCH IGNORING MY SERVICES ALTOGETHER.

London, May 10th, 1809.

SIR, — I have received your letter of the 2nd instant, acknowledging the receipt of the list, containing the names of the officers and men employed in the fireships and explosion vessels on the night of the 11th ult., with my observations on the result of my inquiry respecting their conduct on that occasion; and signifying that you are commanded by their Lordships to acquaint me, that, in order to have before them full and complete information of the proceedings of the several ships employed by me on the various branches of the very important operations carried on against the enemy's fleet in Aix Road, it is their Lordships' direction that I should call upon Rear-Admiral Stopford, Captain Bligh, Captain Lord Cochrane, and any other officer I may have entrusted with any part of that service, to report to me their proceedings, together with such observations and remarks as they may have made whilst they were executing my orders against the enemy; and that I should transmit the same to their Lordships, with any observations I may think proper to make thereon.

You will be pleased to acquaint their Lordships that I have written to those officers to make reports to me accordingly, and shall lose no time in transmitting them to you as soon as they are obtained, but some time must elapse before they can reach me.

From communications I have since had with their Lordships, I am led to understand that a more full and detailed account than I have transmitted of the proceedings of the fleet under my command, during the whole of its operations in Basque Roads, would be desirable. I shall, therefore, in making such a statement, endeavour to omit no incident that may be in any degree connected with those operations, or serve to elucidate the various movements and proceedings of the fleet, persuaded that doing so cannot fail to promote the satisfaction which, in common with the officers and men under my command, I feel upon that occasion, and on the success which has resulted from it.

Their Lordships are aware that soon after I had taken the anchorage of Basque Roads, I stated to them the strong position of the enemy's fleet in Aix Roads; that their ships were moored in two compact lines, and the most distant ship of each line within point blank range of the batteries of Isle d'Aix, explaining, at the same time, that they were under the necessity of mooring in such close order, not for the purpose of opposing a more formidable front, but to avoid the shoals close around the anchorage; and their Lordships will also remember that I then pointed out the impracticability of destroying them by an attack with the ships of the line in the position they occupied; but that I conceived them to be assailable by fireships, having previously suggested to Lord Mulgrave the expediency of sending out twenty or thirty vessels for that purpose.

This suggestion was anticipated by their Lordships, and they were pleased to order twelve sail of fireships to join me, and to direct me to fit out eight others on the spot. Upon the arrival of Captain Lord Cochrane, whom their Lordships had ordered me to employ in conducting the execution of the service to be performed by the fireships, I was induced, at his suggestion, to add the *Mediator* to the number.

These preparations were completed on the 11th ultimo at night, and having previously called on board the *Caledonia* the commanders and lieutenants who had volunteered their services, and who had been appointed by me to command fire vessels, I furnished them with full instructions for their proceedings in the attack, according to Lord Cochrane's plan, and arranged the disposition of the frigates and small vessels to co-operate in the following manner.

The *Unicorn*, *Aigle*, and *Pallas*, I directed to take a station near the Boyart Shoal, for the purpose of receiving the crews of the fireships on their return from the enterprise, to support the boats of the fleet which were to accompany the fireships, and to give assistance to the *Impérieuse*, which ship was still further advanced. The *Whiting* schooner, *King George*, and *Nimrod* cutters, were fitted for throwing rockets, and directed to take a station near the same shoal for that purpose.

The *Indefatigable*, *Foxhound*, and *Etna* bomb, were to take a station as near the fort on the Isle of Aix as possible; the two former to protect the bomb vessel, whilst she threw shells into the fort.

The *Emerald*, *Dotterel*, and *Beagle* sloops, and *Growler*, *Conflict*, and *Insolent* gun-brigs, were stationed to make a diversion at the east end of the Isle of Aix.

The *Redpole* and *Lyra* I directed to be anchored by the Master of the Fleet (one near the Isle of Aix, and the other near the Boyart), with lights hoisted, to guide the fireships in their course to the attack; and the boats of the fleet were ordered to assemble alongside the *Cæsar*, to proceed to assist the fireships, under the superintendence of Rear-Admiral Stopford.

With these preconcerted movements the fleet was at this time unmoored, in readiness to render any service that might be practicable; but being anchored in a strong tide-way, with the wind fresh from the N.W. upon the weather tide making, it was again moored, to prevent the ships falling on board each other.

At about half past eight P.M. the explosion vessels and fireships proceeded to the attack; at half past nine the first explosion vessel blew up, and at ten most of the fireships were
observed to be on fire; the enemy's forts and ships firing upon
them.   Many of the fireships were seen to drive through
their fleet, and beyond the Isle of Aix.

Shortly after daylight, Lord Cochrane, who, in the *Impérieuse*, lay about three miles from the enemy, made the signal
to me by telegraph, that seven of the enemy's ships were on
shore, and that half the fleet could destroy them.   It was
visible from the *Caledonia* what ships were aground, and that
two or three had made their escape up the Charente.   I immediately ordered the fleet to be unmoored, and at half past
nine weighed and run up nearer to the Isle of Aix, with the
view, when the time of tide should render it advisable, that
some of the line-of-battle ships might proceed to attack the
enemy's ships on shore; but the wind blowing fresh from the
N.N.W. with a flood tide, I judged it unadvisable to risk any
of them at that time in so perilous a situation.   The fleet was
therefore anchored.   I made the signal for each ship to prepare, with spare or sheet cables out of the stern ports, and
springs on them, to be in readiness for any of them to go in
that I might judge necessary; in the meanwhile I ordered
three additional fireships to be prepared.

Observing the *Impérieuse* to advance, and the time of
flood nearly done running, the *Indefatigable, Unicorn, Aigle,
Emerald, Pallas, Beagle, Etna,* and gun-brigs, were ordered,
by signal, into the attack; at 2·20 P.M. the former opened
her fire upon the enemy's ships aground, and the others as
soon after as they arrived up.   I then ordered in the *Valiant*
and *Revenge* to support them, and they soon joined in the
action.

The enemy's ship *Calcutta* struck her colours at 4·10 P.M.
and the *Ville de Varsovie,* and *Aquilon,* in about an hour
afterwards; all three were taken possession of by the boats
of the advanced squadron, and set on fire as soon as the prisoners were removed; a short time after the *Tonnerre* was set
on fire by the enemy.

Perceiving, towards the close of day, that there were some of the enemy's grounded ships lying further up towards the Charente, which appeared to be exposed to further attack, I sent in the three additional fireships, and all the boats of the fleet, with Mr. Congreve's rockets, accompanied by the *Cæsar* and *Theseus,* under the direction of Rear-Admiral Stopford, with discretional orders for his acting as he should think fit, and according as circumstances should render it expedient.

On the following day (the 13th) the Rear-Admiral perceiving that nothing further could be effected by the line-of-battle ships, which had grounded, as had also some of the frigates, and how imminent the danger was in which they lay, and being satisfied that the remaining part of the service could be performed only by frigates and smaller vessels, he most wisely took advantage of a providential shift of wind, and returned with the line-of-battle ships to Basque Road. Captain Bligh, on his return, reported to me that it was found impracticable to destroy the enemy's three-decked ship, and others, which were lying at the entrance of the Charente, as the former (which was the outer one) was protected by three lines of boats placed in advance from her.

During the remainder of the 13th the *Etna* was employed in throwing shells, the *Whiting* schooner in firing rockets, and the other small vessels in firing upon the enemy's ships on shore when the tide permitted.

On the 14th, at daylight, I observed three or four of the enemy's ships still apparently aground at the mouth of the river. I ordered Captain Wolfe, of the *Aigle,* to relieve Lord Cochrane in the *Impérieuse,* in command of the small vessels advanced, and to use his utmost endeavours to destroy any of the enemy's ships which were assailable. At 2·50 the *Etna* bomb, and small vessels in shore, began their fire upon the enemy's ships at the entrance of the Charente, and continued to do so during the remainder of the day.

On the 15th, in the morning (the day on which I despatched Sir H. Neale to their Lordships, in the *Impérieuse*), three of the enemy's line-of-battle ships were observed to be still aground under Fouras, and one of them in a dangerous situation; one of their frigates (*L'Indienne*), also on shore, had fallen over, and the enemy were dismantling her.

It blew very strong from the westward the whole of the 15th and 16th, so that no attempt could be made to annoy and harass the enemy; on the latter day their frigate, which was on shore, was discovered to be on fire, and blew up soon after.

All the remainder of the enemy's ships got up the river by the 17th, except one (a two-decker), which remained aground under the town of Fouras; in the afternoon of this day it was observed that another of the enemy's frigates had got on shore up the river and was wrecked, which was afterwards confirmed by the master of a neutral vessel from Rochelle.

On the 19th it blew too violent for any of the small vessels to act against the enemy; but on the 20th, the *Thunder* bomb having arrived, and the weather having become more moderate, I sent her to assist the *Etna* in bombarding the enemy's ship, on shore near Fouras. The *Etna* had split her 13-inch mortar on the 15th, consequently had only her 10-inch effective.

State of the Force of the Enemy, transmitted in Lord GAMBIER'S *second Letter to the Hon.* W. W. POLE, *of the* 26th *March* 1809.

Statement of the enemy's force moored at Isle d'Aix, anchorage in two lines very near to each other, in a direction due south from the fort on Isle d'Aix; the ships in each line not further apart than their own length, and the most distant ships of the two lines within point blank shot of the works on that island.

One three-decker -   - Flag at the fore.

Ten two-deckers (one a fifty-⎫ One flag at the mizen, and
   gun ship, late *Calcutta*), -⎭   one broad pendant.

Four frigates.

(Signed)   GAMBIER.

Caledonia, in Basque Roads, March 26th, 1809.

Statement of the names of the enemy's ships in Aix Roads, previous to the attack on the 11th April 1809; and of the killed and wounded in the action of the 12th of April 1809.

L'Océan, 120 guns, Vice-Admiral Allemande, Capt. Reland. Repaired in 1806; on shore under Fouras.

Foudroyant, 80, Rear-Admiral Gourdon, Captain Henri. Five years old; on shore under Fouras.

Cassard, 74, Capt. Faure, Commodore.   Three years old; on shore under Fouras.

Tourville, 74, Capt. La Caille.   Old; on shore in the river.

Regulus, 74, Capt. Lucas.   Five years old; on shore under Madame.

Patriote, 74, Capt. Mahee.   Repaired in 1803.

Jemappe, 74, Capt. Fauvan.   On shore under Madame.

Tonnerre, 74, Capt. Clément de la Roncière.   Nine months old; never at sea.

Aquilon, 74, Capt. Maignon.   Old.

Ville de Varsovie, 80, Capt. Cuvillier.   New; never at sea.

Calcutta, 56, Capt. La Fone.   Loaded with flour and military stores.

Frigates.

Indienne, Capt. Proteau.   On shore near Isle d'Enette, on her beam-ends.

Elbe, Capt. Perrengier.

Pallas, Capt. Le Bigot.

Hortense, Capt. Allgand.

N.B. One of the three last frigates on shore under Isle Madame.

Return of the killed, wounded, and missing:—Two officers, eight men, killed; nine officers, 28 wounded; one man missing.   Total,—48.

GAMBIER.

Return of the names of Officers killed, wounded and missing.

Caledonia, Mr. Fairfax, Master of the fleet; contusion of the hip.

Cæsar, W. Flintoft, Acting-Lieut.; killed.

Theseus, R. F. Jewers, Master's-Mate; severely wounded in the head and hands by powder in the fireship.

Impérieuse, Mr. Gilbert, Surgeon's Assistant, wounded; Mr. Marsden, Purser; ditto.

Revenge, J. Garland, Lieut.; severe contusion of the shoulder and side.

Mediator, J. Segess, Gunner; killed.

J. Wooldridge, Capt.; very much burnt.

N. B. Clements, Lieut.; slightly burnt.

J. Pearl, Lieut.; ditto.

N.B. The last three blown out of the *Mediator* after she was set on fire.

Gibraltar, J. Conyers, Master's Mate; very badly scorched in the face and hands.

GAMBIER.

Received since the above was written.

Etna, R. W. Charston, Midshipman, slightly wounded.

APPENDIX III.

STATEMENT IN THE ADMIRALTY COURT RESPECTING THE AFFAIR OF AIX ROADS, SHOWING WHY PART OF THE FLEET ONLY WERE ENTITLED TO HEAD MONEY.

Ville de Varsovie.

On Friday, the 15th day of December 1815.

ON which day Pott appeared for the Honourable Thomas Lord Cochrane, late Commander of His Majesty's ship *Impé-*

rieuse, his officers and crew, in obedience to the monition issued in this cause from this Right Honourable Court, citing the said Lord Cochrane to appear and show cause why distribution of the head or bounty money, for the destruction of the said ship and other French ships of war, should not be made to and amongst the admirals, captains, officers, and seamen of all the ships composing the fleet under the command of the Right Honourable Admiral Lord Gambier, at the time of the attack and destruction of the said ships, and on behalf of his said parties objected to such distribution, and in support of such objection alleged that the said ship, *Ville de Varsovie,* was a French ship of war — and together with *Le Tonnerre, L'Aquilon, Calcutta,* and *L'Indienne,* and several other French ships of war, were in the month of April, 1809, at anchor in Aix Roads, on the coast of France, and an expedition was formed under the orders of the Right Honourable Admiral Lord Gambier for the purpose of endeavouring to capture or destroy the said French ships of war. That the said expedition consisted of His Majesty's line-of-battle ships, *Caledonia, Valiant, Revenge, Cæsar, Theseus, Illustrious, Gibraltar, Donegal, Hero, Bellona,* and *Resolution;* His Majesty's frigates, *Impérieuse, Indefatigable, L'Aigle, Emerald, Pallas,* and *Unicorn;* His Majesty's sloops, *Lyra, Dotterell, Foxhound, Redpole,* and *Beagle;* and His Majesty's gun-brigs, *Conflict, Insolent, Fervent,* and *Growler;* and several bomb vessels, fireships, explosion vessels, schooners, and cutters, and on the 11th day of the said month of April, the preparations for that purpose being completed, and the whole of the said fleet at anchor in Basque Roads, on the outside of Aix Roads, and distant about six miles from the said French ships of war, the explosion and firevessels proceeded into Aix Roads under the immediate command of the said Lord Cochrane, who was on board one of the same, and he commenced the attack on the enemy while several of the frigates and sloops, gun-brigs and smaller vessels also advanced on various points to support them; that in consequence of such attack seven of the enemy's ships were driven on shore, and on the following day, April 12th, His Majesty's ship *Impérieuse*, commanded by the said Lord Cochrane, together with His Majesty's ships *Valiant, Revenge,* and several of the frigates and smaller vessels, forming the inshore or advanced squadron, proceeded in and engaged the said enemy's ships so driven on shore; that about three o'clock the said day the *Impérieuse* attacked the *Calcutta,* one of the said ships, mounting 56 guns, and after an obstinate resistance she struck her colours to the *Impérieuse* and was immediately taken possession of and burnt; that the *Ville de Varsovie,* mounting 80 guns, and *Aquilon* and *Tonnerre,* mounting 74 guns each, three more of the enemy's said ships were also attacked by the said inshore or advanced squadron, and after sustaining a heavy cannonade the two former about four o'clock struck their colours, were taken possession of by the boats of the said inshore squadron, and burnt, and the *Tonnerre* was soon afterwards burnt by the enemy to prevent her from being taken by the British ships.

That in *the evening* of the said day His Majesty's ships *Cæsar* and *Theseus,* together with some additional fireships were sent into Aix Roads from the fleet to make a further attack upon the enemy; but the *Cæsar* having grounded before she could get within gun shot of the enemy's ships, the said two ships returned before daylight next morning and rejoined the fleet without being able to effect anything against the enemy; and on a subsequent day *L'Indienne,* another of the said French ships, mounting 36 guns, which had been driven on shore by the first attack, was also burnt by the enemy. And the said Pott further alleged, that during the aforesaid attack and destruction of the said enemy's ships, *Calcutta, Ville de Varsovie, Aquilon,* and *Tonnerre;* His Majesty's ship, *Caledonia,* bearing the flag of the Right Honourable Admiral Lord Gambier, together with the *Cæsar, Theseus, Illustrious, Gibraltar, Donegal, Hero, Bellona,* and *Resolution,* remained at anchor in Basque Roads above three miles distant from the nearest of the enemy's ships, and were *not within reach of shot* and never *were actually engaged*

with any of the said ships; and by reason of the premises
the said several line-of-battle ships are not entitled by law to
share in the head or bounty money payable for the attack
and destruction of the said several French ships of war, and
in verification of what he so alleged the said Pott craved
leave to refer to extracts from the log books of the said line-
of-battle ships to be by him exhibited, and to the despatch
sent by the said Lord Gambier to the Lords Commissioners
of the Admiralty, bearing date 14th April 1809.

Wherefore he prayed the Right Honourable the Judge
to reject the claim of the said ships, *Caledonia, Cæsar, Theseus, Illustrious, Gibraltar, Donegal, Hero, Bellona,* and
Resolution, and to decree the several ships of war belonging
to the said fleet who were *actually engaged with the enemy*
to be the only ships legally entitled to the said head or
bounty money, and to direct the distribution to be made
to them and to the said ship *Impérieuse* accordingly.

APPENDIX IV.

CONFIRMATION OF THE PRECEDING.

IT appears by the log-books of the ships and vessels under
the command of Admiral Lord Gambier, in Basque Roads,
on the 11th and 12th of April, 1809, and also by his Lordship's official letter to the Admiralty, and by the Minutes of
Evidence on his Lordship's court-martial, that, in consequence of an attack made on the evening of the 11th upon
the French fleet, then lying at anchor in the Roads of Aix,
by explosion vessels and fireships, under the command of
Lord Cochrane, the greater part of the French ships cut or
slipped their cables and ran on shore.

It further appears that Lord Cochrane in the *Impérieuse*
frigate remained in an advanced position during the night,

and that at daylight the following morning he made the signal by telegraph to Lord Gambier (who remained with the fleet at its anchorage in Basque Roads, at the distance of about six miles from the enemy) that seven of the enemy's ships were on shore and might be destroyed.

It further appears that, in consequence of the above-mentioned signal, or of subsequent signals of a similar or nearly similar purport, Lord Gambier caused the fleet to unmoor and weigh, either immediately after the first signal, according to his Lordship's aforesaid official letter, or after an interval of some time, according to the evidence of some of the witnesses on his Lordship's court-martial: but that he again caused the fleet to come to an anchor at a distance of more than three miles from the enemy.

It also appears that Lord Cochrane, in the *Impérieuse*, *without assistance* and *without orders*, proceeded to the attack; and that it was not till after his Lordship had made the signal that the enemy was superior, which is coupled with the signal of distress, that Lord Gambier sent in *a part* of the fleet to his assistance; and it further appears by his Lordship's aforesaid official letter, and by a due comparison of the minutes of evidence on the aforesaid court-martial, that the *Calcutta* had surrendered to the *Impérieuse* before any of the vessels ordered to her assistance had joined.

And it further appears that the ships and vessels which were ordered to join the *Impérieuse*, in consequence of the last-mentioned signal, or, according to a further official letter of Lord Gambier, in consequence of the *Impérieuse* being observed to advance, did arrive shortly after the surrender of the *Calcutta*, and joined in the attack on such others of the enemy's ships as had not had time to effect their escape; and it further appears that, in consequence of such attack by a part of the fleet only, the *Aquilon* and *Ville de Varsovie* were captured and destroyed, and the *Tonnerre* set on fire by the enemy.

And, lastly, it appears that the only ships participating in the attack were the following:—

The *Impérieuse,*
The *Valiant,*
The *Revenge,*
The *Indefatigable,*
The *Unicorn,*
The *Aigle,*
The *Emerald,*
The *Pallas,*
The *Beagle,*
The *Etna* bomb, and
The *Insolent,*
    Conflict,
    Encounter,   } Gun-Brigs.
    Fervent,
    Growler,

and that the *Caledonia,* Admiral Lord Gambier,
    the *Cæsar,* Rear-Admiral Stopford,
  and the *Donegal,*
    Resolution,
    Theseus,
    Gibraltar,
    Illustrious, and
    Bellona

remained at anchor with the commander-in-chief, and were *in no respect* aiding or assisting in the attack upon the enemy's ships, or accessary to their capture or destruction.

L'Aigle.

Captain's log erroneous, and date of the *Calcutta's* striking altered.   April 12.

Emerald.

At 12·30 saw the *Impérieuse* and *Etna* bomb open fire upon the enemy. At 1·30 answered signal 236. (*Note.* — By the Caledonia's signal, log 336): one hundred having been added to the numbers that day.   Captain's log.

Growler.

10·30 answered signal 314. Commander went on board   Ship's log the Admiral.   (*Note.* —No notice is taken of the fleet weighing.)

Conflict.

Ship's log.   Weighed at 11 A.M.

P.M. at 1 made sail for the anchorage of Isle d'Aix.   At 3 came to, and commenced action with the enemy's ships on shore.   At 4·30 answered signal as per margin* made by *Imp*   .   At 5 observed four of the enemy's ships on fire! left off action.   (*Note.* — Two of which were not burnt till next day.)

Indefatigable.

Captain's log.
No ship's or master's log from March 15 1809 !   At 11·40 weighed for signal in company with the squadron. At 12·15 shortened sail to let go the anchor.   At 2 P.M. answered signals No. 166 and 366, with compass signal south.   Weighed and made sail in for Isle d'Aix Roads, to assist H.M.S. *Impérieuse.   Then engaged with the enemy's line-of-battle ships.*   At 3·30 shortened sail and came to in seven fathoms with a spring on the cable, and commenced firing on the enemy.

Insolent.

April 12
Ship's log.   At 11·30 weighed for order of the Admiral.   At 2 P.M. anchored in six fathoms.   At 3 weighed and *observed Calcutta had struck.*

Pallas.

At 12·15 anchored H.M.S. *Caledonia.*

Revenge.

No Master's or ship's log.

No Captain's log.

Lieut. Garland, who had sent in previous logs has furnished no account of the proceedings in April 1809 until the 24th, and the date of the commencement of the said log is obviously altered, as will clearly appear both as to the month and the day.

* No signal marked on the margin.

Lieut. Millon, also of the *Revenge*, ends his log on the 31st of March 1809; although on the title-page he states it to contain the transactions of that ship between the 18th of July 1808, and the 19th of July 1809! And the Captain's certificate annexed, is dated the 17th of July 1809!

The logs of the other Lieutenants do not appear.

Etna.

At 11 A.M. the Captain went on board the Admiral's ship. Weighed and made sail by signal, as did the fleet to the southward. At 12, fleet anchored about three miles from the Isle d'Aix. At 1 the Captain came on board, steered in for the enemy's fleet.

Beagle.

At 11 A.M. starboard and larboard division weighed with with fleet — standing off and on. Fleet anchored; the *Impérieuse* and *Etna* bore up for the enemy. At 2·15 *Impérieuse* made signal to Admiral and anchored with springs and opened her fire. At 2·30 Admiral made sign to frigates *Pallas*, *L'Aigle*, *Emerald*, *Unicorn*, *Indefatigable*, *Growler*, *Encounter*, *Insolent* and *Conflict* to anchor in Charente River.

Extract from the Log-book of H.M.S. Gun-brig Insolent.

April 12th, 1809, P.M.

At 3, weighed and observed *Calcutta* had struck.

Extract from the Signal-book of H.M.S. Caledonia.

April 12th, 1809, P.M.

2·50, *Impérieuse* — General, 208. [Being the signal to close, in consequence of which, the *Insolent* weighed as appears by her log-book at 3 o'clock.]

AFFIDAVIT MADE BY ME, DISCLOSING DE BERENGER AS THE
VISITOR TO MY HOUSE ON THE 21ST OF FEBRUARY 1814.

Having obtained leave of absence to come to Town, in
consequence of scandalous paragraphs in the public papers,
and in consequence of having learnt that hand-bills had been
affixed in the streets, in which (I have since seen) it is asserted
that a person came to my house, No. 13 Green Street, on the
21st day of February, in open day, and in the dress in which
he had committed a fraud, I feel it due to myself to make
the following deposition, that the public may know the truth
relative to the only person seen by me in military uniform at
my house on that day.

CochRANE.

Dated 13 Green Street, March 11th, 1814.

I, SIR THOMAS COCHRANE, commonly called Lord Cochrane,
having been appointed by the Lords Commissioners of the
Admiralty to active service (at the request, I believe, of Sir
Alexander Cochrane) when I had no expectation of being
called on, I obtained leave of absence to settle my private
affairs previous to quitting this country, and chiefly with a
view to lodge a specification to a patent, relative to a discovery for increasing the intensity of light. That in pursuance with my daily practice of superintending work that
was executing for me, and knowing that my uncle Mr. Cochrane Johnstone went to the City every morning in a coach,
I do swear on the morning of the 21st of February (which
day was impressed on my mind by circumstances which afterwards occurred) I breakfasted with him, at his residence in
Cumberland Street, about half-past eight o'clock, and I was
put down by him (and Mr. Butt was in the coach) on Snow-
hill about ten o'clock; that I had been about three quarters
of an hour at Mr. King's manufactory, at No. 1 Cock Lane,
when I received a few lines on a small bit of paper, requesting me to come immediately to my house; the name affixed,

from being written close to the bottom, I could not read; the
servant told me it was from an army officer, and concluding
that he might be an officer from Spain, and that some accident
had befallen to my brother, I hastened back, and found Captain Berenger, who, in great seeming uneasiness, made many
apologies for the freedom he had used, which nothing but the
distressed state of his mind, arising from difficulties, could
have induced him to do; all his prospects, he said, had failed,
and his last hope had vanished of obtaining an appointment
in America, he was unpleasantly circumstanced on account of
a sum which he could not pay, and if he could that others
would fall upon him for full 8000*l.* He had no hope of
benefiting his creditors in his present situation, or of assisting
himself; that if I would take him with me, he would immediately go on board and exercise the Sharpshooters (which
plan Sir Alexander Cochrane I knew had approved of*); that
he had left his lodgings and prepared himself in the best way
his means allowed. He had brought the sword with him
which had been his father's, and to that and to Sir Alexander
he would trust for obtaining an honorable appointment. I
felt, very uneasy at the distress he was in, and knowing him
to be a man of great talent and science, I told him I would
do everything in my power to relieve him, but as to his going
immediately to the *Tonnant* with any comfort to himself, it
was quite impossible; my cabin was without furniture, I had
not even a servant on board. He said he would willingly
mess anywhere; I told him that the ward-room was already
crowded, and besides, I could not, with propriety, take him,
he being a foreigner, without leave from the Admiralty. He
seemed greatly hurt at this, and recalled to my recollection
certificates which he had formerly shown me from persons in
official situations: Lord Yarmouth, General Jenkinson, and
Mr. Reeves, I think, were amongst the number. I recommended him to use his endeavour to get them or any other
friends to exert their influence, for I had none, adding that

* Sir Alexander, previous to his departure, had applied to the Admiralty for the employment of De Berenger.

when the *Tonnant* went to Portsmouth, I should be happy receive him, and I knew from Sir Alexander Cochrane that he would be pleased if he accomplished that object. Captain Berenger said that not anticipating any objection on my part, from the conversation he had formerly had with me, he had come away with intention to go on board and make himself useful in his military capacity. He could not go to Lord Yarmouth or to any other of his friends in this dress (alluding to that which he had on), or return to his lodgings, where it would excite suspicion (as he was at that time in the rules of the King's Bench), but that if I refused to let him join the ship now, he would do so at Portsmouth. Under present circumstances however he must use a great liberty, and request the favour of me to lend him a hat to wear instead of his military cap. I gave him one which was in a back room with some things that had not been packed up, and having tried it on, his uniform appeared under his great coat, I therefore offered him a black coat that was lying on a chair, and which I did not intend to take with me; he put up his uniform in a towel, and shortly afterwards went away, in great apparent uneasiness of mind, and having asked my leave he took the coach I came in, and which I had forgotten to discharge, in the haste I was in. I do further depose, that the above conversation is the substance of all that passed with Captain Berenger, which, from the circumstances attending it, was strongly impressed upon my mind; that no other person in uniform was seen by me at my house on Monday, the 21st of February, though possibly other officers may have called (as many have done since my appointment); of this, however, I cannot speak of my own knowledge, having been almost constantly from home, arranging my private affairs. I have understood that many persons have called under the above circumstances, and have written notes in the parlour, and others have waited there, in expectation of seeing me, and then gone away; but I most positively swear that I never saw any person at my house resembling the description and in the dress stated in the printed advertisement of the members of the Stock

Exchange. I further aver, that I had no concern, directly or indirectly, in the late imposition, and that the above is all that I know relative to any person who came to my house in uniform on the 21st day of February, before alluded to. Captain Berenger wore a grey great coat, a green uniform, and a military cap. From the manner in which my character has been attempted to be defamed, it is indispensably necessary to state that my connection in any way with the funds arose from an impression that in the present favourable aspect of affairs, it was only necessary to hold stock in order to become a gainer, without prejudice to anybody; that I did so openly, considering it in no degree improper, far less dishonourable; that I had no secret information of any kind, and that had my expectation of the success of affairs been disappointed, I should have been the only sufferer. Further, I do most solemnly swear, that the whole of the omnium on account which I possessed on the 21st day of February 1814 amounted to 139,000*l.*, which I bought by Mr. Fearn (I think) on the 12th ultimo, at a premium of 28¼; that I did not hold on that day any other sum on account, in any other stock, directly or indirectly, and that I had given orders when it was bought to dispose of it on a rise of 1 per cent. and it actually was sold on an average at 29½ premium, though on the day of the fraud it might have been disposed of at 33½. I further swear, that the above is the only stock which I sold, of any kind, on the 21st day of February, except 2000*l.* in money which I had occasion for, the profit of which was about 10*l.* Further, I do solemnly depose, that I had no connection or dealing with any one, save the above mentioned, and that I did not at any time, directly or indirectly, by myself or by any other, take or procure any office or apartment for any broker or other person for the transaction of stock affairs.

COCHRANE.

APPENDIX V.

King's Bench, Sept. 9th, 1814.

My Lord,—In replying to your Lordship's letter of yesterday, I beg to observe that several applications have been already made to me from several quarters, for the purpose of obtaining the particulars of the conversation between the Honourable Mr. Murray, another gentlemen, and myself, alluded to in your letter, but that I have hitherto refused to comply with such applications, for reasons which must be sufficiently obvious to every delicate and honourable mind. Being requested, however, by your Lordship, to say whether "your name" was said to have been connected "by De Berenger" with the imposition which he had in contemplation," I can no longer hesitate in giving, to the best of my recollection, a statement of the facts relating to your Lordship.

A few days before the late trial against your Lordship and others, I was informed by Mr. Murray, that he was to be examined as a witness on the approaching trial. I asked him what was the nature of the evidence he had to give? He replied, that De Berenger had some time ago told him that he, De Berenger, and Mr. Cochrane Johnstone, had a plan in contemplation, which would be the means of putting a large sum of money into each of their pockets : that he joked De Berenger, and asked him to let him into the secret of the plan : that De Berenger laughed, and refused to tell him what the plan was, saying it was too good a thing to be made known.

Mr. Murray added that this converstion with De Berenger took place a short time previous to the hoax on the Stock Exchange ; and that it was imagined, from a combination of circumstances, that De Berenger must have had the hoax in view when he spoke of the plan between Mr. Cochrane Johnstone and himself.

I asked Mr. Murray if your Lordship's name was mentioned by De Berenger? He replied, " *Oh, no; nothing was said about Lord Cochrane.*"

I observed that I was glad of this, as I conceived De Berenger would certainly have mentioned your name as well as Mr. Cochrane Johnstone's, had your Lordship been in the plot.

Mr. Murray rejoined, " *Yes, I think it very probable.*"

The morning after, Mr. Murray, in accidentally recapitulating the conversation between De Berenger and himself, remarked, that upon recollection he thought your Lordship's name was mentioned by De Berenger, and presently afterwards he observed, that, on reconsideration, your Lordship's name certainly was mentioned. I naturally felt surprised at this statement, it being so contradictory to that of the preceding day, and took the liberty of observing to Mr. Murray, that I conceived he would act wrong, however correct his intentions might really be, to give any evidence respecting your Lordship, after so strangely forgetting himself as to the only part of the conversation which could affect your case.

Other conversation passed, but I am not so positive and clear in my recollection of it as of that which I have detailed to your Lordship.

I have the honour to be, &c.,

RICHARD GURNEY, Jun.

APPENDIX VI.

LETTER FROM LIEUT. PRESCOTT TO LORD COCHRANE.

King's Bench, Nov. 28th, 1814.

MY LORD,—Having been requested by your Lordship to commit to writing the information which I communicated to you some months ago, I have no hesitation in complying with your request.

The substance of the account which I received from the persons whose names I mentioned to you, and who may be called upon if required, is, that they were of the party at a dinner, which was termed, "The Stock Exchange Dinner," provided by order of Mr. Harrison, at Davey's Coffee-house in the Bench, on the day before the *trial;* at which dinner the Honourable Alexander Murray was also of the party, which consisted of seven or eight persons: that after they had dined, and the bottle had gone briskly round, Harrison said to Mr. Murray (who was then, and still is, a prisoner for debt) that he would get his affairs settled; *and as he should receive a large sum from the Exchange for the conviction of Lord Cochrane, if he (Murray) wanted 50l. he should have it to-morrow; proposing at the same time, " Success to the Stock Exchange," which was drunk in claret with loud cheering:* that this took place in the public coffee-room, before many persons both in the room and looking in at the windows, the dinner attracting considerable attention from its style, which was unusual in the Bench: that Mr. Harrison, in answer to a remark from one of the bystanders, that the dinner would cost a round sum, said, it did not signify if it cost 50l., as the Stock Exchange would pay for it: that when the majority of the party had drunk as much as they could or were willing to drink, Mr. Harrison ordered several full bottles to be placed on the table; and the task of finishing the wine which remained devolving at length on the Honourable Alexander Murray, and he being unable to accomplish it by himself, he went into the lobby of the prison, and procured two of the turnkeys to assist him.

The further account of one of the persons above alluded to (who usually messed with Mr. Murray), is, that for some time previous to the trial Harrison was daily with Mr. Murray, dining and drinking with him; and that he was present when Harrison visited Mr. Murray, accompanied by the solicitors, Messrs. H. and R.; on which occasion Harrison said to Mr. Murray, " Here are the gentlemen who will accomplish your wishes; " and one of those gentlemen replied, " *Yes,*

Mr. Murray, after this trial of Lord Cochrane has past, we will then attend to your liberation:"* that he heard Mr. Harrison declare in the lobby, as did many other persons, that he should receive a sum of money *if he could procure evidence which would convict Lord Cochrane;* intimating at the same time, that he was induced to offer his services to the Stock Exchange, in procuring evidence against him, by his personal antipathy to the whole family of the Cochranes, which he said would never subside while he breathed; that, subsequent to the trial, he has *repeatedly heard Mr. Murray express himself sorry for having appeared in Court against Lord Cochrane, and acknowledge that he had been the dupe of Harrison,* in persuading him that his solicitors would undertake the arrangement of his affairs and effect his liberation, provided he would appear as an evidence against Lord Cochrane at the trial. †

Shortly before the trial I addressed two letters to your Lordship on the subject of Harrison's visiting and tampering with Mr. Murray, who was expected to appear as an evidence against you; but your Lordship did not answer those letters, nor attend at that time to my communications. The fact, however, was notorious in the Bench. Of my own knowledge I have only to add, that on the day of the Stock Exchange Dinner (as it was called), my attention was attracted by the noise of the entertainment and the number of people collected; and I went into the coffee-room and saw the party at the table, as did many other persons; and towards the close of the evening I saw Mr. Murray return from the lobby into the coffee-house, accompanied by one of the turnkeys.

---

* Messrs. H. and R. were Harrison's solicitors on the trial between him and the Hon. B. Cochrane, and have since been employed by Mr. Murray, though they have not effected his liberation.

† It is due to the unfortunate Mr. Murray to observe, that his yielding to the arts which appear to have been practised upon him, to induce him to introduce my name into the evidence he had to give at the trial, is solely to be attributed to the imbecility of his mind (naturally good), occasioned by a long-continued habit of excessive drinking.

It was well known *that Harrison was in a state of extreme indigence previous to the trial**; but shortly afterwards, I was present when *he took a considerable number of bank-notes out of his pocket,* and saw him place a 50*l.* note in the hands of a gentleman, to remain till an account with Mr. Lewis was investigated. I have also heard Harrison declare, in the presence of other persons, *that he would ruin the whole Cochrane family.*

I am your Lordship's most obedient servant,

THOMAS PRESCOTT.

APPENDIX VII.

MINUTES FURNISHED TO MESSRS. FARRER AND CO. MY SOLICITORS AT THE TRIAL, AT THEIR OWN REQUEST, AND ENDORSED BY THEM, "LORD COCHRANE'S MINUTES OF CASE."

LORD COCHRANE was not in habits of intimacy with De Berenger.

De Berenger never broke bread in Lord Cochrane's house; and never, as far as Lord Cochrane knows, sat down in it.†

Lord Cochrane's servants never carried a note or letter to De Berenger, or put any note or letter into the post for him.

De Berenger's servants never brought any note or letter to Lord Cochrane, or forwarded any addressed to him.

The only person who came to No. 13 Green Street, on the 21st of February, in uniform, or the appearance of uniform, was De Berenger.

De Berenger wore a grey great-coat, without any trim-

---

* He was imprisoned for defaming Mr. Cochrane, and afterwards detained for debt in the King's Bench, where his acquaintance with Mr. Murray is supposed to have commenced.

† Neither in Green Street, nor any former residence. See answer to an anonymous letter, at the end of this publication.

ming; and had a green coat, or a coat with a green collar, under it.*

De Berenger sent a note to Lord Cochrane, which was delivered to him at Mr. King's manufactory, where he was in the daily habit of going.

The Hon. Major Cochrane was dangerously ill, and confined to his bed, at that time in Spain.†

Lord Cochrane was appointed to command the *Tonnant* but had obtained leave of absence to draw up and lodge the specification to a patent.

His leave of absence was to expire on the‡ and he did write such specification, and lodge it on the§

The man who happened to open the door to De Berenger had been hired for the express purpose of going into the country to relieve Lord Cochrane's sea-steward, and did so accordingly.

No man whatever lived in Lord Cochrane's house, except himself and one or two servants.

The servants, who were discharged, had received a regular month's warning, and left in consequence thereof.

On ‖   , Lord Cochrane directed Messrs. Lance and Smallbone to purchase for him 5000*l*. omnium for money¶; but on going to the office** with the intention to pay for it, he found that he had neglected to bring the necessary sum; and having only about 50*l*. with him, he borrowed of Messrs. Fearn, Lance, and Smallbone, a sum equal to the deficiency, except 200*l*. which was lent to his Lordship by Mr. Butt.

Mr. Fearn was repaid on the following day†† by the sale of the omnium, Lord Cochrane having given orders to sell it, in the event of his not being able to come into the city, which was the case.

---

* See the *second* of the series of questions which I addressed to my solicitors, July 25th.

† At Cambo, in France, on the borders of Spain.

‡ 28th of February.   § Ibid.

‖ 14th of February.   ¶ Which they did on the 15th.

** On the 15th.   †† On the 17th.

Messrs. Lance and Smallbone repaid themselves, and Lord Cochrane returned Mr. Butt the 200*l*. when he received the balance on Saturday the 19th.

APPENDIX VIII.

King's Bench, July 25th, 1814.

GENTLEMEN,— In consequence of what passed in the House of Commons on Tuesday last, I feel it my duty to call upon you, as my solicitors on the late trial, for answers to the following questions : —

Did I ever give you, in writing, any other instructions for the brief, than a few observations contained in one sheet of paper, which was afterwards endorsed by you, " Minutes of Case " ?

Was not the description of De Berenger's dress as contained in those minutes, namely, " a grey great-coat, without any trimming, and a green coat, or a coat with a green collar, under it," understood by you to have reference to what could be proved only, and not to imply a doubt in my mind as to the colour of the under coat, but merely to intimate that the witnesses might only be able to speak to the colour of the collar, on account of the body of the coat having been concealed by the great-coat?

Did not I, at your request, send my servants, Thomas Dewman and Mary Turpin, to your office to be examined by you preparatory to your drawing the brief? And were not you previously in possession of my affidavit, in which the coat worn by De Berenger in my presence on the 21st of February, is sworn to have been green? And were not you aware that my said servants had also made affidavits that the officer they saw at my house on that day wore a grey great-coat, buttoned up, with a green collar underneath?

Did you not particularly question them as to the colour of the under-coat? Did you not expressly ask them whether it was a red coat? And whether they could swear that it was not a red coat? which they could not, because it was worn under a great-coat, which was buttoned up.

Was it not in consequence of repeated questions that they were induced to admit that the under-coat might be red? Did either of my servants admit that any part which he or she SAW of the under-coat was red?

Did you not, in consequence of the examination of my servants, insert in the brief that the under-coat worn by De Berenger was a red coat with a green collar?

Did you ever call my attention to *that* part of the brief, by word or letter? And do you really believe that I was privy and consenting to the fact of my counsel being authorised by the brief to admit that coat to be red, which I uniformly declared to you was green, and which I had sworn to be green?

Did you read the whole of the brief to me, or merely detached parts? Did I peruse it myself in your presence, or to your knowledge? Did you ever, previous to the trial, furnish me with a copy of it?

Did I ever make any alterations in the depositions of the servants, or in any part of the brief, relative to what they could depose on the important subject of De Berenger's dress? Did I ever desire you to re-examine them on that point?

Did I ever, as far as you know and believe, give instructions to my counsel? Did I ever attend any consultation? Was not my defence mixed with Mr. Johnstone's contrary to my orders? and did you inform me that Mr. Johnstone's counsel, and not my own, was to plead my cause?

Was I not, as far as you know and believe, absent from London for near three weeks, previous to and up to the Monday preceding the trial?

Did you ever call the attention of the counsel, by word or letter, to the difference between the statement in the brief and the affidavits of myself and servants, respecting the dress of De Berenger? When did the counsel, to the best of your belief, discover that difference?

Did I not send my servants to Guildhall on the 8th of June, the first day of the trial, to be examined? Did I not send you a note by them, to inform you that I had sent them for that purpose? Did I not send them again on the second day of the trial? and did I not write to you on that day, particularly requesting that they might be examined? When did you receive my second letter? Was it not prior to the close of my defence? and if subsequent, was it not at least several hours prior to the close of De Berenger's defence? Had the counsel, to your knowledge, resolved at all events not to examine my servants? Did you communicate to me such their determination? Have you any reason to believe that I had the least knowledge, prior to the trial being closed, that my servant would not be, or had not been, examined?

If I had been informed that the counsel had refused to examine them, might I not have gone into Court, and personally demanded the examination of my witnesses?

I am, &c.

COCHRANE.

Messrs. Farrer & Co.

Lincoln's Inn Fields, Aug. 3, 1814.

MY LORD, — We were duly honoured with your Lordship's letter of the 25th ult. requiring our answers to many questions relating to the late prosecution; but after what has passed, and the communications we have already made, we hope your Lordship will agree with us in thinking, that it would be highly improper in us now to answer any more abstract or partial questions. We have, agreeably to your uncle's desire, made out, and now beg leave to inclose you our bill in that business, in which you will find most of the facts to which your questions relate stated as they occurred.

We are, &c.

FARRER AND CO.

APPENDIX IX.

WESTMINSTER ELECTION. — LETTER FROM THE RIGHT
HON. RICHARD BRINSLEY SHERIDAN TO ARTHUR MORRIS,
ESQ., HIGH BAILIFF OF WESTMINSTER.

Saville Row, Sunday evening, July 10, 1814.

SIR, — Observing that you have called a meeting to-morrow,
to be held in Palace Yard, to consider of a fit person to fill
up the present vacancy in the representation of the City
of Westminster, and having myself received very earnest
applications from numerous and independent bodies of its
inhabitant householders, requiring that I should meet their
wishes by proposing myself as a candidate, I take the
freedom of addressing these lines to you, to say that I
absolutely decline to be put in nomination in opposition to
Lord Cochrane.

I send you this my determination without concert or
communication with the respectable persons to whom I have
above referred, and towards whom I must ever continue to
give the utmost gratitude.

I trust that I need not declare that I should have felt
greatly honoured by having been again returned the representative of Westminster; my title to aspire to that distinction is simply that after more than thirty-one years' service in Parliament, I can, without fear of successful contradiction, assert that I never gave a vote that was not in
support of the truth of liberty, and in assertion of the
people's rights, duly respecting at the same time the just
prerogatives of the Crown, and revering the sacred principles
upon which was founded and maintained the glory and the
security of our unrivalled Constitution.

Holding these opinions, as a public man, have I hitherto
sat in the House of Commons; and never will I accept a
seat there but on the sole condition of being the master
of my own vote and voice — the servant only of my conscience.

As to the present question, which occasions your meeting to-morrow, I enter not into it. No man feels more the reverence due to the seats of justice, or the confidence due to the verdicts of juries. But under the circumstances of an expulsion from the House of Commons, I do not hesitate to say, that I have a decided opinion that the expelled member has a right to appeal to his constituents, with a view to the restitution of his seat and the rescue of his character.

On these grounds, Sir, I will not allow myself to interfere with the present appeal made on the part of Lord Cochrane, and to which I conceive him to be so justly entitled.

In adopting this determination, I beg leave distinctly to state, that I waive my claim to solicit the suffrages of the electors of Westminster in favour of Lord Cochrane alone.

I have the honour to be, Sir, &c.

RICHARD BRINSLEY SHERIDAN.

APPENDIX X.

[*The Times,* July 12th, 1814.]

WESTMINSTER MEETING.

YESTERDAY there was a very numerous meeting at Palace Yard, convened by the high bailiff, for the purpose of nominating a fit and proper person to represent the City of Westminster in Parliament.

The high bailiff shortly stated the purpose for which the present meeting was convened. He had received two letters, which it would be his duty to read to them. The one was from Lord Cochrane (*loud shouts of applause*), the other from Mr. Sheridan (cries of "*No Sheridan!*" and loud expressions of disapprobation from the multitude who supposed that Mr. Sheridan was offering himself as a candidate).

The letter from Lord Cochrane was first read. He enclosed

to the high bailiff a full and unmutilated account of the defence made by him at the House of Commons, which he requested him to read to the meeting.

(Many voices called out, "*Read, read!*" while many others, both on account of the great length of it as well as the danger of publishing certain passages of it, cried "*No, no!*").

The high bailiff declined to read it. He then read the letter from Mr. Sheridan, waiving his claims in favour of Lord Cochrane.

The high bailiff then asked if any gentleman had anything to propose.

Sir F. Burdett came forward amid the loudest applause. He had on many occasions witnessed with pleasure the generous feeling and independent spirit of the electors of Westminster; but he had never on any occasion witnessed the ebullition of their feelings with such satisfaction as on the present occasion, as there never was one in which it was more important. The question now was, whether an innocent individual (*loud applause*), for so he conceived him to be, should be destroyed by the machinations of corruption and power, or whether he should be supported by the voice of his constituents. He hoped that by the suffrages of the electors of Westminster, that character would be maintained which he thought had never in any instance been forfeited. They had heard a letter read from Mr. Sheridan, who had with great propriety and prudence withdrawn his pretensions, such as they were. Of the value of that gentleman's claims and pretensions he would not now judge; but he thought that it was prudent and polite of him not to press them at present against the popular feeling and the current of public opinion. They had heard also a letter from Lord Cochrane, who wished his defence to be read to them at length. It was not surprising that the high bailiff should decline reading that statement, or that no other person should be found bold enough to do so. At a time when libel was an offence so undefined in its nature that no man knew when he might be speaking or writing libels, he could not himself say whether he was not about to speak libels, but that consideration should not prevent him from speaking the truth. Lord Cochrane had, however, with that fortitude which he had so often displayed in the defence of his country, and which had never been more strongly displayed than during the late trying occasion, ventured boldly to speak his mind in the House of Commons, and was now ready to incur all the additional risks of publishing the statement he had there made. When he had made that statement, the minister of the country, or, as he should term him, the *nose leader* of that illustrious and august body (*a laugh*), not having the power of gagging Lord Cochrane, or preventing his assertion of his innocence, and knowing well the effect that such an appeal to the public would naturally produce, rose, in all the blushing honours of his blue ribbon, to impose silence upon the corrupt and degraded press that is still suffered to exist in this country. At the moment when the House of Commons was going to stigmatise Lord Cochrane with an additional vote conveying censure, the minister thought that it was not proper that the people should hear his defence. Lord Cochrane, feeling, however, as a man of honour must do, that no risk was comparable to the loss of character, wished, at every hazard, to support his hitherto unsullied character and reputation. He therefore wished that his address should be read to the meeting; but the high bailiff must, on such an occasion, be allowed to exercise his own discretion and judgment. When the uniform conduct of their chairman was taken into consideration, everybody must be convinced that his motives were always just and honourable, and therefore it would be most unhandsome in them to press him to act contrary to his own judgment in this particular instance. He felt it now unnecessary to detain the meeting with entering into a detail of the case: the statement of the noble lord had, however, explained those circumstances which appeared to require explanation. He should not now find fault with the jury that tried Lord Cochrane (who were, as he was informed, very respectable persons); but he should for ever find fault with that mode of picking out a jury which Lord Cochrane had called packing them. He did not mean to find fault with the verdict which they found upon the evidence that was laid before them — evidence which was so skilfully and so artfully got up against him by those who had the arrangement of the prosecutor's case, and which had been so feebly met by those who undertook the defence of Lord Cochrane. On such evidence they had found Lord Cochrane guilty of a fraud of which he was sure that he was as incapable as any gentleman whom he had then the honour of addressing. The noble lord had certainly charged the noble and learned judge who tried him with a false statement of the facts of the case, and with a gross misdirection to the jury. As Lord Cochrane had been prevented by the rules of law from having the opportunity of having his case re-tried, he now came before the public for the vindication of his character. He should contend, however, that the rule which was set up against the granting to his Lordship a new trial was contrary to the law, as the law never requires a man to do impossibilities. As, however, some of those who were tried with Lord Cochrane had fled from the country, and others were evidently not under his control, it was impossible that he should have been able to bring them all into court at the time he wished to move for a new trial. The principle, however, that the law never requires of a man to do impossibilities was maintained on another occasion with respect to those proceedings. When, on the part of some others who had been tried with him, an objection had been made to the indictment as not being sufficiently specific, the answer was, it was impossible to make it comprehend every point, and that the law did not require impossibilities. If the law, however, did not require impossibilities in the one case, neither would it require them in another (*great applause*). They must all remember what an impression had been made on the public mind before the trial by the publishing of evidence, if evidence it could be called, which was given before that body that designated themselves the Committee of the Stock-Exchange. He was convinced that almost every man in the court had formed his opinion from this publication of evidence, before the Stock-Exchange Committee, before Lord Cochrane had been put upon his trial. He had heard of what was called the summing up of the noble judge; but his idea of a summing up was, the statement of all the items on the one side and on the other, without addition or subtraction, and presenting to the jury a fair balance. His idea of a judge was that he should be a person free from passion or strong feeling on the case he was to try; but that he was to assist the jury by a clear and impartial statement of the evidence on the one side and on the other.

The noble judge who tried Lord Cochrane was an eloquent person, and, as he thought, his eloquence on this occasion had been unfortunate for himself. He thought that he had been as eloquent as an advocate, and as an impassioned advocate. Indeed, some of his phrases and metaphors appeared to him more nearly to resemble the language of poetry (*a laugh*), and would, as he thought, give him fairer pretensions to the situation of Poet Laureate, than some who had aspired to it (*laughter*). When he had spoken of "hunting down the chase, and getting the skin," it reminded him of the old proverb, "that the man who sold the lion's skin, while the lion was yet alive, was himself killed in the chase." He believed that Lord Cochrane was not yet hunted down; but that, on the contrary, he was now turning against his hunters. It now remained for the electors of Westminster to vindicate the character of an illustrious person who had rendered great services to his country (*loud applause*); services which, if he had even been guilty of the meanness imputed to him, should, as he thought, have protected him from the degrading infamy which it was now intended to have inflicted upon him. ("*No, no!*" from many persons, as expressing a hope that the sentence would not be inflicted.) He should hope that the malice of his enemies would not prevail; but even if he were to suffer that degrading punishment, he would confidently look for his acquittal to the unpacked and uncorrupted verdict of his constituents and his countrymen at large. He say, that if Lord Cochrane was to stand in the pillory, he should feel it his duty to attend also (*loud shouts of applause,* which lasted for many minutes). The disgrace that might be intended for Lord Cochrane, would, so far from stamping him with infamy, remove in the public opinion the idea of infamy from the punishment of the pillory. No man, that had hitherto conceived it an honour to follow the noble Lord would, for the future, conceive it infamy to stand in the pillory in which he had stood. It appeared to him that instead of destroying Lord Cochrane, the infliction of that part of the sentence would destroy the punishment of the pillory for the future. If even Lord Cochrane had been guilty of the offence with which he was charged, would it be supposed that it was for that offence he had incurred such vengeance, or would it not rather be supposed that the real crime, which could not be forgiven, was his bold and independent conduct in the defence of their rights and liberties? (*applause*). This was a crime as unpardonable in the eyes of some men as that which is called by religious men the sin against the Holy Ghost. How marked a difference was there between the punishment inflicted upon him and the treatment of the most notorious delinquents and depredators of the public purse. They, forsooth, are all honest gentlemen, and meant to pay back at some time or another; and by places and pensions they were often enabled to pay back to the public out of their own money. This put him in mind of a story he had once heard of a Scotch gardener, who flourished and grew rich while his neighbours were failing. One of them, however, having got up very early in the morning, met him with a cartful of wall-fruit, which he had stripped from their gardens, and asked him, "Where are you going?" The Scotchman answered, "I am going back again" (*a laugh*). This was the case with the great public delinquents: when they were found out, they were let go back again. He had no doubt but that with the sense they appeared to entertain, both of the innocence and merits of Lord Cochrane, they would enable him again to go to the House, not for the purpose of pruning that hateful system whose branches had extended so wide, but for the purpose of laying the axe to the root of corruption (*applause*), in order that a natural and wholesome vegetation might take its place. He had exerted himself to rescue the property of his gallant brethren in arms from the gripe of legal harpies; he had acted with independence in circumstances where it was not easy to act independently. He thought that a real independent representative, a man not connected with or swayed by any party, stood in rather a forlorn and difficult situation. Having said so much, he should leave the case of Lord Cochrane to their decision; to them he should commit not his life, for that he had freely and often risked for honour at the cannon's mouth, but that immortal-part, which was far dearer to a man of honour than his life, his reputation and his character. To them he now confidently made his appeal, and he trusted that he should not be disappointed. After a few more observations, he concluded by moving the following resolution:—

"Resolved, that in the opinion of this meeting, Lord Cochrane is perfectly innocent of the offence for which he has been sentenced to receive an infamous punishment."

MR. WISHART seconded the motion. Great pains, he said, had been taken to trace one part of the route of De Berenger; but not so much with respect to the other. He did not think that the witnesses on the trial were perjured; but Berenger might have brought the coat along with him in the bundle which he held in his hand. Lord Cochrane came forward like an innocent man, and stated all that he knew of the transaction; nor could it be reasonably inferred that he was implicated in the fraud because Berenger came to his house. The rule of the Court had placed Lord Cochrane in a most difficult and perplexing situation; a rule wholly unknown to the best times of the constitution. Judges thus took the law in their own hands, and encroached upon the functions of Parliament. He did not intend to arraign the conduct of the jury, though the verdict of the juries who had condemned Russell and Sidney had been subsequently reversed (*loud applause*), because it had been improperly obtained, and the memory of those illustrious patriots would remain embalmed in the recollections of the latest posterity. Many judges had been an ornament to the country that gave them birth, such as Sir M. Hale, Lord Camden, and others; and would to God judges like them always presided in the seat of justice. Every man who was actuated by a cause of justice, or by the feeling of humanity, would pour the balm of consolation into the wounded spirit of the noble Lord, who had deserved so well of his country, and who, from some, at least, of his countrymen, had met with such an ungrateful return.

MAJOR CARTWRIGHT said there was nothing in any part of the evidence which warranted the learned lord (Ellenborough) in stating that De Berenger came to the house of Lord Cochrane emblazoned in all the costume of his crime. Such an assertion would only be accounted for upon the supposition, that in his charge to the jury he had trusted rather to his memory than to his notes. The evidence against Lord Cochrane was like a grain of sand in one hand, while that in his favour was like Westminster Abbey in the other (*loud and reiterated applause*).

MR. WALKER thought that it was the duty of the noble Lord's constituents to replace him in his situation as Member for Westminster (*shouts of applause*).

MR. ALDERMAN WOOD, when he first heard of the charge against Lord Cochrane, had said he was innocent, and that he had not the heart nor the disposition to commit a fraud (*applause*). After the trial he was of the same opinion, and everything that had since taken place contributed still more to strengthen that belief. He had heard from one of the jury (who had assured him that others of that jury were of the same sentiment), that had the evidence since produced been brought forward upon the trial, or had Lord Cochrane been in Court and made his own defence, it would have been impossible to have found him guilty (*bursts of applause*). If necessary, he could bring the individual alluded to before them (*" Bravo, bravo!"*). When he first heard of the result of the trial, he, as an elector of Westminster, had been turning in his mind whom it might be proper to propose for their representative. He was happy to think that now there was no opportunity for any deliberation of that kind, for the electors of Westminster would do justice to an injured character, and return him by their verdict to that House from which he had been expelled (*loud applause*). The resolution was then put and carried by acclamation.

SIR F. BURDETT then moved the second resolution :—

"That it is therefore the opinion of this meeting, that Lord Cochrane is a proper person to represent the City of Westminster in Parliament, and that he be put in nomination at the ensuing election."

This was seconded by MR. STURCH, and carried unanimously, and with great applause.

SIR F. BURDETT then moved the third :—

"That a Committee be appointed for the purpose of carrying into effect the foregoing resolutions, with power to add to their number."

This was also agreed to, and Sir Francis proposed several names, among which were Mr. Alderman Wood, Mr. Brooks, Mr. Adams, and Mr. Jones Burdett, &c.

The Hon. Baronet next moved the fourth resolution : —

"That a subscription be entered into to defray the expenses of the ensuing election, toward which it is the bounden duty of every elector and friend to purity of election to contribute."

It was seconded by MR. WISHART, who said that as the City of Westminster had set an honourable example in returning members free of expense, it became their character to continue the practice : but their treasury was not inexhaustible, and he hoped that every friend to the purity of election would come forward and contribute on this occasion (*applause*).

MAJOR CARTWRIGHT moved the fifth resolution : —

"Resolved — That the thanks of this Meeting be given to

Sir Francis Burdett, and the forty-three honourable members who voted against the expulsion of Lord Cochrane."

Sir F. Burdett returned thanks ; and, after a vote of thanks to the high bailiff, the meeting broke up.

APPENDIX XI.

[*The Morning Chronicle*, July 18th, 1814.]

WESTMINSTER ELECTION.

On Saturday last, in pursuance of the notice of the high bailiff, a numerous body of the Westminster electors met at the porch of St. Paul's, Covent Garden, to choose a fit person to represent their city in Parliament. At ten o'clock proclamation was made and the writ read, when SIR F. BURDETT came forward on the hustings, and, addressing the electors, said, that in pursuance to the unanimous resolutions of the electors of Westminster in Palace Yard, he had appeared to put in practice that which was unanimously determined on at that time, by putting in nomination the person whom they had then determined to be worthy to represent them. And such was the effect which that unanimous expression of opinion had produced, that, almost for the first time, they were not faced by any Court candidate ; for such was the weight that it carried, that it had imposed silence in all quarters (*applause*). It would ill become him to detain them long from that great purpose — great it was, for it was the purpose of doing justice and maintaining the oppressed which they were that day assembled to accomplish, but he thought it his duty to add a few words on so novel and important an occasion (*marks of approbation*). The assembly of that day presented the most august spectacle to the mind of man — it was the image of a free people — of a body of free men, appealed to in the last resort, from all minor and inferior jurisdictions, by an oppressed individual — oppressed by corrupt machinations and artful combinations. From whatever cause this oppression arose, it was enough that he was oppressed, and that he had appealed from his oppressors to the justice of the people at large — for the character by which the people of England was most distinguished was the love of justice (*applause*). It was needless to attempt to display any of the merits peculiar to Lord Cochrane, because whatever these merits or demerits, if any such existed (of which he, Sir F. B. was not aware), were of little consequence. It was not in the view of personal merits or demerits, but in the defence of a man oppressed unjustly, as they believed — in support of justice, that they were called on to give their suffrages on this occasion. Though idle reports or malignant artifices had been played off against Lord Cochrane, even had they not carried in themselves their own refutation, they would have had no weight with the electors of Westminster. Free bodies of electors had always shown a disposition to support the oppressed, and particularly in the case of that individual whose apostacy had done such injury to the cause of liberty, and who had always been thought by those who knew him intimately, to have been unprincipled — John Wilkes. In that case, despite of all dislike to the character of the man, he was maintained because he was an object of oppression, and because he had avowed those principles of public liberty which could never fail to vibrate in the hearts of the people of England (*loud applause*). We had lately had amongst us the great sovereigns of distant states, to whom we had shown that respect and kindness which they claimed, from the regard they had shown to human liberty and human happiness; when, had they appeared in their artificial characters of princes only, they might have passed unheeded without any marks of our affection and regard (*applause*). He regretted that they had now departed from this country without seeing what he (Sir F. B.) then saw, and which outshone all the shows and entertainments (*a laugh*) with which, as a mark of respect, they had been justly entertained — the spectacle of a free people in the act of maintaining an oppressed fellow-citizen against the arm of corruption and power (*applause*). Such a spectacle as this no other nation on the earth could afford . . . .

We had heard a great deal lately about hoaxes, especially of that in which my Lord Cochrane had been so innocently and unfortunately implicated. We have been told of a trial by jury, who are supposed to be impartial men, taken at random; now my Lord Cochrane has been tried — tho' I think no blame attaches to the jury who tried him, who, I think, under the circumstances did their duty — not by a jury of the country, but by a packed and selected jury. There is no greater hoax than to try a man by such a jury (*applause and laughter*), — and to tell him he had been tried by a jury of his country. We have been told that the judg should not only be impartial, and sit on the bench as a stone, with no feeling, but with all judgment, but that he should be a counsel for the prisoner. What sort of counsel for Lord Cochrane was my Lord Ellenborough? (*Loud laughter and applause*). Indeed my Lord Cochrane has been the most hoaxed of any man (*applause*).

That very morning he (Sir F. Burdett) had been looking into a newspaper which was famous for hoaxing, and which formerly produced the fabricated French news—he meant the *Morning Post* (*a laugh*). In that paper there was a paragraph, stating that the Princess Charlotte was delighted at her residence at Carlton House, and was highly gratified to see her old friends about her. This he should conceive was somewhat of a hoax (*a laugh*). It was given out to the public that those gew-gaws in the parks, that the childish amusement of squibs and crackers, were all intended solely for the delight of the British public, which public, by the way, would have to pay all the expenses out of its own pockets. Was not this a hoax? (*A laugh.*) But there was one still greater. There was a large body of placemen who grow rich with the public money, and yet were so fastidiously delicate that they could not endure that any peculator of a different stamp should associate with them. Those imma-

culate persons who thus lived by the public purse chose to
call themselves the representatives of the people of England.
He trusted that the example set by the City of Westminster
would spread through every part of the kingdom, and that
the corrupt would be taught that England was not to be so
represented. If other places would act like Westminster, and
return their members to Parliament not only without expense,
but without the least solicitation, in that case Corruption
would receive, if not her death-blow, yet such a wound as
would prevent her from ever re-assuming an influence per-
nicious to the best interests of the country. He would now
propose to them Sir Thomas Cochrane, commonly called
Lord Cochrane, as a fit representative to serve them in Parliament (*great applause*).

Mr. STURCH seconded the motion. He had never had any
personal or political connection with Lord Cochrane till he
visited his Lordship in prison; and he should support his
Lordship because he was persuaded that he had been condemned on imperfect evidence, and because the severity of
his sentence was such as to astonish the whole nation.

The high bailiff then put the question, which was carried
with acclamations and unanimously, and the high bailiff then
declared Lord Cochrane to be elected (*loud applause*).

ALDERMAN WOOD next addressed the meeting. He began
by alluding to some newspapers which had called his conversation with the juryman *chit-chat*. He denied that it was
chit-chat; it was a solemn assertion made by a gentleman
in the name of himself and some of his fellow-jurors. He
begged the electors to dismiss from their minds these calum-
nies which had appeared respecting Lord Cochrane's treatment
of his father. He had made the most anxious inquiries into
that matter, and had gone late last night to gain more particular information; and he was able to assure them positively
that Lord Cochrane had always been distinguished for his
kindness, generosity, and attention to his poor unfortunate
father. It was evident that there existed somewhere a very
vindictive feeling towards Lord Cochrane. As a proof, he

would mention that order of the Secretary of State which directed that the punishment of the pillory should take place on the 10th of August (cries of " *No Pillory*"). Now it had always been usual to leave the time to the discretion of the Sheriff, who never inflicted this punishment at so early a period after the sentence. If he himself were Sheriff he should refuse to obey such an order ; and should content himself with alleging that the time appointed did not suit him (*great applause*). The worthy Alderman concluded by an allusion to the paragraph concerning the Princess Charlotte. He had reason to know, that in spite of all that high satis-faction which she was said to feel in her own residence, she had made three attempts to escape (*laughter and applause*).

The usual thanks followed, and the meeting dispersed.

APPENDIX XII.

[Cobbett's *Political Register*, July 30th, 1814.]

RE-ELECTION OF LORD COCHRANE.

In consequence of the unanimous return of his Lordship to fill his seat in Parliament, as one of the representatives for the City of Westminster, the following letters passed between his Lordship and Mr. Brooks, Treasurer of the Westminster Committee. It is a fact, perhaps not generally known, that, with the exception of one or two newspapers, the London journals have thought proper to refuse giving publicity to this correspondence. Such, indeed, is the degraded state of our press, that the editor of a Sunday paper, in giving his Lordship's letter, omitted several of the most striking pas-sages in it, which, as was done in publishing his defence, he supplied with stars !

Committee-room, King Street, Covent Garden,
July 16th, 1814.

MY LORD,—I am directed by the Committee of Electors of Westminster, appointed at the general meeting held in New Palace Yard, on Monday the 11th instant, to acquaint your Lordship that you were this morning nominated as a fit and proper person to fill the vacancy in the representation of the City of Westminster in Parliament, occasioned by your Lordship's expulsion; and that you were immediately re-elected, without opposition, and with the most lively expressions of universal approbation. The Committee further direct me to convey to your Lordship their sincere congratulations on an event so happily demonstrative of the sense which your constituents entertain of the accusation which has been brought against you, *and of the very extraordinary proceedings by which it has been followed up;* and to assure your Lordship that it affords them the highest gratification to find that you are able to oppose to the envenomed shafts of malice and party spirit the impenetrable shield of conscious innocence. They rejoice to see that the prejudices occasioned by gross and shameless misrepresentation are fast wearing away from the public mind; and they trust that the time is near when your Lordship's character will appear as fair and unblemished in the view of every individual in the British empire, as it now does in the eyes of the electors of Westminster.

I have the honour to be, my Lord,

Your Lordship's most faithful and obedient servant,
SAMUEL BROOKS, *Chairman.*

To Lord Cochrane.

———————

King's Bench, July 18th, 1814.

SIR,—Amongst all the occurrences of my life, I can call to memory no one which has produced so great a degree of exultation in my breast as this, which, through a channel which I so highly esteem, has been communicated to me, that, after all the machinations of corruption (bringing into play her choicest agents) have been able to effect against me, the citizens of Westminster have, with unanimous voice, pronounced me worthy of continuing to be one of their representatives in Parliament. Merely to be a member of the House of Commons (as now made up) is something too meagre to be a gratification to me; but when I reflect on that love of country, that devotion to freedom, that soundness of judgment, that unshaken adherence to truth and justice which have invariably marked the proceedings of the citizens of Westminster, and when I further reflect that it is of Sir Frances Burdett whom they have now, for the third time, made me the colleague, how am I to express, on the one hand, my gratitude towards them, and, on the other, the contempt which I feel for all the distinctions of birth, and for all the wealth, and all the decorations which ministers and kings have it, under the present system, in their power to bestow. With regard to the case, the agitation of which has been the cause of this, to me, most gratifying result, I am in no apprehension as to the opinions and feelings of the world, and especially of the people of England, who, though they may be occasionally misled, are never deliberately cruel or unjust. Only let it be said of me:—the *Stock-Exchange* have accused; *Lord Ellenborough* has charged for guilty; the *Special Jury* have found that guilt; the *Court* have sentenced to the pillory; the *House of Commons* have expelled; and the *Citizens of Westminster* HAVE RE-ELECTED. Only let this be the record placed against my name, and I shall be proud to stand in the Calendar of Criminals all the days of my life. In requesting you, sir, to convey these my sentiments to my constituents at large, I cannot refrain from begging you, and the other gentlemen of the committee, to accept my particular and unfeigned thanks.

I am, Sir, your most obedient, humble servant,

COCHRANE.

To Samuel Brooks, Esq., Chairman of the Committee
of the Electors of Westminster.

APPENDIX XIII.

TO THE ELECTORS OF WESTMINSTER.

King's Bench, Aug. 10th, 1814.

GENTLEMEN, — It is fresh in your recollection that when Lord Ebrington, contrary to my opinion, which was conveyed by letter to his Lordship, and at my request read by him to the House, made his motion for a remission of that part of the sentence which was to have been executed this day, Lord Castlereagh was empowered to state that the Prince Regent had already done that which it was the object of Lord Ebrington's motion to effect. You will also remember that Lord Castlereagh, instead of immediately making his communication, and preventing an unnecessary, and consequently improper discussion, withheld it from the House for a considerable time, and thus afforded the Attorney and Solicitor-General and himself an opportunity of making a new and violent assault upon my character and conduct. Although many of their arguments had been previously refuted, and others were well answered at the time, yet it was impossible for those honourable Members who entertained a favourable opinion of me to answer every accusation which the Solicitor-General and others brought forward by surprise. It remains, therefore, for me to offer some observations in my own defence, in which my reason will appear for having suffered some delay to occur in the execution of this important duty.

In the course of the Solicitor-General's speech he asserted that, in my defence, I had mis-stated the circumstances of the transaction, and had charged my solicitors with a gross dereliction of duty. I shall show that I have neither mis-stated circumstances nor made any unfounded accusation. He further asserted that he would take upon himself to say that the brief had been drawn up from my own instructions. The fact is, I have never denied that I gave instructions for the brief. It is true, however, that I gave no specific instructions to counsel, and attended no consultation; but it is obvious that without some instructions or some information from me to my solicitors there could have been no brief at all. My solicitors themselves applied to me for written instructions, and I, of course, furnished them with such particulars as occurred to me on the subject, which are written on one sheet of paper, and might have been written on one page. This paper is indorsed by my solicitors, "Lord Cochrane's Minutes of Case," and may be seen in my possession.*

I apprehend that it was the duty of my solicitors to have sent me a copy of the brief, which, however, they did not; and I repeat that, previous to the trial, I never read it. It appears that they particularly called my attention to an unimportant circumstance which they had inserted in the brief, or the examinations attached, in consequence of an erroneous communication from my servant, who had confounded the circumstances of two different occurrences.† This was the "one particular" which the Solicitor-General says that I myself corrected. I admitted that this error was expunged by my authority, and opposite the four lines which contained it, is written, " Read this to Lord Cochrane," which I think is an argument that the greater part of the

* It was discovered by His Majesty's law officers that these few hints, or " Minutes of Case," given to my solicitors, at their own solicitation, preparatory to drawing the brief, furnish a contradiction to my assertion in the House, that *I gave no instructions to counsel*. I was desirous of giving these learned gentlemen the full benefit of the discovery by making them public, when I published this Address to the Electors of Westminster, but was prevented by a suggestion that the Address, with the other important documents annexed, were already too long for a communication to the newspapers; and so the editor of one of those prints appears to have thought, for he omitted two very important and inoffensive paragraphs. As the same reasons no longer exist, I insert the " Minutes of Case " between the Address and the questions to the solicitors.

† See this explained, in the answer to an anonymous letter, at the end.

brief was not read to me; particularly as there are twelve lines expunged in another place, opposite which my name does not appear. My solicitors, however, assert, that though I did not read the brief myself, they read the greater part of it to me; and on their assertion I will admit that they did so, though I have no recollection of the fact. But if it could be shown that they drew my attention to every line of the brief, except only to that one most important point, the description of De Berenger's dress, which immediately follows the four lines expunged, I still think that they were guilty of very reprehensible negligence. In my affidavit, which was before them, and was introduced into the brief, the coat worn by De Berenger is sworn to have been *green;* and in the examinations attached to the brief it is stated to have been *red.* It is impossible that this most important difference could have escaped their observation, and yet it is true that they never called my attention to it. I may affirm, without fear of being again contradicted, that I did not know that the dress of De Berenger, which I had sworn to be green, was in any part of the brief, much less in the examinations of my servants, described to be red; because it is impossible, unless I had been absolutely insane, that I should not only have been satisfied with a brief which authorised my counsel to contradict my own affidavit, but have been anxious to send my servants into court to give evidence against me.

If my solicitors actually read this part of the brief to me, it was obvious that I was not giving that attention which a man conscious of guilt naturally would have given. The word "RED," if I had heard it, must have instantly excited my particular notice. But " if the difference between red and green escaped my observation," what did my solicitors "think"* of it? My accusers chiefly depended for my conviction

---

* In more than one account of Lord Ellenborough's charge, his Lordship was represented to have said, "If the difference between red and green escaped Lord Cochrane's observation, what did he think of the star and medallion?"

on proving that De Berenger appeared before me in the red coat in which he committed the fraud. Is it possible that one of my solicitors should have read it to me and not have said, "You observe, Lord Cochrane, that this is contradictory to your affidavit?" To have read it to me without a pause, and have suffered it to pass without observation, is, I think, as negligent as not to have read it at all; and is wholly irreconcileable with the assertion of Mr. Abercrombie, that both parts of the brief were read over to me with the utmost care.

If, in my defence in the House of Commons, I did not state the manner in which I apprehend the difference between the brief and the affidavit originated, it was because I could not have stated it without throwing the more blame on my solicitors than I felt inclined to do. I have been challenged by the Attorney-General to unseal the lips of my solicitors and counsel. My solicitors, however, did not wait for me to unseal their lips, as is evident by what is called the counter-statement, with which they thought proper to furnish Mr. Abercrombie and others; and I think it rather unreasonable to require me to unseal the lips of my counsel to qualify them to give evidence against me, when I could not succeed in unsealing their lips on the trial to speak one word in my behalf. My own counsel, Mr. Topping and Mr. Scarlett, whom I fully expected would have advocated my cause, never spoke in my defence. In saying this, however, I cast no blame on those gentlemen, because I have no doubt that, under the circumstances then known to them, they acted as they thought best. Neither do I mean to blame Mr. Serjeant Best (the counsel for Mr. Johnstone), who, contrary to my expectation and direction, defended my cause in conjunction with that of his own client. He made as able a speech as any advocate could have done, with the information he possessed, and under his then circumstances; but he intimated at the time, and afterwards authorised me to assert, that he was not able to do justice to the cause; and it is a just ground of complaint, that after Mr. Serjeant Best had been exhausted by fifteen hours' close attention and confinement, he was not allowed a few hours to recover himself and prepare for the defence.

To return: I do, however, accept the daring of the Attorney-General, and freely release my solicitors and counsel from every obligation of secresy.* I might perhaps have done this sooner, but the delay has not been occasioned by any doubt in my mind as to the propriety of the step, or fear of the consequences. I thought, however, after the statement which has been circulated by my solicitors, that it was my duty, in the first place, to put to them certain questions, which I was not aware would have occasioned much delay; but after a lapse of nearly a fortnight, they wrote to inform me, that they thought it would be improper to answer those questions. I now lay them before the public.

I particularly authorise the counsel employed for the defence, to state their reasons for determining to defend me conjointly with Mr. Johnstone, contrary to the opinion of Mr. Adam expressed on the 6th of May, contrary to their own opinion expressed on the 24th of May, and contrary to my opinion and direction expressed on the 29th of May; and I also particularly authorise them to assign the reason for their opinion, that no witnesses ought to be examined on my part†; and especially their reasons for not examining my

---

* I have not learnt that any of these gentlemen have made any disclosures in consequence of this release.

† From an item in my solicitor's bill, dated June 6th, only two days before the trial, I extract the following: " Attending a consultation at Mr. Serjeant Best's chambers, when your case was fully considered, and all the counsel were decidedly of opinion that you must be defended jointly with the other defendants; and the counsel recommended your servants being in attendance on the trial, although they still remained of opinion that neither they nor any other witness ought to be examined on your part." In a subsequent item, dated June 7th, the day before the trial, I am represented to have acquiesced; not, however, in the non-examination of my witness, but in the *joint defence*. It appears, however, that I held out to the last; and if I did acquiesce, it was then high time to do so, otherwise, in all probability, I should not have been defended at all.

servants on the subject of De Berenger's dress, notwithstanding my earnest desire to have them examined. I am also willing, nay, I am anxious, that Mr. Serjeant Best should state, whether, when he admitted that the coat was red, and not green, he did not imagine that I had sworn falsely by design? I know that in his speech he attributed my description of the coat to error only, but I am anxious to know whether he did so from his feelings as a man or his sense of duty as an advocate? Until I am better informed, I shall incline to the opinion that he was actuated by the latter feeling only; because, if he really imagined that he had to defend an innocent man, I do think that he would not, without previously communicating with me on the subject, have had recourse to the dangerous expedient of admitting that to be *red* which I have sworn to be *green*, however embarrassed he might have been by the confusion of his brief, or exhausted by the fatigue and long confinement which he had undergone.

I stated in the House of Commons that I gave no instructions to counsel, and attended no consultation. I now see the folly of this negligence; for if I had personally attended to my interests, and conferred with my advocates on the subject, I have no doubt that I should have fully convinced them of my innocence. I believe that, subsequent to the trial, there is not a single individual with whom I have conferred on the subject who has not left me with that impression.

To come now to the manner in which the error in the brief originated, I have no hesitation in acknowledging that I am at issue with my solicitors on that point. Their account is, that two of my servants, whom I had sent to their office to be examined as to the evidence they could give on the trial, admitted that De Berenger wore a *red* coat with a green collar. My servants, on the contrary, assure me that they did not, and could not, admit that it was a red coat; because, when they saw De Berenger, he wore a great-coat buttoned up, and they neither saw the body nor the skirts of the under coat; but the collar, and so much of the breast as

they saw, were green : but they admit, that on being questioned by my solicitors, whether they could swear that it was
not a red coat; they confessed that they could not, and admitted that it might be red, and that the green which they
saw might be green facings to a military coat: but they have
constantly declared that no part which they saw was red, and
they deny that they ever admitted that they saw any red.

My solicitors were in possession of their previous affidavits,
describing De Berenger to have worn a grey great-coat buttoned up, and a coat with a green collar underneath. I shall
not deny that my solicitors considered the admissions of the
servants to amount to an acknowledgment that the coat was
red; but I shall ever believe that such admissions actually
went no further than that, since they did not see the body of
the coat, it might, for aught they knew, be red—and possibly,
that they supposed it was red, because the wearer having a
sword and military cap, they conceived him to be an army
officer. The description which my solicitors introduced into
the brief, in consequence of this examination, namely, a red
coat with a green collar, neither accords with my description
nor with the coat actually worn by De Berenger on his way
from Dover, which, as proved by the witnesses on the trial,
was either wholly scarlet, or turned up with yellow.

If I had been a party to the fraud, and had sworn falsely
as to the colour of the coat, I doubtless might also have been
wicked enough to have endeavoured to suborn the servants to perjure themselves in my behalf; but I should
hardly have ventured to send them to my solicitors to be
examined on the subject, without previously instructing them
myself: and it can hardly be supposed, that if they had been
on their guard from any previous instructions of mine, that
my solicitors, in the common course of examination, would
have obtained from them any evidence which militated against
my own statement. I should naturally, too, have felt some
anxiety to know the result of their examination; yet the
truth is, that I never asked them a single question on their
return from the solicitor's office. Indeed, if I had questioned

them as narrowly as one may suppose a guilty man who had sent his servants on a guilty errand of so much danger and importance would have questioned them, I should in all probability have discovered whether they had or had not executed that errand to my satisfaction.   At all events, I should have been anxious to know the result of their examination as entered in the brief; and if it be true that it was actually read to me by my solicitor, I must, under such circumstances, have lent too attentive an ear to have suffered the ruinous word *red* to have escaped my observation.   I must, too, have shown certain symptoms of uneasiness on hearing that word, which could not have escaped the observation of the reader, particularly as the contradiction between that word and my oath must have been present to his mind.   And lastly, with the knowledge that the brief contained a flat and fatal contradiction to my own affidavit out of the mouths of my own servants, I should hardly have suffered it to have gone to my counsel in that state; and then have pressed, in the way in which I did press, to have those servants examined at the trial.

How my solicitors could admit so fatal a contradiction into the brief, without drawing my attention to it immediately by letter, it is for them to explain; yet they admit that they never wrote to me on the subject.   They very quietly, however, inserted it, and let it remain in the brief until I should happen to discover it; which, as I have pretty clearly proved, never did happen previous to the trial.   It was on the second day of the trial, and not before, that, to my very great surprise, I discovered in a newspaper the admission of my counsel in contradiction to my affidavit.   " Yet," says the Attorney-General, "there was no mistake and no surprise: if there had, the Judges would have dispensed with their rule, and granted a new trial: but, no! there was nothing of that sort here."

In whatever way my solicitors took the examination of my servants on the subject of De Berenger's dress, it is indisputable that nothing can justify their neglect in not immediately drawing my attention to the difference between the result of that examination and the statement in my own affidavit. "It never can be permitted," said the Solicitor-General, "that a person accused should try in the first instance how far he could go without his own witnesses; and then, should the result prove unfavourable, how far he could go with them." How unjust this observation is, as applied to me, is well known to my solicitors—they well know how anxious I was to have my witnesses brought forward *in the first instance.* Those witnesses would and could conscientiously have sworn to the green collar, which would have sufficiently corroborated the description in my affidavit, as it never was pretended that De Berenger wore a green collar to his scarlet coat.

It was asked by the Attorney-General "if the servants could have confirmed the affidavit, where was the advocate who could have been stupid enough to hesitate to produce them?" It is possible, however, that advocates may be prejudiced, may be mistaken, and may be misled by their brief.*

I hope that it will now appear to be satisfactorily proved, not only that I did not see De Berenger in his scarlet coat, but that he did not come to my door, nor *even enter the hackney-coach in that dress.*—(See the annexed affidavits.)

In reply to the Solicitor-General's observation, that I had sought to establish my own innocence by recrimination upon the Judge and Jury, I shall at present merely ask the learned gentleman whether he is of opinion that a like sentence for a like offence would have been passed on any nobleman or member of Parliament on his side of the House? Would a punishment which, according to the unfortunate admission of the Attorney-General, is calculated "to bow down the head with humiliation ever after," together with fine and imprisonment, and the privation of every office and honour, have been thought little enough for a ministerial defendant on such a charge? And if the candour of the learned gentleman impels him to answer in the negative, is it

---

* It is also possible that they may be compelled to attempt the exercise of their duty when incapacitated by faintness and fatigue.

not fair to inquire whether he thinks that such an one would even have been convicted on similar evidence? The Attorney-General observed, "that he was glad that the period had arrived when the trial could be read at length, and thus do away the effect of those imperfect statements which misled the public mind." Reserving my remarks on the trial for a future opportunity, I shall at present just ask the Attorney-General how it comes that he, who is so anxious that the public mind should not be misled, should have made the unfounded assertion, that I not only pocketed a large sum of money by the fraud, but put off absolute ruin? Such an assertion is the more inexcusable in the Attorney-General, who had every facility of obtaining more correct information. His own broker could have told him that the Omnium which I possessed on the 19th of February, when the fraud must have been in agitation, could have been sold on that day at $27\frac{5}{8}$. The average cost was $27\frac{1}{8}$; so that the whole loss on the 139,000l. Omnium, if sold on that day, would not have amounted to above 400l. And when it is considered that the result of my previous speculations was a gain of 4,200l. received, and 830l. in the hands of my broker, how does the Attorney-General make it out that I had so embarrassed myself by such speculations, as to have no other than fraudulent means of escaping absolute ruin? Besides, I can assure the learned gentleman, if he is not already apprised of the fact, that if I had held the Omnium till the 1st, 3rd, or 4th of March, I should have sold it at a profit; and if I had held it till the settling-day, when I must of necessity have sold it, I should not have lost half the sum I had previously gained. But if upon the whole I had lost a few hundreds, or even thousands, how would the Attorney-General be justified in inferring my absolute ruin? It is well known that I had been more successful at sea than almost any other officer of my standing in the navy, and that I have constantly lived, not only within my income, but at less expense than almost any other person of my rank in society. On what grounds, therefore, is the Attorney-General warranted in representing me as a person in such desperate circumstances as to be obliged to have recourse to the lowest knavery in order to avert absolute ruin?

With respect to the other assertion, that I pocketed a large sum of money in consequence of the transactions of the 21st of February, did not the learned lawyer know that the Stock Exchange Committee had seized not only 1,700*l.* of my money, which was my actual profit from that day's sale, but also a further sum of 770*l.* to answer their exaggerated calculation of that profit? and that the aforementioned sum of 830*l.* was also lost through the proceedings of that Committee? If the learned gentleman knew nothing of all this, I can only observe, that he ought to have informed himself on the subject before he made such statements in the House of Commons.

I have the honour to be,

Gentlemen, with great respect,

Your most obedient and faithful servant,

COCHRANE.

APPENDIX XIV.

ADDRESSES FROM PAISLEY.

Canal Street, Paisley, Aug. 18th, 1814.

SIR, — By inserting the following addresses to Lord Cochrane and the electors of Westminster, you will oblige your readers in this place. Accustomed as we have been to the acts of the abettors of corruption, it is with a mixture of pity and contempt we have witnessed the eagerness with which they have endeavoured to heap every sort of contumely upon Lord Cochrane's head. Thanks to his numerous friends, they have in this instance been wretchedly disappointed, and though he has been stripped of those honours which "the breath of kings can bestow," he still retains what they have not the power to give or take away—the applause and admiration of his grateful countrymen.

Yours, with great respect,

JOHN M'NAUGHT.

W. Cobbett, Esq.

At a meeting of a number of inhabitants of Paisley, in the Salutation Inn, upon August the 5th, 1814, for the purpose of celebrating the triumph of Lord Cochrane, the following addresses to the Electors of Westminster, and to Lord Cochrane, were agreed to :—

TO THE ELECTORS OF WESTMINSTER.

GENTLEMEN, — The times in which we live have been denominated a new era. They have produced so many extraordinary and marvellous events, that we cannot help thinking the designation just; but such has been their effect on the public mind, that we almost cease to wonder at anything, however extraordinary. Were it not for this apathy, this callous effect, scarcely anything in modern times would have made a deeper impression than the trial and condemnation of your representative, Lord Cochrane. In spite, however, of this disadvantage, we rejoice to find that this event has produced the very impression it ought to have made; it has produced an impression at once calculated to confound the malice of his enemies, to cheer the heart of every patriot, and to cherish that spirit of justice and independence which has long been dear to every Briton.

Allow us, therefore, to congratulate you and our country on the signal triumph which justice has obtained in your reelection of Lord Cochrane, — an election which could only proceed from a universal consciousness of the innocence of his Lordship, and which has placed that innocence on an immovable foundation. You have had many struggles with corruption, in all of which you have appeared as illustrious examples to mankind. In this last instance you have, if possible, surpassed yourselves; you have appeared as the focus of justice; it has been your prerogative to give the public feeling effect.

We would by no means be understood to insinuate anything to the prejudice of the jury which tried his Lordship. Trial by jury we hold so sacred and invaluable that we deprecate any reflection that would seem to throw a shade on so glorious an institution; but we may freely observe that, like every other human institution, it must be liable to abuse. We can easily imagine that a jury may be placed in such circumstances as to be rendered absolutely incapable of knowing the truth; a villanous arrangement of the evidence to be produced, a malicious and undue influence on the part of the judge, &c. may deceive a jury, and produce as much evil under the forms of law, as private vengeance could inflict. But while it is said that Lord Cochrane was tried and condemned by a special jury, it will also be said that he was tried by the electors of Westminster; he was tried by his country and acquitted.

We conclude by expressing our hope that whenever the hydra of corruption shall put forth her head, you will be found at your posts, ready to strike it off, or inflict a mortal wound; the times are still ominous, and the nation has its eyes fixed on you; we trust that you will not relax in your vigilance till malice and injustice hide their diminished heads, and innocence no longer find its only solace in heart corroding grief.

We are, gentlemen, &c.

JOHN M'NAUGHT, *Chairman.*

TO LORD COCHRANE.

MY LORD, — There is such a dissonance between conscious innocence and imputed guilt, that an upright mind must necessarily be confounded on receiving an atrocious charge; and even when the falsehood of the charge is made apparent, the recollection of it is often so bitter, and its consequences so injurious, as almost to equal the pangs and the deserved punishment of real guilt. Your case, my Lord, is one of a singular complexion. Trained in the paths of honour, habituated to patriotic deeds and high exploits, and possessing in an eminent degree that noble disinterestedness, that open frankness peculiar to a naval life, to you the recent charge

must have been extremely galling. Convinced of your innocence, permit us to approach your Lordship to express the
interest we have taken in that extraordinary affair. When
the charge was first preferred, we considered its improbability
so great as to require the strongest evidence to make it good.
We rejoice to find such evidence was wanting; nay, more,
the lofty spirit of independence, the keen sense of honour,
which you manifested throughout the whole affair; your
astonishing address before the House of Commons, and subsequent illustrations, has destroyed every vestige of guilt, and
placed your Lordship's innocence in the most advantageous
point of view. The universal sentiment in your favour, but
especially the admirable conduct of the electors of Westminster, have raised you to a higher eminence than that from
which you had fallen. You were, indeed, guilty of a crime,
—a crime unpardonable in the eyes of corruption; you had
dictated energy and efficiency to warlike measures; you
sought the glory and happiness of your country, you sought
for justice to your associates in war; was it then to be wondered at that malice should make you a favourite mark?
No, my Lord; but thanks to this enlightened age, her shafts
have been diverted in their course, and by their obliquity
have centred in herself.

My Lord, allow us to conclude by expressing our confidence that the circumstances which have called forth this
address will, if possible, strengthen your habits, and elevate
your patriotic views, that when the time arrives for resuming
public functions, you will be found the same intrepid, fearless,
champion of public and private right you have ever been.

Accept, my Lord, the assurance of our regard,

JOHN M'NAUGHT, *Chairman.*

APPENDIX XV.

ADDRESS FROM CULROSS.

Address presented to Lord Cochrane by the inhabitants of Culross.

WE, the inhabitants of the royal burgh of Culross and neighbourhood, beg leave to offer your Lordship our heartfelt congratulations on being re-elected a member to serve in the House of Commons for one of the first cities in the kingdom; which event may be considered as the verdict of the last tribunal to whom you had appealed from the charges lately preferred against you.   While the firmness with which you met those charges has called forth our highest admiration, we rejoice that they have now been so clearly proved to be unfounded, and that the cloud which threatened your destruction has been dispelled.   In the joy everywhere diffused on this occasion, none can more cordially participate than the inhabitants of Culross; and we beg to assure your Lordship of their unabated attachment to, and respect for, the family of Dundonald.

Calling to mind the many heroic actions your Lordship has performed in your country's cause, we look forward with confidence to a renewal of your ardent and gallant exertions for her advantage, notwithstanding the persecutions you are now suffering.   And we sincerely hope that in defiance of party and faction, you shall again shine forth an ornament to your profession, an honour to your country, and the boast of this place, the ancient residence of your noble family.

We beg also to express our wish that your Lordship may speedily forget those sufferings an honourable mind must sustain whilst struggling against gross and unfounded accusations.

Signed in the presence and by the appointment of the meeting,

W. MELVILLE, B.
JOHN CAW, *Secretary.*

APPENDIX XVI.

LORD COCHRANE'S ANSWER TO ADDRESS FROM CULROSS.

King's Bench, Aug. 18th, 1814.

Sir,—I take the earliest opportunity which the pressure of my affairs afforded me of conveying to my much-respected friends of Culross my heartfelt thanks for the interest they take in my character and welfare, and for the truly gratifying manner in which they have demonstrated their feelings, which are at once an honour to themselves and to me. You may, with great truth, assure our respectable townsmen that their unfeigned congratulations on my re-election add greatly to the satisfaction which I derive from that triumphant event; and that whatever may be the value of my actions, the motives in which they originate ever have been, and ever shall be, such as may claim the reward of their good opinion. I send you a newspaper containing the letter of De Berenger, by which you will perceive that my enemies have now an agent even within the confines of my prison. But I shall eventually triumph over all their machinations.

APPENDIX XVII.

ADDRESS OF THE INHABITANTS OF KIRKALDY TO THE ELECTORS OF WESTMINSTER.

Kirkaldy, Sept. 8th, 1814.

In consequence of previous intimation, a considerable number of the well-disposed and respectable inhabitants of Kirkaldy assembled at the Wellington Inn here, for the purpose of forming a congratulatory address to the honourable, free and independent electors of Westminster, on their re-election of the Right Honourable Lord Cochrane; when the following was publicly read and approved of; ordered to be signed by the chairman in the name of the meeting, and transmitted by the secretary to the Honourable Sir Francis Burdett, Baronet.

WILLIAM DAVIDSON *in the Chair.*

GENTLEMEN,—In imitation of the very respectable inhabitants of Paisley, we now presume to step forward to congratulate you on the laudable and praiseworthy step you have lately taken in re-electing the Right Honourable Lord Cochrane as one of your members for Westminster, whom the base time-servers of the day had, through wicked and deceitful means, unwarrantably deprived of his seat in Parliament. Not satisfied with this, his Lordship's enemies pushed matters so far as to obtain a sentence of pillory, fine, and imprisonment, as if he had been a common felon; nay, more,—deprive him of those laurels he had so magnanimously won, and so justly merited at the hand of his country. His Lordship's firmness and praiseworthy resignation under these uncommon sufferings we cannot too much admire and respect; and we fondly hope that, notwithstanding all these afflictions, his innocence will soon be confirmed by the exposure of those base intriguers and their intrigues, to the utter confusion of all time-serving placemen and their confederate hirelings. We rejoice that his Lordship possesses laurels more noble and lasting, which it is not in the power of princes nor their advisers to bestow or take away. We also trust that when his Lordship shall assume his honourable seat he will be more emboldened than heretofore, in conjunction with your other Honourable Member Sir Francis Burdett, in opposing corruption and its abettors, till the nation, roused from its lethargy, shall unite in behalf of all those who have been unjustly wronged; and thus will our little happy island outvie and triumph over all her enemies, both at home and abroad.

Gentlemen, we hope and flatter ourselves that you will have no cause to lament the re-election of your Right Honourable Member; we have no doubt his Lordship will be proud of the honour you have done him, as it cannot but attach mih more closely to you and to the interests of the nation. We know that many thousands in Great Britain rejoice at the step you have taken, and the victory obtained by his Lordship, who nevertheless are afraid to show themselves lest, like some of old, they are put out of the Synagogue. We still hope, however, that the stigma cast on his Lordship's friends, instead of intimidating them will rather embolden them to come forward and publicly declare the sense they have of his Lordship' innocence. That the honourable and praiseworthy electors of Westminster may prosper and succeed in all their laudable undertakings, and long enjoy the distinguished services of their able and truly honourable representatives; and when they shall have done their duty in their day and generation, that others in succession may fill their place who shall equal them in abilities and fortitude, is the ardent wish of this meeting.

Signed by appointment,

WILLIAM DAVIDSON, *Chairman.*

APPENDIX XVIII.

[*The Times,* July 13th, 1814.]

SIR,—A constant reader of your journal takes the liberty of inquiring whether any measures have been adopted on the Stock Exchange to put a stop to that illicit practice of time-bargaining, which could alone present a sufficient temptation to the authors of the late imposition, and will, if not abolished, continue to hold out similar inducements to the commission of similar frauds. To punish the invention of false news, with the particular view to affect the funds, and yet to suffer such practices in the funds as are both of themselves

illegal, and also give occasion to the invention of the falsehoods, must appear to every one to be highly preposterous;
in fact, the invention of false news and time-bargaining, must
be considered but as different parts of the same act; they
sprung up together—have grown and thriven together—and,
whatever some may suppose, are of no very recent birth.

Lord Cochrane has, in truth, been found guilty of that
which has been, in a less degree perhaps, practised without
disgrace almost every week in the year upon 'Change,
namely, a conspiracy to affect the price of Stock, by the invention and circulation of false news; and if it was necessary
for the noble conspirator and his friends to put in motion a
greater apparatus than usual for the execution of their plans,
they have only thereby facilitated the means of detection, and
proved their want of dexterity in such enterprises, while the
hackneyed jobbers, managing their repeated impositions with
less ostentation, are, in length of time, enabled to effect
much greater mischief, as the mildew does more harm to the
hopes of an honest husbandman than a thunderstorm.

Of the sentence passed upon Lord Cochrane, I shall say
little; but as the most offensive part of it is matter of feeling
and of character connected with feeling, I think that the
characters and feelings of those at whose expense the imposition was chiefly successful, should have been likewise taken
into consideration. If they are men immersed in habits of
that nature of which Lord Cochrane's offence only constituted
a single act, I say that they had not a right to require, or to
be gratified by, so severe a sentence as if they had come into
court wholly unconnected with such proceedings in their own
persons

What I have to demand, therefore, is, whether the gentlemen of the Stock Exchange, with this notable example of
punishment before their eyes, have any idea of adopting some
new system,—of forming some new resolution against those
usages which have hitherto prevailed among them, but have
never till now been visited by so tremendous a sentence? If
they have not, I think it a pity that the learned judge who

passed the late sentence did not endeavour to awaken their
caution by some warning of the danger of persevering in
those courses which had led in the passing instance to so
calamitous a result; in short, an officer in the public service
has fallen by a conviction for conspiring with others to raise
the funds; the public has therefore a right to expect from
all those connected with the sale of national property some
general expression of their detestation of that offence of
which Lord Cochrane has been convicted. Have they, or the
major part of them, seemed by their general practice to
consider it to be a crime till they came to suffer by it themselves, from any alien to their profession? Then they raised
clamours about it, no doubt. I ask farther whether the Committee who advertised for evidence against Lord Cochrane
mean to stop at the exposure of this single offence? or
whether they are resolved, as in justice they ought to be, to
hunt out and eject from the Stock Exchange all time-
bargainers, hoaxers, bangers, and other practisers of fraud,
for the raising or lowering of the funds? Or, if these are
too powerful to be attacked, whether they mean at least
simply to date a new era from Lord Cochrane's conviction, to
proclaim an amnesty of the past, and to give notice that in
future hoaxing, banging, and everything that leads to the
illegal practice of time-bargaining, as well as time-bargaining
itself, shall be no longer practised among them with impunity? I call upon these gentlemen of the Committee particularly to explain to the nation what, in their opinion,
ought to be the future regulations of stock-jobbing from this
time, when a public example is to be made of one, who, to
say the worst of him, has only carried the old practice to the
utmost extent of its limits. I call, Sir, upon the members of
the Stock Exchange, universally, for an answer to these
queries, founded upon facts of which none of them can deny
the existence; and I further denounce prospectively against
them, that, if they will make no rules for themselves, Parliament will interfere, and either make some for them, or will
at least vivify the old ones by such means of discovery as

themselves have used, when they have been the dupes.   In
expectation of a reply,

I remain, Sir, &c.
BYRSA.

To the Editor of *The Times*.

APPENDIX XIX.

[*The Champion,* Sunday, July 3rd, 1814.]

THE PRETENSIONS OF THE LAWYERS, AND THE SENTENCE ON LORD COCHRANE.

AFTER referring to the pretenson of lawyers to being held
infallible, the article continues: "It has, we believe, been
urged by the lawyers that, as the verdict of a jury is to be
considered the voice of the people, the latter can have no
right to rejudge their own decisions, but the idleness of the
plea is evident.   It most frequently happens that the verdict
of the jury is but a small part of the legal proceedings in
any particular case.   A jury may be so trammelled by tech-
nicalities, imposed upon them in peremptory language; they
may be so overpowered by a violent charge, or so confused by
a subtle one, that their decision cannot, in fairness, be regarded but as the result of an overwhelming influence,
leaving them, at least as they fancy, without an alternative;
so that, after all, what have we but an emanation from an
official quarter—tinctured with the interests, the prejudices,
the passions, and the corruptions of a ministerial officer—
in the natural existence of which the framers of our constitution believed, and the effects of which they desired to
check by the healthy and unperverted sense of men who,
being taken from common conditions, were likely to be animated solely by feelings for the common advantage.   But
when the verdict of the jury—however it may be induced—
is pronounced, can it be said that the most important part of
the business is over?   No, certainly not.   The sentence is to
come, which, in many of the most weighty cases, as affecting

the welfare of society and the safety of persons, is left entirely to the discretion of the Judge, so that here there is unbounded room for the exercise of his disposition, whatever it may be. If he be an ill-tempered and vindictive savage, and be, from political or personal motives, irritated against the unfortunate individual who is at his disposal, he may sentence him to a punishment which, as applied to the offence, shall outrage public feeling by its cruelty, and public justice by a prostitution of its penalties to gratify private resentments. Has he ambitious views, which lead him to seek the favour of the court? He may, as the professed guardian of morals, do them the fatal injury, by apologising, in the language of authority, and with all the imposing adjuncts of a dignified and grave station, for those crimes, which, as practised by persons of the highest rank, have the most extensive influence in the way of example. These are mischiefs which, under the cover of legal proceedings, *may* be perpetrated on the country; and it is evident, from their very nature, that we can have no security against them but in the vigilance of the public's observation of whatever passes in the courts of law, and their firmness in expressing their opinion on its propriety.

Secondly. Experience fully supports this reasoning. English history shows that the worst enormities of abused power have been committed through the medium of the Judges. To no other class of official persons is half the execration owing, that is justly due to the lawyers for their frequent perversions of both law and justice in a base subserviency to the temporary feelings and purposes of guilty rulers. And, be it remembered that the most abominable of their proceedings have had the sanction of a jury's verdict, procured by such means as have already been suggested; either by direct intimidation, or by drawing close an artificial network of legal complications and restrictions, which leave to jurymen about as much freedom of finding as he has of motion who is placed with his face close to a wall, and told to jump backwards or forwards, which he pleases.

Thirdly. But perhaps the character and conduct of those

who are at present Judges are calculated to inspire an unlimited confidence in *them*, however distrustful of the profession, and anxious as to its functions, we have reason to be.
This is, in some respects, a delicate inquiry, and, indeed, an
almost unnecessary one, for the vigilance of the people as to
the discharge of public duties should never be permitted to
slumber through reposing on personal qualities. It is, then,
only the arrogant and dictatorial tone of pretension, held by
the satellites of Westminster Hall, that induces us to bestow
a line on those of any one of our present administrators of
the laws. We are told, in the most fulsome terms, that they
are incorruptible,—that it is the boast of British justice to be
clean-handed, &c. &c. This boast, as rested on a contempt
of actual bribery, need be no singular one in these days.
Who now takes bribes from individuals? No one, we venture
to affirm, above the station of a Custom House officer. Perhaps in no department of the public service could a pecuniary
consideration for infidelity be more conveniently given and
received than in the military : a military man, of inferior
rank, and slender hopes, has often an opportunity of giving
the most decided advantage to the enemy, by acting traitor-
ously, and the reward would never be wanting; yet who ever
hears of such an act of baseness? When was there ever an
instance of it in the army? Why then should a Lord Chief
Justice, with an income of twenty thousand pounds a year,
be highly complimented on a virtuous self-denial, which he
only shares with the subaltern who starves on four and sixpence a day? His Lordship's claims to peculiar confidence
and honour must be of a rare kind to be valid. He must
represent to us in his behaviour the exalted attribute of justice
— simple, impartial, purified from passion, partaking of the
nature of a heavenly presidency, rather than of power vested in
a frail and feverish being, liable to be misled by his interests
and habits, and every now and then to be carried away to the
strangest lengths by a storm of anger. If Lord Ellenborough
aspires to deserve this, the best praise that can be bestowed
on one in his exalted station, his ambition is of the proper

kind; but without meaning to convey any imputation against his integrity, we must even take the liberty of telling him plainly what the public think — that as yet he has by no means entitled himself to it. His boisterous vulgarisms in the House of Lords; his impatient fretfulness with counsel, particularly shown in cases where defendants may be supposed obnoxious to the palace, or to himself personally; the extraordinary views he takes of moral questions, so favourable to certain princely profligacies; and the unqualified terms of his charges in those trials that are calculated to rouse political feelings and partialities, are circumstances that have made a strong impression on the public mind. People, therefore, without indecently denying his honesty, are much inclined to doubt his discretion; and it must be admitted, that his Lordship's temper is not precisely of that poised and regulated kind which would be the best plea for an exemption in his favour from that popular superintendence and judgment of his conduct, the exercise of which he finds so irksome, and which his friends represent as so indecorous.

Having thus vindicated the right of the people to express their sentiments freely on the conduct of the Judges, as on that of any other public men, we shall shortly exercise it by joining in the general disapprobation which the sentence recently pronounced against Lord Cochrane has excited. We never remember any sentiment to prevail more universally than this now does: the firmest believers in his Lordship's guilt are loud in their reprobation of that part of his punishment which includes the exposure of the person of a naval officer, whose gallantry in the service of his country has been of the most devoted kind, on a stage of infamy which is trodden by the miscreant whose crime is not to be named. The public feeling has received a shock by this unexpected award, from which it will not soon recover; and surely it must be censured as highly indiscreet, to have turned the horror that ought to have been engrossed by the crime, entirely against the punishment with which it has been visited.

It is not our intention to enter at all on the question of Lord Cochrane's guilt or innocence; it would be very wrong in every point of view to do this at present. His Lordship has signified his intention of defending himself before the House of Commons, and of explaining what he affirms are the misconceptions on which the verdict of the jury was founded. The public will listen attentively to his second appeal; but, in the meantime, we shall confine ourselves strictly to those circumstances which are sufficient to justify the general condemnation of the sentence passed on his Lordship, although the decision of the jury be confirmed.

In the first place, admitting that the evidence may have been such as to compel a conviction, yet there are evident features of extreme hardship in Lord Cochrane's situation when put on his trial, and when brought up for judgment, which enlist sympathy in his behalf, and make it possible that matters of alleviation, affecting *his case only*, may have been concealed by the harsh formalities of the practice of the Court. The law concerning conspiracy is enough to make every individual tremble for his own safety. Through mistake or malice, an innocent man may be included in one indictment with several guilty ones — he is compelled to take his trial with them; the testimony that proves their crime raises a prejudice against him; it is almost conviction to him to have his name called over with theirs; the chain of evidence becomes complicated, and where are jurymen to be found sufficiently clear-headed to mark exactly the connection between the facts sworn to and each of a dozen accused persons? If there is a hostile disposition towards the innocent individual existing in the breast of any in court, who may have an opportunity of influencing the jury, how shall he escape being involved in the deserved fate of those with whom he has been confounded? If, after his conviction, he prepares himself with evidence suited to remove the misconceptions by which his guilt has been presumed, he is granted or denied the opportunity of bringing it forward, according to the conduct of others, over whom he has no control, and who, in consequence of his innocence, and their guilt, have an interest directly the reverse of his. Should they abscond he is denied a new trial, although he presents himself fearlessly to meet its result. These are rules which Sir W. Garrow, the Attorney-General, calls the perfection of wisdom; to common understandings they seem the perfection of hardship. But what legal absurdity or cruelty, that has given way to the growing intelligence of society, has not been so eulogised and pertinaciously defended by the lawyers of the day!

Lord Cochrane, it is clear, has been thus placed in a situation extremely disadvantageous to him as an accused person, and the public sentiment is roused in indignant alarm at the condemnation of an individual to the punishment of the pillory (a punishment more severe than that of death to one in his Lordship's situation of life), who complains in touching terms of hardships, which, to common understandings, involve palpable injustice, and which are of a nature to render any innocent person unable to establish his innocence. It would have been but prudent in the judge to have avoided raising this popular feeling against the sentence of the Court, by keeping it more within the bounds of moderation. Its odious severity sets every one on scrutinising the soundness of the conviction, and the justice of the legal rules applied to his Lordship's case.

The further regards that influence the public to this strong commiseration of Lord Cochrane, and disapprobation of his sentence, are the unsuitableness of the latter for infliction on one of his Lordship's condition, and, we had almost said, its ingratitude, with reference to his very distinguished past services. It is very certain that justice may be as much violated by a disproportionate punishment, as by the offence against which it is awarded; and when we consider that Lord Cochrane is one of the most esteemed officers of the navy, that his courage is of the true Nelsonic kind, that he is a member of Parliament, and a man of rank, the disgrace of the pillory to him must be deemed a thousand times worse than the mere infliction of death, for with this latter his Lordship has been familiar. Now, without meaning to extenuate the crime of spreading false news to raise the public funds, we may say that the state of the general feeling and practice in the country does not at present warrant that a punishment worse than death shall be pronounced against him, who, after the long forbearance of justice, is first convicted of this offence. Statesmen of high name and station are shrewdly suspected to gamble in the funds, and this practice also is illegal;— since such loose and improper feelings as to what is honourable prevail, it would have been but fair, at the first interference of the arm of the law, to have permitted it to fall more lightly.

Lord Cochrane's politics are of a kind to excite the displeasure of the Court against him ; one of his relations has STIRRED IN BEHALF OF THE PRINCESS OF WALES, and, we believe, he has himself made, or assisted, some little scrutiny into LORD ELLENBOROUGH'S PERQUISITES OF OFFICE. These are considerations by which the Lord Chief-Justice will indignantly disclaim being at all influenced ; but we say that he ought to have been influenced by them, inasmuch as they rendered his situation towards the accused extremely delicate.

APPENDIX XX.

[*The Champion*, a London Weekly Journal, Saturday, July 9th, 1814.]

The Case of Lord Cochrane.

LORD COCHRANE'S case is pregnant with the most weighty interests and most touching considerations. Every subject of this country who has access to a knowledge of the facts is bound, as a matter of positive duty, to investigate its merits, with a view to behaving afterwards, according to the means arising out of his condition, in the best way calculated to

assist the vindication of what his conviction shall tell him to
be justice, as it relates to the public and to the party.   It
contains the most forcible appeal to every one distinctly to
bring his opinion to bear on it, that the irresistible strength of
the popular sentiment may either furnish to an injured person
his remedy, or solemnly confirm the disputed decision of the
tribunal which has adjudged him guilty of a serious offence.
On one side, the common feelings of humanity, as well as a
regard for the national honour and the general welfare, as
composed of the safety of individuals, are warmly excited,
that an innocent man should not be suffered to perish, to sink
down and be overwhelmed in the gulf of infamy and ruin,
in the sight of us all standing around him, while he in vain
cries to us for help, and extends his arms to us for protection.
If Lord Cochrane shall be left by his countrymen to be sacrificed pursuant to his sentence, and if there shall nevertheless
appear to be good grounds for disbelieving his guilt, we must
blush for England ; considering the advantages which its
people possess, they would be more disgraced by the occurrence among them of a calamity of this kind, than the French
were by the murder of the Calas family,—we had almost said
than by the wholesale murders of the revolution, which were
committed by a few wretches possessed of power, whose
atrocities were stupidly submitted to by an ignorant and
debased nation.   The judges and others officially concerned
in convicting and punishing Lord Cochrane, have not by any
means their characters implicated in the correctness of these
proceedings to the same degree that the national character is
implicated in the conduct which its people shall now adopt
between the parties.   A Court, during the judicial process,
which only lasts a few hours, may be misled by some great
error ; the administration of the law must be regulated by
prescribed forms, and these, however generally useful, will
often become hardships in their application to particular
cases ;—the accused party may not be prepared with all the
evidence bearing on his cause, or may mar it by his injudicious
conduct, or his employed advocate may take a wrong view

of what is for the interest of his client.　These possibilities
should render us cautious in attributing an erroneous judgment
and unmerited sentence to corrupt motives existing in the
tribunal from whence they proceed; but they also abundantly
prove how much depends on holding no official decision
whatever exempt from scrutiny.　We are astonished when we
hear such a man as Mr. Wilberforce declare that it is improperly disgracing a court of law to submit the correctness of
its proceedings to public investigation; that gentleman, for
whom we have the greatest respect, is even averse to the
interference of the House of Commons to discharge such a
duty, although facts of acknowledged difficulty and of a
nature to excite the keenest sympathy, thrust themselves on
the most superficial observation, forcing doubt, and, therefore,
demanding deliberation.　This, if we understand him right,
he does not deny, but in their very teeth would acquiesce
silently and impassively in what has been done, lest, as he says,
we should throw reproach on the administration of justice
—"the purest among the pure,"—the "fairest among the
fair," and so forth.　Does, then, Mr. Wilberforce forget, that
not only is the House of Commons legally competent to judge
of every act of authority up to the very highest, but that the
real superiority of this country's political condition, and the
conscious feeling which we all have of the value of our constitution are to be traced to its *exercise* of this right.　What
should we have been if this doctrine as to the indelicacy of
scrutinising the conduct of public functionaries had been always
adopted?　What enormities have been the consequence of its
temporary prevalence?　Then, again, how can it escape his
acuteness that, as no human institution or person is infallible,
none ought to claim or receive an exemption from a superintending cognisance?　Farther, admitting, as he must when
put to it, that the Courts may pronounce wrong judgments,
will he affirm that they will be more disgraced by having the
injurious effects of these prevented by timely interference,
than by an acquiescence in that worst of all calamities and
disgraces, the punishment of innocence?　This is the point

which is so unaccountably overlooked by those who take Mr. Wilberforce's view of the question; they think, or at least by their arguments would seem to think, that the correction of an error is more disgraceful to the party who is wrong than its perpetration; they do not seem to understand that the most honourable thing that can be said of the institutions of any country, is that, as a whole, they render it impossible that there should be any wrong without a redress, an evil without a remedy,—and that each of these institutions derives a respectability and strength from this general eulogium, of a far more legitimate and lasting kind, than can result from an impunity which tends to foster its worst errors and assist its progress towards destruction.

We have said enough to show that, in our opinion, the House of Commons ought to have conducted for itself an inquiry into Lord Cochrane's case; more particularly when facts were laid before it which raised grave doubts of his Lordship's guilt in the minds of some of its most respectable and impartial members. It is the object of this article to impress, that it now devolves on the public, and more particularly on his Lordship's constituents the electors of Westminster, to investigate the whole business for themselves, by means of the various documents and evidence which they can command. Our readers must not look for these in our weekly sheet; we cannot among our miscellany furnish them even with a correct outline of the proceedings of the Court, the debates in the House of Commons, his Lordship's defence, and the affidavits supporting it. Most of these, however, are to be procured, and justice, manliness, and humanity require they should be attentively considered. We shall proceed to state and justify our own sentiments on this most interesting affair, as they have been influenced by the progressive information we have received. This will be expected of us; but, we repeat, in a case like this, each ought to investigate and judge for himself. As we have hitherto rested our remarks on the possibility of Lord Cochrane's innocence, it is proper now to add that the voice of the public should now be raised in defence of their legal authorities, and in reprobation of an indecent obstinacy of denial, supported by falsehood wearing its most atrocious features, should inquiry convince them of Lord Cochrane's guilt.

We are impelled to mention first that, whether properly or improperly, we previously cherished no particularly favourable opinion of Lord Cochrane as he was known to the public. He always seemed to us more likely to throw discredit on the cause of honest politics, by joining the word reform with hasty, intemperate, and undignified proceedings, than to accomplish any real good by his efforts, notwithstanding they were generally directed to the removal of what was wrong. Besides this, we thought we observed about him too little selection in his companionships, and too little of what is high-mindedly delicate in his conduct. We heard of the charge brought against him by the Stock-Exchange certainly with no disposition to turn from it as incredible; on the contrary, we leaned, with the majority, to a belief of his guilt, through the weight of the accusation, and a certain weakness, arising chiefly from incoherency, in his Lordship's inconsiderately published defence. The trial came on, and, by the reports of it in the newspapers, our original belief was strengthened: we saw no reason to doubt the propriety of the conviction; we began, indeed, from what we heard and read, to fancy that Lord Cochrane's guilt might be less heavy than that of the others who were included in the indictment; we suspected that he had not been made privy to the mysteries of the plot, although he might have culpably connived at what he knew to be going on, understanding that it would tend to his advantage, but not perfectly acquainted, nor seeking to be, with all the particulars.

With this impression on our mind, we at the same time felt that Lord Cochrane had been exposed to various hardships and disadvantages, in the course of the legal proceedings against him; and that these were sufficient to put even innocence in a very precarious situation on its trial; in short, to justify what an hon. member said in the House — that he had need to be not only *fully*, but *fortunately* guiltless, who should escape conviction under such circumstances. The being included in an indictment with a number of persons, several of whom he had never seen, by which the evidence and the jury's attention were confused, and an odium was thrown on *all* the accused should the guilt of *any* be proved; the refusal of the judge to attend to the counsel, when they prayed that the trial might be adjourned before they commenced the defence, after a sitting of fifteen hours, and when the jury were incapable of giving close thought to the statement, the adjournment taking place immediately when the defence was concluded, by which the prosecutors had given to them a great advantage in framing the reply; the very fierce and unqualified terms of the judge's charge to the jury, putting every fact in the strongest language against his Lordship, and laying little or no stress on the other side of the supposition; — all these things combined, constituted, as we thought, a case of hardship, of which the convicted party might reasonably complain.

The proceedings after the trial were more unequivocally severe. The rule of the court, under which Lord Cochrane was refused a new trial, because others over whom he had no control did not appear with him to seek it, was plainly inconsistent with justice as distinct from law — at least, as it operated in this instance; it therefore shocked the public sense, and raised a strong feeling in favour of the aggrieved party. It is pleasing to find Mr. Ponsonby, who is not only an eminent lawyer, but one by no means to be suspected of a disaffected turn, declare that this rule is as little founded in law as in justice or reason; that it has, moreover, no ancient custom to plead in its behalf, but is of very novel introduction. We have some ground, then, for hoping that this piece of "profound wisdom," as Sir W. Garrow luminously termed it, which every one scouts as senseless and cruel, and which is besides an *innovation*, will shortly give place to a more liberal, and useful, and *ancient* form of practice.

The facts contained in Lord Cochrane's defence, made

personally in court when he was brought up to receive sentence, and which has since been published in its entire form, threw a new light on many important points of his case, and gave an explanation, reconciling with his innocence several matters which served before to prove his guilt. This is a document which our readers should not fail to peruse.

At last came the sentence, and, in common with all the world, we were astounded by it. It thunderstruck the prosecutors, who felt abashed and have petitioned against it; it amazed both sides of the House of Commons; it disgusted all persuasions of people — those who acquiesced in as well as those who dissented from the conviction. It seemed of most forgetful severity, when Lord Cochrane's naval services were considered; of most injurious severity when his political conduct was looked at in connection with the happier fate of certain peculators and delinquents whose turpitude to the public had nothing to relieve its atrocity but their subserviency to the court. In short, the punishment awarded by the judge (we allude to the pillory) appears almost to everyone overcharged, as it relates to the crime, unsuitable as it relates to the person convicted, and unseemly as it relates to him who presided at the trial. It is but fair to notice one exception, by quoting from Sir Francis Burdett's speech: — " The sentence he thought cruel, disgusting, and severe beyond all example. The noble Lord who was the object of it was the only person he had met with who was not of this opinion. His Lordship, when he (Sir F. Burdett) visited him in the King's Bench Prison, said that he had not to complain of his sentence, but of his conviction. Were he guilty, the whole of his punishment, and more than the whole, was justly due to him."

We come now to the proceedings in the House of Commons. His Lordship's defence there ought certainly, in some way or other, to be got before the public: with his feelings highly strung and irritated, as it would seem, in an extraordinary degree, it contained passages reflecting on the conduct of Lord Ellenborough, which the newspaper reporters were told in plain terms they would publish at their peril. Lord Cochrane evidently delivered himself under the almost maddening consciousness of having been the victim of gross injustice; some of his accusations, pronounced with great bitterness, it may be found necessary to keep back; but the narrative and argumentative part of his statement should certainly be printed. It had a prodigious effect on those who heard him: several of the most impartial and steady Members declared that, in their view, it established that there had been on the trial *a misdirection of the jury by the judge of a most material nature*, and to the prejudice of his Lordship as one of the accused; they added, that on the facts which every-one thought told most against his Lordship, he had shed a totally new light, either by offering to rebut them with testimony that deserved attentive consideration, or by explaining circumstances which altered their import, or by showing with much simplicity and indication of general feeling how they had been misconceived, and to what unlucky accidents it was owing that they had operated to his prejudice. Persons whose respectability and judgment will not be impeached from either side of the House protested that under the weight of what they had heard they could not sleep on their pillows were they to vote for Lord Cochrane's expulsion without further inquiry: many affirmed that the case had always appeared to them doubtful, and that now their doubts had become of the most serious kind. A gentleman who interrupted his Lordship in the course of his animadversions on the Chief-Justice, avowed that however injudicious and unfounded these circumstances were, he could not shut up his opinion from facts so strong as those contained in the defence, nor could he reconcile it to his conscience to add confirmation to a verdict of the soundness of which he saw reason to doubt, and bitterness to a fate which it was more than possible might be undeserved.

Yet the House voted the expulsion of Lord Cochrane, not however without a division. Forty-four were for further inquiry, and 140 for expulsion. On the face of this proceeding it appears that forty-four intelligent and honest men

think that there is at least a strong call for further investigation, yet Lord Cochrane has been *sentenced to the pillory!*
But if we read the speeches of the Members, we shall find it
by no means follows that the 144 who decided for expulsion,
are satisfied as to his Lordship's guilt.   Mr. Wilberforce,
for instance, speaks of the case as very distressing, and as
very painful to his feelings — but adds that *he deemed it his
duty to bow to the decision of the judge and jury.*   Now,
this is not an exercise but a surrender of judgment; and,
indeed, we may infer that Mr. Wilbeforce attaches at least
doubt to the case, for otherwise he would not regard it as distressing, but rather as one in which the offender had deprived
himself of every claim to compassion, by shameless obstinacy
and abandoned perjury.   It is observable that the propriety
of expulsion was almost invariably rested on the propriety of
supporting the court of law, and on the many inconveniences
which, as it was truly enough said, would attend a reinvestigation of the proceedings.   The reader sees that these considerations have no connection with Lord Cochrane's guilt or
innocence; yet, judging from the temper and sentiment
manifested by the House, we are inclined to believe that it
was these which chiefly produced its decision, and that a very
large proportion of the majority are far from satisfied in their
minds that their late associate has been properly convicted.

For ourselves, we have no hesitation to say, after a most
impartial study of the various documents, that our opinion is
changed, and that from thinking the weight of evidence on
the side of Lord Cochrane's guilt we now think it on the
side of his innocence.   This, at least, is incontestible, that
great difficulties were imposed upon him by legal forms;
that the most important facts were misrepresented to his
prejudice on his trial; and that if the charge of the judge
was adopted by the jury as a clue to their decision, they have
been misguided.

The best statement of Lord Cochrane's defence that we
have seen was in the *Morning Herald;* the reports in the
Times and *Chronicle* gave no idea of it; but we suppose it

will speedily be published in a more perfect form than any in which it has yet appeared. It makes perfectly clear that the Chief-Justice's most important assertion to the jury, that Lord Cochrane received De Berenger "*in the costume of his crime*," is utterly unsupported by any evidence given on the trial, and that it is in contradiction to several strong probabilities:—it directs attention to the singular fact that Lord Ellenborough, in some instances, quoted Lord Cochrane's voluntary affidavit for proof against him, and in others denied it all authority and truth:—it does all but prove that De Berenger's dress, when he came in the hackney-coach to Lord Cochrane's house, was falsely described by the coachman, and it convicts this witness of other falsehoods, while it justifies a belief that he may have been actuated by a corrupt desire for the reward, by showing that he is a convicted ruffian of the vilest kind:—it satisfactorily accounts for the non-examination of Lord Cochrane's servants by counsel on the trial, for whose examination his Lordship pressed by note when the proceedings were going on, who would have proved that De Berenger's dress was not of a kind to excite suspicions in any breast:—it makes very manifest that Lord Cochrane has suffered by being joined with others whose guilt must be presumed; conscious of his own innocence, and therefore believing theirs, he left to them the trouble of arranging the defence to the indictment, and neither his wishes nor his interests seem to have been consulted:—it establishes that he had no connection with De Berenger's defence, and gives reason to believe that he was but little acquainted with his person:—it tenders fresh testimony, on the oaths of five respectable witnesses, as to the manner in which Lord Cochrane's bank-notes found their way into De Berenger's hands:—in fine, it mentions a multiplicity of circumstances furnishing presumption of innocence, and makes it indubitable that the case might have had much assistance of which it has been from one cause or another deprived.

(Signed) "ED."

I have only selected such opinions of the press as may serve to elucidate what has been advanced. Were I to collect public opinion as expressed at the time, such collection would far more than exceed this volume in bulk. If necessary for my fuller defence, it must yet be adduced, should my life be spared. That my days have been thus far prolonged, is, under Providence, to be attributed to the skill of my physician, Dr. Bence Jones, and to the unremitting care and attention of my constant medical attendant, Mr. Henry Lee, of Savile Row.

DUNDONALD.

END OF THE SECOND VOLUME.